SPEECH: Science-Art

SPEECH

Science-Art

ELWOOD MURRAY
GERALD M. PHILLIPS
J. DAVID TRUBY
EXERCISES BY ALTON BARBOUR

THE BOBBS-MERRILL COMPANY, INC. INDIANAPOLIS · NEW YORK

RUSSEL R. WINDES
Queens College of the City University of New York
Consulting Editor in Speech

Copyright © 1969 by The Bobbs-Merrill Company, Inc.
Printed in the United States of America
Library of Congress Catalog Card Number 79-77823
First Printing

Foreword

The Speech-Communication discipline is in the midst of accelerating change, a change which is challenging long-held theories and traditional pedagogies. The basic textbooks in the discipline, however, have been slow to change; this, in spite of the fact that in speech-communication, as perhaps in no other discipline, the basic text continues to be a key mode of instruction. If the discipline is to reflect the changes which seek to reinvigorate it, the basic textbooks must relate closely to contemporary needs, issues, and theories.

The formal study of speech in American colleges is responding to new thought and theory about communication within the intellectual community and within a turbulent, changing society at large. With acceptance of the belief that complex human behavior can often be best understood through the study of human communication, scholars in the social sciences and humanities during the past decade have turned their attention to new forms of communication and new methods of research. Their studies have produced substantial changes within the discipline because they have ultimately questioned most of the traditional and prescriptive theories and methods for knowledge about and skill in communication. As a result, glib simplicities have given way to engaged uncertainty. Today, the dogmatism of the basic textbook, and the basic course in speech-communication, is a luxury of inertia the discipline can no longer afford.

Beyond these changes in the discipline, the academy also is changing. Concerned students and administrators are demanding that courses engage the analytic and critical faculties of students and that, above all, courses should be socially relevant. Today's youth emphasize and desire communication with the self and the right to develop insight into their own identities. In a real sense the underground movie, the acid-rock phenomenon, and the popularity of encounter and sensitivity groups all represent the search for new modes of meaningful communication; at the same time they indict a discipline which, at best, has given only traditional answers to their concerns.

Seemingly quite oblivious of the revolutions of our times, speech pedagogy continues as it always has. The traditional basic course retains its established format; the speech classroom bears little relationship to reality; the class environment is highly structured, the course essentially recitative, and the student motivated too often by fear of low grades; the basic text is often injurious to learning, for it is used too frequently as a mere catalogue of information which transforms the tentative findings of experts into simplistic nostrums about how to speak well. Little wonder that, though student memories may be developed, their behaviors remain largely unmolested. What should be perfectly clear to all concerned is that speech courses can no longer assume a social model based on Athenian democracy or the American town meeting.

In *Speech: Science-Art,* Professors Murray, Phillips, and Truby develop a socially relevant and socially defensible point of view toward both the speech-communication discipline and the basic course. They integrate both traditional and contemporary theory with the needs and motivations of today's students. While they address themselves to age-old questions about the nature of human life, the meaning of social values, and the organization of society, the central focus of the work is a series of questions which are of concern to all citizens: What are the processes which underlie and motivate communication? What is the role of communication in both the growth of the individual and the development of social culture? How may members of society rationally and profitably communicate to make decisions, resolve problems, and live rewarding lives? How can the individual prepare himself to engage in effective and responsible communication?

In drawing their portrait of the communication process, the authors have placed individual psychology in the foreground, communication with others in the middle ground, and the larger society in the background. Thus speech-communication is placed in a proper perspective, and the study of it incorporates an understanding of psychology, a sense of language and its relation to thought and growth, and a knowledge of the nature and purpose of social organization.

Professors Murray, Phillips, and Truby believe that the student must be motivated and encouraged to discover his own needs for, and ways of, communicating effectively. They stress this belief by emphasizing that personal growth and satisfactions, as well as the successful functioning of social organization, depend on an open and workable theory of communication and its skillful practice. Central to student involvement in the book is a spirit of inquiry, a spirit of innovation and experiment, and a spirit of theory-building and humanistic speculation. This diversity of approach gives the student a special kind of autonomy; the student knows what he *may* do, not what he *must* do. The student is given numerous opportunities to test the hypotheses of the book, and the biases of the writers, against his own experiences and critical faculties. The authors believe that many variables affect the ways in which individuals communicate. In this sense, each individual should be taught on a one-to-one basis, an obvious impossibility in a textbook. Consequently, they have chosen the next best alternative. They have presented *a way of thinking about* communication; they have then indicated alternatives by which the student can relate to and solve his own speech-communication problems. In short, the text, amplified by the teacher, is no longer the "source of knowledge" for the course. The student, properly guided and self-motivated, discovers his own needs, strengths, and limitations, and brings these realizations to both the reading of the text and the realities of the classroom experiences.

Even though the architectonic structures of thought about speech are collapsing, change is difficult to process and program. Traditions are patterns which make life simple, and traditional courses tend to exist because they are often simple for both teacher and taught. *Speech: Science-Art* offers opportunity and challenge to those who are weary of the irrelevant, to those who agree that there is no acceptable alternative to keeping abreast of change. This book will succeed if the speech class becomes not only more responsive to change outside the academy, but also more challenging in itself, and thus far more rewarding. Professors Murray, Phillips, and Truby have presented the challenge of relevancy and diversity, and in this challenge they have brought to their subject the eclecticism and methodological soundness which characterizes thought about speech-communication at its best.

Russel R. Windes
February 1969

Preface

Speech arises out of the *relationships* we carry on. Everyone has some relationships they would like to improve. In order to accomplish this, we must have control over our process of communicating, which includes the processes of perceiving, evaluating, and predicting. This is the major aim of this book: to improve our control, even in a small way, over the relationships we carry on with others. If we can accomplish this, there will be a restoration of the original *logos*—the word as the rational and ordering principle of the universe—as well as a release of our critical and creative powers.

Uncertainty and lopsidedness characterize our understanding of communication today. Communication is used here in its broadest sense—relating, influencing, and interacting with our total environment. Efforts to improve speech differ markedly according to the viewpoint from which it is approached. When speech is labeled "a science," the results of speech training often stop with the barest meeting of the requirements of day-to-day living. When speech is labeled "an art," we tend to be captivated with sound more than substance. Yet, strangely enough, our academic society has produced both technicians to implement scientific speech problems (the speech pathologists who attempt to correct defects in transmission) and critics who deal exclusively with the artistic and cathartic aspects of the spoken and written word. Traditionally, those who have studied speech have approached it from the standpoint of the rhetorician and have examined it as a means of social control. We believe, however, that speech goes beyond all of these orientations, for we feel that the act of communicating with others is so deeply rooted in the human personality that aspects of it cannot be separated out for independent study without losing our grasp of the sensitivity and potency of the act.

Thus, we regard human communication as the end product of the social sciences, the culmination of scientific investigation, and the ultimate of artistic expression. The hyphen in the title of this book, *Speech: Science-Art*, indicates that science and art join in the act of communicating; scientific knowledge and artistic skill are synthesized into one. It also implies that there is a unifying basis for the fragmented communication taught today. This unifying basis is the total human personality in interaction with other personalities. Thus, a physiological view, a physical view, a psychological view, a social view, a linguistic view, a performance view, are all, in themselves, insufficient, but, if taken together, they may provide deep insight into what happens when humans face each other in a communication relationship. Speech is a complex science that virtually defies explanation; and it is a high art that represents the best of man's creative powers.

The understanding of human communication through the ordering of abstractings from our expanding knowledge can enhance all of the specialties, sciences and social sciences, and the humanities. For knowledge is not acquired for its own sake. It has relevance only when it can be shared, communicated, from one human to others.

This volume pretends only to an outline of a science-art of communication. It will need continual revision as results are obtained from scientific investigations and artistic endeavors. Much of what is included here comes from general semantics and related methodologies. There are also important contributions from phenomenal and cognition psychologies as well as group dynamics and sociodrama.

It is impossible to give credit to the many specific sources and the hundreds of people on whom we have drawn. This book is the result of years of reading and thousands of hours of conversation brought together in our own planning and thinking. Thus, we cannot credit this or that idea to a specific person, but we can say "thank you" to all who have helped, and particularly to our students whose questions and criticisms through the years have helped us to clarify our own ideas.

Some special thanks are due to Alton Barbour of the University of Denver whose help in planning and suggesting exercises for this volume have helped us materially in making this book useful in the classroom. The debt to Alfred Korzybski and his successors, M. Kendig and Charlotte Read, is manifest, although they might be disappointed in the way we have extended their classical conceptions of general semantics. The generations of rhetoricians on whom we have drawn also deserve thanks, particularly those modern rhetoricians like Carroll Arnold of the Pennsylvania State University, whose questions and critical comments helped to prevent us from being carried away with speculation. Among the many who have provided specific criticisms and encouragement were Andrew King and Marjorie Thurston of the University of Minnesota, Betty Hinton and James I. Hayes of Murray State University, and Douglas Pedersen and Robert Dunham of Pennsylvania State University. Particular thanks are due to Dean R. Phillips and Georgia Townsend for their scrupulous help in preparing the manuscript. And extra special thanks to Rus Windes for his encouragement and counsel and to our most extraordinary editor Maria Scott for her patience, wisdom, and for being an editor who thinks authors are people.

Most of all, our thanks to the students who have tried and will try in the future; those who sat in our classes and responded to us honestly as we succeeded and failed in the presentation of potential ideas, who helped us to crystallize and focus our efforts. To them, the rebels and critics of the class-room, future and past, we dedicate this effort, for we know that from among them will come the scholars who will correct us, clarify us, and bring to the next generation a more orderly and systematic treatment of this most human of all subjects.

E.M.   G.M.P.   J.D.T.

Contents

Introduction:
A New Philosophy
About a Way to Learn

No subject in the academic curriculum is so dependent as speech on student effort for successful mastery. There seems to be little relationship between the didactic material presented by the teacher and by the textbook and improvement of performance by the student. Most books on how to speak or write are *prescriptive* when they should be *descriptive*. It is easy to say that learning to communicate depends on constant practice. A student can learn this proposition easily and feed it back on a true-false test. But the teacher cannot practice for the student and so mastery of the proposition becomes irrelevant. The only thing that counts is whether the proposition motivates action. This is our goal—an ambitious one we admit, but unless some motivation to participate is created, some relevance to the student established, no progress will be made.

The word *relevance* has become very important on campuses today. Those subjects that do not have a direct application to the students' present interests and perceived needs (or that do not seem esoteric enough) are classified as "irrelevant," i.e., boring. What students are interested in is called "relevant." There is no evidence that a universally relevant course has ever been devised, but if one existed it would probably permit free interaction between student and teacher and allow the student to determine the subject matter and communicate about it as he saw fit to teacher, peers, or anyone else. This actually describes what should go on in a good "communication" classroom.

On campuses where some measurement has been made, students have shown considerable preference for "speech" courses. Some students say this is because the course is "cake" or "mickey mouse," and the chemistry professors are inclined to agree with them. But other students, who will level with the interviewers, declare that in the speech class it is possible to "be a human being, and say something and have it treated with respect." Such a class could, of course, be called "relevant" because it deals in human concerns.

The science-art of communication demands total involvement on the part of the learner. The scientific propositions available to the student cannot be comprehended until there is some experience with the art, yet the art cannot be mastered without internalization of some scientific propositions. And the process of learning to communicate must be carried on in the face of the fact that we have no clear-cut determination of what "effective communication" is, nor do we have a set of objectives against which progress can be measured.

In a great many ways, learning to communicate well depends on the internal state of the learner more than on the critical judgment of a professional observer-critic. In short, total immersion is necessary. Although all of us have been carrying on communication since early childhood, we still evidence considerable inadequacy. The way to improve seems to lie in some kind of a controlled training period, in which the student becomes involved in the solution of his communication problems and the teacher provides guidance as needed and opportunities for the student to take risks as required. In such a controlled training period the teacher would also have opportunities to persuade the student that improvement is desirable. Thus, the art that comes from involvement by the student blends with the scientific control of the teacher and emerges as a synthesis of experience, which presumably will improve communication skill.

Sometimes improvement means nothing more than feeling better about communicating. Improvement can also mean the demonstration of considerable skill at accomplishing goals that only effective communication can attain. Our problem here is to determine how to go about the task of learning to communicate by speaking and writing so that improvement meets your goals. You may only wish to feel a little more confident in what you are doing, or you may have some difficult and complicated goal in mind. Our job is to find a method that can be applied now in your classroom, using the propositions in this book as guides to your personal development. Our view of how to do this differs from most methods now in use.

It has long been presumed in academic circles that setting aside a specific period of weeks with a fixed number of class meetings of a predetermined amount of time permits the instructor to teach something to students. It is further assumed that by doing "exercises" during the allotted time, the student will encounter experiences that will carry learning over into his "life." The procedure usually involves a lecture by a teacher, i.e., "filling in the background," "developing the theroetical underpinnings," or "providing some helpful hints" about the way *it* is done. And, customarily, all this is augmented by a textbook, which usually declares in its preface that it will offer no rules and then proceeds to offer many rules for successful behavior. The teacher and textbook combine to present exercises: themes to write and/or speeches to deliver. These are then criticized, and the student is supposed to ingest the criticism and synthesize it with the "theoretical underpinnings," the "background," and the "helpful hints" so that his performance will improve.

Since there is no standard against which improvement in communication can be measured, the whole process is quite subjective, and the criticism offered is usually more dependent on the instructor's taste than on any other variable. Most teachers recognize this, and to bring some "objectivity" into the course, they offer periodic examinations, usually standardized, which cover the "material" of the course, i.e., the background, theoretical underpinnings, and helpful hints, or they at least test the student's memory of the text and lectures. Because this kind of activity can be standardized, the grading is more often than not based on examinations. Thus the ostensible goal of the course, the learning of communication, becomes subordinated to the necessities of the university, the awarding of grades.

As we will point out in this book, the act of communicating is so deeply rooted in the human personality that it really cannot be dissected for special treatment. Both synthetic and analytic approaches to the learning of communication seem to be ineffective. What does seem to work, however, is a process by which the student discovers his own personal needs to communicate and generates in his own mind some goals he would like to accomplish through effective communication. Then the classroom can become a laboratory in which he tries out his skill and evaluates his success. The teacher can become a mature critic, helping the student both to understand how to set goals and to discover ways of developing techniques to achieve them; his role should be that of referee or facilitater. Didactic material can become meaningful in this kind of learning situation, for there is personal involvement to which the material can become attached. Unfortunately, such a high state of motivation is rarely achieved, and traditional modes of instruction seem to accomplish it only with the few who are already qualified and not in need of learning.

A RADICAL PHILOSOPHY

The philosophy that we present, therefore, may appear to be a bit radical to those who hew to the academic line. We hope, though, that it will offer a way to relevancy and involvement. In this book we have pulled together as many meaningful scientific and artistic propositions about the act of human communication as we could find. These have been simplified, even oversimplified and, of course, do not necessarily represent the preferences or beliefs of the authors. We have taken, for example, both an Aristotelian and non-Aristotelian approach to many of the controversial aspects of communication theory. Our purpose has been not to offer a set of data for the student to memorize or the teacher to elaborate but, we hope, a range of choices which the student will find pertinent when and if he discovers his own personal motivation for learning to communicate. And, we submit, some propositions in this book *can* be used as critical evaluation points against which progress in learning can be measured. The measurement must be done by the student, however, for most of the evaluation points are valuative in nature and concern the feelings of the student about the act of communicating. Measurement by test would be unfair!

The discussion questions in this book may appear a little odd, not what you would expect to find in a textbook. They are provided to suggest for you ways of procedure. They were generated by students in classes taught by the authors. This book should not be used in the traditional way, and if it is used so in your class, may we apologize, for this was not our intent. We advocate something different, yet we do not wish to be too blatant about demanding it, for our evidence of success is meager, although perhaps not so meager as that possessed by those who are more traditional in orientation. In short, we trap you, the student, in the middle of a muddle, in a paradox, where the only determination of what is right or wrong, correct or incorrect, effective or ineffective, just or unjust, true or untrue, must be made by you, the student. In attempting to find your way through the various alternatives offered by this book, or even through the potential conflict between this book and your instructor, or between your instructor and the academic system, you must discover your own way, determine your own goals, establish your own syllabus if you will, and somehow communicate to someone else what it is that is relevant to you. Then you must get on with the business of working it out to your own satisfaction. In a day of unrest among students, where demands for more personal control over academic methodology are legion, this seems to us to be a perfectly rational approach.

There are, on college campuses, many courses that would be hard put to demonstrate their relevance in ways that could be immediately comprehended by students. This is not to say that they are not important both to the scholars who study them and to the expansion of knowledge in general. It is just that they seem remote and overspecialized. For instance, the romantic poets seem to have little to say about the ferment in the ghettos of our large cities; the table of the elements seems distant from the use of napalm in Asian wars; the myth of the "Noble Savage" and the history of the Industrial Revolution are of marginal value when applied to the solutions of the problems of today's poor people striving for a place in their society. In many ways, the subject matter offered by the college represents a refuge from life and the world. Interestingly enough, most students seem to recognize this and find some security in it, despite their demands for relevance.

Getting involved in something real usually takes more effort than people are likely to want to expend. Experiments with a reality-based curriculum, which the students must develop for themselves, are usually accompanied by serious resistance and cries of "You get paid for it, you teach it." When the students are given the opportunity to do the thing for themselves, they are likely to attempt to evade the task and throw it back on the teacher, for they, like any neonate, will resist being thrown out of the comfort of the cradle. The academic establishment has been warm and nurturing for them, and most students really crave the security of academic authoritarianism that has given them the homeostasis of a fixed set of rules for these past years. The students will also seek security in life beyond college. They will take jobs because of pension plans, and they will resist risk! They will do this because they *never* really have been trained in making decisions. Their ability to decide, to communicate their decision, and to persuade others to adopt it has atrophied through years of compliance with the specifications and demands of the academic system. While their conformance has given them security and comfort, it has also reduced their capacity to be human. It is against this sort of "apathy" that the *avant-garde* student, the protester, is screaming.

Human talk may happen with or without substance and purpose. Despite the understanding that scholars claim to have of our talk, and the many propositions that have been generated about it, clearly people will talk and continue to talk whether or not "talk" is defined as a legitimate object for academic study. It is possible for people to use "Aristotelian devices" without ever having heard of Aristotle, and it is possible for people to criticize the language without ever having heard of Korzybski. It is, of course, possible for people to digest food without understanding the digestive process, and to make babies without understanding the reproductive process. The many courses that have proliferated about "decision-making" have about that much relevance. But if we accept the proposition that human personality is basically projected through communication, then decisions about what to say, why it must be said, and how to say it become crucial to the growth of healthy personalities. Thus, without humility, we declare that your systematic study of the science-art of communication in terms of your own needs and wants could easily become the most important thing you are ever called upon to do in your academic career.

The academic world has assumed that students know how to communicate when they come to it. Nowhere in the academic system is there an organized approach to the learning of speech or to the learning of writing. Both seem to have become preoccupied with concern about names for the parts of speech and propriety in the placing of marks of punctuation. Somewhere there must be an opportunity for *you* to approach the study of communication so you can grow into a mature communicator rather than a punctilious punctuator, and we hope this book will show you some possibilities.

PATTERNS OF COMMUNICATION

If you wish to break with the past, you need to take cognizance of that past. We, the authors of this book, are quite familiar with the ways communication has been taught up to now, and we are *not* prepared to toss all of them into the trashbasket. We are convinced that there are ways to adapt even the most traditional of assignments so as to make them meaningful to learners in today's world. After all, we live for utilitarian reasons and not solely for the sake of tradition.

So many books have been written and so many different approaches to the act of teaching have been advocated, that no one could assert that they are all wrong. By the same token, it is specious to assert that *one* way is *the* correct way. It is clear that some people have learned to speak and write well as a result of courses they have taken. Their success came about because of something that happened inside them. They were fortunate enough to have been sufficiently motivated and to have been exposed at the right time to a kind of instruction that was appropriate for them. To maximize chances of this happening, the learner must be allowed the greatest number of possible options, for only *he* can estimate what works and does not work for *him.*

The teacher's role in this kind of learning situation is quite clear. He must be able to propose and promote alternatives, and he should be able to structure the classroom environment so that those who need rewards can receive them; those who need prodding will be prodded; and those who profit most from being left alone can be permitted to find their own way. This may call for some deviation from the format of performance-criticism that is characteristic of the teaching of speaking and writing. Personality improvement, to our way of thinking, seems to be what training in communication is directed at. Whatever happens should happen inside the learner. Presumably, we learn most when we can derive reward from our learning. Learning from reward permits elaboration of personality and growth of the individual.

Traditional teachers of communication, however, have long been trapped by the expectancies of the academic system that presumes that what a student does can be evaluated—the "good" rewarded and the "bad" punished. Criticism and grades have been the rewards and punishments. Intelligent, enhancing criticism is often nullified by the assignment of a grade, for the grade becomes the goal, not understanding the criticism. A good grade may motivate increased involvement, while a poor grade may generate hostility or a desire to improve (the grade) or the decision to give up. In any case, what is said about the content of the communication becomes relevant only when the student is clear in his mind that the content has something to do with the grade assigned. Whether the criticism makes sense is irrelevant. The real question the student asks is whether acting on the criticism will improve a bad grade or sustain a good one.

Students have learned to expect grades. For example, a series of experiments done in speech classes in which the instructors did not grade performances evoked considerable hostility from students who felt that they could not accommodate to so serious a break with their anticipations. Consequently, we assume that before real progress can be made at learning to communicate, some break must be made with the traditional grading system, and the reasons for the break must be understood by teacher and student alike. Hopefully, the following chapters offer enough information about the communication process to reveal the individuality of the stake involved in learning, and can serve as motivation to diverge from the common expectancies of the academic situation. In this case, we would declare, grading is irrelevant. Even if some students regard their communication course as "mickey mouse," the teacher loses nothing, provided he succeeds in motivating part of his class toward personal improvement. Perhaps something akin to a "pass-fail" system might satisfy the academic machinery and yet allow opportunity to learn for those interested in doing so.

We offer now some general suggestions about how a class in communication might be organized. The most obvious suggestion is to use the material in this book as subject matter, augment it with lectures, provide for some sort of student recitation, assign a term paper, and schedule a few examinations. The class would then be defined as "one in which the student would learn *about* communication." This, of course, would satisfy the academic requirements and would demand no innovation on the part of the class or instructor, since virtually anything is honest grist for the academic mill.

When you assume instead that the student wants to learn *to* communicate, then the subject matter of this book and the subject matter on which the teacher is prepared to lecture must be used in a different way. Activities must be discovered that make sense to the student and impel him to take account of the opportunities available to him. He must be permitted to make choices about what he believes and be allowed to perform in situations that enable him to make his errors, understand them, and improve as a result of understanding. He must get the honest impression that *he* is testing *himself!* Most often, the student is not clear on how this can come about. It may be necessary, initially, for the teacher to suggest, prescribe, or assign, because the teacher, presumably, is older and perhaps wiser and has had the opportunity to try things out in various contexts. At this stage of development, the student would play a ratification role, for without some participation on his part, the teacher's suggestions would become classroom exercises and lose their capacity for reality.

We assert that learning the information in this book in such a way that it can be fed back accurately on examinations has very little to do with learning *to* communicate. In fact, most of the material in this book has been written so that it cannot be put into objective test form. The only way this book can become useful is to permit it to function as a source of ideas for a student.

For this reason, the exercises offered at the ends of the chapters are extensive and varied. We raise several questions and point out problems and paradoxes, not with the notion of having students write out the answers as an assignment, but to show ways in which the material in the chapters might be made useful or activated for the students. What is to be done with the exercises, if anything, is the business of the class. The optimum use of this book would be for it to become a source for an individual syllabus made by each student for his own use, with the teacher serving as adviser, guide, and resource person. To further this end, we have presented some additional suggestions, "wild card" exercises, at the end of the book.

Approach 1. The first possible way to learn to communicate is through the use of analysis—that is, discovering ways to determine how successful each attempt at communication has been and to construct strategies for improvement. For example, one basic premise we discuss in this book is that knowledge is dependent on structure. How can a speaker structure his communication effectively? What is the relationship in structural terms between his goals and his behavior? Can he perceive the response he wishes to evoke from a particular person clearly enough to devise a method to achieve it, or does he phrase his goals so loosely that he cannot know whether he has achieved them or not?

One way to implement this kind of approach is to keep a communication diary. This would include a record of all your communications during a specified number of days. The record could then be analyzed to determine what your motivations were at the time you communicated and how successful you were at getting what you were after. You can use this information to determine what modifications are necessary in your behavior, and to determine of what service the class could be to you in assisting you to achieve these changes. Carrying this system to the ultimate would mean that only you could know how much you achieved in the course, and consequently you would have to award your own grade to yourself.

Approach 1 is based on the rationality of self-contained systems. It is presumed that there is a reason present for an act of communication. Merely trying to discover these reasons is useful in revising communication style. The hindsight that comes from the examination of a diary may indicate clearly to you that you are not capable of achieving your purposes by using your present methods. Once this discovery is made, it is easy to begin to pull out new ideas from the didactic information presented in this text. Thus, the material can come alive and be meaningful for you, and while progress may or may not be apparent to the instructor, most of you are capable of making your own decisions about how well you are doing.

The instructor using Approach 1 achieves his maximum function as a guide and consultant. His criticism is meaningful for it is solicited, and his suggestions are made to students interested in using them.

Approach 2. A second procedure for learning to communicate makes use of the formal examination of the content of messages transmitted. This is particularly helpful if your vocational goals include activities in which formal communications are important. Whether these are to be written or spoken is immaterial. There will be a structure to the messages and the bulk of the information transmitted will come through the structure. Bess Sondel, in the final chapter of her book *Humanity of Words,* lists a set of categories against which structure of messages can be checked.[1] By applying these categories to formal messages, you will be assisted in determining how much of your message will be transmitted in the form you wanted it.

An analytic approach, such as Approach 2, tends to be unreal, because it

---

[1] Bess Sondel, *Humanity of Words* (Cleveland: World Publishing Co., 1953).

removes both speaker and listener from consideration and focuses on message content. The addition of a simulation procedure, however, could make it more real. For instance, if you can describe the kinds of situations in which you might be called upon to communicate, you or the instructor should be able to generate some activities in which members of the class role-play with you and serve as live measures of your success. If your purpose is to convey information, you can check your effectiveness by determining how much information was retained by your listeners. However, if your purpose was to change opinions, some simple polling devices can offer a relatively accurate means of determining how effective your persuasion was. The point here is to do something real, and to make the situations as life-like as possible.

In the traditional approach to the teaching of communication, students are required to prepare outlines of various sorts before presenting the completed composition, orally or in writing. (There are several excellent tests that detail techniques of preparing a useful outline.) But one problem has always been that the student has not been able to perceive the purpose of preparing the outline. To him it often seemed a needless chore and many students write compositions and then generate the outline to satisfy the assignment. The purpose of outlining is to simplify the process of preparation by building a structure. Once the student understands this, he can easily develop a personal method of outlining that makes sense as an aid to preparation. Presumably, the outline implants a structure in the brain of the communicator. In speaking, for example, the outline is supposed to help retain the basic structure of the speaker's communication, while permitting him to adapt and adjust his words to the audience.

Most authors of public-speaking texts recommend that speeches not be memorized nor read from manuscript, except in certain very formal situations where complete control must be retained over the words spoken. They advocate instead what is referred to as the "extemporaneous" mode of speaking. This style is characterized by the presence of a plan, an understanding of content, and sufficient fluidity on the part of the speaker so that he can stress those parts of the message that evoke positive response while reducing his emphasis on those that appear to be received negatively. The use of an outline is supposed to help the speaker make these adjustments.

In writing, an outline is crucial, because the greatest hazard in student writing is disorganization and repetition. The random output of a mind, set down on paper, may have a cathartic effect on the writer, but only clear writing ever makes an impact on the mind of the reader. Some teachers must read, literally, thousands of these catharses every semester. Only the most clear have the desired effect of evoking a high evaluation. For this reason, if no other, students must learn to fit their material into structured form.

But the student profits most from the privilege of finding his own method of preparation and structuring. One may choose to put his outline in the form of a computer flow chart, indicating alternate tracks that can be taken if a certain kind of feedback results in the audience. Another, inclined to literary interests, may prefer to write his outlines in dactylic hexameter, and still another may prefer to do his outline in picture form, each picture evoking a stream of ideas in his mind. The point here is that whatever technique of preparation is used, it is most effective when it is generated out of the mind of the user and not lifted from a set of prescriptions in a text. We feel you must have considerable opportunity to experiment with types of preparation, and to make a critical assessment of which style is most effective for you.

Approach 3. Some students may prefer to concentrate on the psychological aspects of communication and use a quite different approach from either described above. They may have considerable interest in what it takes to motivate behavior on the part of others and what they have to do to evoke this behavior. Or students may be interested in communication as an heuristic or problem-solving device, while others may be interested in the formal process of argument. There may even be some who are only interested in communicating to release their personal tensions. Virtually all students, at one time or another, will be interested in creating, in doing something original, attempting to become artistic in their communication.

Most curriculums make some advance specification about the types of communication the student is supposed to work with in the classroom. In speech classes, students are usually asked to do a speech to inform, a speech to persuade, and a speech to entertain, as well as to participate in a problem-solving discussion. Each of these options may have some appeal to a portion of the students, but the greater number will move through the assignment as though it were a pledge duty. A very useful approach to learning is when the teacher outlines the options and then permits the students to work out their own methods of parceling out the assignments. Some students then may choose to work only in one area, because it fits their vocational objectives. There is no virtue in forcing students through activities that they regard as useless, since they will learn little from them anyway. It is useful, however, to have the class understand that its members have some control over their fate—at least in the limited world of a single classroom—and the experience at decision-making they receive while trying to parcel out assignments is invaluable. Students should also be given the task of developing a system of evaluation; they should then be bound by it. There is virtually no opportunity in a traditional college curriculum for the student to experiment with decision-making, particularly in a situation where he is bound by his own decisions.

As authors, however, we are not omniscient. There are many other possible approaches, and the three presented here are only samples. Given exposure to these, we feel virtually certain that you can discover your own ways and means. And, in all fairness, you should be, at least, aware of somewhat more traditional modes of participation. An exposure to the Bobbs-Merrill Series in Speech Communication will give you some idea of what has been happening in communication classes and will provide you with still more alternatives from which to choose, as well as with information presented in a manner very different from that of this book.[2]

[2] The Bobbs-Merrill Series in Speech Communication is a series of twelve paperback books dealing with the various fields of oral communication.

The teacher who uses an approach that gives the basic choice-making privilege to the student must be aware, however, that students at first will tend to resist the responsibility. The opportunity to develop their own curriculum is often jolting to students who, for years, have been compelled to adhere to a preordained curriculum in which the professor detailed for them precisely what they were to do and what they were to derive from it. Once again, the communication classroom offers a golden opportunity for a meaningful educational experience, provided both teacher and students are willing to take the "lumps" that are bound to come when the experimentation first begins.

THE USE OF PUBLIC SPEAKING

The feeling of power that comes from ability to sway the crowd has been a goal of many great figures in history. The lure of the public platform has been manifest to those who seek careers in politics, in the pulpit, and before the bar. The appeal of achieving skill in public speaking, apparently, is so universal that the natural model to follow in teaching oral communication has traditionally been built around the teaching of public speaking.

Sometimes, in fact very often, the desire to achieve skill at public speaking is not very strong in the student, who defines his communication needs as something a bit more immediate. He may be seeking skill at interviewing, so that he may be able to get a job, but most likely, he is unable to see the direct relationship between public speaking and his vocational goal. Most teachers-to-be, for example, really are not aware that the bulk of their work time is spent in public speaking.

Furthermore, the standard pattern of assignments in public speaking does not seem to articulate student needs. As a result, students often attempt to conform to whatever motivates a high grade from the teacher, and, consequently, the instruction has little or no permanent impact on them.

The first step in standard teaching of public speaking is for the teacher to make an assignment, usually a speech to inform, to persuade, or to entertain. The student is supposed to have free choice of topic, but the prevailing legend on campus directs his choice to those topics preferred by the instructor. The bulk of the textbooks make little attempt to guide topic choices into channels suitable to immediate or future needs of the students. But most "fraternity files" contain many speeches that have succeeded with a particular instructor.

Once a speech is given in class, it is criticized. The assumption here is that a "healthy mind in a healthy body" can internalize criticism and consciously bring it to bear on subsequent performance. There is, however, little evidence that this is so. Jurgen Ruesch, in his book *Therapeutic Communication,* states that this notion is firmly rejected in therapy, which assumes that guidance is necessary to evoke healthy self-criticism on which the subject can act.[3] This is essentially true in the public-speaking classroom as

---

[3] Jurgen Ruesch, *Therapeutic Communication* (New York: W. W. Norton, 1961).

well. Criticism is not relevant—unless it is solicited and is meaningful to the student. Furthermore, most classroom criticism tends to focus on the observable, hence the irrelevant. Much is made of pronunciation, grammar, type of delivery, use of gestures, and quality of organization. These are singled out because they are easier to "grade" than whether or not the student achieved the goal he set out to achieve. Furthermore, the performance aspects of public speaking tend to work themselves out if the speaker is properly motivated and concerned about what he is doing, and if this motivation does not exist, all the drill in the world will not improve his speaking.

The acts of criticism and grading give the teacher total mastery over the public-speaking classroom. Even though the preenrollment "advertising" has it that the student is free to make choices and be open in his remarks, the "weapon" of the grade carefully controls his choices, for few students are willing to jeopardize their expected "B" in a "cake" course. As we have said before, the objective of the typical student in the public-speaking classroom is to say what he has to in order to earn a good grade from a single instructor. While this might be an intriguing exercise, and quite useful if carefully motivated, as a steady diet it becomes defeating. The students learn only to speak to one man, and they do not make the necessary connections for carryover into life situations where they speak to many different men and women.

Criticism is defended on the grounds that students seem to "take it" or, at least, don't protest against it. But criticism is normally hard to take, even when solicited. While students appear to accept it because it is part of an academic "game" they understand all too well, their real attitude comes out in Student Union conversations where one often hears protests, loud and clear, about the inequity and impropriety of criticism administered in the speech class. The man who gives the criticism cannot know what goes on inside the person who receives it, and the system prevents the receiver from displaying his concern and hurt. Acceptance may be the order of the day, but the act of accepting criticism without protest does not mean that it is at all useful to the receiver. Furthermore, the only useful criticism is that which comes from inside the performer. The student must understand *in his own terms* what he must do to become more effective, and he must define what he means by "effective." A teacher-critic can offer guidance, but he cannot provide direction. For instance, if a student asks if his outline was sufficiently clear, the instructor can offer suggestions for improvement of organization. But the general lecture on outlining and the criticism offered publicly in the classroom often fall on deaf ears, because few, if any, of the students are willing to admit that either is directed to them.

Criticism offered publicly tends to put the student on the defensive. He seeks to justify his actions and prove the authority wrong, because he must do so to maintain status with his peers. He may also elect the alternative of denigrating the quality of the instructor, thus injuring morale and rapport in the classroom. If the teacher's criticism is administered privately, it is very time-consuming and not directly rooted in classroom activities. If the instructor permits classmates to criticize their fellow students, this criticism can be waved off because the other students are not "qualified" to criticize. It is, in short, easy to evade the impact of criticism and to defend against it.

Recently attempts have been made to apply new technology to criticism by using video-tape recorders and confronting a student speaker with himself. This enables the instructor to point to specifics in the student's performance. While this system may be highly effective with a strongly motivated future lawyer, the typical student is not emotionally prepared to see himself quite so vividly. The simple act of confrontation is destructive and to accompany confrontation with criticism, often before a class, is so defeating as to render some people completely unfit for any later platform performance.

The real question to be considered in a communication classroom is what kind of criticism is most effective in motivating improvement, and how can it be gotten to the speaker so that he can use it? There appears to be no universal system, for different people prefer different sorts of criticism. One student may welcome the suggestions of the instructor, while another may want to use the instructor to help him interpret the meaning of the behavior of the class during his speech. Still another may prefer no formal criticism at all and want to ruminate on what happened on his own time. Some may not care enough for the learning to want any comments at all. Each individual who seeks success at communication must determine for himself what sort of information is most useful to him. The class must be dedicated to helping him get what he wants. And the right to want nothing at all should be honored!

Certainly it is possible to work the student through a variety of challenging situations. For one type of performance, the instructor can criticize in the customary fashion. For another, the student can be asked to generate critical remarks about himself. Another performance can be followed by discussion and comment from the class. Critic panels can be employed, the members of which can be asked to talk about specific behaviors of the speaker. Still another possibility is to have anonymous written criticism turned in and the student speaker can select what is most useful.

It is imperative for teacher and student alike to concentrate on what is important when they consider the effectiveness of their public speaking. In many public-speaking courses and in many classrooms, the main concern has been with voice, diction, and gesture. Some traditional teachers talk about "poise" and "personality," the outward manifestations of the act of speaking. But these matters are not independent of the human who behaves them. They represent signs of the internal state of the speaker. If they are not stylized and controlled, they represent the person as he is, and if they are stylized and controlled, the speaker becomes an actor. Tampering with them may interfere with the flow of ideas, for if a speaker is forced to concentrate too hard on external manifestations, he will lose control over his material.

Yet, there are many mannerisms that are self-defeating and that reduce a speaker's effectiveness. Evidences of uncertainty or lack of conviction and involvement reduce the speaker's image in the eyes of the audience. These must be controlled in order for the speaker to achieve maximum success. Ritualistic behaviors, repetition of words and phrases, awkward pauses, vocalized hesitations, choppy gestures, graceless movements, and unpleasant facial expression can distract the audience from their attention to the meaning of a speaker's message. Thus, effectiveness in speaking seems to be tied up with speaker performance, quality of message, and the mental state of the audience. No one variable can be neglected.

If we accept the fact that the manner of delivery is influential in affecting audience reaction, we must raise the question of how delivery habits can be improved. If outward mannerisms are a sign of the state of the personality, we can reasonably assume that improvement of personality would improve outward behavior. Or, we might accept the obverse of this proposition and declare that improvement of external behavior would have a salubrious effect on personality. This latter assumption was made for many years by teachers of elocution. These teachers were eminently successful financially, although their pedagogical skill could be questioned on many counts. They attempted to teach skill in speaking, appropriate diction, and gestures. So elaborate were the routines that those who mastered them appeared artificial and were as ineffective as they would have been had they retained their old delivery style and their money.

Listeners seek authenticity, that is, they want from a speaker a genuine representation of his ideas and the value he places on them. Some distinction must be made between the speaker and the actor, for though an actor communicates, he is really a vehicle for the words and ideas of others. He may interpret but he may not invent. The public speaker, on the other hand, is responsible for the development of the ideas he presents to others, and audiences hold him accountable. When we talk of a poor actor, we speak of a man who has done poorly at transmitting the message of another. When we talk of a poor speaker, we may mean his message was insincere or that it was transmitted poorly. Once an actor has mastered his "message," careful attention can be paid to the way it is delivered. Furthermore, an actor is committed to his art, and will submit himself to the criticism that is necessary to improve his skill. For the student speaker, prime attention must be paid to development of the message. Only after (and if) he has developed sufficient concern for a worthwhile message will he be amenable to training in manner of delivery. For this reason, we recommend that the main concentration in class be on idea development: conceiving and organizing an idea with the audience in mind. Attention should be paid to delivery only when it is solicited by the student.

THE OLD AND NEW RHETORICS

Specialists will have recognized by now that we have been talking about some ancient categories for the study of speech. We have concerned ourselves with the image of the speaker *(ethos)*, the coherence of his case *(logos)*, and the response of the audience *(pathos)* in a fashion that has not changed very much since Aristotle originated these categories in the fourth century B.C. Furthermore, we have discussed the way a speaker discovers a message (invention), the way he puts it together (disposition), the words in which he phrases it (style), and the manner in which he says it (delivery). The only one of Cicero's original categories we have omitted is memory, since it is no longer necessary to commit large blocks of material to memory, although the retention of ideas and their supports is invaluable to the successful speaker.

An "Aristotelian" would tend to believe these categories and think of the speaker and speaking as split according to these verbalisms. Here is an example where general semantics may help view the speaker (and everything else) as a functioning whole in an environment. However, it is possible to use these categories to display the various alternatives for emphasis in a course of study.

Consideration can be made of the speaker and his storehouse of ideas, the information he carries with him, his ideas and how he derives them. A separate consideration can be made of the way he connects his thoughts and relates them to his audience, while still another investigation can be made of his language, his choice of words, and the way he connects them together. Concern can be shown for the formal aspects of delivery. Methods of preparation and use of notes can also be discussed. Taken together, these would generate a complete speaker. You, the student, can use these categories to analyze your skills and deficiencies, to determine what you can build on and what must be changed.

If you choose the Aristotelian approach, extreme care must be taken to avoid confusing *prescription* and *description*. In a sense, Aristotle was not advising men on how to become effective speakers. He was, rather, describing characteristics of the optimum speaking of his day. It is one thing to say that a speaker should be "well organized" and something else again to lay out the precise steps he must take to achieve this goal. There is little or nothing in the Aristotelian writings that would direct you toward methods of improvement. Once again, these must be generated within your own head.

For the student, the significance of the Aristotelian writings is really that every man is a "rhetorician"; every man seeks, in Aristotle's terms, "all the available means of persuasion." There is no act of communication that cannot be analyzed in terms of a persuasive goal. Even acts of soliloquy are directed toward persuasion of the self. Considered in this light, the act of talking carries with it a high degree of social responsibility.

It is easy to get trapped in complex philosophical considerations when discussing the act of communication. For example, you might assert that the practice of rhetoric involves the search for truth, and try to determine whether truth must exist in the mind of the persuader, or whether truth must emerge in the common mind through the clash of ideas. You might further assert that all men must have equal skill in persuasion if we are to attain the true democratic ideal. All we would need then to achieve the true Utopian democracy is a common course in speech for everyone. This is a splendid idea to contemplate, but it may delude us into believing that what goes on in our classroom has something to do with achieving that goal.

A more cynical view would be that every individual has very little capability to affect the course of history, or even his own destiny. Any effectiveness the common man might have at persuasion would exist for a very small group of people. And sometimes the cards are stacked; children are notoriously effective at persuading their parents, when they can convince no one else. There are very few men who achieve positions of great influence, and the cynic might add that this often has very little to do with their competence on the public platform. Furthermore, fame is fleeting, for even in this day of immersion in the mass media, there are those in America who do not remember Charles McNary, Johnny Ray, Joe Vosmik, and Britt Reed.

We might take a realistic view and note that the use of the tools for communication often results in misleading distortions of our own ideas. Our language is fragile and weak, certainly not strong enough to handle the thoughts and ideas we try to transmit with it. The abstractions in your mind that are brought together to form the concepts you talk about represent your own interaction with the world, which is a unique interaction shared by no one else. The equipment we have to transmit our personal feelings and ideas to others is the language we use, and the fragility of this instrument, both as we use language in our own heads to structure our ideas and as we use it to transmit those ideas to others, cannot be overemphasized. Any words we say have the capacity to distort someone else's ideas, to hurt feelings, to anger, or to disrupt.

The putting together of words into ideas for talk or writing is a complicated process and relationship, not to be undertaken lightly. The communicator may mislead himself by building inappropriate structures in his own mind, by clinging to misbeliefs, by believing the false to be true. He may further mislead others by disseminating his erroneous ideas as true, or he may feel the frustration that comes when others classify him as a fool because of the words he says.

Even if he is honest and his structuring appropriate, what one says can easily be misinterpreted by the listener, through no fault of the speaker. It is manifestly impossible to do a complete analysis that would enable a speaker to predict precisely how an audience would respond to his words. Our history is replete with such misinterpretations. Leopold and Loeb, for example, acted on their interpretation of the meaning of the philosophies of Nietzsche when they committed their "crime of the century." Many crimes were committed in the name of the church and for the honor of God because of misinterpretation of the words of the preachers. And have you seen the "Kill a Commie for Christ!" buttons?

Once an appeal is made to the emotions of the audience, there may be no way to control the response. It seems impossible to avoid triggering unhealthy emotions, even with the most bland communication. When a blatant emotional appeal is made and the audience becomes a mob, spoiling for blood, it is hard for the speaker to resist the feeling of power that comes to him from evoking such a response. Even if he succeeds in avoiding being carried away with his capability to impel people to action, he may be impotent when it comes to "turning them off" and deterring them from dangerous action.

Once you have achieved real skill at public speaking, it will become clear how much power the spoken word has over the minds and behavior of men. There are many instances of skillful speakers who have become prisoners of their own power, and find themselves playing for the response of the crowd rather than for acceptance of their premises. The concept of audience does not mean that the speaker has to change his ideas to fit those of the crowd. The man who does this is a demagogue. The real challenge in speaking comes in gaining acceptance for ideas from an audience that is unwilling or apathetic. This, incidentally, is the problem faced by most teachers, and the reason we have so much bad teaching is that so few teachers have recognized their rhetorical responsibility.

A major problem for the learner of public speaking is how to develop an active ethical code that will enable him to function as a responsible communicator in a free society. There is no such formal code neatly drawn up for your perusal. Most of the issues involved in the development of such a code are not clear-cut and cannot be resolved with a series of "thou shalts" and "thou shalt nots." It is recommended that the beginning speaker read *Ethics of Speech Communication* by Thomas Nilsen and attempt to generate a personal code from his ideas.[4] This problem of ethics is a worthy topic for class discussion and could take considerable time and evoke considerable interest, but it should be approached only after the students have developed sufficent skill so that they understand what the issues really are.

As a final caution, we see no point to forcing the learning of public speaking. The student who cannot perceive a place for it in his life ought to be spared the rigors of training, because if he can see no reason for it, he will not become effective. Even the wisdom of the teacher who can see a direct connection between skill at public speaking and achievement of the student's life goals is not particularly helpful, unless the teacher is sufficiently skillful as a persuader to inculcate this belief into the student. Even here, caution is necessary, for the wisdom of the teacher may not extend to predictions that are always accurate. The teacher's perception of what is relevant is refracted by his life experience and his vocation, a combination that often causes him to see what is not there. This is one of the many reasons for permitting the widest possible range of options for performance in the communication classroom.

INFORMAL PATTERNS OF SPEAKING IN THE CLASSROOM

While it may not be clear to you as a student just how public speaking will fit into your life, it is clear that considerable interpersonal activity is required of all of us. It may be necessary for your speech instructor to use

[4] Thomas Nilsen, *Ethics of Speech Communication* (Indianapolis: Bobbs-Merrill, 1966).

"all the available means of persuasion" on future teachers to get them to accept instruction in public speaking, but no such effort should be necessary to convince students of the benefits to be derived from acquiring skill at social interaction.

For most of us, the speaking that we do is purposive and set in a social context, but it is generally not public, in the sense that there is a formal audience addressed by a designated speaker. Our daily conversation may not appear to be purposive, but when we consider the relationship of speech to personality, each act of oral communication has at its root the desire of the individual to achieve a high evaluation in the eyes of others. Thus conversation is patently persuasive and rhetorical. You shouldn't have to stretch your imagination to understand that much of your future behavior will be evaluated by superiors largely on your communication skill, and your economic and status advancement will come about in some proportion to your ability to communicate your competency to those whose job it is to make decisions about it. In short, the way we "reach the power" is to communicate with it.

What we are is largely determined by the response of other people to us. The initial perceptions based on personal appearance can be overcome, for good or for evil, the moment we begin communicating. All of us have been startled by the attractive-looking girl with the whiny voice, or the suave-looking man whose speech smacks of incompetency. However, the more-lasting impressions are based on communication and response to communication.

The preoccupation of students with "conformity" indicates that they understand this folly, and fear the loss of personal identity through conformity based only on the requirements of social situations. We seek identity but, regrettably, sometimes the only way we can find it is to lose ourselves in some organizational or social structure, to which we conform with great rigidity. The problem for each of us is to discover a way to preserve our individual identity and personal integrity yet still evoke a positive response from the people around us. Flaunting our differences before society may be moderately satisfying in the short haul, but it does not enable a man to exert much control over society. Too much flaunting of differences relegates a man to a peripheral role where he is classified as irrelevant, foolish, dangerous, or sick, and where he no longer finds his views considered by those around him. In our interpersonal relations, we are involved directly in the rhetorical task of making our identity clear and our ideas pertinent in ways that others can understand and respect.

In many ways, success at interpersonal interaction comes from the same sources as successful public speaking. There must be coherence inside the speaker. His goals and purposes ought to be clear in his mind, and his motivations in any context should be equally obvious to himself. He must understand those he deals with and be able to adjust his words and sentences to them, so that they will understand and believe. This does not mean he must change his opinions to suit those of his listeners, but it does mean that he cannot (if he seeks success) slam others over the head with his ideas.

It is hard to conceive of a situation in which people talk to each other that is devoid of rhetorical process, even if the encounter calls for nothing more than finding a pleasurable way to structure time. People seek ascendancy in their relationships with others, and in each attempt to communicate all parties to the transaction seek ways to gain control of the situation and derive some advantage from the contact. Much interpersonal conversation is really a struggle for accommodation, a situation where all parties to the transaction try to feel relatively comfortable, so that they can all believe they have won. The man who can bring this feeling about in others is, of course, the big winner.

Is it possible to apply our learning about public speaking to acts of social intercourse? Can we be as conscious about the structuring of communications in social situations as we are in the more formal context of public address? To what extent can the process of analyzing an audience be applied to typical social encounters we have with others? If we are speaking to one person, it is clear that we have an audience, and we know it is possible to alienate our listener and evoke hostility, which may have unpleasant ramifications for ourselves. In this interpersonal situation we are in much closer contact with others than when speaking to a more formal audience. In direct confrontation, however, we can see what the other person does. We do not deal with a mass. We can respond at once to what we see and feel. It may well be, because of this, that the act of social conversation is more difficult than public speaking.

Returning to the problem of the student in a world that he perceives as one of alienation, we think that the most valuable service an academic course can provide is to offer him some insight into his personal role in developing his own identity and show him some ways in which he can cultivate and develop a real image of himself. The writing of George Herbert Mead makes it clear that we all develop much of our personality through interpretation of the behavior of others in response to our own behavior.[5] It is hard to identify and classify the responses that others make to us, and often we act on our own faulty interpretations. Yet, we tend to behave in our society the way others expect us to. Failure to live up to the expectations of others may evoke the classification of "unpleasant" or "mentally ill." Furthermore, any desire on our part to change calls upon us to make considerable adjustment in our personal behaviors, and sometimes demands that we discover a new and more appropriate social milieu in which to operate, one in which our behavior might be evaluated more positively. These ideas will be elaborated in the chapters to follow.

There are many people who seek to withdraw from social interaction because of their inability to adapt their behavior in such a way that it will consistently evoke satisfactory responses from their partners at interaction. They may seek to control, to remain superficial, or to remain silent. They seek a consistent pattern of response that will "work" with all social audiences,

---

[5] George Herbert Mead, *Mind, Self, and Society* (Chicago: University of Chicago Press, 1934).

but since they cannot adapt to others they cannot succeed at interaction. After many failures, they may attempt to withdraw and cease their efforts to make verbal contacts with others.

Once avoidance has been habituated, it becomes wrapped up with self-fulfilling prophecy. Interaction has failed; therefore subsequent attempts at interaction will fail; therefore no attempt is made to interact; therefore, failure is absolute. People of this sort may seek occupations that require as little interaction as possible regardless of their interests. Thus they deny themselves the possibility of self-fulfillment, and often they deny society their maximum services, which may be potentially valuable. Your class in communication must take into account the possibility that some of you may be on the verge of becoming this type of person, and provide the means for learning how behavior can be adjusted so that it tends to evoke more rewards.

Those who are strongly motivated to dominate tend to become obvious and blatant and defeat their own purposes. They may talk too much or try to bludgeon their listeners into submission through an intense outpouring of words, or they may bore their listeners into oblivion by not permitting them to take part in the transaction. These people, too, need training and understanding of the cooperative nature of the social transaction, and particularly they need a clear understanding of what they do to others through their dominant behavior and how they defeat their own purposes by doing it. They must acquire a way to evaluate their own successes and failures so that they do not perceive themselves, unrealistically, as being charming and delightful when they are intolerable bores in the views of others.

Still another group with which we must be concerned are those who seek to change their behavior style. This is particularly pertinent for the so-called disadvantaged, who are expected to take on new speech styles as they move into different economic and social strata. If such changes are to come about, however, considerable acceptance and support is necessary. As a person changes speech style, he must also change audience, because often the new patterns are unacceptable in the old society. Many an immigrant was appalled by the Americanization of his children, which he interpreted as a flat rejection of the "old ways." This may have been superficially a process of language acquisition, but learning new language styles really reflects changes in acculturation, and consequently, it forces a drastic change in living behavior, as drastic as that required of Eliza Doolittle when she was trained to talk like a duchess. The person who seeks change by acquiring new speech styles usually appears initially as a fraud. The person who has the capacity to change will do so once he is given the opportunity to move about in society. Finally, those who do not wish to change should not be plagued with the requirement of change by the schools, for their communication styles are quite useful and suitable to their own purposes, even though they may offend those in other segments of society.

Existential writers tell us that we seek "authenticity" in our communication, but the definition of that word is hard to come by. When we function as listeners, we are quick to utilize the opprobrium "phony" applied to either speaker or message, and when we use it we can associate it with all manner of characteristics that cue us to the fact that the person speaking is not communicating his real self. This may account for the considerable emphasis on technique in most writing about speech communication, because, as speakers, we seek to be genuine; we feel that inappropriate technique will betray us and make us appear to be counterfeit in the eyes of our listeners. Thus, all our interpersonal contacts are potentially fraught with emotional involvement of the entire personality as we strive for positive evaluation.

In examining an individual listener, however, no one can say for sure what constitutes an approving response. We seem to have only a series of assumptions, existing as myth or legend, that purport to tell us what constitutes approval. Empirically, however, it is clear that all people do not approve in the same way. For some, rigid attention constitutes a positive evaluation. For others, nervous involvement may convey the same message. Some will smile approval, but some will smile smugly to show superiority. It is not possible to distinguish between the two without considerable prior contact with the individual doing the smiling.

Restlessness is not necessarily a sign of inattention and sitting still is not a sign of total attention. The act of social conversation requires us to develop an impression of our partners over a period of time and in different contexts, so that we can gain an understanding of what constitutes their approval and disapproval. We learn then to play to what we see, and we can build our friendships on this accurate interpretation of their responses. But when we attempt to apply our understanding to initial contact with new people, we are prone to error, for each person's response style is unique.

There are many activities that can be carried on in the classroom which will help the student practice and sharpen his conversational skills. Role-playing is a particularly useful device. In a role-playing situation, a person is asked to assume the position of another and to act him out as he perceives him. The result is both an opportunity to work through a situation of simulated reality and an opportunity to examine our own perceptions of other people's behavior. These are equally important, and if role-playing is attempted in the classroom, both opportunities should be considered.

There are many possible ways to approach role-playing. The simplest is merely to assign roles, e.g., "You are the professor," "You are the dean," "You are the student in trouble," "Your problem is . . ." —now work it out. A more complicated format is required to build private agendas into the roles. Assignments are made publicly, but each role-player has a private role, known only to him, assigned as well.

Public: You are the professor   **Private:** You resent the dean and want his job

Public: You are the dean   **Private:** You seek the professor's support

Public: You are the student in trouble   **Private:** You really did it and are trying to get off the hook

Sometimes it is useful to make no private assignment, but instead to plant another role-player behind each participant and have these people function as alter egos, i.e., periodically say out loud what they perceive is going on inside the person who is playing the role. There are many other variations that can be developed in your own classroom to fit your needs.

When you deal with role-playing, you are dealing with perception. This activity helps you to see inside social situations and helps you to understand how you perceive these situations and what you use as a basis for evaluation. To achieve this purpose, however, you need to have considerable analysis and discussion of the scenes, concentrating both on discussion of the nature of the situation and the way the role-players perceived it and each other. It might be useful, for example, for a student to discover how he perceives the dean, for this awareness might help him better control his behavior toward that authority. Discovery of a negative perception might also help explain previous inabilities to interact well with that person.

Application of originality to the common problems of the student can result in the development of challenging and useful role-playing situations in the classroom. This is one situation where the students' expertise clearly outranks that of the teacher, for the students are thoroughly familiar with situations of concern to themselves. In fact, a strong teacher seeking honest reactions might even risk allowing the class to role-play him, in order to find out how he is viewed by the students.

There are some cautions that must be observed in using role-playing, however. We are not all consummate actors, and in role-playing situations while we tend to act out the way we view a situation we are limited by our capabilities to project a new personality. For this reason, role-playing sometimes is dull and lifeless. Certainly, it is an activity that cannot be required of everyone. In any group of students, however, there should be some who can perform well, and these ought to be permitted to act. The others can be encouraged to take part in the discussion that follows.

Also, it is hard to determine whether a role-player is performing himself in a situation or reacting to the typology of the person he is portraying. One way to control this ambiguity is to have students play themselves in various unfamiliar situations with other students enacting familiar roles. At least some of the role-playing will be unambiguous, and the players might get an idea of how they might react in those situations. Furthermore, role-playing frequently results in a kind of grossness of behavior which almost makes a caricature of the person being portrayed. Subtlety of internalized value projection cannot be expected of a role-player. For him, it is almost like opening the head and dumping in a new personality. Most of the action will be frontal and not subtle. Anger will be more angry than is natural, frustration more obvious and physical. Subtlety will only emerge when the role-player's own personality takes over. It is at this point that some complicated and refined analysis of perceptions can be done.

If you use role-playing in your class, don't expect success the first few tries. You must become familiar with the techniques and develop some ease at acting out. Your instructor will be required to extend his natural tolerance limits and set himself for the unexpected. In the comment and analysis period, it is wise not to discuss the quality with which the role was played, because the concentration cannot be on acting skill. It should focus on problems raised by the simulation. While it might be interesting to discuss how other persons would have acted out the role, such discussion can disrupt the freedom with which students role-play. If they think they will be criticized for their lack of acting skill, they will concentrate on technique and raise many inhibitions to their natural behavior. As a result, it will not be so easy to get to the problems the role-playing is supposed to clarify.

Through role-playing it is possible to accomplish many important goals. One of these is the capability that role-playing gives each of us to test oneself against unfamiliar or unpleasant situations. We can discover our own strengths and weaknesses and take steps to adjust our behavior for a real encounter. It also tends to reveal some of our concealed bigotries and barriers to clear thinking. The tension of the role-playing situation enables us to drop our defensive masks and reveal ourselves to ourselves and to others. We can display real beliefs and values that we would not care to talk about in a public speech. Role-playing is effective in the psychological clinic for just this reason. For example, the psychiatrist can discover hidden attitudes toward parents and siblings that may have been suppressed but yet contribute to failures of interaction. Revelations of this type are highly volatile, and care should be taken in the classroom to avoid situations that may compel players to give away more of themselves than they care to. Most instructors have neither the experience nor the credentials to cope with psychiatric emergencies, so in casting for roles, caution should be exercised to preserve some neutrality and not force individuals to participate who do not want to.

Empathy can be heightened through role-playing. It is possible for us to act out the position of the person with whom we disagree and thus gain insight into the reasons for his behavior. This kind of role-playing has been successfully used in various kinds of negotiations. Once the underlying reasons for the behavior of the other are understood, it is possible to work with them more effectively to derive solutions to mutual problems. This technique can be appropriately applied to differences of opinion between teacher and student.

Throughout, in the use of role-playing and similar sensitizing devices, care for the individual must be paramount. We must ask how much of ourselves we are willing to expose before we begin to participate in a role play. Do we really want to know some of the things we hide from ourselves? What if we discover that we are really unpleasant and incompetent? Would we be able to adjust to this information? Once we have opened ourselves to others, how much control can we exert over subsequent transactions? Is it possible for two people to assume something approximating a normal relationship after they have role-played each other? Is the normal relationship more desirable than what would come about after role-playing? These questions are solid meat for classroom discussion and should be considered in depth after the first tentative efforts to use role-playing. The technique is so power-ful that students are entitled to know what they are dealing with, and what the possible gains and risks are, before committing themselves fully to the activity.

There is, however, considerable analogy between the communication classroom and the mental health clinic. In each case, the supervisory au-thority, teacher on the one hand, psychologist on the other, seeks to make possible a behavior change on the part of another person. Care should be taken, however, to insure that the classroom does not become so clinical that learning is subordinated to personality change. It is wise to assume that the students who come to it are basically normal and that the teacher does not have a monopoly on truth about what constitutes desirable behavior. If students have been permitted to generate their own goals and activities, this will not be of so much concern, for they will act of their own accord and take their risks as they find them necessary. Arbitrary imposition of role-playing in the typical classroom without apprising the students of the potency of the tool takes serious liberties with their personal right to protect their self-esteem, and generates risks for the teacher that he is not entitled to take.

If role-playing appears to be excessively volatile, or if the students prefer not to use it, other methods can be used to get to the heart of some inter-personal transactions. Sensible and controlled observation of people acting in a relatively natural state can offer some insights. Observation of interaction in the Student Union, at fraternity parties, and on the campus in general can provide substantive material for discussion about what constitutes a normal transaction. Personal testimony and introspection are also useful.

Sociometric techniques can be used to develop situations in the class-room that can be examined intelligently. One such technique, for example, can be applied as follows:

1. The class is asked to divide itself into groups to work through a series of problems. The initial groups are set up at random, with students rotated so that they have contact with most or all of their fellow students.
2. Students are then asked to fill out a simple questionnaire in which they designate those persons they would prefer to work with and those they would prefer to avoid.
3. Groups are then reconstructed, sometimes with people who mutually choose each other, and sometimes based on mutual hostility.

After a series of such experiences, the student can analyze his own be-havior and derive for himself information about how he functions in situa-tions of friendship and hostility.

Problem topics are easy to generate. They may be drawn from the class-room, campus, or community. For example, try some of these (and then generate your own):

1. How can grades be made to represent the real man?
2. Is there any other time, more convenient, when this class can meet?

3. What recommendations would we like to make to the editor of the school newspaper?
4. What should be done to protect students from suffering double punishment for misdemeanors, that is, on campus and in the community?
5. How can the high rents in the dorms be reduced?

It helps in working through problems like these to prepare a written report at the end, so that you get the experience of working through the problem and then finding out if you really agree on the written solution.

Although this sociometric approach lacks some of the reality of role-playing, if the problems the groups are called on to work out are relevant to their interests, solid improvement results. The "Eureka" type problems that have one solution should be avoided. It is more successful to ask groups to prepare brief written statements about their collective attitude toward contemporary problems. It is helpful if the students are willing to submit to grading on these activities. Grading, if it is done, should be competitive, so that some legitimate stress is built into the transaction, i.e., the instructor or a team of neutral referees should rank the outputs and award grades on his rankings. For example, if your problem deals with the college library, the head librarian could be asked to rank the reports.

Another possible approach is to demonstrate to students that it is possible for them to make considerable self-exposure to others without any particular risk. Although most students perceive themselves as quite friendly and outgoing, the typical college campus has considerable xenophobia, and students tend, for the most part, to adhere to the familiar, both in choice of situations and social contacts. Friendship patterns can be broadened and a successful experience at interaction provided through the use of dyad interviews between pairs of students who do not know each other very well. In this activity, a format is provided for the interviews; students are asked to interview each other on their background, education, goals, values, interests, dreams, hangups, immediate wants, etc., and perhaps to explore in depth values in politics, religion, sex, friendship patterns, use of drugs, the draft, etc. The more personal the topics, the more effective the transaction. Each person then prepares a report on the interview and details in words the picture that has emerged in his mind of the other person. The problem can be extended by asking each party to predict how the interviewer will react to him, or by having each participant read the report and present a rebuttal. Experience with this system has demonstrated it to be quite popular with students, most of whom testify that it enabled them to make a friend out of a casual acquaintance or total stranger, and further they discovered that most of their personal problems and beliefs were not unique.

The formal teaching of interpersonal transaction is relatively new, and few people are demonstrated experts at it. Any class that attempts it should define themselves as innovators and experimenters and be prepared to make some educational history. There is simply not enough tested material to devise anything approximating a foolproof system. Consequently it is legitimate for common decision-making by teacher and class, and in the view of the authors, it is most appropriate for learning of communication in general.

THE USES OF GROUP DISCUSSION

Most often, in the traditional speech class, interpersonal interaction is taught through group discussion. The textbooks approach discussion primarily as a problem-solving methodology, but in practice, students are asked to consider problems far outside their scope of competence and interest. Trying to solve integration problems or foreign-policy impasses represent a simulation activity so far from reality that learning does not really result. About all that can be gained from using broad problems is some familiarity with method.

Group discussion can be made more real by using it as the tool with which the rest of the class is shaped. If students are given, at the beginning of the semester, the problem of discussing their class and determining what should be done, they will attend to the business at hand, and since they have a stake in the outcome, they will receive more experience with the reality of interpersonal contact in a small problem-solving group.

Rules and regulations of group discussion need not be repeated here. A concise explanation can be found in *Communication and the Small Group*.[6] Learning the rules of group discussion is merely an academic exercise, however, unless it is accompanied by working through real problems.

THE USE OF ORAL READING

The technique known as oral interpretation of literature can also be useful in generating ideas about communication and the individual's role in it. Commonly, this activity is taught and used as an artistic method, a sort of theater, and training in it is accompanied by many critical comments designed to improve both the understanding of the selection and the technique of reading it.

The device can also be used, however, to expose the class to ideas about communication in literature by presenting selections that reveal the commonplaces of human tension and confusion in interpersonal transaction. Some of the commentary of Holden Caulfield in *Catcher in the Rye*, for example, may strike a familiar chord with some students. Kafka's *Castle* is a splendid revelation of the universality of alienation of men from one another. Students with a literary bent can be asked to select from their favorite literature and read to the class passages that involve human communication. These selections then can become the substance of class discussion, which may help to open some individual explorations. There are

[6] Gerald M. Phillips, *Communication and the Small Group* (Indianapolis: Bobbs-Merrill, 1966).

a number of good texts about oral interpretation. Most useful are the three chapters in *Speech: A Course in Fundamentals.*[7]

SUMMARY

We have, in this Introduction, dealt with many activities that can be used to assist the student in learning something about himself as a communicator. Suggestions have been made about individual responsibility in improvement, and some options have been proposed for the class to facilitate individual progress. Clearly, the classroom is an essentially artificial arena for learning to communicate and steps must be taken to bring into it a vestige of reality, if the student is to do something more than master didactic prose about communication.

We have encountered a paradox in approaching the problem of how to learn to communicate, in that the act of performance in the classroom may be studied and dissected but, because it is in the classroom, it is not real. Behavior outside the classroom is real, but it cannot be observed systematically enough to provide a cogent study. Our only recourse seems to be to make the classroom as much of a model of reality as is possible.

The process of learning to communicate cannot be compared to any other segment of the traditional academic curriculum. There is a body of subject matter about human communication that is interesting to learn and often is useful to the learning communicator. Both interest and use, however, are personal matters. There is no reason to believe that mastery of subject matter alone will improve communication skill.

There are, also, several generalizations that have been made and methodologies proposed, the use of which are alleged to improve communication skill. No doubt they do so in *some* cases. But what of the others? What about the student for whom the class in speech is pure pain or the class in written composition a terror? Can society permit him to remain locked in, without seeking ways and means to permit him to make contact with his fellows? We cannot forget that speech is *all that is specifically human,* and the logical corollary is that *inability to communicate reduces the capacity to be human.*

So much is at stake in the learning of communication. For a long time speech has been left to chance, almost to casual development. The schools and society have assumed that because people speak at the time they come to the schools, they know how to speak. Little attention has been paid to expression of ideas, although there has been much attention paid to the form in which the ideas are expressed. There has been almost no attention paid to the object of communication, the listener or the reader, and much of the purposiveness of the communication act has been lost through the requirement of standards of presentation.

The ferment of our time is a sign of communication breakdown, a gen-

[7] S. J. Crandell, and others, *Speech: A Course in Fundamentals* (Glenview, Ill.; Scott, Foresman, 1963).

eralized disorder in our society. The channels through which people make contact with each other seem to be blocked. We talk of generation gap and credibility gap without being aware that these gaps are really signs of ineffective communication, inability of the parties to a transaction to make themselves clear to the others. We assume that mere contact or repetition, improvement of form, or renaming of the elements will work some magic, but the real magic must be worked inside human beings.

The need to communicate well must be appreciated by the individual. The teacher has the persuasive task of inducing the student to appreciate it. Once the student comprehends the cruciality and centrality of his task, opportunity for experimentation must be permitted and full opportunity offered for the individual to expand and improve in his own way and on his own terms. Accomplishment of this kind of learning would do much to make relevant and meaningful other aspects of academic study. Equipping a man with the feeling that he is an effective communicator enables him to make what he learns come to life as he talks and writes about these things with facility and confidence. He can experiment with ideas and concepts; he can think, speak, and write aloud; and he can interact with others to improve his ideas. Thus, he can improve his contribution to society—to the good of all around him.

This is not hyperbole. This book hopes to assert the complexity and the imperative of human communication and the learning of it, because the skilled communicator is the maximum human being, someone sorely needed in a world of rigidity, anonymity, and barriers to humanness.

And it's your ball game now. . . .

No one else's!

SUGGESTIONS FOR FURTHER READING

Keith Brooks, ed., *The Communicative Arts and Sciences of Speech* (Columbus, Ohio: Charles Merrill Books, 1967). This book is a thorough index of the speech discipline and its related fields. It is literally a survey of the field and is thus a valuable reference.

Thomas Griffith, *The Waist High Culture* (New York: Harper and Row, 1959). Although somewhat dated by over a decade, this book describes some trends that are evident today. It points out a need for effective communication; the events of the past decade have served to underscore the importance of Griffith's message.

S. I. Hayakawa, *Language in Thought and Action* (New York: Harcourt, Brace, and Company, 1949). Like many classics, this book will never be dated. It is highly rated as a primer on the how and why of effective human communication.

John R. Searle, "Human Communication Theory and the Philosophy of Language," in *Human Communication Theory*, ed. Frank E. X. Dance (New York: Holt, Rinehart and Winston, 1967). Dr. Searle presents a concise and scholarly overview of the major technical points covered in several interrelated theories of human communication.

SPEECH: Science-Art

1

That Man May Talk
and Live

Not so long ago, the rose was a thorny, wild flower.

One of the wonders of our age has been the improvement of roses. The horticulturists brought this about by studying the rose in its total environment. Larger roses are now grown, more varied and more beautiful; they bloom longer and have fewer thorns.

But outside of science fiction, there is no horticulturist scientifically to improve the strain known as mankind. We must improve ourselves as we change with our changing environment, and as we attempt to probe our special relationships within that environment.

The purpose of this book is to contribute to an understanding of the way man accomplishes *relationships*—that is, his communication and his speech.

The proper study of communication and speech requires far more understanding of human behavior than is usually associated with the traditional approach to the subject. In a sense, human communication is the end product of the social sciences, and within that context, speech is probably man's ultimate behavior. Man's speech, which is taken for granted by so many, is our most complex behavior, and it can be studied only by thorough examination of both its scientific and artistic features.

Of all the animals on this planet, only man must learn to live with two kinds of change—natural change and his own change within nature. As self-titled rulers of our planet, we have become a living paradox: as we change our environment to better our lives, we often destroy what nature has produced for us. Up to now, the earth has managed to survive. If land is left alone, it tends to develop species fit to live on it. Though its life conditions may be chaotic, the chaos seems to be orderly. If there is no gross interference, events seem to reoccur that reveal nature's ability is sufficient to sustain life. Of course, doomsday criers remind us that we live in the omnipresent shadow of a gigantic nuclear cataclysm which could shatter and destroy both earth and universe. Others say that our ancestors predicted that the crossbow would destroy the human race and that the invention of gunpowder doomed the world. Happily, life seems to have the edge over death in the historical win column—for now, at least.

Part of survival must be attributed to pure chance, and part to the beautiful rhythm that nature develops if left alone. Most animals do not attempt to interfere; they have a sense of participation in natural cycles and they win or lose as they compete with natural conditions, each on his own level. Man, alone, has the ability to interfere with his ecology and, as a result, he is doubly threatened. Each time he surmounts a natural obstacle, he creates an artificial one for himself. Once more, we note the paradox. Man seems to be the best and worst thing that has happened to the earth. We can disrupt the balance of growth to produce more food, but at the same time we may deplete the land. Archeology testifies to vast man-made deserts and the buried ruins of extinct civilizations. As we drive across our country today, we see wastelands that are the results of man's exploitation of irreplaceable treasures. The things we use quickly outlive their usefulness, and with much inefficiency, we discard them, polluting our air and water or piling them in untidy heaps of junk on our land.

The damage we do to our environment is small, however, when compared with what we do to ourselves through war, crime, and incredible waste of the human mind. It has been said rather cogently that the most underdeveloped territory in the world lies under our hats. If this is so, we can safely say that, of all the things which make us unhappy, we are guilty of creating most of them ourselves.

When and if we learn to form suitable relationships, we will not defeat ourselves so often. When we learn to cooperate with nature, we will be able to make natural forces work for us; and when we learn to cooperate among ourselves to achieve our full potential we may be able to build a world that is fit for us to live in.

Generally, as our physical discomfort has been reduced, our social discomfort has increased. It is most questionable whether the modern jungle of Desmond Morris' *Naked Ape* has progressed further or is more secure than the primitive jungle world of Raymond Dart's *Adventures with the Missing Link*. The threats we now face are far more subtle, but no less deadly, than those confronting our little ancestor *Australopithecus Erectus* in the basal period of the Pleistocene Epoch some 2,000,000 years ago.

As primitive man discovered that he must band together with his fellows to contend against natural threat, today we know it is imperative that we unite to overcome the self-made travails of the twentieth century. The same science and technology that produces our physical comfort and security and enables us to overcome today's travails has also placed us in the jeopardy of one final war. And if war does not erase us by nuclear bombs, we may be destroyed instead by the implosion of each human as he discovers that frustration and boredom is his lot in life and that his unique identity is irrevocably lost. We live in the "worst of times and best of times," and once again, our ever-present human paradox raises its head. All man's achievements have brought him to this place where we must now decide for survival or total destruction.

Our major hope in this struggle for survival is communication. Today's problems are so complex that no one man can solve them alone. Men must work together against war, against persecution, poverty, starvation, frustration, boredom. Communication—the science or art by which humans relate to each other—must be universally learned and practiced well.

Yet communication is not a skill to be taught like watchmaking or swimming. It must be learned in the context of vital problems. Today our communication patterns and techniques remain primitive, because we have not yet discovered scientific techniques by which to improve them. Attempts to improve our ability to communicate have been made by grammarians, linguists, philologists, rhetoricians, and general semanticists. Like the paradox of man's evolution, each effort has introduced both confusion and progress. No single system is an Aladdin's lamp, of course, with the magical means to solve our communication problems; the problems are too firmly rooted in the subtle complexities of our world. But one thing is certain: that the answer lies somewhere within ourselves, and somewhere within the society we have created for ourselves. Let's look for some clues.

THE CYBERNETIC REVOLUTION

After the bomb was exploded, the years since 1945 have been designated as the Atomic Age. Yet, despite the awesome power of the released atom, it is the computer that has had more actual influence on the life of most people. Several years ago a science-fiction writer wrote about a computer-run civilization, dull, with little creative force, but a civilization in which the destructive potential of man's ideas had been quelled and suppressed. Today there is virtually no area of human intellectual endeavor to which the computer cannot be applied. It has been used in the analysis of ancient manuscripts, to translate from one language to another, to write poetry, music, and drama. It has been used to match cattle in dairy herds and to arrange marriages between men and women. It can solve unbelievably difficult mathematical problems and compute statistical operations impossible by hand. It can play tic-tac-toe and checkers, simulate wars and corporate operations, and both catalog and retrieve information. It has extended our capability of knowing far beyond the imagination of history's scholars.

The computer has been used by some scholars as a model for human communication. Because the computer must be "talked to," these scholars have assumed some similarity to human communication. The analogy, of course, breaks down when we observe that a human is a self-contained communication apparatus, capable of communicating with himself as well as with others. However, the computer does reveal some essential ideas about *how* communication is carried on. Computer programmers translate an idea into a language that the computer can understand and to which it can respond. Of course, the language was put into the computer by man, but once a machine has been programmed certain of its capabilities surpass those of the men who "feed" it data.

While we learn how to communicate with the computer, we must also learn something about how men respond to communication. Our understandings can be built into new and advanced techniques of teaching and learning, so that communication, in general, is improved. This cannot be done if we regard man solely as a self-programmed computer. Our ultimate goal is not to talk to computers but to communicate with others. The initial step is to understand each other and the rules and territories we set for ourselves. These consist of our mores, traditions, and laws. We call them civilized society.

THE RISE OF THE MIDDLE CLASS

There was a time, at least in the Western World, when man could withdraw from his community, move elsewhere, and attempt to build precisely the type of life he wanted. He could work toward an agrarian or industrial society to suit his needs. If he wished, he could maintain a mere survival existence. His aspiration level often could be satisfied by the work of his own hands. He did not need to depend on others for goods or ideas. Even though his economic lot was poor, he could be relatively independent of others in his decisions. In our day this is impossible.

Modern technology has brought a proliferation of affluence, gained largely at a sacrifice of independence. To achieve prosperity, we have found it necessary to cluster populations in cities. Thus, it is no longer possible for a man to avoid communicating with others. In many cultures, where life is hammered from the land, silence is a symbol of association. But the complex industrial society in which we live is the result of men talking together to solve mutual problems. In so doing we have constructed a society in which it is no longer possible to be alone.

Though acquisition of necessities is no longer a problem for most Western people, our facility to satisfy our needs has confronted us with problems of congestion, transportation, air pollution, billboard proliferation, racial conflict, crime, and boredom—problems indigenous to a middle-class, urban culture. The problems we face in our modern society are so complex that one man cannot handle them. The leisure that has come to us because of expanded technology makes it necessary for humans to talk with each other at work and at play.

THE POPULATION EXPLOSION

The phrase "population explosion" has been used so often that it is now a cliché, but that does not make our population explosion any less a problem. The full implications of the problem have been diluted by over-use of the phrase, yet no problem faced by man makes improvement of communication more urgent.

There are so many people on this earth that the search for solutions often ignores the individual human. Gross solutions, manipulation of whole populations, seem to be the only ones. If one man disagrees, it is techno-logically simpler to destroy, imprison, replace, change, or ignore him than it is to understand and adjust to him. There is little room for individual thoughts in the big, money-colored worlds of business, industry, or gov-ernment.

Science's advances have created hardship too. Agricultural technology now keeps food production in pace with the increasing appetite of a grow-ing world population, but the world's economy and the balance of produc-tion and distribution systems have lagged in certain territories and cultures. The result is some people actually starve to death, while others throw away surplus food. In underprivileged lands, the struggle for food is hope-less, and societies dream their dreams of comfort and ease while their citizens starve on the streets. To keep their people in line, leaders usually resort to base totalitarian methods and use a kind of political witchcraft to perpetuate a state of virtual slavery. "We starve because we are at war with the enemy" is the slogan used to rationalize deprivation. Often, more sympathetic societies fail to realize that they are in the twentieth century and permit age-old superstitions and taboos to get in the way of human survival. Only to the extent that we can communicate about these prob-lems have we hope of solving them.

But man's paradox creates new ironies, as he faces the truth of the 1970's and the population explosion becomes a cultural proliferation.

AN EXPLOSION BECOMES AN IMPLOSION

Expansion of societies and close groupings of people have reduced the possibility of a man finding his identity. Human intellects, striving for uniqueness, have generated a stream of art, poetry, literature, and drama far beyond the capacity of our society to utilize. Scholarly writing has in-creased to the point where no one can keep track of the developments in his own field, much less be able to select pertinent literature elsewhere. Each writer and artist is a communicator seeking a mass audience. There is so much from which to select, however, that works that might have been successful 50 years earlier are rarely read today.

Creative talents seek rewards where they find them. Many of our most gifted artists and writers find financial rewards in writing slick pieces that make little pretense at being anything other than prurient for television, the movies, and the popular magazines. The creative output of the advertising industry, which fuels our economic life, utilizes the best of our writers and illustrators and rewards them fabulously.

Once the written or spoken word was a powerful tool for social change Today our society is filled with unread words and unheard orations. Direct-mail advertising ends up in the wastebasket, and commercial messages fall on ears made insensate by the throbbing beat of the "rock and rollers." Escape in film and slicks characterizes the routine life of man. The theme of our time was expressed by some lyrics:[1]

. . . and in the naked light I saw ten thousand people, maybe more, people talking without speaking, people hearing without listening, people writing songs that voices never shared. . . . No one dared disturb the sound of silence, . . . and, the people bowed and prayed to a neon god they made. . . ."

Today's flood of books, radio, television, and films has brought a semblance of literacy to millions, and now it is possible for people to communicate with all parts of the world, to understand other people and other times. Transcultural understanding is a moral imperative, because only as cultures communicate and interact with each other can they insure mutual understanding, which, as we have said, is the initial step toward survival.

Threats to our survival continually mount. In our land, the underprivileged threaten us with violent, seething unrest. Overseas, racism rears its head as new cultures emerge. Starving people have discovered that there is a better way to live. Before destruction befalls us, we had better learn to talk with each other. Let us suppress action by making use of words, our distinctive gift of communication. The petty, chauvinistic issues, which so often in the past led to war between nations, must now be suppressed through nations speaking reason and logic, for the threat of total annihilation makes international understanding imperative.

Our world has become so intricate that it seems hopeless to find solutions through the slow democratic process, while the totalitarian rule by men who "know" all the answers is undesirable. We seem to be on the verge of being pushed into universal-authoritarian control. Increased participation in society and government by the individual is urgent, so that personal freedom can be gained for those who do not have it and maintained for those that do.

Above all, the individual human being must communicate with and receive communication from his fellows, so that he may find his personal identity, so that he may communicate to avoid choosing the path of mental derangement that accompanies anonymity within the great supersociety.

---

[1] From Paul Simon, "The Sound of Silence," Charing Cross Music. © 1964 Charing Cross Music. Used with the permission of the publisher.

INCREASING FOLLY IN THE MIDST OF INCREASING KNOWLEDGE

For Cicero, the educated man was the man who knew all about everything, who could speak with grace and elegance on any occasion. This may have been possible in Cicero's day when "all" knowledge could be found in a compendium. Sadly for us, no library today can pretend to have all knowledge. Our mammoth dictionaries contain many words that become obsolete with frightening rapidity. Every area of knowledge and every profession has its special library, dictionary, and language. The products of research laboratories increase fantastically, for today more scientists are alive than lived in all past time. Yet their jargons are so formidable and specialized that few of them can communicate with others.

H. G. Wells's comment that civilization is a race between education and disaster was never more true than today. We have knowledge available to help us solve almost any problem. Our journals are glutted with scholarly discoveries that must be taught. More and more it becomes imperative that there be a body of knowledge held in common. The main need in education today is to open communication among scientist, humanist, and technologist.

Teaching is a rhetorical process, a study in persuasion. The major contact between student and teacher is motivational, carried on through talk with one another. The successful teacher is a happy combination of ethos and pathos, and his entire image and being is the key to learning by the student. Real motivation to learn comes from the persuasive power of the teacher, because his attitude toward a subject matter is the crucial factor in motivating a student to learn that subject. For this reason, it is critical that educators lead in the search for improved communication.

The teaching profession, however, is not the only occupational group with a need for speaking ability. Among all the academic disciplines speech is perhaps the only skill that crosses the often inflexible borders of occupational specialization.

Specialization has come to us without balance. Science has raced us into a gadget age, a space age, and a computer age, while the humanities and arts, not sure which scientific advances are important, continue to focus their efforts on the old, and often tired, excitement about the irrelevant and the trivial. As a result, the arts tend to communicate less than ever with the sciences. This academic inability to talk together, as each specialized field diverges farther from the others, confronts us with an intellectual Tower of Babel. The disciplines *must* talk to each other, share knowledge, and work together to solve problems. The "art" of science must be explained to humanists, while the "science" of art clarified for the engineers.

The *behavioral science* and *humanistic art* of communication is the potential channel through which disciplines can speak to each other and provide a common denominator for all man. To dig this "channel" requires an understanding of the nature and purpose of communication, as well as mastery of the artistic elements of presentation. It cannot be assumed that, because men have been speaking since birth, they are adequately trained to communicate. Neither can it be assumed that mastery of didactic wisdom will automatically result in intelligent activity. The man who wishes to learn to communicate must master ideas and behaviors.

Our follies are evident. Attempts to communicate something new still arouse tremendous resistance. The new math and the new grammar are still fought in the schools. Fluoridation and birth control are fought in various communities. Our politics are marked with sloganeering and our international relations with chauvinism. We punish the mentally ill for their sickness by imprisoning them, while we reward our criminals by providing security for them. Despite discoveries on every side, it seems impossible for scholars to reach the community. This cannot be blamed on the stupidity of the ordinary citizen. Most scholars are inadequate speakers and writers, unconcerned with the communicative impact of their reports. They talk to each other and decry those who attempt to popularize. In the community, listeners and readers take the path of least resistance and heed the slick magazines and the shrill cries of TV, or they talk vapid bromides to each other.

Small children, free of resistance to learning, are the ones to whom sensible communication systems can be taught. The adult community, however, cannot be ignored. Every effort must be made to expand communication training on all levels. Our so-called educated elite are by no means free from responsibility for making intelligent communication.

The youth of today, ironically, seem separated and alienated from the problems of their times. They seek leaders and causes, but they resist analysis and understanding. A few years ago, pedants deplored apathy among students. Today these same pedants look in bewilderment at the myriad of movements to which young people commit their lives. What is now happening to students represents the failure of the academic to communicate with the real. The gap has widened and the academic community stands in bewilderment at the emotional ferment of the young people they must teach.

Cicero would not be a worthy model of communication for today. His "either-or" logic would be considered dangerous. Charismatic leaders of this century, such as Mao, Castro, and Hitler, utilized two-valued, oversimplified ways of viewing complex situations and accompanied them with brainwashing, systematic twisting of vocabulary, tremendous pressures to force learning by unscrupulous rewards and punishments, and exploitation of behavioral sciences to control the minds of men.

The purpose of science is not to control men's minds but to free them. If this is to be accomplished we must understand that communication no longer has social control as its only legitimate goal. Rather, its main goal must be social cooperation and understanding. Speakers and writers alike must prepare themselves for this new use of communication; listeners and readers must be ready to receive new types of messages.

BINDS AND DOUBLE BINDS

The harnessing of our resources—earth, water, tides, solar energy, the atom—can enhance human welfare beyond anything we can now conjecture—provided we are able to distribute the benefits to all mankind. The development of sophisticated tools has reduced the use of human muscles to a minimum but has not compensated by conferring on man increased ability to cope with environmental problems.

Food, clothing, and shelter are easier to come by than ever before. Nature has given up her secrets to revolutionize agricultural production and food processing. New construction methods result in secure housing. Natural resources have been converted into energy. Throughways contour the landscape. Skyscrapers and suburbia accommodate the living needs of man. Transportation around the world is available to all, while food chains, supermarkets, banks, and insurance companies organize and minister to other human needs. The society of today reflects the limitless resources and imagination of the coordinated human mind.

The complexity of increasing power is reaching a point that is dangerous to us all. It is another paradox. The individual man had to be submerged in the great organization. The consequent search for individuality leads to wild anarchy. The riots in our large cities, libertinism and the decline of moral values, slaughter on the highways, mass murders—these are signs of striving for individuality in a society where the individual loses his worth as the worth of his organization increases. Excessive freedom of organization leads to misuse of power. Our century has witnessed a high-powered national state run wild when controlled by a madman named Hitler.

This great issue of the use of power and resources pervades our lives and influences all our decisions and messages. The stuff of society is the fabric out of which all communication must be fashioned. The old problems of freedom and order have not been resolved. Indeed, communication about them is more and more imperative. Man finds himself today in what Gregory Bateson calls "binds and double binds," which begin when a young child senses that mother's loving words mask a feeling of rejection, or, that what mama wants the child to do, papa disapproves of. We prize our organizations because they provide us with goods. We hate our organizations because they deprive us of individuality.

We are in a bind if we go forward, backward, sideways, or even if we stand still. Ask any executive about the problems of decision-making, or any student about the everyday paradoxes he confronts in high school or college. Ask the Secretary of State or the head of any state. Ask yourself. Most men cannot even say to themselves what their real problems are. The system of balances characteristic of Western culture is a vast improvement over the one-way communication system of tyrants. We rely upon the two-way system to bring justice into families, industries, organizations, and institutions. But the two-way check and balance system no longer is fully satisfactory. It has not prevented power from running wild. Its conservatism has retarded needed reforms necessitated by massive changes in our ecology. For many underdeveloped nations, traditional democracy does not hold out the hope for the future that it offered the United States.

Communications systems must become multidimensioned. In the new society, men must be able to talk to one another, so that all can find dignity and a sense of personal worth in their lives. Only by increasing the communicative power of the individual can we prevent the anonymous "organization" from destroying what we have built. By teaching men to communicate with each other, we can preserve the best of our society. Through broader and more authentic interaction, we can be spared anxiety, neurosis, withdrawal, and apathy.

Nature has provided the grand analogue, for the mind of man can learn about her multidimensioned workings. Science has gone far toward doing the same. Science no longer is a search for a first cause or a philosopher's stone. Science today is multidimensioned, with many men and many phenomena interacting to develop systems and understandings.

As we go on, we hope to combine some of the results of scientific discovery with the empathies of human art and shape them into a communication theory and methodology which might improve relationships between people. There is a paradox here, also, for we do not yet know enough about human communication to call it a science, yet it is so vital to personal expression that we must regard it as an art. Thus, we will examine the science-art of speech. Where we have data, we will offer it; where we do not, we will present our honest feelings. In any case, what you, the student, should have at the end of this study is your own personal kernel of a theory of what speech is all about.

SUGGESTIONS FOR DISCUSSION

1. What do you think about the possibility of the "scientific improvement of man"? What expectancies did you have about your university in regard to your personal improvements? Can you think of some rules and regulations you learned somewhere that helped you "improve"? Is there anything you would like to say about this to your professors? To the college administration? To your classmates? (Would it make any difference if you could write your thoughts down anonymously? If it would, do it.)

2. Man has made many improvements on this planet. Was the invention of the automobile an improvement? The development of heavy industry? Discuss some other improvements. Some young rebels claim that industry takes a "be damned" attitude toward the American public as it pollutes the air and fouls the streams, for example. Do you have any comments on industry's attitude? Who would you like to talk to about it? How would you go about getting someone to listen?

3. Some of you will undoubtedly get married. What is your feeling about using the pill? Is it really important to have general population control? Are we concerned any longer with the morality of sexual intercourse? What comments do you have on this, based on your personal experience, for the professor? What would you say if you knew the professor was a conforming Catholic? Would that make you

drastically alter your comments? Would it make you change the way you phrased your remarks? What ways would you change?

4. The authors of this book seem to assume that everyone has communication problems. Do you agree? What is a communication problem? In a class or group discussion you have had recently, did you have a communication problem, or did you notice somebody else having one? What types of communication problems can you identify among people you know?

5. You have probably been urged to "drop out." Is it possible to "drop out"? Aristotle said that man is a political (social) animal. How applicable today are the remarks made by a philosopher who lived over 2,000 years ago? How would you go about dropping out if you wanted to? Who would you talk to about what? Is there anything you would absolutely have to communicate about?

6. Have you ever been in a crowded room and felt alone? Have you ever talked to someone for a while and felt that absolutely nothing that was said made sense? How would you describe these situations? What do you and your colleagues do to overcome the feeling of loneliness? What prescription would you give to an incoming freshman at your school to help him overcome loneliness? What skills would he have to have?

7. Television—some people call it a vast wasteland, but for millions it is a major form of recreation. How important is it in your life? What do you want from a television program when you sit down to watch? To what extent is it filling your needs?

8. The authors apparently are trying to interest you by quoting from Simon and Garfunkle. That's because many students have told the authors that "pop" music is important, that it carries a message. Listen to the local radio station or someone's record collection, and then, using a tape recorder, see if you can illustrate what the current music is trying to say. What would you say to someone who called "pop" music "contemporary poetry"? Do you think it is possible for people over thirty to understand pop music, or is it all a put-on?

9. Who are you? Do you have an identity? We, the authors, probably will never get a chance to meet you (unless you are in our class). If you were going to have one of us as your teacher, what would you like us to know about you in order to evaluate you fairly? Now look at what you just said and try to figure out how much of it you said because you thought we would want to hear it, and how much represents a real and honest expression of what you believe. How honest can you be and still remain in society?

10. Do you agree with what the authors said in this chapter? If not, what is the basis of your disagreement? How do the authors reveal their biases? Do you accept their goal or values? How do yours differ?

11. Everything is scientific these days, even communication. Some day, some professor is going to come up with a textbook on scientific love-making or scientific beer-drinking. But isn't science "objective and inhuman"? How do you think it can solve human problems? Do you think the authors can really defend their definition of speech as science and art? Or are they just following an academic fad?

SUGGESTIONS FOR FURTHER READING

Edward T. Hall and William Whyte, "Intercultural Communication," in *Communication and Culture,* ed. Alfred Smith (New York: Holt, Rinehart and Winston, 1966).

The major contribution of this work is that it demonstrates that non-Americans think like non-Americans, and thus, more than verbal translation is necessary for understanding.

Alfred Korzybski, *Selections from* SCIENCE AND SANITY (Lakeville, Conn.: Institute of General Semantics, 1948), Chapter 8.

Max Lerner, *America as a Civilization,* Volume 2 (New York: Simon and Schuster, 1957). This is old, but good. Read it in bits and pieces, tying in the information with other courses and other disciplines. It will show you how you live.

Edward Shils, "Mass Society and Culture," in *Culture for the Millions,* ed. Norman Jacobs (Boston: Beacon Press, 1964). This is the classic anthology of recent American culture and communication. The contributors plead a good cause, and Shils is particularly good.

Charles Erskine Scott Wood, *Heavenly Discourse* (New York: Vanguard Press, 1927). Don't let the date or the title keep you from reading this book. A rare treat awaits the reader of this witty look at man talking to God talking to man talking to other men, etc.

2

To Talk Is to Be
with Another
Human Being

A magnet "talks" with other pieces of iron. It may attract or repel them. It ignores everything except iron. A person also attracts, repels, and ignores other people who, in turn, attract, repel, and ignore him. While a magnet has only three messages, "come," "go," "ignore," people may transmit many messages. Just as a magnet's message may be strong or weak, people's messages can have different charges of energy, e.g., ideas about politics, religion, sex, or other people. Such words as *communism, socialism, racism, birth control, war* are capable of inspiring intense reactions. We are so pushed, pulled, and saturated by the words around us that some of us lapse into self-centered apathy. Words and ideas lose their reality and meaning for us. We overuse words until we finally drag them into the mass grave of triteness. This semantic excess creates today's clichés from yesterday's catchwords, for example, *uptight, groovy, escalate, brainstorm,* etc. Of course, one may argue that clichés really communicate but without impact or precision. A clichéd vocabulary leads to mental apathy. Once apathy dulls our senses, our power to send and receive messages is almost nonexistent. We have willed off our magnetism, and we die a "semantic death."

While a magnet cannot volitionally turn its influence on or off, people (at least in part) are able to do this. Through training we can increase our power to attract others to us and our ideas. When we allow ourselves to be defeated by the forces around us, we lose this control. If this loss of attraction becomes acute, our communication gap becomes a veritable chasm of emotion, which if deep enough could drive a person to choose to become mentally ill, as Thomas Szasz puts it.[1] So it is vitally important that each of us rub minds with others to maintain our power of useful discourse.

The personality of a person may be metaphorically represented by a magnet. But while the behavior of a magnet has a theoretical limit, the behavioral possibilities in the personalities of people are limitless. An idea cannot be isolated from the person who has it, nor can it avoid being influenced by the person who hears it. When two magnets are brought together, something must happen. The same is true when two or more people are brought together. One magnet may attract all the filings, the other none; there are critical points in the relationship of magnets to filings. Similar complexities, only more varied and unpredictable, occur when two or more people and their ideas interact. When lines of influence clash, the results usually are muddled and unclear. The potential of people to attract and repel cannot be described in clear mathematical terms as can the potential of magnets. Some ideas are at first vague, ambiguous, and confused. Later they may become explosive and destructive.

This analogy to magnets may be applied to groups, institutions, nations, and societies. They can hold together or fall apart because of the way millions upon millions of human influences arrange themselves. The people in a society shape the society, which, in turn, influences the individual. A society is something more, something different from the sum total of the people that make it up. On the other hand, remember that society *is* people and is the product of the people who comprise it.

All analogies, including this one, fail at some point. Magnets cannot communicate about communication and therefore cannot improve their messages. They cannot interact to improve interaction or influence their own influences. They cannot be aware of their own awareness and sensitivity. They cannot have a perspective on their own perception. The power of humans to communicate confers the ability to do precisely what magnets cannot do. Man's power to create and use symbols gives him power over his own magnetism.

Speech is the human force field. It consists of meaningful oral symbols that people use to transact the business of the day, to do the world's work, to think, create, idle away time, get in trouble. The ability to use symbols is what most clearly differentiates man from the other animals. This is the source of our ultimate paradox. Communication, our technique of survival, also gives us our capacity for destruction.

SYMBOLS AND LANGUAGE

A *symbol* is anything that takes the place of, stands for, or refers to something else. X or 3 are mathematical symbols. Do, re, mi stand for musical sounds. Dog and cow refer to objects that can be perceived. Love and hate

---

[1] Thomas Szasz, *The Myth of Mental Illness* (New York: Hoeber-Harper, 1961).

refer to feelings. A shrug can convey a feeling, a hand motion can give instructions. Symbols can be both verbal and nonverbal, oral or written.

Gesture symbols, for example, may be defined as the physical actions and bodily movements we make when we communicate. The expressions on our faces, the movements of our hands and arms, even the position of our bodies, are important ways of transmitting ideas to others. One appropriate and interesting example is the meaningful motion of the exotic dancer. Whatever else you may say about her, she *does* communicate!

Gestures may be used to reinforce words or to substitute for them. Gestures add depth of meaning for those who perceive them. Gestures often are more accurate expressions of feeling than are words, which can be carefully controlled. In fact, some authorities declare that if a person inhibits his verbal communication, the body will take over and make involuntary communications for him. One authority has even constructed a theory that physical states of the body will communicate needs to others as surely and as accurately as words. A whole new field called *semiotics* has been developed to study the nature and impact of nonverbal communications.[2]

Pictural symbols depict relationships of objects from which conclusions can be drawn. The furniture in a room or the way clothing is worn can communicate about the person who lives in the room or is wearing the clothes. The artifacts and potsherds studied by the archeologist communicate about early civilizations.

Symbols may also be *written.* However, printed or written words are nothing more than code representations of oral symbols. Written symbols make redaction possible. Redaction is the process by which oral information is put into writing for greater permanence. Statistical methods, chemical formulas, and mathematical notations are some obvious examples of written symbols that functionally shorten verbal or written messages. Poems and novels are filled with written symbols that help us share emotions with men of the past.

Basically, however, human communication is made up of the spoken word. One authority estimates that over 75 percent of our day is spent in speaking and listening. We must master verbal symbology in order to communicate with another. In short, we are very much in need of capability at oral communication to perform effectively in our daily life.

A *word* in its most basic sense can be defined as a combination of sounds to which society has given meaning. That is, people have agreed in advance that a specific combination of sounds shall refer to some idea, emotion, process, or thing. Furthermore, human societies agree on the way words must be combined so that they can be understood. The rules for these combinations are grammars. However, it should be clearly understood that grammars are not prescriptions for the use of language. More properly, grammars should be considered descriptions of the way society uses language.

In addition to words and grammars, there is the matter of speech de-

[2] Thomas S. Sebeok, Alfred S. Hayes, Mary C. Bateson, *Approaches to Semiotics* (London: Mouton & Co., 1964).

livery. But speaking is not an instinctive activity; it is a process that must be learned. All the parts of our complex vocal mechanism have some other major physiological purpose than to create speech. The lungs, which provide the power for speech sounds, serve mainly to oxygenate the blood. The vibrating mechanism in the larynx which produces characteristic speech sounds, is actually a valve to prevent food from entering the lungs. The articulatory mechanism—tongue, lips, and teeth—that differentiates sounds has as its primary function the chewing of food. The sinuses and other cavities in the head and neck are for drainage, though they also provide the resonance and quality of speech.

Speech is taught by society. An infant can vocalize, but he does not learn to speak until he discovers that he can get others to respond to his vocalizations. In fact, a few children do not learn to speak until they begin school, because until that time they had no real need for speech. Older brothers and sisters or overly attentive parents did the talking for them. There was no need to speak, so why learn? Communication could be carried on through gestures. Once the child has symbolic capacity, however, he is ready to use communication to regulate his own behavior and that of others.

Because verbal symbols are intrinsic to society, some fundamental concepts about language and culture must be understood before the communication process can be analyzed.

1. The symbols that make up a language are arbitrary. Meanings are not necessarily associated with things. Some early theorists about the development of language suggested that there are characteristic sounds associated with certain situations or objects. More intensive examination indicates, however, that verbal language is an arbitrary code developed by a culture. The symbol often has no necessary connection with the thing it symbolizes. That which we call a *table* will remain essentially the same if we called it *zog* or *quork* or whatever we wish.

2. A language is not static. It is continually changing. It may alter both its form and its structure. It may add new words and new dialects. It necessarily adjusts itself to suit changes that come about in the culture that employs it. A dictionary, as we have said, is a historical record of meanings given to words in the past and not necessarily a catalog of current usage. The existence of cognate languages and regional dialects most graphically illustrates the ability of language to change.

Language provides a historical record through place and family names. Changes in a civilization may be deduced by examining archaic words referring to objects and events no longer meaningful in the contemporary society. What is important in a contemporary civilization may be discovered by examining the living language.

Languages replenish themselves by dropping useless words and creating new ones to refer to new events. The adoption of Hebrew in Israel as a living language after 2,000 years of disuse illustrates some of the problems of language change. Biblical Hebrew makes no reference to typewriters and airplanes. Hence, it was necessary for the Israelis to borrow words from other cultures in order to communicate in their own. The ability to do this

indicates the viability of a civilization. Our English language has been en-
riched by terms borrowed from the various immigrants who brought their
own languages to our shores.

Languages can also develop sublanguages of occupational interest.
Technical jargons and taxonomies, ranging from "hip talk" to the mathematics of nuclear physics, provide specialized tools with which various
groups can carry on specialized interaction.

3. Language can be used for phatic purposes. That is, words can be ex-
changed merely to indicate that human beings have met and recognized
each other. Such social activity helps show how deep a relationship could
become. Each society develops its own formulas. An Arab wants to talk
about his family and the weather before he does business. The usual format
for Americans is "Hello." "How are you?" "What's new?" The speaker is not
interested in hearing about symptoms or current events; he only wants to
pass the time while he sizes up the potential of the relationship. This kind
of communication, called *phatic communion,* prevents self-exposure while
people determine how far they wish to carry the relationship. Two dogs
carry out a form of phatic communion when they sniff each other upon
meeting.

Language can also be presymbolic. A set of words can convey impressions without necessary reference to the specific meanings of individual
words. Virtually any ceremonial illustrates this use of language. Few Roman
Catholics can understand the Latin of the mass, and few Jews can comprehend the Hebrew of their liturgy. In both cases, however, real emotive communication comes about through the sounds of the words and the familiarity
of the ceremony as it is related to the symbols of worship.

4. Finally, language can be a source of aesthetic stimulation. Words can
be connected together to convey emotions of joy, sorrow, and excitement.
Such communication as poetry and music are effective ways of motivating
an audience to laugh or cry. Fiction and narrative prose may also convey a
message. Communication does more than enable people to collaborate or
conflict with each other; it enables them to express their inner feelings,
thoughts, dreams, and fantasies. In this sense, language is a social function.
The transactions of society are based on the ways in which language is used.
Political and religious structures are linguistically built. Most important of
all, knowledge is transmitted through time by language. The past can be
connected with the present to influence the future. Only man possesses this
capability to *bind time,* which is an important concept in understanding
language. And man is the only time-binder among animals.

USES OF LANGUAGE

Though people express their ideas and emotions mostly through speech
and writing, it should be clearly understood that the term *communication*
means more than speech and writing. Communication is *interaction.* It is
dynamic. Any sensory stimulus that interacts with the sense of a perceiver to

transmit meaning may be said to communicate. The wooden bench at a football game interacts with the spectator to communicate hardness. The perceiver responds by placing a cushion, signifying softness, on the bench. It has been said that the kiss is an effective communicator, and with the myriad of our empirical evidence, it would be difficult to reject the hypothesis. Ponder on that for a moment.

As we have explained, all communication is certainly not on the verbal level. The verbal symbols of speech and writing cannot be separated from nonverbal associations. Silence may communicate the emotional inner state of a person. The empty spaces that surround words may be so powerful that they cancel out the impact of the spoken words. The movements of faces, eyes, hands, or bodies may transmit more meaningful ideas than our words. Speech is a behavior and it can never be considered apart from the other behaviors in which it is embedded. Together speech and surrounding behavior represent a projection of our total personality. Often meanings we wish to conceal are transmitted by nonverbal behaviors; all our words cannot mask our real intentions. So powerful are nonverbal communications that our bodies can communicate ideas we have suppressed or do not wish to admit we have. A psychosomatic ailment, for example, may communicate a need for sympathy and attention that we would not wish to admit verbally. Interestingly, one medical authority has estimated that 85 percent of the ailments he treats which do not involve a distinct pathology are of this emotional-source nature.

Some nonverbal expressions can be controlled to reinforce and amplify the meanings of words. Often, however, our body movements are beyond our direct control. To alter our basic communication patterns requires a change in our personality. We may learn general rules about communication behaviors, but the application of these rules must be idiosyncratic and volitional so that they fit our personality.

Humans can control only to an extent what they transmit, and they can only exert some control over the relationships they establish. We can consciously plan the use of symbols to develop a relationship with another person, but we cannot predict his responses with certainty. We can also use symbols about our symbols, a form of criticism, and thus correct future communications in order to raise the level of predictability of the responses. If we desired to make the force field of a magnet stronger, we would have to "pump" electricity into it. The magnet could not do it alone, nor could it persuade us to do it. Humans, however, can increase their own communication "force fields" by responding to the responses of others and consciously controlling symbols.

Everything communicates to the person who can tune in. The nail you are hammering talks back through its rigidity. It tells you enough about itself so that you can respond by controlling your use of the hammer. The same holds true for relationships between people. We receive responses from other people, and these determine our own behavior in relation to the people. The cues we receive are processed internally, and we prepare directions for ourselves that we hope will control the subsequent relationships. The directions are stored in our memory bank, so that appropriate action or reaction may occur when we find ourselves in a similar situation some time in the future.

Awareness of and sensitivity to all kinds of symbols add dimensions to thought. Awareness and sensitivity imply relationship to the environment, including other people. A thing or situation is meaningful only as we see connections, associations, and linkages to ourselves. These connections are made by processing our sum total of experience, adjusting both our memory of experience and our symbols. This relationship is used well by writers to sell paperbacks, television shows, and motion pictures to the public, i.e., the audience finds it rewarding to identify with the characters in the book, show, or film. Such identification was the basis for the fantastic acceptance of the James Bond books and films a few years ago.

It is impossible to think about the future when we separate people from their natural relationships. Dr. Victor Frankl, who survived the Nazi death camps, pointed out that when inmates lost the hope of fruitful relationships with others, they tended to become inert vegetables and died. Those who could cling to the hope of a future in which they could "relate" to some person or things in new relationships survived.

There are five basic relationships that can be expressed through symbolic communication. They are symbol with object, symbol with prediction, symbol with evaluation, symbol with explanation, and symbol with control over others. These five relationships can be explained by examining the five fundamental ways in which we use language. Remember that the substance of our communication comes to us silently through perception. Perception provides input for us; communication is our output—but it may also be an input for we cannot ignore our own symbols.

1. *Language can be used to express identification and description.* Our initial contact with the outside world is silent. We perceive an ever-changing process, and only after we have learned to classify does the world take on some meaning. We note similarities among groups of objects and give names to them, though the names are arbitrary at the outset. However, once we have attached a label, a whole series of associations develop between the word and the characteristics of the thing the word represents. Sometimes this distorts our subsequent perceptions of objects, so that we fail to see differences among them. Many of our prejudices arise because we cannot separate the qualities intrinsic in the use of a word from the unique characteristics of each separate entity. Unfair and prejudicial generalizations, such as "Polish people are stupid," "Jews are greedy," "Negroes are oversexed," "The British are snobs," or "Italians smell," typify this failure to recognize differences.

No two persons experience sensory data the same way. We can never be sure what another person actually "sees." However, words are used to relate people to each other by relating the words to common experience. When we perceive "X" we can use the word *ex* to refer to what we see, and regardless of whether we see it precisely the same way as the other person, we can share a common experience by using a word to point to a thing.

While we cannot know what impact either "X" or ex made on the other person's nervous system, we can know our responses and infer that they are, in some ways, congruent to those of the other person. Communication about sensory stimuli merely means that you are aware of a relationship a verbal symbol has with an object. It does not mean that you can sense in any way the internal feelings of the persons to whom you are relating. For this reason, total communication and/or total agreement is virtually impossible. Sufficient relationship can be expressed through verbal symbols, however, so that society can run and people can associate with each other. We have a capacity to relate, though never completely, to other people.

When we use the words to describe objects, we develop a relationship with a listener in which he examines his own symbols to form an image of what we are talking about. A communicative relationship results in similar, though not identical, images. Description remains basically subjective. The congruity between the description and the object images formed by the listener depends on the perception mechanisms of both people. It also depends upon their previous experiences with the object and on evaluations made previously about similar objects. The extent to which the communicators possess common symbols, moreover, determines the nature and quality of a relationship. Some examples would include, "an ideal day," "a terrific figure," "a sweet handling airplane," etc.

Likewise it is exceedingly difficult to describe objects to a person who has never seen them. If you talk about a large, gray elephant, your words will make sense only if your listener has had experience with "largeness" "grayness," and "elephants." Through description, however, it is possible to classify and organize information. We can explain "large" to a person who understands "small." The idea of "grayness" can be demonstrated by mixing black paint and white paint together or by showing your perceiver a color-scale card, such as the photoengraver's gray scale of tonal values. We can describe an "elephant" by referring to familiar objects—"it is like a huge pig with a snout elongated into a thick, bristly hose and large, fanlike ears."

Achieving understanding through description is imperative if higher levels of communication are to be reached. We must remember, however, that even on the descriptive level of communication, we are already far from authenticity. Truly authentic communication is the silent relationship between a human and the object or event he perceives—before it has been given a name and before a communication relationship with another person is attempted. As we move to more complex types of relationships, we progress even farther from the world of idiosyncrasy, uniqueness, and personal contact with the environment. As we manipulate symbols in a sophisticated fashion, we tend to lose our simplistic view and our joy at perception. This is almost a worthwhile sacrifice, provided the more sophisticated manipulations help us to gain greater control over our environment and ourselves.

2. *Language can be used to infer missing details and to predict the future.* An inference has been defined by one authority as a "statement about the unknown based on the known." This simply means that our perceptions are

often incomplete and fallible, and it is necessary to fill in details. If a person is sitting in a room, we assume that he entered the room, probably through a door. The inference tends to preclude the slim possibility that he entered through a window, but our past experience with similar situations tells us that a door is the most likely mode of ingress. Since this explains what we see, we are willing to accept it as almost fact.

Our tendency to confuse inferential and factual statements often gets us into trouble. The archives of criminal law are full of examples of how circumstantial or inferential evidence has been used to convict innocent men and free the guilty. Consider the possibilities of the controversial trail of events in the Dr. Samuel Sheppard murder case for example. What was seen led to a variety of inferences, some of which convicted him and some of which acquitted him.

We must, however, act to take the risks of decision-making. We cannot proceed with the work of the day without making inferences to predict the future. When we get out of bed in the morning, we infer that nothing will happen to us. Otherwise we would probably never get up in the first place. Of course, there is a possibility that we may get hit by a car or a meteorite, but our past experience tells us that it is sensible to act as though we will live through the day. After all, our prediction can fail only once, and then it could not possibly matter any longer—at least in a worldly sense.

When we state facts, we are directly experiencing or observing things or events. Inferences can be distinguished from statements of fact by their reliance on probabilities. Consequently, an unlimited number of inferences can be made. Since they cannot be confirmed, they represent only degrees of probability. A factual statement can be confirmed by other observers. Statements that refer to things or events others can see and confirm bring us as close to agreement as humans ever get. If we confined ourselves only to factual statements, however, we could never make progress, for only a limited number of factual statements can be made. Solving problems means predicting the outcome of events. To the extent that we infer competently, we can plan our activities. However, when we speak inferentially, we must be prepared for uncertainty and expect the unexpected. If we act as though inferences were facts, we maximize our chance of trouble.

For example, during the Congo unpleasantness of 1964, two United Nations soldiers in the full uniform of their nation were walking down a street in Leopoldville talking in their native tongue. A group of Congolese set upon them and beat them brutally. A later investigation revealed that the Congo natives overheard the conversation, decided that the soldiers were Belgians speaking Belgian, and attacked them. The soldiers, however, were Canadians speaking in French. Without reference to dubious justification for the beatings, the Congolese got into trouble because they could not distinguish a fact from an inference.

It is hard to live in a universe of probabilities. Most of us prefer certainty and would regard it as instructive to "know" the future. However, very few things are certain, and it is impossible for humans to communicate sensibly with each other and still remain on the factual level. The mature man will anticipate the hazards that can arise when he leaves the factual level and will be ready for the unexpected.

3. *Language can be used to form and express evaluations and reactions.* Past experiences shape present reactions. In addition to strong images and words, we store evaluations or reactions to what we see and say. It is impossible to think of a situation about which we do not have some attitude, however mild. Some events are almost neutral, but further exposure to them helps us to assign them values. When we see a person for the first time, we respond mainly to the impact of his appearance. We associate him with similar-appearing people we have formerly encountered and evaluate him accordingly. Further contact enables us to respond to specific activities, and we can revise our attitude. Our initial response may be modified or changed completely. Surely each of us has gone through the situation of meeting someone for the first time, forming an opinion of that person, then having to alter that opinion a full 180 degrees following later instances of interaction with the person.

Our evaluation system provides us with expectations about our experiences. We may respond to our perception of appearance, and sometimes alter our perceptions in line with our evaluations. Our evaluations have been shaped slowly over time and can be altered only by careful and slow exposure or by sudden shock. It is rare that a speech requesting us to change our attitudes has any affect on us at all, unless it happens to recommend changes we were about to make anyway. The speech becomes an excuse to change, not a reason for it.

This same concept explains the political phenomena that Democrats listen only to Democratic speakers, and Republicans listen only to Republican speakers. Very few of either party will listen to a cross-party speech. You are not likely to encounter a racist at an Urban League gathering or an SDS member attending a John Birch Society meeting unless they come to heckle and disrupt. We seek reinforcement of our ideas, values, and beliefs; we do not voluntarily seek change or conflict of ideas.

We try to understand the world by applying verbal labels. It would be impossible to react to everything we experience as unique. Classifications are created by applying a single word to an aggregate of similar things or events. In a sense, we create a set, all members of which can be regarded as similar in the characteristics that define the set. Any evaluation we make of one or a few items in the set apply to all. When we evaluate, we respond to similarities. Our evaluations may be called "prejudice" when we ignore individual characteristics. Obviously this is a rejection of one of the simplified basic premises of Aristotelian logic: that A is always A. A is A only verbally. All of the A's are different in some way. Awareness of the *principle of non-identity* helps us to make specific distinctions between the various A's while the symbols help us respond to them as a group—we can know something about Presbyterians and still regard individual Presbyterians as unique humans.

Again we find ourselves in a bind. Many of our simplest decisions could not be made if we did not use language to express evaluation. For example, when we eat at a restaurant, we read the menu and respond to the words that denote possible choices in food. If a word evokes a positive response, we order it. If we choose a lamb chop, we predict that we will respond to the lamb chop as we did to previous lamb chops. On subsequent occasions, both our choice of restaurants and of menu items will be influenced by our evaluations of present situations in the light of past experiences.

The composite of our value judgments and attitudes may be referred to as taste. *Taste* can be defined as a personal set of standards used for evaluation. Our taste is formed primarily by our personal experiences, and secondarily by the standards that prevail in the society. As members of our society, we tend to accept verbal evaluations and act on them when we are confronted with similar situations. An American child, for example, could be expected to show a greater interest in football than in soccer, because his society accords a higher and more positive value to football than to soccer. As children grow up, they encounter conflicts in taste between their parents and their peers. It is often annoying to parents to find that their children reject parental judgments and rely on the judgments of their friends. By this process the child fits himself into the society, however, and it is essential to his intellectual growth. Taste dictates the selection of activities and objects. Society maintains its mores by inculcating the proper values into the child. Members of one class in society who seek to move to another level must first display their willingness to verbalize and then to act on taste patterns of the stratum they aspire to.

4. *Language can be used to conceptualize about objects and events and to explain relationships among them.* A *concept* is a group of words that explains something. A concept may express similarities in obviously different things or differences in similar things. It may detail relationships of cause, sign, trend, or association. Our attempts at scientific or creative thinking are manipulation of concepts. A textbook on logical reasoning deals with the use of verbal symbols to form concepts. Religious creeds are also built on concepts as they attempt to explain the nature of man and the universe.

The ability to use words to create concepts or explanations has enabled us to carry on scientific investigation. Words can be used to form an analog that can be examined and tested by performing an experiment or making an observation. We call verbal concepts *hypotheses;* these are statements or propositions to be tested by scientific or statistical methodology. Before embarking on a study, a scientist will examine his hypotheses and the assumptions that underlie them. Conceptualization is perhaps the most advanced use to which language has been put.

Literary forms are also conceptual. Metaphors and the various figures of thought used by novelists and poets attempt to display original relationships between things and events. In such cases, the relationships reveal the unique directions a creative mind can take when it contemplates the world.

5. *Language can be used to influence and persuade others.* The man who seeks political power, the salesman who wishes someone to buy his goods, and the clinician who wants a change in behavior on the part of his client all seek to influence and persuade others. This process is called *rhetoric*, defined by Aristotle as "the art of finding in any given case all the available means of persuasion." There are some who feel all communication is persuasion in one form or another. Each time we interact with someone else, we seek some response from him. Our quest for favorable responses is carried on through the use of rhetoric.

Virtually all uses of language bring about a relationship between people. Underlying any relationship is the desire on the part of a communicator to bring about a change in the behavior of the person or persons with whom he is communicating. Description, inference, evaluation, conceptualization—all can be used as devices by which others can be influenced and persuaded.

In order to persuade effectively, a communicator must be able to conceive a clear image of purpose. He must know what effect he desires if he is to be able to exert conscious control over his ideas. He must also understand the response behavior of others so that his expectancies are sensible.

Both conceptualization and persuasion will be considered in later chapters of this book. They are the essence of communicative transaction. Through conceptualization we seek to understand and explain and to transmit our knowledge and wisdom to future generations. Through persuasion we seek to take action; to compete against our environment and organize our world so that we can live in it. In both cases, serious damage can be done by inappropriate usages. Faulty conceptualization can lead to superstition and error. Persuasion toward anything less than noble ends can stir up conflict that threatens the survival of man. There is much that must be understood before we can explain these sophisticated uses of language. First, it is necessary to examine the many relationships men have to one another when they communicate.

COMMUNICATION RELATIONSHIPS

Autocommunication

We talk to ourselves all the time, though rarely out loud. According to some authorities, the process called thought consists of manipulating verbal symbols internally so that we make our sensory impressions orderly.

People tend to follow an orderly process when they think through a problem. John Dewey described thought process as proceeding through five steps:

1. A difficulty or perplexity is felt.
2. The problem is defined.
3. Solutions are proposed for the defined problem.
4. Solutions are evaluated and one is chosen.
5. Action is taken.[3]

[3] John Dewey, *How We Think* (New York: Macmillan, 1906).

All but the first are carried out in symbols. All but the last are carried on in the mind. Though people often talk with others about their thinking in order to find correction or confirmation, the final decision is internal. If the wrong problem has been identified in step 2, the solution may not be appropriate and the feeling of difficulty may persist. If the definition is apt but the solution is inadequate, perplexity remains. People try to dispel their feelings of bewilderment, frustration, and anxiety by taking actions to solve problems. Action is based on thought carried out in symbols—a form of communication with the self.

Some psychologists contend that all behavior is rational from the point of view of the behaver. This means that no matter how peculiar an act may seem to an observer, to the person who does it, when he does it, the act is based on his thought and seemed correct at the time. Immediately afterward, it might be obvious that he did not succeed in dispelling anxiety, and it may be necessary to think through the problem and act again. When we persist in using solutions that do not work, society may evaluate our behavior as "irrational" and attempt to help us through psychotherapy. Psychotherapy seeks to add new dimensions to thought processes so that more adequate decisions can be made.

Education may also be considered a form of therapy, because in addition to adding new symbolic data to our minds, it also offers methods for manipulating the symbols that, hopefully, will result in more effective problem-solving. Essentially the same organization and structure we used in communicating with ourselves is also appropriate in our communications with others. Conversation is a sharing of symbols between two persons, while mass persuasion via public address is an attempt to bring the symbols of others into harmony with our own.

If we think in terms of structuring symbols, we can have an overview of the communicative process on all levels. To the extent that we can project our own internal consciousness into others, we can understand how others think. These understandings help us to control the use of symbols for more effective communication with others.

One-to-One Communication

As we said earlier, two dogs meeting on the streets will sniff each other and determine whether they are to be friends or enemies. In much the same way, we make initial contacts with others through verbal formulas, which we call phatic communion. The interchange of such symbols as "Hello," "How are you?" "What's new?" give people a chance to observe each other, make evaluations, relate appearances to past experiences, and make some decisions about what the nature of future contact ought to be. Phatic communion is a socially accepted method by which human beings can come into contact and determine how far the relationship is to go.

Two people may also carry on complex social transactions in which many kinds of relationships can develop, characterized by the purpose of the participants. For example, we may say to each other:

1. I like you and your ideas.
2. I like you, but I do not like your ideas.
3. I do not like you, but I like your ideas.
4. I do not like you, and I do not like your ideas.

Our view of the position of the other tends to determine the nature of our relationship. In primitive societies, people can identify only members of their tribe; others are classified as enemies. More sophisticated societies develop a variety of subtle relationships. Americans can identify immediate and extended family, friends, acquaintances, job associates, casual passersby, and strangers. We do not identify all strangers as enemies as primitive tribesmen do, but often, as our associations become routine, we may tend to do so and thus limit our power to make friends. Sometimes we set the nature of the transaction because of verbal classifications we can make of our respondent, such as the snobbery of economic or social class differences.

There can be relationships of superior to inferior in which one person issues directives and the other follows them. There can also be relationships of equals in which a common activity is controlled by the communication. There are relationships of weakness in which two persons mutually support each other. In any case, the context of the relationship will determine communicative behaviors unique to the transaction.

The communicative relationship between two people can be examined through the psychiatric concept of transference. In early life, a child develops relationships with others that are necessary to survival. A mother who beats her child still maintains a relationship. In later life, as the growing individual encounters other people and new situations, he will respond to them in the light of early experiences. The child or growing adult will react to teachers and peers, to bosses and colleagues, in somewhat the same way that he responded to his parents and siblings when he was younger. The attitudes and needs of earlier relationships are "transferred" to the new acquaintances. To the psychiatrist, when the patient is ready to break this transference and make his own mature, adult decisions, he can be released from therapy. But in developmental stages, the transference relationship, the essence of which is carried on through communication, represents the foundation of the process by which a human learns how other people around him behave. He transmits symbols based on the role he wishes to play in relation to others. They evaluate his symbols to determine whether the role he desires fits their view of society, and then send messages back to him to show their approval or disapproval. When cues are misinterpreted, there is awkwardness in the relationship, usually culminating in hostility or conflict. The jargonized term for this common occurrence is *communication failure,* and we are fond of saying, "There has been a breakdown in communication here."

Through the interchange of communications people seek their roles in a community, society, or culture. If they do not wish to accept the place to which society assigns them, they are treated as mental patients, outlaws, or rebels. Sometimes they may decide to reject the communication style of their society and form a new one. The so-called hippies exemplify such rejection.

The structures of human organization can be perceived as interacting networks of dyad communicating. Each participant is directly influenced by face-to-face contacts and secondarily influenced by past and peripheral contacts. These references, external to the immediate situation, help him choose the symbols he transmits and the way he interprets the symbols he receives. Past experiences provide criteria with which present situations are evaluated. Previous contact with authority, for example, will tend to determine the nature of a present contact. More important, experiences will shape our ideas about ourselves and our relationships with others.

To the extent that the individual is a unit in a larger group, he loses part of his ability to decide his own actions. His ability to interact will help him find a satisfying role acceptable to the others in his society.

One to Many

All of us have the potential to influence our group, organization, society, or culture. For more than 2,000 years wise men and philosophers have been concerned with the art of rhetoric. They have aptly shown how we can use symbols internally to develop ideas about the future. Once these ideas are clear, we can specify the role of others in achieving them. The persuader develops a picture about how things will be when he has exerted his influence; he then plans a set of messages to project at others, his "audience."

The methods used by a speaker or writer to influence his audience is referred to as "rhetoric." According to classical principles, there are three sources of rhetorical influence: pathos, logos, and ethos. It is important for the persuader to affect his audience. To affect them emotionally is *pathos;* to affect them with logical reasoning is *logos;* to affect on them the persuader's own image is *ethos.* Ethos, according to tradition is the most important of the three classical concepts.

Unfortunately, it is not possible to construct at will a satisfactory image or ethos. Our ethos is a product of our personality, experience, reputation, and skill. Things that others say about us are as important as the things we say ourselves. Our physical appearance, the record of the things we have done, and the ideas we have expressed shape the response of the audience to us. Furthermore, each member of the audience will have a different impression of us. Some will respond to emotion, some to logic, some to their evaluation of our personality. The audience is formed of individuals who are also influenced by the behaviors of the people around them. Some may be self-persuaded, seeking a speaker who agrees with them to whom they may respond. Others may be confused, seeking a man to lead them. Still others may be objectively seeking data from which to develop ideas. Some may want a speaker to give them an excuse to act. A speaker will rarely, if ever, find an audience in which all members will respond the same way.

The man who communicates to many must, therefore, be prepared to receive a variety of responses from the people who hear him. The problems of communicating to an audience have been discussed by many authorities. What all agree on is that the "one-to-many" speaker succeeds only to the extent that his goal is consistent with what is possible for the individuals who make up the audience to believe and do.

Many to One

The people around us communicate with us all the time, sometimes with nonverbal symbols, sometimes directly, sometimes traditionally. We learn our personal behaviors from what society says to us. As we identify consistent behaviors, we learn what behaviors are expected of us.

As children, we learn behavior from the significant adults in our life. Later we accept direction from people our own age. Sometimes these cues are incompatible. What is permissible with peers is not permissible with parents. What is desirable among parents would evoke hostility from peers. These conflicts must be resolved if we are to achieve a satisfying role. In the normal individual, the parental/peer cues often appear at polar ends of an emotional scale within the individual. These polar extremes tend to reconcile themselves, however, as the individual matures and interacts within his society. In any event, our image and our standing within our society are determined by our perception of cues and by our interaction based on that perception. When we receive defective cues or interpret them wrongly, we may interact awkwardly with the people around us and become focal points of hatred, ridicule, or pity or perhaps be ejected from the community.

When a man elects to leave the farm and become a physician, he must accept the communication pattern of the medical community. When he returns home, he may find it very hard to communicate with old friends and relatives. This may explain why it is so difficult for college students to interact harmoniously with their parents. As Thomas Wolfe put it, "You can't go home again." The society we have left changes, and we are not there to tune in on the change. We bring to our old society new symbols we have acquired from new associates, and often these symbols are meaningless to our erstwhile companions. Before we can control our own communication effectively, we must be aware of what the surrounding society is saying to us. It is impossible to make intelligent decisions about how to communicate unless we know how to listen to the communications transmitted to us.

Many to Many

People communicate with each other in groups for many reasons. Some may be seeking to discover facts about a problem. Others may be evaluating an event as to its gravity or perhaps assessing the merit of a literary work.

People may engage in joint educational activities. Problem-solving may be the goal, or perhaps the goal is rehabilitation of one or more members. Groups or factions may struggle against each other to win some sort of victory. Or people may come together merely to enjoy each other's company. Whatever the reason, when people gather in groups, they must subordinate some of their personal sovereignty to the achievements of a group goal.

What goes on in a group can best be understood in terms of *references*. A reference is an impression of a group, idea, or man, from which values are derived. A religious denomination may be a reference, as may a political party or an individual important to you like parents, friends, and personal heroes. Each individual comes to a group situation with many personal references, and as he communicates with the other people around him, those references are altered by new references developed within the group, as he makes full or partial commitment to the group goal. A group truly develops as the goals of its members blend into a goal to which all or most can commit themselves. While no one member will have all his personal goals included in the group goal, an effective group will become so thoroughly synthesized that all members can commit a portion of their beliefs and value systems to achievement of what the group seeks.

Sometimes, however, we are not able to make such a commitment. When this happens, conflict arises, and a group may divide into subgroups that contend with each other for power. If a group succeeds in resolving its problems, it may achieve *consensus*. A consensus is a set of words with which the members of the group can agree. If a group is fragmented, the goal of each subgroup becomes victory; someone wins and someone loses. Or, as an alternative, a coalition may be formed among the hostile factions. This way, the group continues to function, although far less efficiently and effectively and with less chance for consensus. Usually harmony and consensus are unknown in the coalition situation. Harmonious group communication leads to solutions that satisfy all members to some extent, as well as meet the requirements of the group problem.

When the activity of small groups is projected into a complex society, a number of potential conflict points arise, and it becomes important that society find a way to resolve the disparate claims of the various groups. Some societies develop authoritarian structures in which one person, alone, establishes what the goals shall be. Others develop an elite oligarchy. In our democratic society, an arbitrary method of resolution called "voting" is imposed. Once again, communications patterns determine the nature of the group's activity, as well as its output.

Any group of communicating people develops its own personality, which includes some idea of what constitutes an effective participant and a worthy goal. Commitment to the goal provides a framework for the activity of members. The ideal participant may range from Babbitt to abstract scholar, but whatever idea a group develops about who is a suitable member determines the nature and style of participation and leadership. True leaders are not imposed. Instead they emerge from the group and generally fit a model of leadership that represents the style of the group. Groups may voluntarily submit themselves to authoritarian leadership; they may demand anarchy; or they may develop complex patterns of protections and privileges in a democratic format. Whatever the final format of leadership, it carries the functional responsibility for the ultimate satisfaction of the group's purpose.

A synthesis of individual communicative behavior and communicative behavior within groups may be described in terms of a game. "Game," in this sense, refers to routine stylized operations that satisfy certain goals of the participants. A message evokes a relatively predictable response. In order to play complex games in society, we must develop understandings of personal and group goals that provide us with rules about what can be communicated and how it may be done. For example, a group member has an approved method of contacting his leader. The leader, in turn, has certain options and prerogatives in his response. If a regular, nonleader member attempts to communicate like a leader, other members may call a rule infraction and ignore or attack the aspiring leader. The group member may also be misled and follow the new leader. Finally, he may elect to transfer allegiance altogether. The established leader may elect to compete to retain his position; he may voluntarily withdraw; he may win or lose.

Each individual must play this game in a myriad of interlocking influential groups: his home, his job, his ethnic or religious center, his social locus, etc. Sometimes he may be out of phase with a specific group because of influences from some other group, equally important to him. Young people are especially vulnerable to this problem. For example, the youngster away from home for the first time feels dissonance when his peer group invites him to participate in an activity that collides strongly with the mores of his family group. Or a normally respectable man attending an out-of-town convention may drink too much or pay too much attention to an unattached female in order to transmit the cue of "being one of the boys." Of course, there are less extreme examples of dissonance, but these will serve our purpose here.

Trouble arises in our society when roles are misinterpreted. Establishment of consistent roles within a society is the surest guarantee that the society will become authoritarian and the individual members will lose freedom. Somehow a balance must be struck, so that every man may retain some individuality without totally disrupting the society. Techniques to achieve this will be discussed in subsequent chapters.

SUGGESTIONS FOR DISCUSSION

1. Man, that's "neat," "cool," "tough." He's "square," "cool," "turned on," "a drag." What are some of the words and phrases people use that annoy you? By yourself or with your class, make up a list of annoyance words that you would like to have banned from conversation for a while. You haven't had much contact yet with your professor, but maybe he has a few to put on the list. Do you have any favorite phrases that might wear on your friends?

2. Students at one of the institutions represented by the authors of this book came up with "A Standard Lexicon of Campus Mini-Language" in which they identified "nerds," "gapers," "flamers," "screamers," "yo-yos," "clods," "bananas," "wrinklies," "dingos," and "gross-outs." Do these designations mean anything to you? Do you have some kind of language that you use to communicate with your friends that outsiders can't understand? Is there a "native language" in use on your campus? Try making such a lexicon. Share it with your professor. He may be willing to share with you his private language in return.

3. We all use gestures. Are they substitutes for words or do they reinforce words? Why do you use gestures? Do you feel that people resort to gestures when they have a poor vocabulary? (That is often said to be the reason for using profanity.) Talk for a while about some of the motions people around you make and what they tell you. Does the phrase, "your actions speak so loudly I can't hear a word you say," mean anything to you? Talk it over with your classmates. How do you know when the professor is angry, offended, pleased? Does he often tell you about his emotional state? What do you have to know about his response style to help you program your behavior to get the maximum grade?

4. If it is true that a child has learned nearly all of the language he will know by the time he is three years old, what on earth goes on in English class?

5. Too many academic people use terms that ought to mean something different as though they meant the same thing. For example, in this book, the authors talk about "communication," "speech," and "language" as though they have different meanings, but they still come out sounding the same. Can you distinguish different meanings for the words? Which is most general? Most specific? What relationships do they share?

6. Harry Truman used to say that a president cannot function well unless he has a sense of history. It seems that almost every academic discipline at one time or another gets into the "debt to the past" syndrome. What *is* the debt of the present to the past, and how does it affect the future? What events happened in your past that have something to do with the way you are now and what you plan to be? For example, what influenced your vocational choice or choice of a major? Did anyone influence you to make that choice and when did they do it? Is it possible to resist the past? Is it possible to look at the present and make sense out of what might come? We have used here the term "time-binding." What does this have to do with history? Talk for a while about present social institutions that look like atavisms. How much of the foolishness that goes on in the world now is the result of time-binding? Is there a sensible way that a group of you can find to improve time-binding at your school?

7. Did you notice how the authors seem to get carried away with metaphoric analogies? For example, this business of spectators at a football game interacting with benches. Is it possible for a human to interact with a non-human? Aren't the authors just a little far out when they indulge in this sort of anthropomorphism?

8. It is said that "misery loves company." The authors suggested that much of our physical illness is emotional in origin. Sit down with a group of your classmates and investigate this phenomenon as it affects you. What happens to each of you under stress? Do you feel physical symptoms? Are you familiar with the phenomenon of the "down" or the "blahs"? When does this happen to you? How can you get yourself out of that state? What recommendations can you make to each other?

9. Did you ever feel the taste of acid that comes into your mouth when someone says something very hostile or threatening to you? What does this do to the

operation of your mind? Can you think of any instances where your remarks
might have caused this feeling in others? Would you ever try to do this on purpose? Under what circumstances?

10. One student who read some of the manuscript of this book in its early stages
remarked that, "It sounds like atheism to me." Look at some of the things your
authors have said to you in this last chapter: they have denied truth by saying
that people cannot see the "same" thing; they have denied a "fact of life" by
asserting that it is not a fact that you will die; they have even denied certainty
in their talk about a probabilistic world. What is your reaction to this? What do
you regard as certain or universally true?

11. "I talk to myself because I like to talk to an intelligent person, and furthermore,
I like to hear an intelligent person talk." How does an intelligent person go about
talking to himself? What does he talk about? What is the purpose of his talk? Do
you talk to yourself? Does the rest of the class?

12. Is it possible to talk without trying to persuade someone of something? Examine
your normal talk. What is the persuasive force of "Hello, how are you?" What
persuasion does a chemistry lecture have in it? Is there any persuasion in your
literature books? What does the following mean: "In any conversation, there is
something up for grabs. Someone wins and someone loses. Sometimes win means
the absence of loss. Sometimes loss means a non-win. The optimum is when
everyone wins together, but most of the time, when we talk, everyone loses"?

13. John Dewey had the audacity to write a book called *How We Think*. What do you
think? Do you think it is possible to set down rules for thinking? Do you think
it is even possible for anyone to describe the act of thought and apply it to
everyone? Take another look at Dewey's propositions and see if you can role-
play some situations in which you strive consciously to avoid working through
Dewey's steps.

14. Everyone is trying to hustle "relationships." One colleague remarked, "In the old
days, we would find a girl and talk to her for hours and hours, days and days,
running on into months, to see if we could talk her into a 'relationship,' but these
days, the guys find a chick and hustle her into a relationship in order to find out
whether she is worth talking to." What is a "relationship"? What role does communication play in forming a relationship? In sustaining it? Can you find some
rules you all have in common for forming and sustaining relationships? Is a person with whom you are having a relationship also a "friend"? What are the differences you have in relationship with a fellow student of the opposite sex, a
student of the same sex, a male professor, a female professor, dean, the kids
you went to high school with who didn't go on to college, your parents, your
aunt with the money, your drinking uncle, the man who interviews you for a
job, a black student on the move, a member of SDS? Are there any generalizations you can make about "relationship" in the midst of all those differences?

SUGGESTIONS FOR FURTHER READING

Paul Chauchard, *Language and Thought* (New York: Walker and Company, 1964).
Pay particular attention to Chapters 2, 3, and 6. This French scholar's style is not
easy, but what he is saying is well worth the time and effort it takes to read it.

John C. Condon, *Semantics and Communication* (New York: Macmillan, 1966).
Although only Chapter 6 is appropriate to this portion of our book, take an hour or so
and read the rest of this splendid book.

Jerrold J. Katz and Jerry A. Fodor, "The Structure of a Semantic Theory," in *Readings in the Psychology of Language,* ed. Leon A. Jakobovits and Murray S. Miron (Englewood Cliffs, N.J.: Prentice-Hall, 1967). If you like complex and precise models to explain the theories of communication, you will enjoy this selection. It contains valuable information, but it is not casual reading.

George Herbert Mead, *Mind, Self, and Society* (Chicago: University of Chicago Press, 1943). This chapter owes a great deal to Mead's work. *Mind, Self, and Society* is a pioneer classic in general semantics, even though Professor Mead never thought of it that way.

3

A *Structure to View* the World

In their book, *Individual Behavior,* Combs and Snygg point out that ". . . what one assumes about the basic causes or reasons for events in this world will broadly determine the kind of theory he is going to articulate."[1] That means, simply, that the way we act in response to the things we see is based on assumptions we have made. This explains why you would probably jump back if you suddenly encountered a rattlesnake poised to strike you as you walked in the woods. But often our assumptions are naïve and disorganized. We may assume, for example, that all people learn to speak in the same way, that other people understand words precisely as we do, and that it is possible to use words to conceal meanings. Likewise, what we believe will determine our behavior. Our retention of a message will also affect our behavior. For instance, one authority has tested message retention, and after many years of work in this area concludes that we retain only about 5 percent of any given message over a period of time. This means that 95 percent is not retained and is essentially lost. We must do better, and to improve our ability to communicate we must understand the complex nature of human communication.

One of the most effective ways to understand communication is to build a model of communication as we understand it. For example, if we think of society as real, then we would learn meaning from common practices we

[1] Arthur W. Combs and Donald Snygg, *Individual Behavior* (New York: Harper and Brothers, 1949).

see. We would have extensional communication by relating to real things outside our skin. Each person would base his own translation and analysis on the perception he receives. If, however, we feel reality is developed in the mind, then the meaning of messages would be determined by the person alone. Each person would base his own translation and analysis on the perception he receives of what we are saying. Communication becomes intensional when it deals exclusively with personal meaning. Neither extensional nor intensional communication by itself will result in satisfactory understanding. If we look only at extensional data, we may lose sight of personal creativity, and become merely scientistic. If we look only at what happens in the mind, we tend to lose our grip on reality. We must understand how communication relates to reality as well as the effect it has on the mind. In this chapter we will consider communication from both an intensional and extensional perspective.

Communication cannot be regarded as divisible from other features of human personality. Most evidence leads to the conclusion that communication is a function of the complex interaction of three basic influences on human beings, and to get a holistic picture we must examine these *social, psychological,* and *physiological* influences.

Communication is in part a product of human physiology. The sound of the human voice is produced by the combined activity of the lungs, vocal cords, resonating chambers, and articulators, and the way the voice sounds is determined largely by the size and condition of the components of the vocal mechanism. (Pathological conditions affecting some part of the vocal mechanism can alter the sounds of speech.)

Content and style of communication depend on the central nervous system and the brain. The nervous system receives stimuli both from the outside and from the body of the individual. These stimuli are interpreted and processed by the brain, which, in turn, selects messages to transmit to parts of the body. The reaction of the body to the command of the mind is the ultimate result. The action may be verbal, such as a message, or it may be nonverbal, such as a shrug, or it may be both, such as a verbal assault and a physical battery—to use legal terminology. In any event, we call this action *behavior.*

To a large extent, behavior is limited by the structure and state of the brain and the nervous system. We are, in that sense, prisoners of our own physiology. In addition, our general tonicity, which has a decided influence on communication, is affected by the neuro-endocrine system. The output of hormones will tend to determine the degree of vigor of communication. However, a totally physiological explanation of behavior is not satisfying. The sociologist lists at least sixteen functional definitions of behavior, all related, yet all different, which seem to be more closely allied to sociocultural perceptions than to physiological ones. For example, no one is altogether certain physiological change alters behavior. It may be the reverse; interaction may change physiology. We can make a scientific exploration of the effect of physiology on behavior or we can explore behavior and its impact on physiology without getting a complete picture.

How a person sees his role in society tends to influence his own picture of himself as a communicator. Our communication behavior is shaped by the many cultures in which we live. For example, you were born into the specific linguistic culture of your parents and siblings from whom you initially learned language. Later your communicative activity was reinforced and stylized by schools and interactions with your peers. Hence the language that you now use has developed over many years from a variety of cultures and has constantly changed to meet new needs. The jargon you used as a teenager was quite different from that of your parents at that age, but quite functional and adapted to your immediate needs. Let's elaborate on this.

The primary linguistic culture, usually the family, sets the tone for behavior in cultures encountered later. No child can participate in a family culture until he has learned its language use. Once he can control his communication with the family, he may move into other cultures in which the family lives: the neighborhood, the extended family, socioeconomic, ethnic, religious, etc. The school and play peers provide a channel for movement into cultures not shared by the family. Eventually a vocational culture must be mastered to achieve economic survival. All this movement in and through cultures is based on communicative contact, and without this no adaptation could take place.

Each culture we encounter as we mature leaves an imprint on us. Our response to new groups is shaped by the style of responses we made to previous groups. If we are able to adapt to the cultures in which we find ourselves, we can be classified "socially adjusted." If we cannot harmonize our communication with that of our present culture, then we are termed "disrupted," and our behavior evokes the classification "deviant" from those who observe us. In an earlier chapter, we introduced the concept that we interpret the world by manipulating symbols and images so that perceptions from the outside are processed by comparison with previous perceptions in order for us to find appropriate symbols with which to classify them. Once we have labeled a behavior or event, we find an evaluation. Each new set of stimuli we receive is evaluated and stored away in memory to be used in subsequent behavior in identical situations.

The world inside our head is different from the world as seen by anyone else. No matter how much alike we may seem, each of us carries some unique characteristics that make up our personality. These individual differences may create an honest bumping together of ideas, which let us rub minds together, or these differences may produce hostility or conflict. The fact that each of us sees the world differently does make conflict between people possible. The uniqueness of every person permits the exciting ferment of society and confers identity upon individuals. Our personal view of our surroundings is called *phenomenal world.*

Maintaining our unique identity seems to be a goal for all of us. The fact that there are biological differences leading to differences in perceptions makes this uniqueness possible. We can synthesize what we see in common with what we see alone to develop ideas of goals by which to guide our actions and to aid us in communicating with (or is it persuading?) others to accept our particular models. Our past experience helps us assess our ability to exert our influence to persuade others to accept us in the role we seek. We attempt to communicate in such a way that the world will become as we think it should be. Our image of what we think it should be is our model.

This approach to communication shows us that communication must be considered as holistic. What we've been leading up to is that those three behavioral disciplines which consider communication are not separate and unrelated. Our view of communication must, obviously, be interdisciplinary.

Physiological, social, and psychological behavior cannot be separated for study. The attempt to build *models* of human communication is based on the desire to discover how the three variables relate to each other. A *communication model* is an attempt to explain through diagrams and pictures what happens during communication. To the extent that the model is an accurate map, representing in some way what actually goes on, we can derive from it hypotheses or statements of probability, which then can be subjected to empirical tests. The tests, once replicated and extended, give us information about communication that is useful both in understanding and teaching the process. Sometimes it even gives us ideas about how to become better communicators.

REQUIREMENTS FOR COMMUNICATION MODELS

To develop a sound theory of communication from the various models, we must apply certain basic criteria.

First, since communication is intrinsically rooted in the human being, both subjective and objective methods of examination must be used. The communication process can be studied both horizontally and vertically. *Horizontal study* is the examination of similiar behavior across many samples of many people, using the methodology of the natural sciences. The results can be generalized into propositions about many human beings. *Vertical study* is the examination in depth of a single person, which helps explain his behaviors. This is the familiar case study, the results of which can be applied to other individuals with characteristics similar to those studied. Both methods must be synthesized to derive a sound theory.

Second, no theory of communication can focus on only one of the three behavioral variables. The interactions between them must be analyzed and understood. Our psychological state affects our social behavior; social behavior, in turn, structures our perception of data that we process and store as our physiology permits us to do so. Interactions among them are reciprocal; each affects the other, so that serious distortions in understanding result when we attempt to study physiology, psychology, or sociology alone. A theory of communication must be holistic in its view of behavior. No known influence on human behavior can be omitted. Yet, since there is no known method by which all the variables can be handled, it is impossible, at this time, to develop an all inclusive theory.

Third, the communication theorist must clearly understand the limits of his model system. Some models take into account only the transfer of symbols from one person to another, ignoring internal processing. Others attempt to take into account sources of messages and the meanings of the symbol to both sender and receiver. The latter, a *content model,* permits a more general explanation of behaviors. The former, a *transmission model,* results in a more precise explanation of specific behaviors.

Fourth, both personal and social meanings of communication must be considered. Communication must be understood as a process through which individuals obtain both meanings unique to them and meanings consonant with those of society. Each message must be regarded as capable of evoking many images, some rooted in society, some unique to the individual, and some ambiguous. It must also allow for the fact that any message may mean something different to both speaker and listener, so that complete understanding is unlikely.

Finally, any theory must take into account that communication is the only method by which phenomenal worlds can be brought into contact. Communication is also used to adjust the phenomenal world of the communicator. People monitor their own messages, and use their own words to adjust their ideas.

Modeling is used to help clarify our ideas about communication and thus bring about improvements in understanding.

THE PROBLEM OF INDETERMINACY

There are limitations on model-making and theory-building. The research methods of the natural sciences are used as prototypes for investigation of social phenomena. Werner Heisenberg, "father of quantum mechanics," for example, did his initial experiments in the behavior of electrons. He discovered that it was not possible for him to measure the velocity and the path of an electron simultaneously. In order to measure the path of an electron, he found its velocity must be controlled, and vice versa. He could only calculate a probability that an electron would be in a specific place at a given time. The implications of this are important to us, for if certainty is impossible in the physical sciences it cannot be a goal in the study of human behavior. The investigative procedure we choose tends to qualify what we see. What we do not or cannot measure can influence what we are looking at or measuring. What Heisenberg showed is that scientific statements are normally made in terms of probabilities (or "chance," if you prefer). There is no scientific theory that can account for all the possible behaviors of all the happenings in our universe. We must, in our explorations, accept the idea that behavior may be random, and all we can do is discover patterns of occurrence, to which there are many exceptions.

The insight that the *orderly universe* was a human construct opened the eyes of scholars to exceptions, and to the study of unique phenomena. Once scientists dropped the notion that order was sitting out there waiting to be discovered, perceptions ceased to be distorted by false expectations. The behavior of the universe, and of everything in it, can be regarded as a random set, in which behavior can be described on a normal curve. In any distribution, some behaviors will be perceived to occur more frequently than others. Under the normal distribution curve, the researcher can predict certain statistical probabilities, correlate factors, and draw inferences, and, he can test his hypotheses for statistical significance. However, his decisions will be wrong a certain percentage of the time because of chance. This percentage of error is based partly on the significance level of his experiment, in which he sets his error level in advance, as much as if to say, "I'm willing to gamble that 95 or 99 times out of 100 I'll be right; I'll be wrong only 5 percent or 1 percent of the time." What the investigator looks for is a modality of behavior recognizing that any statements he makes will not describe certainty but only probability. An understanding of the normal curve of probability and its statistical method helps us to understand that any theory has its exceptions.

When we study human beings, we must understand that some generalizations can be made that are likely to be applicable to all people, but that in any given case the behavior of a single person will not necessarily accord with them. It's been said that we can generally predict the behavior of 95 percent of the population in most instances. The grim news headlines, though, are found among the behavior of that remaining 5 percent. If we fully understand the limitations of our observations systems and our method of making generalizations, it is possible to examine some communication models and attempt to evaluate their contribution to the understanding of human communicative behavior.

Claude Shannon, an engineer for the Bell Telephone Company, developed a communication model in an attempt to improve the *transmission* of messages over wire, so his model must be adapted to make it applicable to human communication. The model operates without reference to the meaning of a message. It begins with a source or message sender. The model then traces the message through a coding process, transmission through a channel, to a receiver who decodes it for its destination. The channel is subject to interference from extraneous influences called *noise*. In the case of mechanical transmission of messages, the spoken word would be coded into an electrical impulse sent out over a wire channel, decoded from impulse to word, and put into the ear of the receiver. The model can serve as a basis for understanding what happens when humans transmit words to other humans.

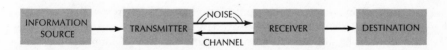

Figure 3–1. *Shannon's Model for Communication Transmission*

From Claude E. Shannon and Warren Weaver, *The Mathematical Theory of Communication* (Urbana, Ill.: The University of Illinois Press, 1949). Reprinted by permission of the publisher.

Some of the technical concepts Shannon introduced into his system are quite pertinent in a study of human communication, as follows:

1. *Entropy* refers to the tendency of the system to disintegrate. Human communication likewise tends to break down unless effort is expended to make it succeed.
2. *Redundancy* refers to portions of a message that are not absolutely necessary. Telephone messages must be amplified to overcome noise. Human messages must be repeated to overcome misunderstanding.
3. *Probability* refers to the likelihood that the correct messages will be selected from other possible messages. In mechanical systems, it is possible to make technological changes to increase the probability of accuracy. In human communication, probability of understanding can be increased through striving for mutual understanding of speaker and listener.
4. *Noise* refers to interferences in the channel that tend to distort the message. In human communication, it can also refer to social, psychological, and linguistic differences that increase the probability of misunderstanding.
5. *Feedback* refers to a method of monitoring a system, which signals correct and incorrect operations and permits correction of the system. This term has become important in the study of human communication, because it suggests that the chance of accurate communication will be increased if some concern is shown for responses to communication and efforts made to accommodate to them.

If we can temporarily accept the proposition that communication can be studied without considering the meaning content of what is communicated, then Shannon's model can be useful in studying aspects of human communication such as accuracy of reception of vocal transmission. We could measure how well the listener received the words that were sent, then derive propositions about improvement of word choice and how to enhance accuracy. Some modifications are necessary, however, if we wish to study meaning or influence of messages on our receivers. If we were to apply Shannon's model to human communication exclusively, we would have to adopt a mechanistic view of communication as a "separate" facet of human behavior. Before accepting the model though, we should clearly understand that it was designed to describe the behavior of mechanical devices.[2]

Though many of the concepts introduced by Shannon have already become part of the technical lexicon of students of human speech, the model must be adjusted to account for the capacity of humans to endow symbols with meaning. The application to machines takes into account only the transmission of symbols. It is tacitly assumed that the meaning of the

[2] Claude E. Shannon and Warren Weaver, *The Mathematical Theory of Communication* (Urbana, Ill.: University of Illinois Press, 1949).

sender will reach the receiver, if the transmission is accurate. If we assume that meanings lie in the sender and receiver rather than in the symbols, the model must be adjusted to accommodate to this idea if it is to be useful in studying human speech. The Shannon model implies that it is theoretically possible to design a perfect transmission system of nonsense words. Both the accuracy and efficiency of such a transmission could be calculated mathematically. But communication between humans is more than simple transmission of symbols. Meaning must be considered, if for no other reason than to understand how a speaker influences himself while talking.

Preoccupation with the Shannon model has led to many experimental studies of transmission behavior. While these tell part of the story of human communication, they obviously offer few insights into what goes on in the human mind when communication is carried on. Most of what is presently regarded as learning theory is based on some form of this transmission model of communication. In order to deepen understanding of the communication process, meaningful content must be included in the theoretical model. While this idea has been attacked by some behavioral purists on the grounds that it would make communication a "philosophical" study, those concerned with a holistic view of human behavior contend that "philosophical" is not a bad word, and that such an approach must be taken with behavior that cannot be empirically measured.

A model based on Shannon's which at least fits the mystery of meaning into the system was devised by Charles Osgood (Fig. 3–2). Osgood's model adapts the concept of sender and receiver by combining them into a single unit, i.e., into a human system. Each communicating unit is both sender and receiver. His major modification was to insert a *mediator* between input and output. The model is oriented to stimulus-response. Any input can be a stimulus for output that, in turn, acts as stimulus for his communicative response. This process results in a circular or active view of communication. The mediator is defined as a *cognitive unit* containing meanings, attitudes, emotions, and possible reactions. The message originates inside the mediator as a result of stimulation, and is coded there into symbols for transmission. The nature of the mediator is not actually specified, but it includes the ability to translate stimuli or perceptions into communicable symbols. Thus, the mediator helps to clarify our thinking about communication by including meaning in the model, but it is not regarded as amenable to objective inquiry.

Philosophers and scientists often find it necessary to construct words to refer to processes that cannot be associated with anything concrete or real. These *fictions* help scholars to speculate about a process and to avoid oversimplifications that might arise from total reliance on empirical data that we observe. By using a fiction like the mediator, we are able to understand the limitations of experimental information based solely on observable processes in the Shannon model. Osgood's model helps us to understand that subjective inquiry is necessary to broaden our thinking about communication. In the next sections, we will consider some additional models, as external interference, such as static or background noise in a channel.

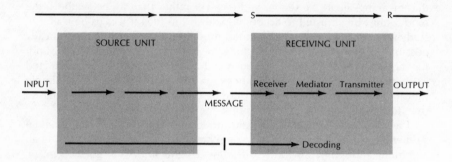

Figure 3–2. *Osgood's Modification of Shannon's Communication Model*

From Charles E. Osgood, "Psycholinguistics: A Survey of Theory and Research Problems," *Journal of Abnormal and Social Psychology*, XLIX (October 1954), p. 1. Copyright 1954 by the American Psychological Association, and reproduced by permission of the American Psychological Association and the author.

Osgood's modification enables us to consider the possible influence of noise inside the mediator. Psychological, social, and linguistic differences in speaker and listener may be considered as possible reasons for failure in accurate communication. If we wish to restrict our study of communication only to what is measurable, Shannon's model is adequate. If we wish to attempt to study meanings as well as processes, a modification (such as Osgood's) must be made. Although both of these models deal with communication behaviorally, Osgood does introduce a degree of active involvement. Neither, however, goes very far beyond a static view of communication. In the next section, we will consider some additional models, more dynamic in nature, which better express human interaction.

INTERACTION MODELS FOR COMMUNICATION

Human communication is an interaction relationship. When we talk to others, we respond to their responses. The method by which this interaction is carried on is through symbols, beamed back and forth, so that both parties are active. An effective communication model should take into account the dynamic nature and mutuality of this relationship. One of the interesting concepts involved in interacting is the idea of *feedback*.

Intelligent understanding of feedback helps expand understanding of interaction. In the simple transmission model (Fig. 3–1), feedback refers to measurements made in the system and the programming of various negatively entropic activities into the system to compensate for deficiencies. In the more complex human systems, feedback refers both to initial response and to later response to response, etc., for the human is capable of exerting his own negative entropy. A major question, however, is how you, for example, as a communicator select your responses. *Integrated field theory* offers some help with this problem.

INTEGRATED FIELD THEORY

If dynamic interaction is to be considered, the relatively simple stimulus-response model is not adequate. J. R. Kantor attempted to extend the stimulus-response principle in his communication model, based on integrated field theory.

Integrated field theory deals with the interaction of an individual with objects considered as stimuli modified by his previous contact with similar stimulating objects. The field of contact becomes integrated as the individual increases the number of his responses through repeated contacts in various settings. In other words, each contact with a stimulating object or event is stored away in memory to be referred to when another contact is made with a similar object or event, and various similar contacts can be grouped, or "integrated," in broader terms.

A frog, for example, can perceive only living flies. It may starve to death in the midst of dead flies, because it simply cannot see a fly unless the fly is moving. In much the same way, what a human stores in memory depends on the nature of his "viewing" mechanism, which includes the physiology and memory of previous perceptions. Humans cannot see outside the visible spectrum or hear high-frequency sounds. We design complex equipment to translate this information for us into scales we either can see or can understand and relate to previous knowledge. For instance, sounds we cannot hear can be translated into light patterns that we can observe visually on an oscilloscope.

Kantor's model (Fig. 3–3) suggests some of the activity that might be carried on inside Osgood's mediator (see Fig. 3–2). A stimulus is recorded as an image in the brain, and a symbol is attached to the image. The particular symbol is screened from among many possible symbols based on comparison of the image with other stored images, and the best-fitting symbol is selected. Those evaluative and inferential symbols attached to the stored image are extended to the new image, which is then stored. The new data modifies the old slightly, but mostly the new is shaped to fit the memory of previous experiences. Whatever happens, however, is controlled by the nature and state of the receiving mechanism.

The human brain permits us to relate new data to what we know, but we also can adjust what we know to the new data. Our ability to respond to stimuli by assigning symbols provides us with "scales" by which we can scan the unfamiliar. Unfortunately, each set of symbolic scales is unique to the individual and consequently only amenable to measurement in its observable projections.

Kantor's model helps us understand what inferences we can make about symbolic behavior of people in general. Thus, we can state that a perception

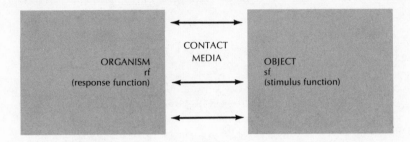

Figure 3–3. *Kantor's Conception of Integrated Field Theory of Communication*

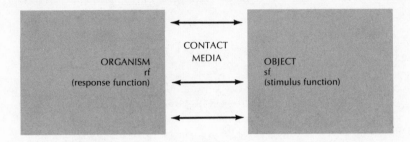 From J. R. Kantor, *Interbehavioral Psychology* (Granville, Ohio: Principia Press, 1958). Reprinted by permission of the publisher.

will evoke a response, i.e., the selection of a symbol. Selection of a symbol is associated with an evaluation of the worth of the data, which, in turn, shapes the nature of the behavioral responses. The response will, in turn, alter the environment, so that a new perception is received and the process started again. In no case, however, can we get sufficient information to predict with 100 percent accuracy the nature of individual response. We cannot penetrate into someone else's mind and see the way values interact to shape his behavior. Even verbalization of attitudes helps little, for an attitude, while related to a value, does not necessarily express value conflicts that precede behavior.

Another theory is that of Kurt Lewin.[3] Lewin's "field theory" helps us find the connection between the subjective and objective view of human behavior as it is expressed through communication. Essentially we assume that an individual's response to "society" is expressed through communicative behavior. "Society," in this context, refers to the totality of people and things around us with which we make perceptual contact . . . your own little world, in other words. Thus, communication in a normal person may be construed as a response to society, which is also a stimulus for alteration in society, which stimulates more behavior, ad infinitum. As you see, the process is in a continual state of flux. However, excessive emphasis on the individual's manifest reactions to society can distort inferences about his behavior. Valid predictions cannot be made about an individual either from knowledge of his society or from observations of his behavior, because each individual sets his norms of behavior internally, based on his unique experiences in and perceptions of his society. Concentration on interaction between the individual and his society may, therefore, lead to misunderstanding of that part of an individual's behavior which he does not reveal

[3] Kurt Lewin, *Field Theory in Social Sciences* (New York: Harper and Brothers, 1951).

to the society. A society demands of an individual that he play various roles, and his evaluation of responses to him in his roles helps him to adjust his behavior to what he perceives as necessary to "survive in society while remaining consistent with his values." Each man has a wide range of behavior choices available. Society, then, does not "cause" individual behavior; rather, it is a field in which human behavior can take place.

Lewin's field theory is designed to locate individual behavior internally and externally and is based on three principles:

1. Every behavior is a result of interaction among the various aspects of a given situation.
2. Description of behavior cannot focus on any single influence or aspect.
3. Causation is primarily contemporary and is exclusive of the past or future, in that it is a synthesis of past experience and fantasied expectation at a particular time.

Field theory, then, is an approach that attempts to treat a psychological phenomenon in its total setting. Communication, as one psychological phenomenon, must be broadly analyzed and approached through the concept of *life-space*.

Life-space is a concept somewhat similar to that of *phenomenal world*. It stems from the concept that the behavior of the individual depends upon his own internal state and the nature of his environnmet. Person and environment are interdependent variables. A field or space that includes everything which affects his behavior must extend totally around and inside each person. Life-space is neither psychical nor physical exclusively. The individual-in-motion exerts influence on life-space, which, in turn, exerts influence on the individual. Life-space would include physiological and psychological aspects of behavior as well as social, cultural, and conceptual influences on individuals as they affect individual behavior. Field theory is a mode of analysis that regards the total environment and the inner structure of the person as decisive in shaping behavior.

The model in Figure 3–4 is based on the concepts of life-space and field theory. A stimulus is received. It is processed through memory, and an appropriate set of symbols is selected for it. A verbal response is prepared commensurate with the symbols chosen. The response is then projected both inward or outward. Inward projection alters what is possessed in memory. Outward projection may also alter the external world and evoke new stimuli. The process becomes more clear when we consider the diagram of a specific act in Figure 3–5.

The behaver is now presented with a "spider-free" external world to which he responds. The diagram could be extended to include another person, and if the internal world of that perceiver has also included a fear of spiders, his response may have been to direct another person to "squash the spider" or to take flight. If the fear had been paralyzing, gross physiological changes would have resulted in nonverbal cues about the state of

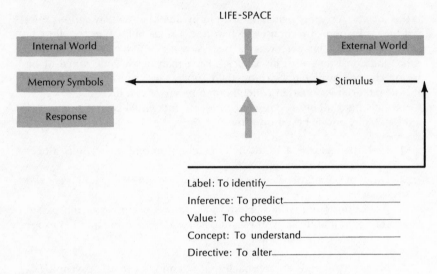

Figure 3–4. *Life-Space and Its Influence on Communication*

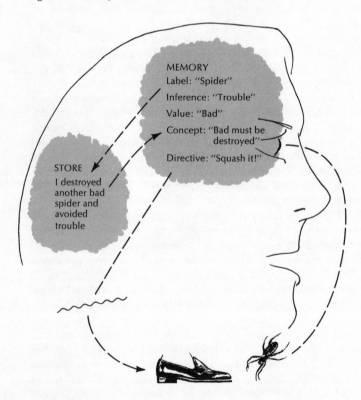

Figure 3–5. *Specific Communicative Response in Field Theory*

the individual. In any case, communication is directed both to the internal *and* the external world. The act of squashing the spider will have some influence on subsequent encounters with entities classified as "spider." What happens in the way of communication in the inner world will be considered under Vygotsky's model (Fig. 3–6).

Life-space may now be defined as a totality of acts or events real or remembered, which influence individual behavior at a certain moment. Life-space cannot be regarded as a simple additive function; rather it must be looked on as a complex process-in-motion of all variables in constant interaction. Nor can it be regarded as real, because there is no way to define, map, block out, or point to a life-space. It is a personal phenomenon, internalized by the individual and impenetrable to the investigator. Life-space contains the person and his environment, and it is generally divided into region and boundary, with the boundary being the outer limit that connects life-space with sensory perception. Life-space continually changes, because each new perception from the outside world influences the inner world, which changes the individual and alters his behavior, which, in turn, changes the appearance of life-space. Perceptual psychologists refer to this concept in terms of "ground" and "figure." The *ground* is composed of everything perceivable, while the *figure* is that which is directly perceived at a given moment. Figure cannot be separated from ground, nor can ground be looked at without some part of it being in figure.

Each new experience you have helps to process subsequent experiences. Each time you communicate, your response to the act and the responses to you influence your future communication. If you receive satisfying *feedback* into your life-space, you are encouraged as a communicator. If you get negative data, you might be apprehensive about future attempts. In general, your ability to communicate well is related to that stored-away "image" you have of yourself as a communicator. Improving communication skill implies receiving stimuli that will result in a strong and positive image.

Each influence on life-space has a "valence" and a "vector." *Vector* refers to the direction of influence, positive, negative, neutral, etc, while *valence* refers to the strength exerted. Behavior can be described in diagrams showing how the valences and vectors of various influences act on each other. What is present in life-space cannot be specifically isolated for study. Images, words, evaluations—all act on each other to influence behavior.

So, we have moved from model to theory. Now, let us consider some basic assumptions. The basic assumptions of field theory are of considerable importance in building a total theory of communication. The three assumptions are as follows:

1. It must be assumed that an individual reacts as a holistic unit whose reaction to stimuli cannot be analytically separated into basic elements and then synthesized without losing some important understanding. Communication can be understood as the process by which an individual receives information into life-space and transmits information to alter it. Each communication has an effect upon both external and internal life-space, i.e., both the environment and the individual. Each transmission and receipt will, of course, alter life-space.

2. It must be assumed that, because life-space is always in a state of change, each new perception alters the ability to communicate. The alteration may encourage or retard ability to exert influences through communication. There is no stimulus integrated into the individual that does not influence subsequent behavior in some way. It is for this reason that in learning communication, the extent to which an individual has positive, reinforcing experiences will determine his ability to communicate in other times and places.

3. It must be assumed that time is an important element in field theory. At any given moment, the life-space includes all that exists for the individual and excludes all that does not. Only the "now" of life-space can have effect at any moment. To study the communicator in terms of life-space would require momentary stoppage of the system, which is, of course, impossible. Thus any study is limited to its references to past behavior.

This concept of life-space makes it clear that the study of communication behavior is incomplete if it focuses only on a few variables and omits others. While the expediency of scientific investigation may make it necessary to isolate specific data or variables for study, the interpretation of the findings must be tempered with the realization that the investigator does not have the complete picture, and his generalizations, though accurate in terms of statistical probabilities, may not fit a given person at a given time. Human speech behavior is one of these areas in which the statistical "map" doesn't always account for the behavioral "topography" of the human territory.

VYGOTSKY AND INNER SPEECH

An intriguing problem in studying the speech behavior of humans is what happens to the speaker himself, while he speaks, and what role does his symbolizing capacity play in the development of his personality. The Russian pyschologist Lev Vygotsky has developed an approach to this problem in which he regards thought as *inner speech*.[4] Vygotsky is called an *associationist,* because of his belief that words have meaning because of an association made between the symbol word and the signal object.

Scientists only recently have turned their attention to the neurophysiological aspects of thought, and, as yet, their discoveries have not offered any solid information usable in training speakers. The neuropsychologists can work only with what they can see and measure. On the other hand, the associationists attempt to bridge this empirical gap by postulating that thoughts are "formed" by reproducing images from the past and connecting them with present images. They use neurological descriptions to build

---

[4] Lev S. Vygotsky, *Thought and Language* (Cambridge, Mass.: The Massachusetts Institute of Technology Press; New York: John Wiley, 1962).

analogies. For example, while some experts attempt to compare man's mind directly to a computing machine, the analogy breaks down when we discover that man responds to internal stimuli as well as external ones. The stimuli to action developed inside the man can be regarded as thought, according to Vygotsky.

Vygotsky's explanation tends to show that pure behavioral analysis cannot explain thought. He regards thought as a process that can coordinate what we have previously perceived to evoke original associations that become part of our life-space. Because of the capacity to develop an original idea out of stored data, thought cannot be studied as a stimulus-response activity. In short, thought is a process with which man can exert control over his environments.

We create part of our own internal world through the process of manipulating symbols and associating them with images we receive of objects or events. We "speak" to ourselves to build structures of symbols that are necessary to control our own behavior. Thoughts are formed of both old and new images associated with old and new symbols. Each new input is capable of expanding the potential for association. In human communication, one simple interaction can change a life.

If we accept these premises, then we can understand the reason for teaching both speech and writing in the manner we have been teaching them. The careful and conscious planning of an essay or a speech is, in reality, an internal rehearsal in which we convince ourselves before attempting to convince others. We understand communication in terms of "what is convincing to others must be convincing to ourselves." But, we must understand the uniqueness of each human mind in order to do an effective job of speaking. It is necessary to recognize that each mind with which we communicate will process the data somewhat differently, and consequently we cannot expect total and perfect success, no matter how well we prepare. In preparing a political speech, for instance, the writer will often use a "shotgun" approach to his speech composition, attempting to provide "something for everyone" in his content. Compare this kind of writer with the writer who approaches his audience as a master marksman approaching a paper target with a highly accurate target rifle. Which is more effective? Whatever the answer, the speech communicator works toward betterment, sharpening his language, honing his symbols, and, hopefully, whetting his audience's perception for behavioral reception.

Although our knowledge of the world and our ability to symbolize are mutually dependent, language serves to integrate and bind the two. Language is the external projection of man's ability both to think and to symbolize. Elimination of language would not eliminate the symbolization process. However, elimination of the symbolization process would destroy language. For example, nonverbal, universally recognized picture symbols of common objects, such as "telephone," "man," "airplane," etc., could remain as meaningful symbols even though they were not a part of the spoken language. This is the theory behind travel signs that use pictures rather than words to inform visitors who do not speak the language of the country. According to Vygotsky, thought is carried on through manipulation of symbols, and any external projection of symbols is in some way a projection of thought.

But the theory goes on to show that inner speech is a function of outer speech—that is, the inner processes of attention, image formation, inferring, conceptualizing, and directing cannot fully develop without the outward projection of language. This means that speech and thought are not precisely the same thing, but neither are they separable. Figure 3–6, based on Vygotsky's work, illustrates this.

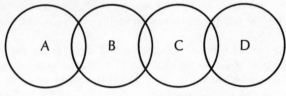

A—Thought
B—Inner speech (Verbal thought)
C—Thoughtful external speech
D—Non-thinking external speech

Figure 3–6. *Vygotsky's Model of the Relationship of Thought and Speech*

In the child, a prelinguistic thought process can be identified. This occurs before the child is aware of the symbolic processes of his culture. At the same time, he may be engaged in producing sounds and projecting them. Next, he forms an *algorithm,* an understanding that a symbol can take the place of a thing or event. Gradually "A" and "D" merge and blend, so that both "B" and "C" are now possible. The precise nature of this prelinguistic process is not clear, nor is it important right now. We shall consider it again shortly. What is important are three implications, if we are to understand Vygotsky's ideas:

1. Speech cannot be learned solely through observable performance.
2. Since outward projection of symbols depends on concept formation through inner speech, training must be directed toward inner attitudes and concepts.
3. Satisfactory training of inner speech may make performance training unnecessary, if a person can be given a positive image of himself as a speaker and can develop his own skill at performance. Without such an image, performance training will be superficial and temporary.

To improve communication, it is necessary for you to conceive an idea of the role of communication in your life and of your role as a communicator. Such understanding will help you discover the ways in which you can improve.

THE VYGOTSKY MODEL AND DEVELOPMENT OF ORIGINAL THEORY

Classical study of the art of speech is usually based on the *five canons of rhetoric:* invention, disposition, style, delivery, and memory.

Invention refers to the conception and selection of an idea for communication.

Disposition focuses on the organization of ideas.

Style focuses on the selection of words and phrases.

Delivery relates to the actual utterance.

Memory refers to the ability to hold the idea from start to finish.

Classical scholars and their modern disciples have attempted to instruct students in speech by dividing training into the five canons. The Vygotsky model illustrates how the canons can be tested scientifically by establishing some hypotheses about them in terms that can be manipulated for experimental study. The Vygotsky model makes it possible to reverse the five canons of rhetoric and show how the classical concept can be used to describe the development of speech in human beings. Here's how the model (Fig. 3–6) is explained.

Memory is that feature of human behavior which separates man from other speaking animals. A myna bird cannot speak in sentences, because it has forgotten the beginning of the sentence before it reaches the end. Memory capacity develops in human infants in order that symbols, which are learned arbitrarily and at random can be stored. We would postulate that the "A" portion of the diagram develops first. Shortly afterward, the infant begins babbling random symbols, then delivers meaningless messages, "D." Style develops as the child becomes able to connect symbol with image and build them into meaningful units. "A" and "D" connect to produce part of "C," although the child is totally imitative at the outset. The change from single symbol to integrated chains of symbols permits the child to issue simple directives and commands, but later the child is able to arrange these symbols so that it can attempt to control the environment through transmission of organized ideas. Now another part of "C" has developed. Finally, the ability to manipulate the symbols into conceptions, projections, and fantasies gives the speaker the ability to conceive an idea as well as predict the potential effect of his idea, and "B" and "C" become complete. The emerging ideas can be tested clinically by observing the developing language in children of various ages.

This applies to teaching through an approach to the child characterized by reinforcement of learning that enables maximum control of speech to result in the mature adult. Exposure to many images and symbols should expand memory capacity. Exposure to much talk and conversation would offer a variety of models for imitative verbal play and would improve delivery. A free, permissive atmosphere, enabling the child to experiment in the control of his life-space, should improve style. Confrontation with problem-solving situations should assist in developing the ability to organize logically. Finally, maturation, assisted by consistent exposure, example, and careful training, should assist in the growth of inventive capacity.

The foregoing is a somewhat imaginative approach and one you are probably not used to. It is presented as an example of what can be done with original models. You should, by now, realize that the development of communication models is limitless. Many fine examples have been constructed by noted scholars. Perhaps the most definitive model is that of Harold Lasswell, who asks simply: "Who says what, in which channels, to whom, and with what effect?"[5]

Whatever the purpose stipulated—learning to speak or learning about speech—it is necessary to have a model as a sensible guide to your speech activity.

WE HAVE PROBLEMS!

Researchers in communication attempt to answer questions, of which very few are simple questions. In fact, virtually all of them involve complex model-building, theorizing, and testing. This book does not purport to answer such questions, because most demand a personal solution, by you, if the answers are to be used. However, some guidance based on the best available evidence will be offered throughout this book. You, however, must discover your own personal answers.

Here for your edification and confusion are a few of the problems we face:

1. What is the impact of ideas about communication on the major problems of our society and our world?
2. What is the significance of stimulus-response ideas for communication? Can communication actually be reduced to a stimulus-response explanation?
3. What is subjective and what is objective in speaking? Is it possible to evaluate speech performance objectively? What modes of evaluation are possible and available?
4. How can a communicator find out what it is necessary to do to "reach" his audience?
5. What effect does communicating have on the communicator? How can we understand the various types of influence communicating has on various people?

[5] Harold D. Lasswell, "The Structure and Function of Communication in Society," in Lyman Bryson, ed., *The Communication of Ideas* (New York: Harper and Brothers, 1948).

6. What can be done about hostility to training in communication? How can we teach better the needs of people to communicate?

7. How can communication behavior be used to analyze adjustment of an individual? If speech is a significant projection of the inner self, to protect our egos should we not be more guarded and careful in its use?

On pages 58–62 you will find several other models for analysis and study. Your main job as a student is to discover a model that explains your communication activity to *you*. If you cannot find a satisfactory one here, build one!

SUGGESTIONS FOR DISCUSSION

1. The authors talked about value in this chapter. What gives a thing value? Talk in a group about the things around you—things like TV sets, cars, clothing, cameras, skis. Have each person rank-order a set of things. Why are the lists different? Is there any way you can come to agreement on the value you assign to the various things? Is there any reason why you even have to come to agreement on matters like this?

2. Surely you have been in a classroom where one person is sitting absolutely still; one is taking notes furiously; one is staring off into space; one is writing, but it is a letter home; and another has his eyes closed. Is it possible that everyone could be communicating? Is it possible that they are all communicating something different? Could they possibly be communicating the same thing? The man who doesn't move at all—is he communicating? A man in his room alone denouncing the world—is he communicating? Is it possible to communicate all the time? Is there ever a time when you are not communicating?

3. Look at the letters to the editor in your local paper. See if you can find examples of mental illness expressed by the communications in the letters. Working as a group, can you construct some letters that reveal obvious hang-ups?

4. Following is a verbal model written by one of the authors. Does it make any sense to you? Can you draw a picture of it? Why was it written?

Toward a Model for the Operational Unification of the Sciences-Arts

The unification of what is called Science with what is called Art emerges from different ratios of "emotion" and feeling to "intellectual" and logical operations of the human brain in response to accumulated experience. There are no dichotomies in this common process of communication. For the scientist, rigorous reasoning and checking to his fact-phenomena predominate and guide the structuring of his messages. In the artist, feeling predominates, leaving whatever structuring there is far more often to the perception of the receiver.

With isomorphism (semantic structural similarity) as the basic variable, the generation of ideas and their control proceeds through cybernetic subvariables. Emotively powered by positive feedback to release inferences, fancies, and imaginings, the ideas are brought into isomorphism, relevancy, coherence, and organization through the inhibiting action of negative feedback. The process is given direction in line with purpose as there is a joining with the feedforward variable by the positive and negative feedback variables.

Productivity of the Scientist-artist as well as of the Artist-scientist is limited by how much he knows, and the ordering he is able to bring about in these abstractings.

This "model" of the communication process is offered as only one way of viewing the contents of the library. Perhaps there will be a fuller mobilization of resources for communication and learning as the model becomes more complete, verified, and brought into use.

5. The most important goal of this chapter is to assist you in developing some models of your own. One way to do this is to gather in groups of three or four and share some common experiences about communication interactions that go on at your campus. See if you can draw a model of interaction between student and professor; between male student and female student; between professor and professor; between professor and administrator; between students of the same sex. What variables do you have to account for in your diagrams? (What are variables? What do we do with a variable in a model?) From this, and from examination of the models in the text, perhaps you can come up with your own model which describes what goes on in the communication process as you see it. After you have done this, can you answer the question: why is it so important to have models?

6. Allusion was made in this chapter to the problem of preserving uniqueness in a mass, conformist society. What kinds of problems does this cause? Is it possible for anyone to remain unique in society without controlling society? One student remarks, "My soul is on the computer card. It's like the picture of Dorian Gray. If I change, the card changes. I think that's why they won't let people mutilate or spindle computer cards. If they do it to mine, I'll die." How does technology subvert uniqueness? Can you build a rationale for the president of your college regarding you all as quite similar and not permitting much idiosyncratic behavior? What would he have to do in order to make you think he thought you were a unique individual? Is it possible for him to do it for everyone? (And if he doesn't do it for everyone, would you want it done just for you?)

7. Most "scientists" will resist the use of the Heisenberg Principle applied to the study of human communication, but it does seem very applicable. Does the Heisenberg Principle apply in your classroom? What effect does the presence of the professor have on your behavior? Does your presence do anything to his behavior? Do you behave differently when you know you are being watched? Can you think of a way in which you can gain experience under supervision without the Heisenberg Principle affecting you? What if you were asked to practice speeches on a video-tape recorder, without the professor in the room? Would you behave naturally?

8. Why does it seem to be important to you and others to be "unique"? Why can't people just settle down and accept the fact that they are all pretty much alike? If people did that, society would be a lot easier to run. What defense can you make of the concept of uniqueness to your professor? To your dean? The college president? Your mother and father? Your friends? The administrator of the Federal Security Agency or Income Tax Bureau? Why do people fuss about "big government"? If it could be proved that big government and centralized administration in which all people were presumed to be the same were the most efficient methods of government and provided more goods and services for all people, would you be willing to give up your quest for uniqueness?

9. What does the fact that frogs can only see live flies have to do with your own view of the world? If you can't distinguish a Blue Spruce from a Douglas Fir,

do you see either of them? What do you think of the proposition that humans can only "see" what they can name? Is it possible to see things to which no words attach themselves? Why is it important to know the limits of your viewing mechanism? Discuss in a group the implications of seeing and naming in race relations, drug usage, or any other current and vital topic. What do you suppose the typical racist "sees" when he looks at a black man?

10. What is your "life-space" and how does it differ from that of the person sitting next to you? Talk about it with him for a while. See if you can determine where you share a life-space and where your life-space differs. When you find some differences, explore the possible misunderstandings you could have with your respondent because of the differences in life-space. You might continue talking for awhile and see what kinds of profiles you can draw up of each other.

11. Take another look at the models in the chapter. Can you discover their flaws? Obviously none of them are perfect; otherwise there would only be one, not several. Starting with the Shannon model and working through to the last one, try to apply each model to a kind of investigation. Why are models essential to scientific investigation? What variables are involved in each model? Do you have any suggestions about how the investigation could proceed? Why don't we use models in artistic performance? (Well, some artists use them, but we are not talking about that kind—or are we?) What is an artist's model? A playwright's model? A composer's model? How are they similar to, and different from, the models in your text?

SUGGESTIONS FOR FURTHER READING

David K. Berlo, *The Process of Communication* (New York: Holt, Rinehart and Winston, 1960). Chapter 2 is pertinent to our discussion in this chapter. Dr. Berlo presents the basic detail and style of communication theory.

Frank E. X. Dance, ed., *Human Communication Theory* (New York: Holt, Rinehart and Winston, 1967). Dr. Dance's compilation of original essays presents a myriad of scholarly thoughts and opinions about human communication. Your best bets here are Chapters 1, 6, 8, 9, and 11. You can safely ignore the ponderous footnoting that outweighs the text in several cases.

Alfred Smith, "The Theory of Human Communication," in *Communication and Culture* (New York: Holt, Rinehart and Winston, 1966). This is another large bite of theory, but it presents the topic in a truly, interdisciplinary light.

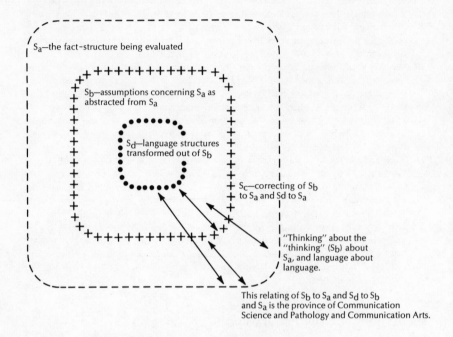

The diagram labels read:

S_a—the fact-structure being evaluated

S_b—assumptions concerning S_a as abstracted from S_a

S_d—language structures transformed out of S_b

S_c—correcting of S_b to S_a and S_d to S_a

"Thinking" about the "thinking" (S_b) about S_a, and language about language.

This relating of S_b to S_a and S_d to S_b and S_a is the province of Communication Science and Pathology and Communication Arts.

Figure 3–7. *Interplay in Language-Thought Relationships in One Person*

Figure 3–7 is an attempt to represent the interplay and circularity between an environment and the ensuing speech back into the environment. At the highest order of abstraction, c (communication) may be described as a series of isomorphic transformations from S_a into S_d When the different orders of abstractions (transformation to transformation) are kept in correspondence with S_a the conditions for adequacy, mental health, and creativity remain favorable. Communication pathology is concerned with the array of physical, semantic, psychological breakdowns and disorders in this whole relating-functioning.

The principles of relating as diagrammed in Figure 3–7 are further exemplified in Figure 3–8, a modification of a diagram by Wendell Johnson. Both combined would be the model we have in mind, but it seems impossible to put both in a single diagram.

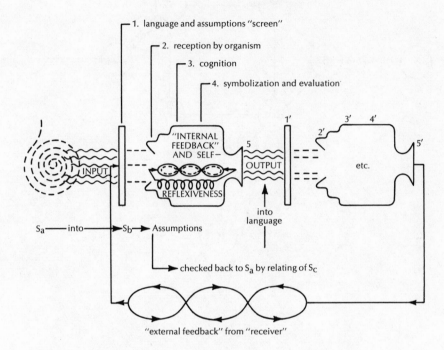

Figure 3–8. *A Fact-Structure Transforming Isomorphically into Language*

Elwood Murray's modification of Wendell Johnson's diagram (Fig. 3–10) from *Your Most Enchanted Listener* (New York: Harper & Brothers, 1956). Modification used by permission of Harper & Brothers.

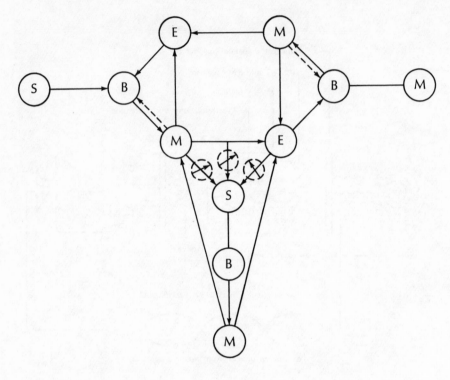

Figure 3–9. *The Peterson Model*

A schematic representation of a simple communications link, with the speaker in the upper left and the listener in the upper right: S—generalized sensory system, B—brain, E—ear, M—motor mechanism of speech. The three circles in the lower portion of the diagram represent an experimenter: S—generalized sensory system, B—brain, M—generalized motor system. The dashed circles and arrows represent measuring instruments.

From Gordon E. Peterson, "Speech and Hearing Research," *Journal of Speech and Hearing Research,* March 1958. Reprinted with the permission of the American Speech and Hearing Association.

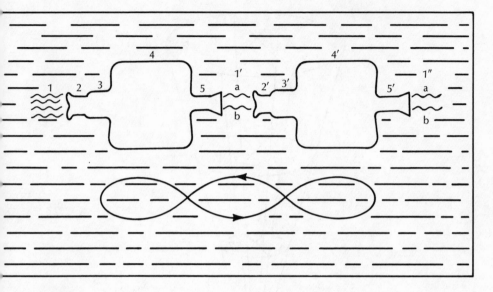

Figure 3–10. *The Johnson Model*

Key: Stage 1, event, or source of stimulation external to the sensory end organs of the speaker; Stage 2, sensory stimulation: Stage 3, pre-verbal neurophysiological state; Stage 4, transformation of pre-verbal state into symbolic forms; Stage 5, verbal formulations in "final draft" for overt expression; Stage 1', transformation of verbal formulations into (a) air waves and (b) light waves, which serve as sources of stimulation for the listener (who may be either the speaker himself or another person); Stages 2' through 1" correspond, in the listener, to Stages 2 through 1'. The arrowed loops represent the functional interrelationships of the stages in the process as a whole.

From Wendell Johnson, *Your Most Enchanted Listener* (New York: Harper & Brothers, 1956). Adapted from previous diagram by the author in "The Spoken Word and the Great Unsaid," *Quarterly Journal of Speech,* Vol. 32 (December 1951). Adapted version used by permission of Harper & Brothers and the Speech Association of America.

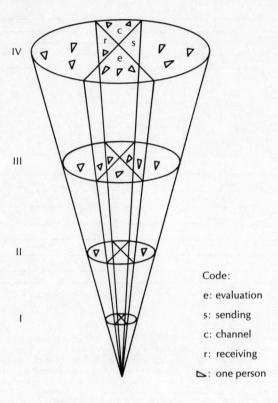

Code:

e: evaluation

s: sending

c: channel

r: receiving

◁: one person

Figure 3–11. *The Reusch-Bateson Model*

From Jurgen Ruesch and Gregory Bateson, *Communication: The Social Matrix of Psychiatry* (New York: W. W. Norton, 1951), p. 275. Copyright 1951 by W. W. Norton & Company, Inc. Reprinted by permission of W. W. Norton & Company, Inc.

4

Variations on a Theme:
Isomorphism

There are many ways to view communication. Each of the models described in the last chapter approaches communication from a different perspective. We can examine speaking atomically and look at the neural synapses, or we can examine speaking wholly and look at the broad patterns in the anthropology of behavior, of how people act and react. We can see insight by examining what goes on in our own minds.

VIEWING OUR VIEWING

You can examine your view of communication as a broad human activity, the substance of cultures and civilizations, the fabric by which the past and future are bound together. You can also regard communication as a minute behavior through which the trivial wants of the moments are satisfied. When we communicate about communication, we can consider the potential and actual behavior of human beings and their societies. In brief, the more vantage points we choose from which to view communication behavior the higher our degree of personal understanding of behavior and communication.

The viewpoints presented in Chapter 3 have been constructed by scholars. They were not presented as "facts" to be memorized or opinions you must believe. They were presented to guide you in developing *your* own viewpoints, valid to meet *your* goals. They will be useful to you only as they enable you to understand how you discover what you talk about, when you talk, how much you talk, whom you talk to, what you hope to achieve by talking and how well you do it. It's like a cookbook. Each chef/author feels that his blend of ingredients, in his proportions and order, provides the most rewarding result. Similarly, each of us can add a pinch of our own values here and a pinch there to season our talk to our own subtle satisfaction. In this way, we add our own unique personality to the recipe. Your awareness of these subtle, individual differences is the rewarding part of the communication process. As you recognize the many variaables that influence your success in speaking, you will be able to discover the subtle influences that seem to help you succeed as well as those frustrating influences that so often defeat you. It is easy to remain rooted in accustomed behaviors. Consider the man who enters the army and never rises above the lower enlisted ranks throughout his entire career, or the man who retires at the "junior executive" level at the end of his career. Whatever the root causes, it often becomes easier to accept the consequences than to change behavioral patterns. Learning effective communication, like advancing professionally in life, demands active participation by you. It cannot be taught to you. You must learn it through your own efforts at mastery of the variables of communication.

SPEAKING WITH A PURPOSE

In football, a tackler pursuing a pass receiver shortens his route as he predicts the place where the runner will be. A cat places itself in position where it can leap most easily on the mouse as the mouse comes out of hiding. Human beings make hundreds of predictions as simple as these in their day-to-day behavior. A pilot must predict where his plane will land on the runway and the ratio of speed, altitude, and distance to make it in safely. You must be equally accurate in your predictions when you drive your car in heavy traffic or when you are a pedestrian.

Human beings differ from intelligent animals in that they can predict over wide ranges of time, about more things, in far more complex situations. If we make no effort to predict outcomes we can expect to be pushed around, shocked, frustrated, eventually demoralized, and then destroyed. Unless we are able to make a considerable number of accurate predictions, we are unable to cope with even the simplest situations. We can exert control over our environment to change it better to suit our needs, but this involves prediction and action of even higher orders.

Our communicative behavior not only gives us some control over the external world, but it also helps us order our own ideas so that we can interpret what we see and our relation to it. We use recognizable symbols in order to make the world seem more orderly to ourselves. Inability or unwillingness to interpret messages properly or respond to them intelligently can be symptoms of social disorders, such as delinquency or mental illness.

In fact, most social and emotional problems are described in terms of communication inadequacies. Consistent out-of-phase communication is a sign of disordered thought characterized by inappropriate evaluation and inadequate decision-making, i.e., mental problems. The person with mental problems refuses to take part in the orderly use of symbolic communication used by his peers in society—the so-called "norm." However, we do not generally isolate these people until they replace disorderly symbolism with overt behavior that may be harmful to society, to individuals, or to the self. For example, an extremist may speak hatefully, even violently, about other people, and society will not really take notice until his symbolism threatens to become harmfully active or actually leads to an overt threatening behavior.

Decision-making and evaluating are similar in that both are based on prediction. We exert control by thinking out how an act will affect us and others and trying to shape the act to maximize chances of achieving our goals. We evaluate goals by predicting our response to their achievement. We make decisions by predicting their effect on the world we seek to control. Each change in our environment demands new evaluations and new decisions, continued assessment and prediction. This is evident in the everyday world of "cat-and-mouse" games played in politics, business, education, etc., and reported in the mass media.

What all of us must understand is that what is important to one person may be trivial to another. Evaluations are specific as people encounter specific events at a specific time, based on their own interpretations. When we are not aware of the unique relationship of person and thing, we tend to misunderstand people. If we assume that everyone sees the world just as we do, our relationships with others are going to be awkward and unproductive. Our behavior is inappropriate if we do not understand that the words we may use for one purpose may evoke different evaluations in the person to whom we speak. Intelligent prediction depends on awareness of uniqueness, and the attendant realization that there are widely different behaviors possible in response to each of our acts. When we speak to others, we must attempt to predict in their terms, not ours. Relying on our own sense of the world ignores the fact that difference is more common than similarity.

In writing, the author acts from this knowledge when he adapts his style to his readers. Similarly a speaker relates his message to the perception and evaluation levels of his audience. You can gain insight into this concept by studying the contrasts between a teacher whom you evaluate as being "good" and another who is "boring" in terms of your evaluation. One is communicating *with* an audience, while the other is communicating *to* an audience. Observe the two teachers in action, and you will be observing the personification of *the two-way-street* principle of communication.

Ignoring differences by no means stops communication. Messages can be misinterpreted to mean "You are not important!" or "What you are saying is not important." People will not tolerate deprecation of themselves. After all, "I am the most important thing in the world" is an idea that cannot easily be shaken off by any of us. But the effective speaker must shake off this idea if he is to achieve maximum success. He must adopt the idea that each person in his audience is the most important person in the world at that particular moment, and that communicating his message *with* the person is his most important goal. Within this context audience evaluation, or prediction, becomes very important.

Satisfactory prediction can be assisted by regarding the people around you as a "set" in which all behaviors are possible. In any set, however, some behaviors and responses will be relatively common and consistent. The good speaker will search for these commonalities, regardless of whether he shares them.

An effective speaker seeks to maintain as much control over the communication situation as possible. While he cannot predict the responses of his audience with complete accuracy, he can select and arrange words in such a way that his ideas evoke the most positive of the many possible responses from his listeners. Again, this is prediction.

Characteristically, the effective speaker is focused on his environment, which includes the situation that causes him to speak, his listeners, and external influences on them. First, he must discover ideas sufficiently important to warrant communicating about them. Second, he must feel competent to exercise an influence. Third, he must control his mental processes to select words and phrases that will accurately express his ideas so that his audience will understand them, and he must behave continually to evoke the kind of response he desires from his audience. Fourth, he must have a methodology for understanding his listeners and their attitude toward his goal. Finally, he must be sufficiently self-critical so that he can evaluate accurately his level of success or failure.

Speaking with a purpose involves many levels of evaluation and prediction. The speaker must be able to use his past experience to predict his own behavior in a given situation. He must be able to evaluate his own performance in a given case with a given group of listeners. He must be able to discover reasons for ineffective performance and change to more effective behavior. What we are saying is that practice does not make perfect, only habitual. What does lead to communicative improvement is understanding, evaluation, and control.

Perfect control is virtually impossible, however, even for the best of speakers. Performance must be considered in terms of probabilities. Oral communication involves total personality in a total situation. For instance, a speaker cannot control weather, and he may have to present an outdoor talk in a downpour. The rain may be a negative variable or a positive variable, but the main thing is he cannot control it. The speaker can, however, relate his message to the environment so as to take advantage of the situation.

The speaker's voice and body movement often cannot be stylized to conceal meanings. To an extent, the speaker is controlled by the evaluations of him made by his audience. If his listeners negatively evaluate things he cannot change, there is nothing he can do about it. He must attempt, as

best he can, to control the controllable, i.e., the material content and structure of his speech, as well as his personal responses. For the most part, a
speaker can learn to control his responses to cues transmitted to him from
his audience whether it is an audience of 1 or 1,000. Care in planning formal
communication is assisted by our natural training in society—that is, our
daily association with others teaches us how to respond to others. Most of
us can indeed interpret the responses of others and accommodate to them
with great accuracy. Those who cannot, become outcasts or rejects. But
careful attention to successes in private communication can help all of us
to understand the responses we receive from larger audiences.

There is really very little difference between public and private performance. One authority, James Winans, declared that public speaking is
nothing more than "extended conversation."[1] You must take care to avoid
feeling that public speaking is a special situation which demands that you
alter your voice or body movements. It was once thought that special training in voice, diction, and gesture was necessary to success on the public
platform. That notion has long since been rejected. Now it is believed that
understanding communication, sound and sensible preparation, and the
ability to evaluate yourself and your audience are vitally essential elements,
far ahead of skill, in all oral communication.

SEEKING THE BASIC VARIABLE OF COMMUNICATION

Our prediction can be accurate only when our knowledge of the situation and people we are predicting about is sound. The thoroughness and
accuracy with which we acquaint ourselves with our changing environments
control our ability to exert influence over them. Like the experimentalist,
to predict B from A, you must assume some knowledge of A. The more complete and detailed your knowledge of A, the better able you are to predict
B, if B and A are associated. If such prediction is our goal, we must be very
careful in our observation of A, and how it changes.

Thus, the more control a speaker wishes to exert over others, the more
knowledge he must have of his medium and his audience, and the more involved he must be in the total situation. He must understand that his
chances of failure become greater as he seeks more complicated goals,
especially if he has additional knowledge on which to base prediction. He
must evaluate his prognosis accordingly.

The power plant of the human evaluater is the brain. The instrumentation system is his perception apparatus. The interplay between *self* and *situation* determines his chance of success. The wider the range of adjustments
he can make, the greater is his potential as a speaker. Thus, experience in
many situations, carefully analyzed, is the most effective road to success.

The brain and central nervous system control the interplay between ourselves and our environment. The central nervous system, controlled by the

[1] James Winans, *On Public Speaking* (New York: Appleton-Century-Crofts, 1915).

brain, is a mechanism for the transmission of signals received from the sense organs; the brain handles integration of this information and the activation of behavior. Activities carried on in the spinal cord are simple and invariable. Those carried on in the cerebral cortex are complex and, if not intelligently controlled, are relatively unpredictable.

Man has a tendency to seek order or *homeostasis*. Once a child learns to control his brain, he can manipulate the way the world looks to make it appear controllable and orderly. Through management of symbols and images in the brain we try to achieve proper evaluation. Such evaluations help us to achieve productive behavior—communication patterns capable of influencing and motivating others. If, however, we are excessively concerned with making the world predictable and secure, we may lose our capability to influence reality.

Alfred Korzybski offered the analogy between a symbolic map and the territory it represents.[2] He pointed out that, while a map is *not* the actual territory, to the extent that it shows relationship among locations in proper proportions it can be used to guide movement through the territory it purports to describe. Inaccuracies in the map result in inappropriate behavior. Following this analogy, we use our brains to map relationships among the things we perceive. We act, then, on the basis of our mental maps, which represent "reality" to us the only way we can know it. To the extent that our mental maps correspond to the world outside, we can exert control. That means we must continually adjust our maps through accommodation of new information.

If we map others as having the same emotions as ours and speak to them as we would speak to ourselves, our words may have no effect. If we map information about the knowledge level of our audience as higher than it is, we are likely to speak over their heads. If our mental map is an inaccurate representation of the audience's territory of perception, we can get lost when we follow it. We can even arrive at the wrong destination, i.e., blunder into the wrong conclusion at the end of the message.

Our behavior is based on our predictions based on the maps we make. Communication training can be compared to steps in map-making. We must consider our goal and the "terrain" we must traverse in order to get there. Then we select symbols according to the extent we think they will carry us to that goal.

Before we propose some methods of map-making, we must consider the various ranges of limitation people have on their ability to think and behave. The goal of communication training is *not* to bring everyone up to some arbitrary level of performance. Humans differ widely in their capabilities. The goal we must strive for is training that will enable each man to go as far as possible toward his physiological and psychological limits in understanding, predicting, and acting.

Some people will be able to draw accurate maps and follow them suc-

---

[2] Alfred Korzybski, *Science and Sanity* (Lakeville, Conn.: International Non-Aristotelian Library Publishing Company, 1933).

cessfully. Others will be able to draw the maps but lack sufficient psychic energy to travel the ground. Some will not be able to map at all yet will be able to "muddle through" with some success. Still others will be inadequate at both mapping and moving. Communication training must take into account the human limits and set goals for training within these limits.

THE PRINCIPLE OF ISOMORPHISM

Hundreds of pieces of man-made paraphernalia that have been boosted beyond the gravitational pull of the earth are racing through outer space. Man-made assumptions and evaluations may be similarly out of orbit and just as useless when they pull free from their factual orbits. They are worse than useless if they have never been questioned or examined by the people who made them, because unexamined ideas often have little correspondence with reality. Our lives are built upon hundreds of assumptions about the "way things are," and we have acquired those assumptions through our experiences from childhood to the present day. We have already noted that each experience we have alters our view of reality. All our past experiences refract and distort each current experience. Taken together, our sum total of experience provides us with a set of premises on which we interpret and evaluate the world so that we can behave in it. When our premises result in reasonably high predictability, we feel successful and capable in our interaction with society. When our premises do not help us cope with the world and its frustrations, our personalities dissolve, and we feel the pangs of anxiety and dissociation, which can lead to the mental problems mentioned earlier in this chapter.

What we have just said states another way of looking for the main variable in communication. We are concerned with correspondence between inner maps and the external territories they represent. We are concerned with ways of moving our symbols around, so that the world inside our heads bears some resemblance to the world outside—the world that gave us the stimuli on which our internal world of symbols and images is based. In brief, we try to improve our mental maps so that they more accurately represent the external world we perceive.

Applied directly to speech behavior, your verbal activities must be consistent with some internal model. You may not be conscious of this model, but it is the result of the processing your brain has done with the data it received from all of your previous attempts at contact with the world. If you become aware of your model, you can test it to determine how effectively it helps you behave. Then your evaluation of each experience may lead you to modify the model, your behavior, or both.

This process by which communication keeps us in tune with our universe is called *isomorphism,* which one authority defines as "one-to-one correspondence between objects in different systems which preserves the relationships between the objects." Another says it is "structural similarities in different fields." In very general terms, isomorphism is the evaluatory proccess by which our "maps" are altered so they will more accurately represent territories. However, as we stated before, this accuracy never becomes statistically or realistically perfect. We will deal with this concept more specifically in Chapter 7.

An isomorphism resembles the changes that occur from one generation to the next. A pine tree transforms into another pine tree, not into a cottonwood. Each of the two pine trees is a different individual (system), but the younger tree preserves fidelity to the identifying characteristics of previous generations. Each new generation, however, is unique and has characteristics of its own.

An artist generates isomorphism in his painting transformation. The more closely he perceives the meadow, the more detail he can preserve in his painting. The more closely he looks into his mind, the more abstract and individualized his painting will be. If he were to attempt to capture on canvas the meadow in minute, photographic detail, we could perhaps locate objects there by using his painting as a map. If, on the other hand, he was representing the emotional impact of the meadow on his own psyche, the best we could hope for is an insight into his inner emotional state. In either case, we might glean some information about his dexterity by watching his movements. Scientists follow the same procedure as they manipulate symbols. So do poets as they capture subtle word associations. Both accuracy and evaluative impression are important if man-made isomorphism is to have any real meaning.

If communication could be perfect throughout the stages in the process from environment to language, it could be said to carry through with "invariance under transformation." Originally used by mathematicians, *invariance* applies to the transformation of one set of symbols or a formula into a different sets of symbols or another formula. Very simply $X = \frac{A}{2} + B$ could be transformed into $A = 2(X-B)$. Such an invariance carried through from input to output implies perfect communication, which, of course, is impossible for humans. In fact, complete fidelity is by no means always necessary except in very important mathematical situations. In human decision-making, approximating is sufficient. The process we have called *feedback* and the speaker's response to it, control the nature of each isomorphic transformation. This will be discussed in detail in the next chapter.

Anything we perceive undergoes isomorphism as it is stored in our brain. Evaluation begins on contact. Communication from the outside to our inner world puts *us* into contact, so that *we* become a part of every situation we encounter. Perfect objectivity is impossible, because we are participants in every situation we speak of, even by virtue of just knowing about it. Our responses sometimes seem independent of our awareness of response. We are forever bombarded with peripheral stimuli that register on our consciousness and influence behavior, even though we are not making a consciously controlled observation. Also, responses to a situation begin immediately. Those that are spinal require no symbolic manipulation; they are virtually automatic. Responses controlled by the cerebral cortex, however, demand symbolic manipulation before behavior.

Symbolic manipulation in itself is no guarantee of accurate assessment. Planned behavior, regardless of its rationality, may be useful and appropriate in terms of the system planning it, and it must be evaluated in terms of its utility. While our behavior may be perfectly rational to us at the time we behave, we have, in most cases, an opportunity for hindsight. It is a common irony to speak of 20/20 hindsight as being far superior to our normally myopic foresight. We can evaluate our behavior in terms of its success in satisfying our needs and wants, if indeed we know them. The evaluation we make is then stored to influence subsequent behavior.

Other persons evaluate our behavior and often attempt to apply correctives. Those we respect may help us to modify our behavior, while those who push their evaluations on us may alienate us and impel us to negative responses and reinforcement of inadequate behavior. Parents, teachers, and friends are frequent evaluaters of the behavior of others. Because they are often not tactful or subtle, it is essential that we learn to evaluate evaluations, lest we be destroyed by an excess of negative cues.

Our behavior, modified by our own evaluations and those of others, will help form a personal style. We will construct a "counterpart of reality" around which we will organize our behavior. To the extent that our mental counterpart of reality is isomorphic with events, we will be effective in exerting an influence on reality. Our failures can be analyzed by examining the extent to which our counterpart is not isomorphic or "how accurately did the map fit the territory?"

We can describe the processes of learning to be an effective public speaker in terms of isomorphism. Your voluntary behavior the first time you speak in public will be shaped by your image of how you should behave in order to hold the interest of others. To the extent that your impressions are isomorphic with reality, you will perform adequately. If they are not, then you will need to adjust the "counterpart." Reading and experience will help you do this. So will criticism from your instructor and classmates. You must remember that it will primarily be your feeling about the situation, represented by your "map," that will control the evaluations you make of your own performances. Involuntary behavior, such as stage fright, is not part of your plan. However, it somehow intrudes and becomes an unwelcome guest—but there just the same. To a great extent, this unplanned behavior can be positively utilized through such devices as gestures and vocal expression, which release the tension you feel. This feeling is something all beginning speakers experience to some degree or other. However, that word *experience* seems to be the magic cure for most people too.

Though performance will be an isomorphic transformation of those other performances that preceded it, each new performance will also have some unique qualities. Improvement comes about by altering your view of performance, so that you can capitalize on what you found effective, reject the ineffective, and be personally capable of responding to uniqueness as well. You may facilitate this process through an understanding of both parts of the isomorphic process, the "inner" and "outer" environments.

Our inner environment is a "phenomenal world" of images and symbols stored in the brain containing everything we know, think, or fancy. It includes ideas and feelings plus an assortment of images from art and interaction. It includes a record of all the assumptions, false and true, which we have previously made. It includes what we have learned or half-learned: our prejudices, hates, and fears; our loves, ideals, principles, and wisdom. It includes all of our memories, some of which have faded to subconscious levels, but which have not been totally forgotten. Much of our inner environment is unconscious. Furthermore it is unique.

If we could "know" our inner environment, we would know ourselves. But we tend to conceal much of ourselves from ourselves. We push below consciousness those things we don't want to know in an attempt to bury unpleasantness. We often communicate with others to conceal what we do not want to know. Our masks, deceits, and poker faces are also an important part of our inner environment. Our inner environment is for the most part inaccessible to direct observation. We can see only part of it reflected in behavior. Even our own internal world remains somewhat of a mystery until we behave in response. It is here that we meet our most persistent communication problem: that of making an appropriate isomorphic transformation of parts of our internal world, so that we can communicate with another internal world in understandable terms.

A vast amount of our inner environments have emerged from our minds in the symbolic forms of art, music, poetry, sculpture, thousands of textbooks, literatures, scientific journals, architecture, etc. Massive collections of communications from inner environments are found in libraries and museums, and they multiply constantly. We live in a sea of symbols, fed by torrents from the press, radio, TV, classroom, job, governments, and churches. Advertising assails us from all sides—in our homes, on the highways, and in the mails. This flood of symbols must be processed by our mind. Every impact on our nervous system is another message from outside that we must evaluate and store and make some decision about. If the data is isomorphic, the change it makes in our inner environment will help us behave more effectively. If we permit too much alteration in our inner environment because of messages that are not isomorphic with reality, our behavior will be awkward, ineffective, or bizarre.

Our communication is the way we reach out to influence the outer environment. Our inner environment is built on communication, symbols, and behaviors we perceive. In order to make our inner and outer worlds isomorphic, we must have a good understanding of what goes on in both. We must also have an opportunity to try various kinds of communication and be able to evaluate our successes. The closer we can come to making our map fit the territory, the "happier" we will be as individuals.

SUGGESTIONS FOR DISCUSSION

1. All the authors of this book have been doing is wasting time, trying to make you believe the act of one person talking to another is more complicated than it really is. We've all been talking for several years. It is nowhere near as complicated as they make it seem because . . . (Fill in several hundred missing words—out loud!).

2. Get together in groups and play a hand or two of poker. Start with an ordinary game of poker (and keep the money off the table). Keep a record of the number of times you get four of a kind dealt in a hand of Seven Card Pete. Now make deuces wild. Is your record any different? For sophisticates, try Woolworth's (fives and tens wild) and see if this raises the chances of getting four of a kind. Assuming that four of a kind is desirable, which game would you prefer to play? Why? What does this have to do with the chapter? How do evaluations and predictions interact as you decide which poker game you prefer? Now get some menus from various restaurants. Let each person pick an item off the menu and defend his choice to the others, attempting to convince everyone that his was the right pick. How rational are the defenses? Is one man's prediction, another man's rejection? How come we all can't have the same values?

3. The notion of appearing and talking in public was introduced in the preceding chapter. How different is this from talking with a friend in private? James Winans said that public speaking was merely enlarged conversation. Do you agree? How do you think public speaking differs from private speaking? Look beyond circumstances, at speaker motivations and audience options. Are you sure that they are so different? Take a moment or two to figure out some commonalities between the two situations. Do you think that if you could master some successful principles of behavior from a study of interaction with your friends, they would be useful to you in an appearance on the public platform?

4. What is the relationship of Korzybski's map-territory analogy to the various models presented in the last chapter? Using the map-territory analogy, see if you can map out "success in college." Some students did this by preparing a game (like Monopoly) which included some of the local campus vagaries. Perhaps a committee could be formed to prepare such a game. Or you might take a look at a game called *Careers*. This game purportedly "simulates" life goals. How relevant is it to your goals as you see them? Is the playing of games a useful way of learning how things work or how people interact? George Herbert Mead believed that the small child learned to grow up by playing games. Using a bit of collective brainstorming, what kind of games can you come up with that would help you learn to survive on your campus?

5. "Isomorphism? Sounds like a disease." Why is it necessary to use terms like this? Can you find another term in general American English that might mean the same thing? Would "transformation," "transmutation," "topological manipulation," or "metamorphosis" be more apt? When Shannon first developed his model, he said that interferences with communication on electric wires had to be overcome by increasing redundancy. By that he meant by reinforcing or amplifying the message. What ways can you discover that redundancy is used in human communication? What relation does redundancy have to isomorphism?

6. Most of the things you consistently do and believe in are based on some inferences you have made at one time or another. Take the words: "Nigger," "Kike," "Spick," "Dago," "Polack," "Bohunk," and "WASP," and write descrip-

tions of the people to whom the epithets might be applied. Now do the same thing for Afro-American, Israeli, Mexican, Italian, Pole, Hungarian, and Anglo-Saxon. Are there any differences in the association? Would you respond differently to someone if he had been labeled by someone you respect with one of the epithets? Would it help improve relations if you were taught to think of him by one of the generic labels? Now isn't this a sort of euphemism process? What do you think happens to people because we use terms like "terminal illness," "sexual intercourse," "the Great Beyond," "kill-ratio," "low-yield explosion," etc? How do manipulators of human behavior employ this process to get you to fall in line with their goals? Find some examples in mass periodicals of this sort of manipulation.

7. The following is a good experiment in projective devices. Administer the following test to everyone:

> I am a_____
> I am happy when I_____
> I am sad when I_____
> Ten years from now I want to_____
> This school is a_____
> Next Saturday night I want to_____
> My three heroes are_____
>
> _____
> _____

Now divide up into interview teams and have each partner try to make inferences about the other partner based on his answers. Try them out on him. Ask him how accurate you are. Then let him try to figure you out.

SUGGESTIONS FOR FURTHER READING

Melvin DeFleur, *Theories of Mass Communication* (New York: David McKay Company, 1966). Read Chapter 5 for a valuable insight into communication and language, stripped of the usual jargon and confusion.

Harry Weinberg, *Levels of Knowing and Existence* (New York: Harper and Row, 1959). Start with the first chapter, which is relevant to this chapter, and then read on in this excellent introduction to general semantics.

5

The Basic Variable:
Language and
Life-Space

The basic variable of communication can be defined as the interaction of language and thought with our human ecology. Ecology refers to the interaction of an organism and its environment, and this interaction results in mental map-making as we move through the terrain of our environment. The information we receive from our world and the signals we emit that are designed to control our world combine into a series of isomorphic transformations leading to human adjustment. Our brain is constantly reviewing signals, then organizing and arranging them, and preparing our appropriate responses to them. A satisfactory coordination of perception, thought, and behavior represents our communication process, by which we seek to assert our control of the life we live.

Many animals appear to have more freedom of behavior than people have. The sea gull, for example, exhibits a wide range of flexibility, ingenuity, and purpose as it soars in flight, follows an ocean vessel for food, or rests on air currents above us. Gulls exhibit purpose as they behave to stay alive. The apparent freedom of animals is controlled, however, for they can only behave in response to stimuli. They cannot use symbols to plan long-range behavior, and their communication with each other, as far as we know, is limited to very rough reflexive signals. Man, on the other hand, asserts his freedom through his ability to manipulate symbols and plan for both long-range and short-range goals.

As we've noted earlier, our behavior involves choice-making. Of course, our choice-making is not absolute, because certain laws operating in nature do not always permit us choice. We cannot choose to be hungry, nor can we choose the ability to float freely through the air. Social barriers also hinder our freedom of choice. After all, you cannot really choose to be wealthy or famous.

What we have just said can be shown in the model pyramid in Figure 5–1. The broad base of natural barriers narrows to the social barriers, and, finally, we are left with the top portion in which we have choice. The lines between the barriers are not static and are moved by factors of age, law, mores, wealth, education, fame, etc.

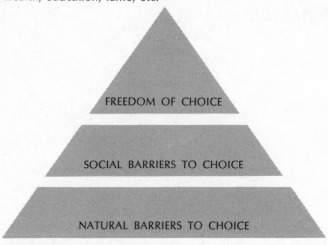

Figure 5–1. *Model of Choice Barriers*

In order to understand the more subtle features of the communication process, the concept of isomorphism, which we considered in the preceding chapter, must be divided into subvariables and considered in more detail. Our ability to make isomorphic transformations has already been identified as the major variable in the human communication process. The big question is, however, "Is it possible to teach people to improve their communication?" It certainly is not sufficient to assert that everyone should "pay attention" to isomorphism. Such a directive would be meaningless unless it were accompanied by some specific advice about manageable subvariables. Bear in mind that in this discussion we are not concerned just with speaking in the classroom. The subvariables we will discuss apply to all phases of oral communication, e.g., conversation, decision-making, social control, clinical practice, teaching, and intercultural understanding. Our purpose throughout is to make each person able to contribute the maximum to his society, to improve the lives of all of us. We wonder why there are so few Lincolns, Kennedys, and Churchills, when such men as these are sorely needed by our troubled world. Part of the answer lies in heredity and culture, but the largest part lies in training—the training of men and women to discover, present, evaluate, adjust, and accept worthwhile ideas. Communication is the process through which men make their contribution.

DIRECTIONALITY AND PURPOSE WHICH SUCCEEDS

The old, gnarled, twisted piñon tree growing out of a crack in the rocks high above the timberline on Kenosha Pass in the Rocky Mountains is an example of purpose that succeeds. More than a century ago, the little pine cone from which it sprang had been wafted into a small rill of melting snow. With the aid of expansion and contraction, from freezing and melting, roots found their way into a small crack. Through the cruelties of nature, the tree continued to interact selectively, cooperating with what protected it and gave it energy while evading the forces that would destroy it. It succeeded because it remained consonant with its environment and organic to its ecology. In this sort of successful functioning we can observe the purposive operations of nature.

Nearby, at the Continental Divide, another example of purpose and direction is to be found. Many tiny rivulets from underneath the melting snows gather into a small lake. Here the Platte River originates and starts on its journey down the canyons, across the plateaus and the plains to the Missouri, Mississippi, and finally into the vast Gulf of Mexico. The water has no choice-making doubts about the selection of the route it travels and the goals it seeks, although it is capable of instant change as better alternatives open around the thousands of barriers it encounters. It persists in seeking its goal. However, nature is not always so successful. Beetles can ruin whole forests of beautiful spruce, if lightning does not set the trees on fire first. A crop of grain can be wiped out by hail or flood, and across our prairies, weatherbeaten houses stand lonely in the dryness of the dust bowls created by human intervention. As we've just seen, nature illustrates the conflict between freedom to seek goals and the restraints that interfere with choice-making.

The balancing of freedom and restraints is a human goal. The ego goals of the individual are impeded by the id restraints of the group. The man who first thought about the wheel as a way to reduce men's burdens may have been the first example of such conflict, if his "thinking" seemed "wild" or "muddy" to everyone else in his tribe. The same sort of vague, half-baked, loose, and perhaps speculative thought characterized the inventors of the steam engine, of vaccination, of putting a gas engine in a buggy, of the Constitution of the United States; it also characterized the composer of the Ninth Symphony and the man who believed pictures could be transmitted through the air. Virtually every idea that has helped us to live better has met with opposition from established forces. The inventors hit on new ideas by free-wheeling, creative thinking, often with excursions into the irrelevant, where one thought triggered another and another.

But thinking alone was not sufficient to insure adoption of a new idea. The ideas had to be made practical and proved relevant. The forces that oppose new ideas act to suppress the irrelevant. Each new idea had to be balanced by rigorous investigation, test and retest, and the results had to be proved to the people the new ideas would affect.

The man who invented the wheel had to show others how his wheel could save them labor. The steam engine had to be shown superior to human work, and those who made the first automobile had to prove their machine's superiority over the horse. In addition, the effects of the products of the human mind had to be dealt with. When automobiles became popular, an inordinate amount of space was set aside for junkyards and parking lots. Men had to be trained to sell insurance and cemetery lots. The cancer of billboard blight spread across our landscape to expose the automobile driver and his passengers to commercial messages. And new kinds of labor unions emerged, so that cities selected for our manufacturing processes have grown into complex social and economic entities replete with new problems. The problem is to harmonize the new with what already exists, to balance creativity and conservatism so that newness and innovation are not prized for their own sakes nor social inertia allowed to stifle creative urge. Thus we come to equilibrium.

THE GOAL OF EQUILIBRIUM

Equilibrium can never be attained unless all activity ceases. The life of man is like the process of nature, because the necessity of constant interaction with other men precludes the possibility of a static or a permanent state.

Despite this, it is natural for all things to seek a state of equilibrium. Research in modern physics shows that all matter seeks a state of random behavior, while order seeks to break down. What we are saying is that all tangible matter is subject to decay of some form. This process is known scientifically as *entropy* and is defined as the random decay of physical structure. Only the interference of processes with each other, the influences of outside forces, restrain this disintegration. Such an outside force is known as *negative entropy*. It is these negative forces that assist objects and events in attaining unique characteristics by which we identify them. But inevitably all things change; matter decays and is reformed by new forces which impose change.

The human animal has the power to impose forces on himself, to prevent disintegration into random behavior, and to seek goals. Tension in self results when we set a goal and are uncertain about how to achieve it. This same tension impels us to move ahead, for the discomfort of tension actively prevents us from remaining static. So we must proceed to our goal in order to release our tensions.

As each goal is reached our tensions are reduced, which permits us to develop a new goal, and thus develop new tensions. This continuous process of goal-setting, tension, goal achievement, release of tension, new goal, and so on motivates our behavior throughout our lives. For many people, the goal may be secondary to the means of achieving it. The means may become a goal in itself. For example, a speaker may obtain his resolution of purpose and his release from tension solely in the applause and attention he receives, rather than through the convictions he plants in his audience or in the information he transmits. His evaluation at some later time, however, may motivate him to try again, this time to go beyond the immediate means and concern himself with the depth of his goal success. In goal-seeking, we must distinguish between the pleasure derived from accomplishing vs. the pleasure to be derived from accomplishment. The most effective speakers, artists, or people in general, however, may obtain great satisfaction along the way to ultimate achievement of a goal, yet derive their greatest pleasure from the final step. Thus, means should be kept subordinate to ends; then they can be made to serve their purposes effectively. The conflict between ultimate satisfaction from means or ends has a decided effect on the nature of society and man's life in society. And, we're back to the idea of human balance, which we termed equilibrium.

This tendency toward equilibrium seems to characterize every object, thing, and situation that is human or nonhuman. The critical balances, crises, and issues that arise in human affairs most often stem from conflicts among goal seekers. Hopefully, people—their ideas and technologies—can be brought together so that there is mutual success in goal-seeking. Success permits us to set higher goals, which serve to keep man away from the lethargy of equilibrium and act as an outside force to offset entropy.

PURPOSE: THE COORDINATING POINT FOR SELF-DIRECTION

The organizing center of a living plant is first in the seed and continues in the growing tip of the bud as a plant seeks to achieve its *purposes*. A bird building a nest does not say "I am going to build a nest." However, when it sees a straw and also a crotch in a tree, it begins to build, *if* building will serve its purpose. Plants and animals have a built-in singleness of purpose that enables them to coordinate themselves with what they respond to, and to ignore the irrelevant in their environments. The migration of birds and the hibernation of bears does not need to be learned. In human infants, some prenatal programming of the organism was done with the joining of sperm and ova. So we conclude that physiological development in humans and animals goes on precisely according to the time clock of the species. Environmentally, of course, it is a different story.

Both plants and animals seem to have considerable leeway in their responses to the environment. However, the responses are *locked in,* and events never before encountered must be handled with present programming or the species will be overcome by the event. The human, however, because of his ability to symbolize, may make choices and adapt behavior to suit different purposes. Thus, his capacity for both survival and self-destruction is consequently much greater than that of plants and animals.

The science of cybernetics as developed by the late Norbert Weiner[1] is based on the application of systems in nature to an understanding of men and their affairs. One of the most effective ways, for example, to understand the communication act is to apply the terminology of cybernetics to the steps in communication. While analogies often break down, and while the cybernetic system is not completely applicable to men and their affairs, some of the basic concepts of cybernetics are immensely useful in developing understandings necessary for effective mastery of communication. The basic analogy between man and nature involves the use of such terms as *feedback* and *feedforward,* plus some other terms drawn from the science of machines patterned after nature. Man, in his inventions, can build something analogous to himself and then, by studying it, can make new discoveries and inferences about himself and his behavior. An examination of the relationship between human communication and cybernetic systems offers a model around which the improvement of communication behavior can be built.

THE BASIC ANALOGY

Directionality and purpose in nature provide a basic analogy for the world of communication of ideas. The development of ideas may be compared to the process of evolution in nature. Contact between men, however, makes the evolution of ideas move at a much more rapid pace than natural evolution. Furthermore, the forces that may threaten destruction of ideas are as powerful as the ecological changes that can destroy species. The worth and merit of an idea does not insure its survival, any more than an animal's usefulness guarantees its natural survival (with the passenger pigeon and American bison being two obvious examples). In another sense, many beautiful species of animals have died out because they could not defend themselves against natural forces, while worthwhile ideas have been destroyed because the men who espoused them could not give them adequate defense. The cockroach survives because it can defend itself. The concept of Christian love sustains a tenuous existence because it has not defended itself as well as some counter-ideas have been defended.

What we are saying is that directionality and purpose determine survival. In plants and animals, direction is built in by genetic codes. Man also has these same primitive built-in directions for the body, which operate unconsciously, but his power to speak and symbolize enables him to make his own purposes.

When the built-in purposes for air, food, sex, bodily safety, and comfort do not succeed in plant and animal organisms, retardation, disease, deformity, and death take over. Of course, man cannot escape his physiological purposiveness; but, unlike other living things, he can go beyond it.

[1] Norbert Weiner, *Cybernetics* (New York: John Wiley, 1948).

Literally, the ability to establish purposes is what endows man with his life-sustaining humanity. Our first conscious goal-setting takes us out of the realm of physiological determinism and puts us into a dynamic society of family, groups, and nations. Thought and communication are our tools for survival, and, just as our body processes implement the goals of the genetic code, so communication serves to implement the goals of thought. While failure of physiology may spell the end of the organism, failure of communication may mean the end of human personality. In that which makes us human, we exercise our abilities to make goal designs for our lives. Thought enables us to plan, predict, and decide about courses of action that will help us meet those goals. Thought enables us to support even our physiology, again through communication. Communication is the action we take once we have thought out a course of behavior.

Figure 5–2 shows the relationship of genetic code, physiology, thought, and communication. Our body processes and our intellectual limits are set by the genetic codes. Our physiological processes seek to balance biology and protect us from threats, like disease or systemic upsets. Our capacity to process ideas—that is, think—is also limited by our physiology, but within these limits there is no necessary physiological barrier to effective thinking. Thought is largely carried on through symbols, and thought is transferred to others through symbols. Thus communication is both the substance of thought, and, frankly, it is about the only evidence we have that thought is going on.

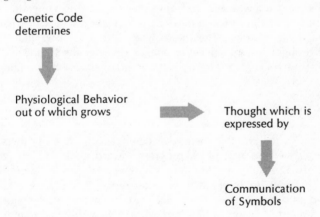

Figure 5–2.

As humans we must take *in* and put *out*, both physiologically and intellectually. Just as the organism cannot continue to function without food, thought must be continually nourished by stimuli from outside. Sometimes these stimuli reveal threats to goal-seeking behavior. In these cases, we must respond by attempting to manipulate or control the environment, and *communication out* is the method used. It is in this way that man may be considered a *cybernetic creative,* for he adjusts his behavior in accord with his plans for control. His communication out may be regarded as *feedforward* and the message coming in as *feedback.*

Most animals respond to situations as they occur. When they are hungry, they seek food; when their physiology dictates, they seek sexual outlet. When the needs are not present in their bodies, apparently they do not think about the activities. However, because of our capacity to make symbols, we can plan ahead. In fact, the basic product of planning ahead, which is *society,* has become the most potent force in the development of man and his institutions. We are essentially weak. For example, we cannot survive as infants without nurture. We cannot survive in some of our climates without artificial protection. We can neither outrun a jackrabbit nor block a hog from a trough. Without the aid of our minds, plus useful tools and weapons, we would fall easy prey to other species or to our environment or most probably to both. Yet, in all our dealings we need the cooperation of our fellow creatures. Our very survival depends on the way we and others like us organize together to defend ourselves, mutually, against external threats. But with each step in the organization process, more threats are generated within and through the act of organization itself.

Initially, man is dependent not only for his physical survival but also for the symbols he uses. You received food and the capacity to think from your parents and your early peers. As you reached maturity, you became able to provide food for yourself, and now you are able to generate ideas about the future and then plan your steps to achieve them. Goal-making is the sign of a mature man. The internalized verbal symbols that are used in active thought serve to develop images of what the future might be like, and they serve as guides to the way the goals should be sought.

HUMAN GOAL-SEEKING BEHAVIOR

People often find that their goals conflict with those of others. There are unforeseen events that block progress toward goals. In fact, goals themselves often cause problems, so let's look at goals in a bit more detail.

Goals may be long-range or short-range. Long-range goals may be divided into subgoals or steps. Each goal, whether it is major or minor, must generate tension, which is resolved when the goal is met. However, achievement of each goal permits the idealization of another goal. Thus, no activity can be carried out rationally in human society unless it has been planned or has some reason. While it may not be possible for an observer immediately to determine the rationale for a behavior at the time it occurs, the behavior must be presumed to be rational and in harmony with the goals of the person behaving. It is indeed true that all behavior is rational to the person behaving at the time of his behavior. The answer to "why" is often some form of "it seemed like the thing to do at the time."

Goal-seeking can be shaped through the traditional systems of reward and punishment. Thus, it is possible for teachers, psychiatrists, parents, and friends to assist others in developing goals and achieving them. Frustration in goal-seeking behavior may lead to disturbance of the equilibrium of the human system, and may result in development of new and more reasonable goals, or it can go the other way, to disorganization and illness.

We said that the process of manipulating symbols internally to force outcome is called *feedforward*. Feedforward operates consciously and unconsciously in what we are going to think about next, what we are going to do in the next moment, in the next day, week, or year. It guides our behavior, much as the target programmed into the nose cone guides the flight of a missile. The missile does not always hit the target, nor do we always hit our goal, but, fortunately, the human has the capacity to respond by readjustment. Unlike the missile, he need not be destroyed when he fails.

Feedforward is an important variable in communication. It guides our senses and perceptions, focuses our attention, and it determines largely what we see and hear and our reactions to these stimuli. It shapes our behavior as we prepare messages designed to restructure the environment, so that it falls in line with our goals. The effective behavior, the man who can communicate so that his goals are most often met, is the man who has learned to exercise considerable control over feedforward.

If the moralists will forgive us, we might analogize the thought process to the wheels on a slot machine. Each perception we make is stored in the brain and is associated with a word and with a value. The word tends to reduce variety, and to make things we see seem similar by classifying them into verbal groups. The value tends to determine the way we will bring the image and the word out of storage. Each perception we have may exist on many wheels, all at once, just as the images on the wheels of the slot machine. The dials may spin, just like on the "one-armed bandit," for each new perception or event that we encounter requires the alteration of the position of our wheels. Often our behavior is incomprehensible to us, because we are not in control of the way the wheels spin. We permit the values in the third ring to operate without being aware we are evaluating, and this forces us into faux pas, gaffes, awkward situations, situations of threat and stress, somewhat like coming up one needed fruit short on the third wheel when you have jackpot fruit on the first two wheels. Feedforward seeks the conscious control of the movement of our wheels so that we can control our behavior and keep it in line with our goals. The moral of our analogy is that we should be able to control our own behavior, just as the casino owner can control the behavior of his slot machines.

Sometimes, however, our goals are unconscious, and reasons for our behavior are concealed from us. When behavior becomes primarily motivated by unconscious concerns, we tend to act in ways that evoke negative evaluation from society. We may choose to become mentally ill—repeating the words of Thomas Szasz.[2] On the other hand, failure to use the power

---

[2] Thomas Szasz, *The Myth of Mental Illness.*

of feedforward may mean atrophy. As behavior comes more and more under the control of unconscious forces, it becomes harder to exert conscious control. The important point for you to remember is that for the normal and for the mentally ill, there is a seemingly rational, or at least free-choice, reason for behavior. Behavior happens because of some processing in the brain that seems perfectly reasonable to the behaver. There may be no outside control or intervention.

Every human reacts and responds because of what he has stored in his head, which includes his immediate perceptions, his images stored away, the symbols he has available about those images, and the values he has attached both to the images that came from outside and to those he has created inside by processing data. It becomes evident that the contents of the mind are manufactured by the data-processing capacity of the brain as surely as the cells of the body are manufactured by the digestive process of the stomach.

SELF-REFLEXIVENESS

This capacity of the human mind to manipulate images, symbols, and values is called *self-reflexiveness*. As far as we know, man is the only self-reflexive animal. A self-reflexive animal can create another animal. For example, you can take a concept of "horse" and a concept of "horn" and put them together in your mind, attach a label drawn from other data in storage, and thus create a "unicorn." You can then respond to it with literature and poetry, or you can draw its picture on paper. Of course, you must understand that you cannot go and photograph it, for it was never perceived *externally*. In like fashion, you may also create such concepts as "private enterprise system," "gross out," "gross national product," or "kill-ratio" out of data and symbols you have stored away. Now you begin to realize that you build analogies in your mind. Sometimes the analogies fit reality, so your estimates and predictions made on the basis of the analogies seem to work out. Sometimes the analogies do not fit, and men and societies become self-destructive because they cannot distinguish between analogy and reality. As man is the only self-reflexive being, he is the only being known that can destroy himself by responding to the unreal, much the same as a Siamese Betta will fight its reflection in a mirror.

Self-reflexiveness may be random or controlled—that is, thought may trigger other thought in an associated pattern, wandering freely over the gamut of what is stored. To be relevant, however, some conscious control must be exerted over the process of associating, e.g., learning when to stop and report when a valuable or beautiful association is found. Hanging images and words together does not necessarily mean the production of literature, for conscious critical judgment in the form of feedforward must be exerted in order to stop the creative process at the proper moment and write it down.

Often, self-reflexiveness must be controlled, particularly when man is presented with a problem that must be resolved in cooperation with others in logical ways. At these times, feedforward offers a guide to data processing to make self-reflexiveness an orderly procedure in which each step serves to implement achievement of the goal. This is usually the major problem found in group work, where individual self-reflexiveness is working independently and often at cross-purposes to the common needs of the group. In this common situation, individual goal-realization signals are fed forward, with the group ideas being secondary. Thus, feedback is subjugated to feedforward.

Self-reflexiveness may express itself in spontaneity, a capacity some people have to make connections and see relationships that may be denied to others. The popular characterization of this, of course, is Whyte's *The Organization Man,* in his rapidly tattering, nearly two-decade-old gray flannels.[3] However, spontaneity is more than random withdrawal of images and words from memory. It is the ability to move rapidly through stored data to find exciting and original connections. Often this ability is suppressed by the traditional and noneducational insistence our academic systems place on the storing of information in order and pulling it out the same way during examination ordeals. But mere memorization and rote communication do not make an effective participator, a good thinker, or an interesting conversationalist. The ability to utilize memory so that it produces both wit and wisdom, logic and inspiration, is the highest achievement of the capacity of self-reflexiveness. So, we can now look at a summary picture of *feedback.*

The raw materials of behavior—ideas, symbols, values, inferences, interpretations—are multiplied as the base of knowledge expands and the range of perception widens. They are made operational when the mind imposes a system that permits the identification of a creative idea, an exciting thought, a reasonable and effective solution. In order to establish such a system, contact must be made with the world of men and events outside the brain. The behaver must know how effective his behavior has been. He must get some impression of the impact he is having on the world outside. Such information returned to the mind of the behaver is called *feedback.*

POSITIVE AND NEGATIVE FEEDBACK

Any behavior influences what is happening around it. Sometimes this influence is in accordance with the goals, the *feedforward,* of the individual. Sometimes it is not. Satisfactory goal achievement comes from continuing behaviors that are fruitful and in revising behaviors that prove to be diverting or damaging. But the only way to obtain an evaluation of the effect of behavior is to observe what happens to the world in which the behavior is being carried on, and to interpret the information's effect on feedforward. If the interpretation serves to continue or reinforce the behavior, the feed-

[3] William H. Whyte, Jr., *The Organization Man* (New York: Simon and Schuster, 1956).

back is said to be *positive*. If the interpretation tends to inhibit or revise the behavior, the feedback is called *negative*. Note, though, that these are relative terms, and should not be thought of as supporting establishment or resisting change. Think of the terms strictly in a definitional sense, and not as a sociopolitical value judgment.

The simplest analogy that explains positive and negative feedback is the thermostat on a furnace. The feedback mechanism is the thermometer located somewhere away from the furnace. If the temperature is not equal to the setting, the thermometer sends back electrical information that keeps the furnace system producing, just as the mind processes positive feedback. If, on the other hand, the temperature equals the desired setting, the thermometer sends back inhibiting information designed to stop the furnace, just as negative feedback encourages the brain to direct a revision of behavior. The main difference between machine feedback and the feedback received by the human mind is that machine feedback is pre-set and usually digital, i.e., the machine can either continue or cease what it is doing and a clear criterion point is established for each alternative. In the human, information received by the brain is not so easily processed. It is necessary for the behaver to interpret what he receives, then compare it with his goals determined by feedforward to decide whether he will continue, modify, or desist from his behavior.

It should not be assumed that positive feedback is always good because it encourages and negative feedback is always bad because it inhibits. Sometimes misinterpretation of data results in positive feedback that maintains a behavior which is dangerous to the person. The chap playing the role of life-of-the-party often misinterprets polite attention as complete approval and feeds back positive data into his system. He feels that he is attaining his goal of popularity and approval, when the information would appear to other observers to indicate that he is becoming a bore and being rejected. Negative feedback, on the other hand, in the form of intelligently interpreted criticism can result in improvement of the behaving system, e.g., better speaking and better writing.

In the communicative process, a man seeks to maintain some sort of connection with another person or persons. The connection has some purpose, some goal, and the feedforward system has developed a picture of a desired behavior outcome. The communication seeks to attain this behavior. Most of us know that total success is impossible, but in order to maintain the communication system in motion, it is necessary to sustain an image of one's self that is characterized by approval and success. Without this image it is necessary either to modify behavior or modify feedforward and alter goals.

A salesman, for example, has as his goal the act of purchase on the part of his prospect. As he moves through his sales talk, he must watch his potential customer for indications of approval. If the customer is politely nodding but not hearing the words, and the salesman interprets this behavior as approval that will eventually lead to a sale, he is in danger of disappointment when the customer answers his crucial sales-closing question the wrong way. Likewise, if a teacher interprets movements on the part of her students as inattention and requires them to sit silently and motionless while she speaks to them, she may succeed in forcing positive feedback that is spurious. The act of motion on the part of a listener cannot be automatically interpreted as negative feedback, because it is impossible to know what is the natural state of attention of another human, without having considerable contact. The student who fidgets or talks with his class "neighbor" may be totally involved with the teacher's discussion.

Of course, there are many opportunities to misinterpret cues and obtain erroneous information about feedback. One of the most important things a communicator has to learn is the ability to pick up appropriate cues and interpret them intelligently, lest he inhibit behavior or continue behavior at the wrong time. The answer lies in his interpretation of information, not in the information itself. Sometimes, an individual will be so shaky and uncertain about his own behavior, and his feedforward will be so misty, that he will tend to interpret almost anything as negative feedback, and eventually will inhibit himself so badly that he will not be able to cope with communicative situations. On the other hand, a speaker may have such an exaggerated image of his own ability that he will become insensitive to negative feedback and continue to behave in the face of total rejection. He will soon become equally ineffective as a communicator.

Understanding and orienting to positive and negative feedback have been referred to as *audience analysis*. The goals established as a result of feedforward have been referred to as *speaker's purpose*. Many writers about communication have attempted to develop formulas as automatic as the formulas that govern the operation of the furnace thermostat, so that speakers can develop purposes and respond to listeners infallibly. Rejection of the possibility of infallibility of response to feedback in the human is necessary before a truly sensitive job of communication can be done.

In later chapters we will present a concept of audience analysis through analysis of feedback, and consider some of the possible goals communicators can have and how they can be effectively achieved. In the following chapter, however, it is necessary to turn to the substance of the communication process—the symbol itself—in order to complete our understanding of the basic transaction of communication.

SUGGESTIONS FOR DISCUSSION

1. The word "ecology" applies to the relationship of animal or plant with environment. As the word is used in this book, it seems to imply something else. Or does it? Acting as a group, try to describe your ecology. What effect would a change in topography have on your life? How about double the amount of rainfall? An increase in year-round temperature? What people occupy your ecology? What is your role in relation to them? Are they as influential in shaping your life-style as the plant and terrain features around you? If we were to create a phrase, "communication ecology," what would it mean to you?

2. Thinkers have been discussing existentialism for some time now, and very few people can define what "it" is. It appears to involve choice-making. Set up some "suppose" situations. Role play them. For example, suppose you were confronted with the problem of sitting on a committee to oversee the administration of a limited supply of a life-saving drug (prevents radioactivity sickness) to the population of your college, what criteria would you use to make your selections? Have one group draw up some biographies of students, and present them to your group anonymously. Suppose there are seven students and you could only pick three. How did you make your choices? Where would the word "existential" fit in? What is the opposite of existential? Are there only two alternatives in choice-making? Why is it that when you tried to choose people to receive the drug, there was disagreement? (Develop some more cases and work them out.)

3. Some people oppose scientific approaches to problem-solving because they claim it stifles creativity. Some professors grade on creativity. What does the word "creativity" mean operationally? If you were advising teachers about grading, what advice would you give them about rewarding creativity? Can you prepare a list of criteria that would help your teacher recognize a creative activity carried on by a student? As you set these items down on paper, to what extent is the act of scientific investigation impeding your creativity? Can we work to become creative, or is creativity always a function of spontaneity? If it is, do you think it is possible for anyone to be creative at your college?

4. Zorba, in *Zorba the Greek*, told his young boss that "Life is trouble," and that only in death is there absence of trouble; and in the last few lines of *Oedipus Rex* it is said that a man is not considered to be lucky until after he is dead. What do you think about a trouble-free life? Are there degrees of trouble? What problems might you encounter as a group if you tried to brainstorm a trouble-free college? What would you have to do to make the school run perfectly, a place where everyone has his needs and goals satisfied? Is it worth the effort? Does trouble make any contribution to your pleasure at living?

5. "All behavior is rational to the behaver at the time of behavior," say two psychologists (Combs and Snygg). The authors declare that all behavior is purposeful. Now if this is the case, there can be no such thing as mental illness. As long as a man behaves rationally all the time, then he cannot act irrationally. Can you make sense out of this? Suppose you said to your teacher, "I'm sorry the assignment is late, but I had some trouble at home," and your teacher answers, "Tough rocks, Charlie, the piano player eats potato chips." Is there any way that you could classify your teacher as "rational"? Develop a few more situations like this, act them out, and then try to figure out what the players might have in mind.

6. How much of your behavior is predictable? What things do you do every day, in the same way, at the same time? How much of your roommate's behavior can you accurately predict? What accurate predictions can you make about your instructor? How accurate are his predictions about you? If we have difficulty predicting the behavior of people close to us, not to speak of ourselves, how can there be a "science of man"?

7. The concept of a random universe sounds like atheism, doesn't it? Why do you suppose the authors included it in this book? Given the premise that all three authors are regularly "religious" in a socially acceptable way, how is it possible that they believe what they have written?

8. The terms positive and negative feedback can be rather confusing. Does negative feedback mean that the information transmitted is negative, or that it does some-

thing negative to the speaker? Or does negative feedback mean criticism and positive feedback mean encouragement? Then positive feedforward would mean successful planning, and negative feedforward would mean unsuccessful planning? Or does positive feedforward mean continuing to act while negative feedforward means stopping whatever you are doing? In this case, would negative feedforward be the response to positive feedback, and positive feedforward be the response to negative feedback? Is this clear?

9. An interesting exercise is to speak to the class while the class is being taped on a video-tape recorder. If your college has such a machine, try it. After the audience has heard one person speak, have them write their honest reactions to the speech on a slip of paper and hold it on their desks. Then have the speaker watch the tape of the audience responding to him and try to interpret from the feedback just what each person's attitude was toward his speech, or toward him, or both. Then check the inferences made by the speaker with the slips of paper written by the audience.

SUGGESTIONS FOR FURTHER READING

Abraham Maslow, "Isomorphic Interrelationships Between Knower and Known," in *The Human Dialogue,* ed. Floyd Matson and Ashley Montagu (New York: The Free Press, 1967). This is an interesting paper by a leader in the field of humanistic psychology. Mr. Maslow's style is most readable.

Ted McLaughlin, Laurence Blum, and David Robinson, *Communication* (Columbus, Ohio: Charles Merrill Books, 1964). Although this is primarily a business-industry oriented book, the initial chapter contains a great deal of material applicable to our subject.

Harry Weinberg, *Levels of Knowing and Existence* (New York: Harper and Row, 1959). Chapter 10 is relevant to this chapter.

6

Abstracting and Symbolizing: Processes and Patterns

Not until descriptions of processes become less ambiguous and the body of knowledge is better ordered can the study of speech be considered to be a *science*. But in the meantime large numbers of speakers, actors, teachers, and clinicians go ahead improving their speaking, because they have found some consistent and reliable descriptions which enable them to practice their *art*.

Many speakers who did not pretend to know much about the nature of speech succeeded in their efforts to move the minds of others. The speeches of such men as Franklin D. Roosevelt and Winston Churchill changed the course of history, although neither man, presumably, spent much time ruminating about the complex relations involved in their performances; yet their speeches still serve as models to which other speakers aspire. Speech that is natural, spontaneous, effective, and pleasing to an audience may be considered an art.

We can examine effective speeches and speakers and infer that a good speech must meet certain standards. Cicero's conception of a good speaker was "a good man who speaks well," and modern critics, in their consideration of speakers, often focus on the ethicality of a speaker's cause and loftiness of purpose as well as his specific speech behaviors, such as composition and language.

Today we must combine literary criticism of speech as an art with recently derived propositions about human behavior, and consider speech to be a science-art. Speech is science in its relationship to human physiology, psychology, and social behavior; speech is art because it is so complex and so organic to humans in social situations that as yet no one has developed propositions that let us predict behavior and control. Every communication contains elements of scientific control and artistic expression. And since we think of speech as a unity rather than a dichotomy, science-art seems the appropriate term to use.

Whether study of speech is labeled as "science," "art," or "science-art" is not important as long as we consider the process holistically, as an interaction among people and events. Language and speech are the products of the human brain as man integrates himself with his environment. Part of what happens when people communicate can be described scientifically, while part can be described only in terms of artistic effort and effect. Neither description, however, is complete alone. For the present, if we desire understanding as complete as we can get it, we must content ourselves with being scientific when warranted and artistic when justified, taking care not to distort our view by becoming pseudoscientific or effete.

In order to get a sophisticated view of our communication, we need to understand the wide range of behaviors of which we are capable and the number of possible meanings such behaviors can have. When we attempt to analyze our own communication we become a part of it and the Heisenberg Principle applies, i.e., we affect the situation that we are viewing. It is likely that other observers, not so involved, might view our behavior in a different light. Of course, once we are involved, in a strict sense, our objectivity ceases. But, as we have seen before, this is true whenever our minds become cognizant of any situation in which we are a part.

Few speakers and listeners have the ability to see themselves honestly as they participate in the communication act. As soon as a speaker is aware that his behavior is being watched, it changes, somewhat like the behavior of little Johnny told not to look at Aunt Sarah's withered hand. As soon as Johnny's attention is focused on the hand, he cannot look away. He is consciously aware of it all the time, and his attempts not to look at it are more embarrassing than if he had been staring. So it is with the speaker who becomes aware that he is going to be subjected to critical evaluation. He begins to focus his own attention on his performance output. He loses sight of the audience and concerns himself with gestures, pear-shaped tones, proper enunciation, and often becomes so agitated about suspected inabilities to "do it right," that his tension causes him to botch.

A famous experiment conducted many years ago in an industrial plant demonstrated that it made little difference what changes were introduced in work conditions; the simple fact that changes were being made was sufficient to encourage the employes to greater output. This so-called Hawthorne effect seriously distorts what we know about the oral communication process. What we can observe about behavior in a normal speech class may have little relationship to actual behavior in life situations. It is necessary to make formal training realistic enough to carry over into real situations—that is, to make instruction relevant to life. In order to accomplish reality, we must learn something about perception, abstraction, and symbolization, which are basic to oral communication.

PERCEPTION AND ABSTRACTION

Perception begins with attention. We are constantly aware of peripheral stimuli around us, but until we focus attention on a small part of what is available to us to perceive, we do not get useful information. The act of focusing, however, blocks out other details. We risk the same limited view as when we use a telescope to focus on one object, blocking out the view of the area surrounding the subject. This focusing is also like looking down a tunnel. Our first caution is that we can really see only a small part of what we see, and this is further "tunneled" by the fact that we are, in part, programmed for what to look for. It is literally true that people will see what they want to see. Consider the axiom that designers of women's fashions supposedly keep in mind: Man's imagination is woman's best friend.

Unless we exercise some selective judgment, however, all we can get is a mass of jumbled perceptions. If we had to rely on this kind of information for what we know, we would not advance beyond the animal stage. Our ability to codify perceptions and store them away in convenient form has enabled us to develop skill at data processing called *symbolic thought*. What we perceive is abstracted and then fitted into categories designated by verbal labels. We abstract by blocking attention to differences between things and trying to fit what we see into categories shared by similar objects or events. We label this category and store images of reality in it. This, of course, is the data-classification and storage function of the brain.

The process of abstraction requires omitting more characteristics than it includes. As long as we classify tangible objects into simple groups, there is little possibility of trouble. However, when we move to more complex classifications, we may find it easy to abstract but far more difficult to get the abstraction back to a reality others can understand. Your concept of the "American Free Enterprise System," for example, may come from your set of images of poor young men opening small stores and gradually expanding without limitation into major entrepreneurs. Someone else, however, may start with the image of a man taking a job in a corporation and advancing to the presidency. Another person may see gigantic corporations and industries growing to towering heights against the sky, all in a picture totally without humans. While there is some vague similarity between the ideas, the three applications of the image will be different. Until all three of you returned to your initial idea, agreement among you would be difficult to achieve. Generally, the greatest difficulty we encounter in communication is that it is easy to express what you know but very hard to get someone else to understand it. Once you have decided that it is necessary to get someone else to understand, then you must consider possible differences in behavior occasioned by differences in the abstraction process.

THE ABSTRACTION PROCESS

Our sense organs are limited in their capacities. They offer limited data about the environments in which we live. Basically, we "know" only the world we can perceive, and we can only make inferences about the rest. We are never fully aware of what we do not see. The experiment in which a frog starved to death while surrounded by dead flies, referred to in Chapter 3, illustrates this. We humans are capable of finding out what frogs cannot see, but it is hard for us to comprehend that there are some things that we do not see, and that our attention to what we perceive leads us away from attention to potential danger. We receive information through our sense organs, but the information becomes useful only as we process it symbolically. Let's look at some of our personal information sources.

Vision is probably our most widely used source of information. Our eyes enable us to observe details and predict direction of movement and relationships in space. We may infer relative size, shape, form, and speed from what we see. Much of this predictability does not come solely from perception, however. We learn inferences we can make about relationships of objects in space. For example, a child does not immediately learn perspective. Experiments have demonstrated that he will see a man far away and decide that the man is smaller than a child standing close by. Interesting experiments have been conducted with children riding in airplanes and reporting on the respective sizes of familiar objects seen from the ground and from the air. Similarly, it is necessary for us to learn about the relationships of the things we perceive.

Vision, however, cannot be totally relied on. Our eyes can play too many tricks. When we see the rotating blades on an electric fan, they appear to be solid. We must learn somehow that we cannot touch these blades because they will rip off our fingers. A series of experiments done some years ago, called the Ames Experiments, demonstrated the many distortions that can occur in viewing.[1] Given a room distorted in shape, our eyes will give us false information. We may see large things as small and the reverse. We cannot fully trust what we see until we have made some adjustment to the field in which we see it.

We can extend our viewing through instrumentation. By the use of microscopes and telescopes we can see things that escape our normal vision. For most of us, however, all this does is to make us aware of the existence of microbes and nebulae. In our daily living, the microbe and the nebula exert little influence, because we do not constantly receive messages about their existence. We are never sure we see what "really" is, because we know very little about how others see things and we have no way to check our accuracy. When we see a color called "red," we do not really ever know whether we see exactly what someone else sees. We know that the use of the symbol cues us both to look at what is apparently

[1] W. H. Ittelson and F. P. Kilpatrick, "Experiments in Perception," *Scientific American,* August 1951.

the same object, but the development of different tastes in color and form indicates that people undoubtedly do see the "same" object differently. The saying of the word, however, can point to some common agreement about the "red" object that we perceive.

Hearing is a second major source of data. It can supplement and deepen the impressions we get by letting us associate visual with auditory stimuli. Differences in combinations of visual and auditory information explain partially the reason for differences in choices. Our hearing operates within a range from approximately 16 to 7,000 vibrations per second. Our vision also operates within a limited range. (Some animals can see out of human range; others can hear frequencies that we cannot hear.) The sound we hear must conform to a range of loudness and be of a certain quality in order for us to make sense of it. Excessively loud or distorted sounds assault our ears as noise and have little or no meaning and much emotional value. Indeed, excessive sound can also impair our hearing apparatus.

Of more importance to us is the duration of the sound. Given a sound in the proper range, we tend to make sense of it as we abstract its qualities in the time we hear it. A series of short beeps, for example, may eventually seem to us to be a continuous sound, while excessively short or prolonged sounds may make no sense. Even the intelligibility of human speech is affected by duration, for we can effectively hear only a given number of words per minute. Continuous duration, or words uttered constantly at the same rate of speed with consistent pauses, may be monotonous to the listener. Furthermore, we can listen comfortably at a rate that is usually different from the optimum speaking rate. Generally, speaking at a rate slower than 125 words per minute may seem slow, unintelligible, or boring to a listener.

The sense of *touch* also gives us information to abstract. We receive information about pressure, pain, warmth, coldness, vibration, tickle, and texture through our skin. These sensations can deepen our understanding of what we see and hear, and they tell us about other qualities of things we come in contact with. Tactile stimuli are also subject to distortion, however. When you step into an air-conditioned room on a hot, humid day, you may receive a sensation of extreme coldness, but if you remain in the room, you may begin to perspire. In this case, the absolute temperature and humidity is irrelevant, while the comparison of sensation is important. For example, if you hold one hand in a pan of water at 105°F, and the other in a pan of water at 65°F, after a few minutes the water in both will feel about the same. Then if you suddenly plunge both hands into 85° water, one hand feels a sensation of heat and the other of coldness. Thus, much of the information we get from our senses is subject to some kind of distortion, and our judgments are made comparatively, not absolutely. To respond as though a comparative judgment were absolute may result in serious disruption of the communication process.

The senses of *smell* and *taste* give us other information, although taste is greatly influenced by smell. Certainly our choices of food are determined by the responses of our taste buds and our sense of smell, which has somewhat atrophied in our evolutionary development. For some animals, though, the sense of smell gives cues about the physiological state of the organism. A dog, as we have said before, will decide whether another dog is to be ignored, played with, fought with, or made love to depending on what he smells. No one can say for sure whether or not our sense of smell influences our behavior. Despite the way we mask our body odors with perfumes and deodorants, it may very well be that some of the information that shapes our responses to others comes to us from our sense of smell, though we may not be consciously aware that this is so. Evaluations can be drastically altered depending on what we smell. Adjectives, such as "fragrant," "fruity," "spicy," or "putrid," play some role in determining how long you would choose to remain in a place. With regard to taste, some authorities feel that man can actually distinguish only three different tastes—sweet, sour, and bitter—and that refinements in taste, such as gourmet abilities, are more the result of discriminating olfactory sense.

The human brain, somehow, manages to sort out all five sense stimuli. It has the capacity to associate messages from all of them to present a relatively complete image for storage. The abstraction process through which we store the information reduces stimuli to prototypes associated with verbal symbols, although some of the details may be omitted. Yet there is reason to believe that some sensory impressions leave no memory. Mothers have known this for years, for who would bear a second child if they had a specific memory of the pain of the first?

COMMUNICATION AND MEMORY

Communication with others depends on images evoked when words are transmitted, as follows:

1. Developing a sensible statement begins with association of images and words.
2. Understanding a statement is a decoding process in which the words are reduced to images.
3. Communication takes place when there is relative concordance between the images that led to the sending of the message and those that occur as a result of receiving it.

This process, which takes place inside the mind, is not amenable to the kind of scientific investigation that often explains the relationships between external stimuli. For example, a speaker's potential depends to a large extent on the way he can crystallize his ideas and express them to evoke similar ideas in others, but he is denied the power to observe what goes on in others' minds.

Inner senses and the messages we derive from them are probably just as potent as what we get through our external senses. There are few people who can avoid having internal messages block out stimuli from outside. Stomach upsets, sore feet, any sort of pain, can distract attention from what is received from outside. While some people can transcend pain and remain effective behavers, most people need to feel well in order to make sense out of stimuli from outside. This phenomenon is known as the *threshold of pain,* and the level to withstand pain differs in individuals, as does the variable of the way in which the pain is inflicted. For example, a woman can calmly give birth to a child but go to pieces emotionally when she nicks her finger while paring apples. A famous professional football star can play week after week with injuries that would hospitalize a normal man, yet this same athlete has been known to panic on a routine trip to his dentist!

Body kinesthesia is also important. The way muscles work together and coordinate with the nervous system will exert control over the kinds of behavior of which a person is capable. Sometimes people have difficulty speaking because they cannot coordinate mouth, tongue, teeth, larynx, and lungs with messages from the brain. Such people may have to learn special techniques, receive special remedial training, in order to become competent speakers. In general, any impairment of muscle or nerve will affect behavior.

Throughout our daily behavior we respond to sensations from inside our skin. Our attention at a conference, for instance, may be distracted by sensations of hunger or somnolence, or our ability to speak in public may be impaired by physiological symptoms evoked by our nervous state. Our listeners may also have their attention distracted by their own internal cues. Their inattention may not be owed to speaker inadequacy, but merely to a personal discomfort or distress identification. If we are too quick to blame ourselves for failure to excite our listeners, we may injure the image we have of ourself as a communicator and thus reduce our effectiveness. Consequently we must take care to determine how much of behavior we see is motivated by external stimuli and how much by the state of our activity.

As important as our internal physical cues are those that come from subconscious or random activation of memory. As you know, it is exceedingly hard to predict what sort of images will be evoked inside another person by a set of words transmitted to him. Many mental health problems result because individuals get impressions that are unpredictable, which cause them to act in ways that are evaluated negatively by society.

Memory is of critical importance in the communication process. This does not mean that messages must be memorized and transmitted in order to be effective. What it means is that every transmission will evoke some response from the memory of the listener.

There is no clear agreement among authorities about how memory operates. It appears that information is keyed in storage with associated values. Various images and symbols interact, and relevant responses are made according to their values. Values in memory are a potent force in determining how messages are prepared for sending and how they are to be received. Some messages, for example, may inadvertently trigger powerful interferences that overwhelm all possibility of understanding the way the speaker desires. These responses distort evaluation and judgment and may severely impair the possibility of comprehension by others.

For the normal person, the brain acts like a filing cabinet in which he stores impressions of everything he has experienced before. The more that is stored, the greater is his capacity to make subtle connections and respond to complex material. Memory is useful, however, only if information can be pulled out of our "filing cabinet" systematically, because the mind tends to store data in some sort of coherent order. That order is determined by the abstraction process, and by the fact that storage is coded and activated by verbal symbols.

It is impossible to separate biological inheritance and influence of environment in memory. The capacity to remember is limited by the biological capability of the brain, and can either be expanded or inhibited within those limits by contact with the environment. Personality may be regarded as behavior resulting from the interaction of inheritance-environment. Patterns of personality and communication become established from memories built in during the growth process. They are adjusted by new experiences and the addition of new memories.

Psychologists contend that nothing is ever really forgotten, although some information is more readily accessible than other information. For example, our ability to calculate a square root may recede as we learn the operation of a desk calculator, but our capacity to relearn it would be greatly assisted by the memory of having done it before.

Memory may keep operational both useful and useless information. It is as easy for us to retain error as it is to retain the relevant and practical, so our total output of communication will combine both. Information we receive will be altered by information in storage. To motivate, it is necessary for a speaker to assess the range of possibilities of behavior open to his listener and to work to trigger the kinds of responses that memory will assist in his cause. He must understand how minds, in general, structure and organize information for storage, and he must attempt to structure his communications in ways that make them easily understood by his listener by relating them to what is stored away.

Memory of disconnected bits of data is often short-lived. The literary selections and lists we learned for various classes remain with us long enough to satisfy a teacher's assignment and then fade, perhaps to return again for no reason whatsoever in adult life. Graduate students report the same reaction to their traditional comprehensive examinations, which they regard as being more of an academic hurdle or barrier than part of a meaningful educational process. Thus, so called "intelligent assignments" seek memorization in a structured form, associated with what is already known. Generally we become competent listeners and speakers as we retain material in the form of relationships, associations, and connections and try to think in patterns and structures. To accomplish this, let us look at our own memory process and observe how we store data and how we activate it. We must literally observe our own process of observing and become aware of our own awareness, in order to make our systems conscious.

Feedback operates in memory as well as in observation of our own behavior through the eyes of others. What is fed back to us may inhibit or promote memory function and shape it to make it useful or irrelevant. The small child, for example, when the teacher speaks of life on the farm, may find it pleasant to think back on experiences he had on a farm last summer, but he would find it more useful to think of the farm in relation to his present experiences in the city. For the adult, talk of race riots may evoke pleasant memories of how life was in the good old days before he was confronted with such problems, but it is more useful to him to attempt controlled feedforward about what must be done to eliminate the trouble. Conscious control of memory can suppress the irrelevant so that the relevant may be activated.

All behavior is subject to control through feedback. The operation of our arms and legs, for instance, depends on the evaluation we make of how well they are working. We learn to dance by observing, controlling, and evaluating the movements we make. We perceive our movements visually and kinesically and suppress them through negative feedback or continue them through positive feedback. In short, we direct them through feedforward toward the idea in our mind of what we would like them to do.

The speaker must exert similar control, not only over his verbal output but also over the thought process that underlies it. A speaker may hear his own voice and make necessary internal corrections. He may also observe the behavior of his audience, draw inferences from them, and correct accordingly. In order to achieve any sort of correction, however, he must attend to his mental data processing and alter it as well. If his speaking does not seem to be evoking the desired response, it must be revised. This implies changing the processing of images and symbols inside, for external expression reflects what is processed in the mind. However, the way both internal and external events tend to control behavior concerns total personality, and will be discussed in detail in Chapter 11. Here, it is sufficient to say that success at expressing the self and in achieving feedforward goals is the product of disciplining the mind and its control over behavior. The process of discipline is the result of learning techniques of isomorphic transformations, making information relevant, meaningful, and useful when it is received and when it is transmitted.

We will now proceed to a discussion of how data is ordered as it is transformed from perception to information, to language, to speech, and to total behavior. We are mainly concerned with the way internal environments are structured from external stimuli, and how these are codified into language and then transmitted to others in the hope of altering their external world.

ABSTRACTING INTO INFERENCE

The process of abstraction starts with perception. Thus far, we have been concerned with how we abstract sensory information so that it can be systematically stored. Going farther, there are, actually, no known limits to man's power to abstract. It is questionable whether other animals abstract at all. If they do, it is only rudimentary classifying into categories of threat and support. The human, however, once in possession of a stimulus, may arrange and rearrange it, associate it, reclassify it, and engage in all manner of "creative" processing.

We have already pointed out that information we derive through our senses is relatively incomplete. To make sense of it, it is necessary to fill in details. Providing details to assist storage and activation in this situation is called the *inference* process. An inference goes beyond what is known— that is, it may be uncontrolled and random, or it may be intelligent and coherent. In either case, it transcends data; and it adds something to what the senses provide.

On receipt of data, it is necessary to fit it into some storage point or category. In responding to Figure 6-1, some people will perceive a "beautiful lady," while others will see an "old hag," while still others will see nothing at all. Figure 6-2 may appear to be a vase to some people, two faces to others. Whatever label is applied to either picture is a result of inference through abstraction. Neither picture is complete in itself, and in order to make sense, details must be added. Once a label has been attached, however, it becomes very difficult to see the other alternatives, for the process of viewing is itself affected by the process of drawing inferences.

Differences about the labels that ought to be applied to the two simple pictures illustrate the source of much difficulty in human relations. As perceptions become more and more complex, the inferences will become more detailed and more personal, and the possibility of getting similar perceptions in two people will consequently be diminished. To resolve those difficulties, it becomes necessary to ask questions about what the other person is seeing and drawing inferences about, rather than debating the inferences *per se*. Before sensible questions can be asked, however, we need to understand how the inference process operates and to understand that some of what we accept as factual information is really inferential.

At this point, it is necessary to distinguish between impulsive making of inferences and thoughtful estimation of what is missing. In practically all animal behavior there is impulsiveness, i.e., little delay between receipt of stimulus and response to it. Rabbits, for example, either immediately freeze or run when they perceive something as a threat. They do not sort out the nature of the threat nor are they able to distinguish between a real and a spurious threat. Some people tend to respond to stimuli in rabbitlike fashion; in that they may snap out disagreements, freeze into silence, or give uncritical assent before allowing themselves to analyze and process the information they have received. Such instantaneous activity characterized by immediate response to inference as though it were fact is called *signal response*. In contrast to signal responses, thought requires delay to permit the mind to scan and order the information it needs to make the best estimate of what is missing, to fill in the details, and determine a sensible response. Such processing is called a *symbolic response*, because the individual recognizes that what he is responding to is a symbolic construct in his mind, not necessarily reality. The user of a symbol response recognizes that his inferences may not fill in details accurately, so he is set

Figure 6–1.

Figure 6–2.

to revise his behavior if it does not seem fruitful. Those who use signal responses seem to believe honestly that they respond to reality, and they are usually upset when things do not work out well.

The basic difference between signal and symbolic response lies in the delay. A story that illustrates this well involves a London bus driver during World War II. When the driver had stopped his bus full of passengers at a red traffic signal, he noticed a German buzz bomb coming directly at the bus. Even though the red light evoked the signal to stay stopped, he was able to process symbolic data and move his bus through the red light, thus saving his passengers from death. His ability to transcend response to the immediate signal was responsible for his act of heroism, but his data processing and response to the symbol of the situation motivated his intelligent response.

A monkey could not have behaved this way. While a monkey can be trained to respond automatically to red and green lights, he cannot be trained to respond to complex and subtle situations. To make sensible predictions, to see relationships, to generalize meanings—all require the conscious processing of a great many symbols.

As long as inferences are consciously processed, intelligent behavior can result. Of course, the signal-responder thinks that he is acting in line with fact. However, sometimes the symbols to which we respond may take on the overtones of signal. Such symbols as the flag, the cross, or the swastika, and rituals like the boy scout oath and the pledge of allegiance may lose their meanings and their impact as people begin to respond to them instantaneously and emotionally without spending some time on their meaning. Contributing to this kind of behavior is the monotony of the intonation often associated with some of our greatest pieces of symbolic literature. The Declaration of Independence, the Gettysburg Address, or any other symbolic work can lose its meaning and become a signal if care is not taken in presentation of the message. Sometimes, when we deplore the lack of patriotism in modern youth, it might be useful if we look back on the way they were exposed to our great democratic symbols during their school experience.

Conversations may also become signalic and ritualized, and the conversationalists may become unutterably bored, if care is not given to the substance of the talk. If the members of the conversational group participate mutually in explaining and deepening the meanings of the ideas they transmit, if they permit questions, if they converse with the interests of others in mind, it is possible for them to derive great pleasure and a good deal of wisdom. If, however, the members respond impulsively by responding to remarks as signals, there is usually conflict. If they respond phatically with polite nods "how true" and "mm hmmm," no progress is made. But in a good conversation you can almost see, feel, and hear the meshing of mental gears as the participants think and speak about their topics and rub their minds together in the communicating process.

To be able to move from the level of an impulsive response to communication to a more mature level of delayed thinking and conscious data processing takes a great deal of practice and thought. There must first be conscious awareness of the communicative trap people fall into when they confuse signal and symbol and respond to inferences as though they were fact. Awareness and introspection about our responses helps us to understand the possibility ranges of responses of others. That is, while no two people will react in precisely the same way, the many ways in which others may respond can be understood simply by analyzing the range of our own replies to communication and defining what it is that motivates us to behave in that way.

Many situations, for example, may leave us cold, may leave us bored, or make us want to ignore them. Mature communicators recognize that they have the capacity to block out stimuli, to respond ritualistically, and take steps either to overcome it or avoid such situations. The less mature may respond signally, without recognizing that they are doing so. And, more important, if these people do not recognize their own boredom, they may not be able to recognize it in others with whom they speak. Many people do not understand that no response is often a response in itself—a potential negative feedback that symbolizes the fact that the listener is not receiving information, for any number of reasons—demanding that the speaker adjust his message or his method of presentation. The lack of movement in a class taught by a dull teacher does not mean that everyone is listening intently. It may well mean that somnolence has set in and that nothing whatsoever is entering the minds. If the speaker interprets lack of movement as attentiveness, he feeds forward in such a way that he continues the kind of activity that encourages nonlistening, and thus defeats his own purpose through defective interpretation of feedback.

By the same token, what emotionally motivates you to anger may also stir the ire of others. It is not wise to expect your listeners to stay calm if you speak words to them that might well provoke you to rage if they were directed at you. Awareness of what triggers your signal responses may assist you to avoid triggering them in others, thus sparing them the necessity of anger that blocks the receipt of your message.

However, quiet contemplativeness and delayed reaction should not be equated with apathy, just as quick response should not necessarily be classified as impulsiveness. People differ as widely in their data-processing capacity as they do in personality, so that it takes time and contact to determine what constitutes an intelligent response from any given listener. Indeed, generalization about responses are hard to make. That is why it is so difficult to plan ahead for speeches to large audiences. In any aggregation of people, many different data-processing styles will be represented. Only observation and intelligent inference on your part will enable you to be able to predict with relative accuracy the kinds of responses that are possible from the people to whom you speak.

The inference process is so complex that it is better to avoid learning rules about it. For example, the "old wisdom" that a *quiet class is a busy class* has long since been disproved. Experiments have demonstrated that some people listen and learn well when they are quiet; others have to move about and involve their bodies while they listen and learn. One of the problems faced by teachers in our Negro ghettos is the inability to accustom themselves to styles of listening and data processing which differ culturally from those they are used to. It is easy to draw the inference that age determines the kind of response that a child will make, and so teachers, unfamiliar with the influence of environment in shaping response pattern, will encounter consistent failure with black children, if they expect from them what they consider to be normal in white, middle-class children.

It is useful at the beginning stage of learning effective communication to suspend generalization, or at least make sure generalizations are well tested by spending considerable time observing the behavior of the people around you, trying to check their behavior against the types of questions they ask and the words they transmit to you in response. This is essential before you can begin to draw any conclusions about what constitutes good listening behavior.

INFERENCE, INTERPRETATION, AND PREDICTION

There are at least two sorts of inference. One, called *interpolation,* adds information to what is observed. For example, if you see several apples decaying on top of a barrel, you might infer that the rest of the apples in the barrel are also decaying. Another example might be the analysis made by an economist about a consistent decline of the use of electric power in areas where natural gas has just been installed. He might infer that industries and homes are shifting to the use of gas. Interpolation attempts to fill in data about the past or present by providing cause-and-effect "clues" for inferential decision-making.

Extrapolation attempts to make some prediction about the future. The economist who made the observation about electric power and natural gas may also note other activities, such as reduced use of means of transportation and decline in purchasing in retail stores. He may conclude from this data that a recession is ahead. He may then refer to data about how a previous recession was met and proceed to make recommendations about what to do in months to come. This would be an inference about an inference, and our economist friend should not be surprised if things did not work out exactly as he planned. Sound all too familiar? If he were sufficiently perceptive, he would make his plans open-ended, subject to change to meet feedback about unexpected conditions.

In either inference—interpolation or extrapolation—accuracy can be estimated only in probabilities. An inference can never be classified as "true" or "false," because it is a manipulation of symbols characterized by adding details in the mind. To the extent that the details approximate reality, the inference will be accurate, but in no case can you expect that complete certainty can result from inferential statements.

One of the most common inferences made by speakers is that the listener understands him. If a speaker assumes this, he must also assume that any breakdown in communication is the fault of the listener, which may also be a faulty assumption. He may attribute misunderstanding to willfulness on the part of the listener and absolve himself from any blame. He must also take the consequence of this kind of reasoning, which is usually a failure to achieve his goal. The wise speaker recognizes that any statement which he makes about his listener is only an inference, and he will then be prepared to adjust his own communication to meet new and unexpected behaviors on the part of his listener.

In our sophisticated society it should not be necessary to make the point that our world is in a constant state of change. Everything we see and evaluate changes from moment to moment. However, most of us tend to act as though the world were static and things will continue to be as we experience them. Our failure to anticipate change prevents us from exercising the widest range of inference potential. Furthermore, it tends to tunnel our expectancies so that we are not even aware that our belief that things will remain the same is an inference of a very low order of probability. For example, people do not remain as we experience them. They change from moment to moment, day to day. In communicating with others, we must constantly be aware of the immediacy of the transaction and act in line with the feedback we are receiving at the moment. It is simply just not wise to expect our listener to behave in the same way he did the last time we spoke to him. His physical state may have changed; his evaluation of us may have undergone a transformation. Whatever happened in our last transaction will affect the way he behaves toward us now. In an attenuated communication like a public speech, the state of mind of the audience will change from the beginning of the speech to its end. Whatever you think you know about the audience when you start will be altered by your performance in front of them, and by the time you finish the speech there should be considerable harmony between you and your audience, with mutual response characterizing the relationship.

Of course there are some things which change very slowly. Inferences we make about the rotation of the earth or the combination of elements are fairly safe, yet even these inferences have only a degree of probability. The discovery by a physicist that two atoms of hydrogen and one of oxygen do not always produce water led to the discovery of a whole system of isotopes, which, in turn, led to the discovery of ways to release power from the nucleus of the atom.

Another assumption that tends to disrupt our thinking is that things or events are alike. Even apparent similarities should not necessarily be construed to mean that two things or events are exactly alike, even in similar circumstances. No two Presbyterians, Republicans, college students, or parents will behave in exactly the same way. Despite the fact that our data-processing equipment tends to group things in symbolic categories, the things in the categories have identity only in the characteristics that identify the category. For example, parents are alike in that they have children. This will be the only *necessary* similarity, and it has been imposed verbally by the mind through the inference process. Any attempt to extend similarities beyond the criteria of the symbolic category can lead to errors in the inference process and reduce the possibility of accurate prediction. Thus, parents can be expected to behave quite differently toward the very children that caused them to be parents in the first place.

We tend to make progress in our thinking as we can find similarities that help us fit people and events into classifications. In the experimental method, we may find things out about college students in general, or about male and female college students, about high achievers and low achievers, about freshmen and sophomores, about Greeks and independents. Any confrontation with an individual student, however, must be characterized by response to the unique person. If our expectancy is that the student will respond according to some modality we have already established through research, we are very likely to be disappointed. With that in mind, it is safe to assume that we are likely to discriminate against things and people, to make faulty inferences about them, to the extent that we cannot perceive individual differences. We try to mold our opinion of people and things to the preconceived "map" in our minds. In this case, reference can be a great mind molder, although the mold may be highly inaccurate. Scientific progress is based on discovery of similarities, but satisfactory human relations must be based on perception of individual differences. Once again, a speaker may calculate generally what preparation he may need to succeed with a group. He must, however, permit himself considerable leeway to adjust to the particular behavior of his audience, which may not do what he expects. Most teachers have discovered this as they attempted to apply what worked last term to this term's new class; they didn't succeed because the individuals in the new class were sufficiently different from the first group to warrant an entirely different approach.

Our predictions become more accurate as we search beneath the surface of events to find structure or patterning regularities that seem to serve as bases for accurate predictions. Casual abstraction of qualities without a penetrating look may be highly misleading. Unfortunately, most of what we see is shaped by what we have seen before, because it is natural for people to try to connect new information to that which they have already organized.

It is easy for us to find similarities in animals and rocks because of different behaviors or shapes. Furthermore, faulty identification of a rock would cause no particular harm, unless we were a geologist. (In that case, we would very likely be equipped with sophisticated criteria for identification.) Our defective identification of animals might be more serious, if we chose to eat something that has the potential of being fatally inedible, say, uncooked pork.

Our identification of people into classes and categories, however, can also cause serious harm, largely because the complexity of people makes them defy casual categorization. Our understanding of where people fit, for better or worse, is shaped by our understanding of science. We know about regularities in nature, about how seasons come around once each year, how animals tend to group themselves into hierarchies of ever more complicated behavior. We may confuse the issue severely if we assume that people can be classified in the same way. Despite the fact that some people appear smarter, wealthier, more charming, more capable at times than others, generalizations about groups of people rarely seem to weather empirical test. Human behavior somehow manages to defy consistent classification.

Whatever generalizations we do make about people must take into account both similarities and differences. Prediction of outcomes generally becomes more difficult as the object or event about which we are predicting becomes more complicated. We may make specific predictions about the behavior of chemical elements, because we are dealing with basic units of matter, the rate of change of which is relatively slow and regularly paced. The predictions we make about a more volatile element, such as a radioactive substance, must take into account a wider capacity for behavior.

In the social sciences the problem of prediction is much more complicated. The man who attempts to force the outcome of some activity designed to stimulate business or quell race riots must base his prediction both on what he has observed in the past and what is going on now. He does not have the power to impose the same kind of entropy on the system as a technician has with basic chemical elements. He doesn't have the power to control the variables, as he can in a "clean" laboratory experiment. Because he cannot control the variables, the social scientist must base his assumptions on the premise that behavior will be consistent with what it has been in the past. This is not always a safe assumption—as the mayors of many large American cities began discovering in the summer of 1967, when communities of people with which they had been dealing exploded, despite the fact that the city fathers were still attempting to "do something" for them. "Do something" had heretofore seemed to placate the people. The social scientist, working with large aggregates of people, can still count on certain modalities, however. Although he may not be able to predict behavior in a given person or in a given neighborhood, he can be relatively accurate about the extremes which behavior will take, and what form *most* behavior is likely to take.

So the social scientist will feed forward and attempt to develop feasible goals. He will infer that application of certain techniques or activities will help to achieve these. Once his program is activated, it is necessary for him to respond to feedback, to move ahead only when his feedback is positive and to be prepared to alter course when the feedback is negative.

Thus we cannot help structuring the information we have. In fact, let it be clearly understood that structuring and ordering information is crucial to the information process. What is also important to remember is that in dealing with human beings our structures are guides, not absolute plans or formulas. The extent to which we can revise structures to accommodate new data we receive from feedback will determine our general effectiveness in motivating other humans, through speech, to fall in line with our goals.

SUGGESTIONS FOR DISCUSSION

1. If you have some science majors in the class, have them try to explain to you what scientists do. After they have made themselves clear(?), try to apply some of their propositions to the study of human communication. What is it about communication that makes it defy scientific analysis? After all, we can measure degree and quality of sound; we can describe the muscles of the vocal mechanism; we can count the verbs and nouns in a speech and make ratios. Why do we continue to insist on the term science-art?

2. Just how vast and sophisticated is your science of art? Get some evaluation teams or spokesmen designated and deal with such questions as: Are the Beatles artists? Is modern art really art if no one can understand it? What relation is there between the folk idioms and art? Is Stokely Carmichael an artistic speaker? How about George Wallace? Robert Welch? Carl Ogilvie?

3. Suppose your class were asked to set up an art display in your student union. The display is to be called, "The Art That Speaks to Our Youth on Campus." Assuming you can understand the title of the exhibit, make some decisions about what you would put on display. You might even want to lay out the displays. If you do a good job, you might want to talk your school of fine arts into sponsoring the exhibit. Who knows what you could get yourselves into!

4. John Locke once said, "Nothing exists in the intellect which has not been previously experienced through the senses." Do you believe this? Is there a "pot" smoker or an "acid-head" available that you can interview to find out if he believes it? What can you conceive of that you never saw before? Draw some of those things!

5. Where do you suppose science-fiction writers get their ideas? Check out something like Robert Heinlein's *Stranger in a Strange Land* and see what it tells you

about nonhuman sensing. You might want to get some of your classmates to role-play intelligent roaches on another planet. What do you think they will talk about?

6. Is the memory of the mind like a file drawer, a wastebasket, a closet in the attic, a junk yard, a toy box, a pantry, a swamp, a mismanaged library, all of the above, none of the above? If none of the above, what do you think it is like? Don't say "a computer." Everyone does that.

7. Do you think there will ever be brain transplants? Why do we know so little about the brain, when we know so much about heart and livers? What are some of the problems you would encounter in doing research on how the brain works?

8. The great detective entered the room and found Tom dead on the floor. The television set was on. The window was open about five inches, and showed no evidence of having been open wider. There was a puddle of water and some broken glass directly under the window next to a small coffee table. An examination of Tom showed that he had not been shot, killed with a knife, or poisoned. How did Tom die? (What inferences will you have to make to answer this question?)

9. Ready for another one? You are an anthropologist going ashore on an island populated by two races of people, the Redbloods and the Bluebloods. They look alike, but because of quirks in their language, it is impossible for Bluebloods to tell the truth and for Redbloods to lie. You see three natives. You ask the first one, "Are you a Redblood or a Blueblood?" He answers, but you do not hear the answer. You ask the second, "What did he say?" The second man responds, "He said he is a Blueblood, and he is." The third man adds gratuitously, "He is not, he is a Redblood." Now which of the three is Redblood and which Blueblood, and what kind of inferences do you have to make to answer the question?

10. You can spend a good deal of time discussing whether a traffic light is a symbol or a signal.

SUGGESTIONS FOR FURTHER READING

Hubert G. Alexander, *Language and Thinking* (Princeton, N.J.: D. VanNostrand, 1967). Chapters 2 and 3 are highlighted by a thorough and well-written treatment of thinking and abstracting, all related to creative communication.

Rudolf Flesch, *The Art of Clear Thinking* (New York: Harper and Brothers, 1951). Dr. Flesch presents first aid for word trouble in Chapter 7, which deals with abstractions.

Walter Weir, *On the Writing of Advertising* (New York: McGraw-Hill, 1960). Forget that this is a book for advertising majors and enjoy Mr. Weir's thoughts in Chapter 31, as he applies communication principles to everyday topics.

7

Abstracting and
Symbolizing:
Concepts
and Classifications

In the previous chapter we introduced some basic ideas about abstracting and symbolizing, and emphasized those that involved our thought patterns and behavior, based on the way we view and interpret stimuli. In this chapter, we will continue the discussion and emphasize the role of language in establishing classifications and explaining concepts.

DEVELOPING CONCEPTS

Humans tend to develop concepts to help them understand the mass of information they receive from their environment. Conceptualizing is at the center of our reasoning and our critical and creative thinking. Inability to form subtle and sensitive concepts forces a man to live on a mundane, mechanical level, often disappointed because his predictions do not work out and his effectiveness in society is low.

Conceptualizing itself requires a delay of reaction. Long and penetrating observation of a situation is needed to perceive both similarities and differences. It takes a while for a child to learn, for example, about "chairness"; the quality that confers verbal identity on objects normally referred to as "chairs." He must learn that neither shape nor color but use makes an object a chair. The child's observation of easy chairs, dinette chairs, barber chairs, chairs on the subway, may initially tell him that these things look different from one another and consequently do not belong in the same category. He must develop considerable sophistication before he learns to define the category "chair" operationally, in terms of its primary use for humans to rest their posteriors on. An adult's selection of a chair for a home, however, requires some concern for differences between chairs and the fitting of chair into a concept of position in a room. Chair then moves into a new verbal category of "home furnishing." Feedforward must relate the chair to decor and space allotments, and the chair finally selected will be unique from other chairs, although it may fit nicely into the category of "tasteful furniture in my living room."

Most speakers attempt to transmit some kind of concept to their listeners. Whether in social conversation or at a political meeting, the speaker seeks a response from a listener which is in harmony with his feedforward of a goal. As we've said in Chapter 6, the speaker who assumes that his listener will automatically accept the concept transmitted and fall in line with his goals is dangerously misled. To be successful on the public platform or in social conversation, the speaker must understand the kinds of concepts his listeners may form, and then fit his goals into their conceptual framework. It is possible that some ideas which might evoke strong emotion in you may be entirely irrelevant to your listener. For example, even if you are very angry about the treatment you received from the local police department, you cannot expect similar anger from a listener. Even when you show him what his stake is and how he will lose if he does not take the action you recommend, his concern will differ from yours. Or, in another case, you may feel that you are quite desirable socially, but you will not win social acceptance in conversation with others until you take the time and trouble to appeal to their needs for expansion of self-esteem through utilization of concepts they will perceive.

There are limitless concepts. They form at any level of abstraction and are embedded in memory. They formalize the chains of associations we make between images, symbols, and values, and they give us the substance of what we fear, love, hate, or believe in. Most of us can be trained quite easily to manipulate concepts that are not emotion-laden. For instance, we can learn about relative size or use of dogs. However, when we are asked to apply the concepts, strange things may happen. A child who has been bitten by a small dog may express inordinate fear at being exposed to another small dog, while showing no fear of a large one. A man who intellectualizes that he is safer in an airplane than he is in his own car may still choose to drive to his destination, if he has another concept of personal danger in high places. A speaker tends to use concepts by drawing from his memory a set of symbols that will express concepts as he knows them, because this represents an initial substance of communication. To do this alone may be cathartic, but it is rarely sufficient to communicate. In order to complete the job of communication, the structure of concepts pulled from the speaker's mind must be made to coordinate with those of his listener. Otherwise there is confusion, misunderstanding, and potential conflict.

The beginning speaker must master many concepts before becoming a skilled communicator. If he seeks to communicate in writing, he must learn some basics about structure of language and how to arrange words—the grammar of his tongue. If he seeks to communicate in speech, he must learn about appealing to the needs of others, developing and arranging his material to meet these needs, and then presenting his materials in ways that are easily understood and organized by his listeners, according to their own cognitive process.

One of the most effective concepts a speaker can use to transmit ideas to others is called *analogy*. An analogy abstracts characteristics from two dissimilar things and attempts to explain one through use of the other. For example, the statement that "pearls should not be cast before swine" is a statement analogous to "wisdom should not be wasted on fools." A *literal analogy* compares two things in the same category, such as two dogs, two people, two cars. A good example of a literal analogy would be to say that because anticensorship laws are useful in Pennsylvania, they will also be useful in Indiana. A *figurative analogy* is built on metaphor. For example, President Franklin D. Roosevelt in attempting to explain the workings of the American government compared the legislative, executive, and judicial branches of the government to a three-horse team, an analogy used later, by the way, by the Soviet Union in its demand for a "troika" leadership in the operation of the United Nations.

Such expressions as "the oil tanker plowed the seas" or "he loosed a volley of oaths" capitalize on the capacity of metaphors to illustrate and highlight the characteristics of something unfamiliar through the use of the familiar. To a farm child, the movement of a boat through an ocean he has never seen becomes considerably clearer by the analogy between the wake of the boat and the furrow of the plow. The rapid-fire delivery of imprecations becomes highlighted by analogizing it with bullets fired from a gun. Very often, in attempting to make ourselves clear, we become excessively literal or excessively abstract, with the result that an analogy making something unfamiliar share a relationship with something that is familiar to our listener helps to get a message through to the audience.

CLASSIFICATION

Accuracy in communication is built on appropriate use of categories. If we are not clear in our minds where things fit, our attempts at communication result in confusion and defective inferences by our listeners. It is even more difficult to transmit precise categories to a listener, who may not see the reason for "splitting hairs." To clarify ideas and to work down from high-level to simpler abstraction requires careful attention to *categories*. A category can best be understood through the analogy we have used before of the storage file. We file away relevant information under the appropriate designations. Many of the designations we use may be relevant only to ourselves, however, and not at all meaningful to our listeners.

In a cross-cultural situation, inability to perceive categories may easily arise. A Laplander will have several categories dealing with the concept of conserving reindeer, a notion alien in our society, which associates reindeer primarily with tales about Santa Claus. The Laplander is equally bewildered when confronted with the wide variety of words we use to talk about football. In professional fields, the process of carefully developing categories is very important. The physician, when he diagnoses your ailment, must distinguish carefully between various types of viruses, for each of which he has a name. However, he may tell you simply that you have a virus infection. For him to spew forth the complex Latin name of the virus he had diagnosed might generate disturbance and unhappiness in you, his patient. Similarly there are hundreds of different antibiotics, but they are all known to the layman as "a shot." Likewise, a lawyer must be able to distinguish between a felony, a misdemeanor, and a tort, all of which may be irrelevant to the person who has never run afoul of the law. Many words that teachers use are irrelevant to their students. Most college students do not know the difference between full, associate, and assistant professor, although the difference may become a matter of life and death to their teachers.

It becomes obvious that every profession or occupational commitment generates its own technical categories, and most homes have developed some unique ones to describe their peculiar relationships. The "drinking relatives" or the "neighbors" means nothing to people who live four blocks down and are not in the "family." The categories represent a kind of shorthand used to deal with the relevant, the commonplace, and the meaningful that simply must have their own unique slots in our minds.

We experience little trouble in trying to explain our precise categories to others. The physician can distinguish for the layman between various kinds of viruses merely by describing them and their effects on the body. The lawyer can define the categories he uses by talking about the gravity of the crime or differences in the legal implications. However, many concepts, used by all of us, float around freely in a kind of semantic limbo. Such concepts as *life, freedom, education, democracy, sociocultural, moral,* or *progress* are remarkably difficult to pin down. They serve as "wild cards"; each man can make them represent whatever he wishes. Politicians may use categories of this sort for precisely that reason. They need never be bound, for they have not defined their own boundaries, but allow each listener to include precisely what he wants in the category. For example, to a middleclass white American, progress may mean a split-level home and two cars. To a Negro, it may merely mean a job; to a city planner, it may mean destruction of the central city; to the slum landlord, it may mean preservation of things as they are. The politician who calls for "progress in solving the problems that beset our city" beams a generalized "to-whom-it-may-concern" appeal to all these people, and has reason to believe that he will captivate each of them.

Regrettably, listeners often make false judgments, because they assume that the speaker means what they do when he refers to his "wild-card" category. Speakers as well simply may presume that listeners have the same things in mind when they hear the words spoken. One of the problems encountered in many great works of literature and philosophy is the number of high-order abstractions. Consequently, once such a work leaves the desk of its author, it is open to a variety of interpretations, and frequently serves as the basis of unnecessary controversy, much of which could be avoided if people would not assume that it is possible or necessary to attain agreement on what the concepts meant to the author when he wrote them.

Concepts attach themselves to nonverbal symbols as well. The American flag, the cross, the hammer and sickle of communism, the skull and crossbones on a bottle of poison, or the placing of a wrecked car at a dangerous intersection convey a wealth of meaning to the viewers. Yet the images evoked in any of the viewers are different. Each person will respond to his flag somewhat differently; the feelings of patriotism will evoke different behavior.

Continuing contact with the symbols, and continued manipulation of verbal concepts, will in time reduce the potency of the message. This presents a problem, particularly for professionals, because they may begin to deal with difficult concepts quite matter of factly. For the psychiatrist, the word *schizophrenic* refers merely to a category of diagnosis, while it may strike terror in the heart of the potential patient who hears it. The warning on the side of the cigarette pack has exactly the same effect. After the smoker has seen it many times, it ceases to impress him; it is merely something that he buys along with the brand name on the package.

Whatever categories are employed in the mind, it must be remembered that they will be associated with emotion, to greater or lesser degrees. The emotional loadings of a verbal category will differ widely from person to person, depending on the contact they have had with the category and upon other information they have stored that may have some effect on it. No one can assume that his thinking, expressed in words, will have anything like the impact on another mind as it has on his own. Care must always be taken to predict and appeal to the types of emotional loadings the listener has, for without this kind of planning, there is little possibility for intelligent feedforward, and considerable opportunity to misinterpret feedback. In addition to conceptual categories, other factors must be considered in our communication of words in meaningful fashion.

MULTI-ORDINALITY

Words, particularly those referring to abstract categories, tend to change in meaning through time. Emotional loadings consistently applied tend to give words coloration and, eventually, may even change the categorical meaning of the word. An excellent example of this phenomenon is the word *propaganda,* the categorical meaning of which is quite different today from its original categorical meaning. The characteristics that lead to the development of a verbal category are referred to as *denotation.* The emotional loadings surrounding the category are called *connotation.* A good example of connotation is the word *dynamo.* When it was coined from the Greek word *dynamis,* meaning "force," it referred to a machine that converts mechanical into electrical energy. Then someone began to respond emotionally to the word and built an analogy to a person, so that today *dynamo* has two applications. Others went on to coin words based on the Greek root, and we now talk of "dynamic personalities," "group dynamics," "dynamism." The term no longer has a single application. Standing alone, its meaning cannot be checked in a dictionary. The only way to find out what a user has in mind when he employs the word is to analyze the context.

A word that takes its meaning primarily from context is referred to as *multi-ordinal.* Such a word can take on specific meaning only if the context is specific. If the context is vague or ambiguous, so is it. For example, the word *speak* in the phrase "to speak of war" has considerably more emotional loading than it does when used in the phrase "to speak at the next meeting." The word *tradition* employed in "the tradition of American freedom" does not mean the same thing as in the "tradition of Christmas lights in our city." The word itself is the same, but the meanings are vastly different. There are many words of this type that consistently can take on many different levels of meaning depending on the emotional state of the user and the other words with which he nests them. Words such as *critical, knowledge, problem, agreement,* or, for that matter, any word expressing an evaluative description, like *beauty* or *truth,* are examples. Just one word by itself can refer the listener to a series of possible meanings listed in the dictionary. The word in context, properly pinned down, can lead the listener to reasonable understanding without the necessity of using the dictionary.

Some of our colleagues in the harried halls of academia have a tendency to proliferate meaningless multi-ordinalities. The terms "know about knowing," "meaning of meaning," "theoretical construct," "model for behavior," "theory," "principle," "law," "hypothesis" all may have some meaning inside the head of the scholar, but the traditional method of transfer of meaning doesn't seem to work, as generations of college students can attest. Obviously, Lamont Cranston is not the only one with the power to cloud men's minds!

Words employed in such a way that they are meaningful only to the user can do nothing more than generate confusion. Surely you know at least one poor soul who has ingested impressive words without associating an appropriate meaning, and has blurted them out awkwardly in conversation at some inopportune time, much to the glee of his listeners and to his own discomfiture. Sometimes, too, people become preoccupied with differential meanings to the point where it is not clear whether they are reacting to a thing for which a concept word stands or to their feelings about the thing or concept.

This last idea is evident in the person who worries (reaction) about worrying too much (concept). There is also the person who fears to be fearful. This is a frequent phenomenon among novice speakers. They have heard the emotion-laden words *stage fright* to the point where they decide they do not want to have stage fright, even though they may not know its symptoms or effects. They begin to fear the idea "stage fright" and are thus rendered unable to speak, not because they are afraid to speak, but because they are afraid to be afraid of speaking.

People also get very comfortable in their emotions. The teen-ager falls in love with love and develops many spurious relationships with others of the opposite sex merely because he likes the emotions generated, not necessarily the people. Prejudices and hatreds may be very comforting to have. There are people in this great democracy who freely admit a hatred of a Negro or a Jew, simply because "they" are Negro or Jewish. Similarly, there are black men who hate everything and everyone connected with "Whitey," simply because "they" are white. However, for most people, such terms as *love* and *hate* are too strong for generalizations, and are often diluted to the *like* and *dislike* level. Most of us need a set of likes and dislikes that make the decision process easier for us. From the simple act of ordering food from a restaurant menu to the infinitely more complex act of deciding who to hire for an important position, we are helped if we have a clear-cut set of criteria for what to like and dislike. For instance, if we can reject those people who have long hair and beards, those with low-grade point averages, those who have graduated from denominational colleges, those who are married women, or those who are over 35, the task of selecting graduate students becomes much easier. When we have fully developed these neat, prejudicial rules of thumb, however, they become so facilitative for us that we begin to defend them to the point of finding rationalizations for them. We become quite hostile when these rules of ours are threatened, for to threaten them jeopardizes the ease with which we have been thinking up to that point.

While we must recognize the comforting nature of our prejudices and multi-ordinal responses, we must remember that they are highly personal and consequently may conflict with other people's multi-ordinality, if we express them or attempt to act on them too vigorously. While it may not always be possible for us to sort out our own multi-ordinal responses, attention to negative feedback from our listeners will at least cue us in to points where corrections need to be made if we are to communicate more effectively.

HIGH-ORDER ABSTRACTIONS

We have discussed the way abstractions of sensory information result in storage of images and symbols, how these symbols can be abstracted into inferences, inferences into concepts, and how concepts become complex associations of words and ideas, such as analogies, categories, and multi-ordinal responses. We have also noted how abstracting may stop at any time, how it may move ahead in spurts with little connection between the steps, or how it may proceed with deliberate pace through close-reasoned associations. Now it is necessary to turn our attention to the way words connect together to make longer statements about relationships with and connections to things we think about.

In order to become a perfect communicator, it would be necessary to be aware of all the events in the universe, and to be able to connect them together through symbols in ways that others can understand. It would also be necessary to have complete knowledge about how others think, so that precisely the right phrases could be selected to evoke precisely the right images in the mind of the listeners. Some classical writers on communication had the notion that men could be trained to perfection, and several ancient works detailed methods to reach this perfection. They tried, in addition to giving advice about speaking, to develop compendiums of knowledge so that the speaker could learn all there was to know about everything.

Today we understand that mastery of complete knowledge is impossible, and we no longer seek to attain it. We understand that our potential vocabulary is limited to about 1,000,000 words that must stand for an infinite number of things and ideas. We operate now in the realm of probability and try to give a student speaker enough information so that he can make intelligent guesses about what he needs to do to achieve his goal within the limits of what is possible. By now, you should be aware that it will not be possible for you to communicate perfectly with everyone. You will experience many failures, and at best, your success will only be partial. This is the reason we stress the concepts of feedforward and feedback. Both are process terms. Both imply that it is possible for a speaker to adjust to meet the needs of the situation as he observes it. Neither term offers more than the expectancy of partial success. Both are *continuous* rather than *discrete* variables, i.e., both feedforward and feedback are continuing processes that operate all the time there is communication—neither is static.

What a speaker has to say can be no more reliable than his input and data processing. It is manifestly impossible for anyone to come in direct contact with all the things, ideas, and events that might be relevant to talk about, so much of our input comes from abstracting the knowledge of others from what we hear and read or see. If we are expected to exercise our critical faculty in processing the information we get directly, we must apply even more important critical judgment to the information that comes from others. We must constantly ask how they know what they know, what kind of abstracting they have done with their information, and what multiordinal responses might distort the information they are transmitting to us. We plan our own communication as though our listeners were doing precisely this. When we are in the role of listener or reader, we cannot afford to do less; otherwise we might become masses of distortion and emotion and either lose our capability to transmit information coherently or turn into an unethical demagogue who seeks approval and acceptance at any ethical price.

Whenever possible, it is a good idea for us to get back to lower levels of abstracting in listening to or reading the words of others. A great deal of distortion comes about as the abstractions become more and more complex. The lowest order description, for example, contains some emotional loading and potential distortion in and of itself. Consider the following descriptive statement:

A two-pound cellophane sack of Derk's tomatoes contains four or five tomatoes. The water content averages 98.2 percent. Not less than 10 percent of green remains before each tomato turns bright red. There are no spots. Stems have been completely removed. Freshness and vitamin content are preserved, since no tomatoes delivered are more than two days picked from the vine.

This level of abstraction provides details in somewhat the same language an observer might use if he were in contact with the objects described. It may help a listener to identify the object. It is detailed, but it is not entirely free from inference. For example, the comments about 98.2-percent water content and 10 percent of green are inferential in nature. Furthermore "freshness" is an evaluation.

Conscious attempts to get a purchaser to buy the product may lead to deliberate attempts through language to induce the listener to manufacture inferences:

The secret of soup made from Derk's tomatoes is in the most luscious choice tomatoes grown in the clear, bright air and irrigated from the snows of Colorado mountains. Blended in fine table butter there is just a rightness of seasoning. One look or whiff and you want a spoonful. One taste and you want a bowlful.

Details are lost, and the inference words begin to blend so that they make the listener give the response desired. We can go still further.

The words can be made even more general to gain a higher order acceptance of the product:

Derk guarantees high quality in the vegetables distributed. Control of moisture and freshness keeps nutritional values at a maximum. Careful selection and packaging provide for products which meet the expectations of the housewife. Efficient customer service has always been a major policy of Derk.

The listener may now infer that all Derk tomatoes will be delicious, that they will be filled with food value, and that they will satisfy you regardless of what use you intend to put them, and that if anything goes wrong your money will be cheerfully refunded. The housewife may see these tomatoes as an image, rich and red, on a platter in the center of her table, may even see her guests eating them and complimenting her on her fine choice of foods. The language of that message is calculated to evoke just such an image, particularly when the housewife comes into contact with the brand name. Associating the name of the product with such pleasant images makes the name take on connotations that should lead to purchase of the product.

We may go even further and make broad conceptual generalizations, in this case, political and economic in nature.

The great food chain stores are a feature of the American economy. They are also a feature in making available the variety and balance of particular energy resources of the planet which must sustain human life. In combining modern agricultural technology with efficient distribution facilities, the whole welfare of our people is advanced.

And if Mr. Derk believes this, it justifies his whole operation and makes his life meaningful, although the statement may make absolutely no sense to anyone else.

When language reaches this level, it is exceedingly difficult to draw any information from it. When ideas are expressed this vaguely, they may be meaningful to the speaker, but they permit the listener to insert whatever meaning he desires, whatever happens to be evoked, which may not concord at all with what the speaker has in mind. In a sense, though, through generalization, we have something for everybody, even though we may not have communication between speaker and listener.

Some authorities have offered the analogy of the road map to describe the requirements of communicative language. In order to be useful, a road map should show the proper relationships between cities, the direction and course of the roads, and the natural hazards, all in proportion to the territory it purports to map. No road map can be precisely up to date, for it probably cannot take into account road repairs, bridge washouts, and other detours. Generally, however, the usefulness of a road map is determined by how effectively it can guide travelers from place to place.

The road map is relatively useless, however, to the man who is primarily interested in topographical features of a terrain. He will want other kinds of information, including data about elevation, course of rivers and streams, nature of obstacles in the terrain. A petrologist might want a map of what lies below the surface of the land, rock formations, shale deposits, location of natural gas. A service man for the electric power company will be concerned with location of utility poles and the course of underground lines, and he will want junctions of power lines clearly noted on his map. Attempting to blend all this information into one map would render the map useless to everyone because of the probable confusion. Nor would an artistic representation of the territory make a useful map; it might express an emotion about the location but not convey specific information.

The authorities who offer the analogy of the road map go on to point out that the speaker ought to be aware both of the kind of map he is drawing and the kind of map his listeners can understand and use. If the speaker is trying to guide people from one location to another, he must concentrate on roads, because details about power lines and shale deposits would only distract his listeners. If, however, his listeners are primarily interested in prospecting for oil, directions from place to place might have to be associated with oil locations in order to make them relevant and acceptable.

The speaker must first of all be aware of his own map-making and its inherent hazards. He must then become aware of the maps his listeners can understand and need, and he can try to adjust the *method* of achieving his goal to the kind of information they can understand and accept. He must, in short, use isomorphism to the fullest extent possible.

THE PRINCIPLE OF ISOMORPHISM RETURNS

The term *isomorphism,* as we use it here, refers to the capability speakers have of altering appearance while preserving the essential structure. The effective speaker seeks isomorphism in his communication. He develops a clear structure in his own mind and attempts to transfer it to others. Although the "appearance" of the structure as it enters the listener's mind may be different from its "appearance" in the speaker's mind, the basic and meaningful core is the same; both speaker and listener can perceive the structure in essentially similar ways. The speaker understands that he cannot transfer the structure directly because of differences in the mind of his listener. He knows that, somehow, his message must be made to fit the mind of his listener. He must do this without destroying the message he believes in, and he knows that he will not be successful in every case. He tries to raise the probability of success through isomorphism, by varying the appearance of the message to reach as many minds as possible.

TECHNIQUES FOR ACHIEVING ISOMORPHISM

There are several techniques for creating and using isomorphism in speech situations. Three basic ones—narration, exposition, and argumentation—are described below; analysis and definitions in abstraction are discussed in the next section.

Narration is the most common technique used to describe and report. Narration abstracts details of an event as it moves through time. Narration consists of a starting point and an ending point with subevents described in sequence between the points. Attention to the way two different newspapers will report the same story indicates that narration is not so simple as it seems. Examining news reports of the six-day war between Israel and the Arab states, one finds it hard to determine the precise sequence of events. No one reading the reports can be certain who started the war, when or whether the Egyptians were surrounded, what points of land were occupied, in what sequence, and so on. Only a few specific main guideposts can be determined, i.e., the war started and it ended, and several things happened in between. Narrating to listeners relatively familiar with events demands that great care be taken to avoid distortion, for any event placed out of the sequence they are familiar with will jar them and reduce speaker effectiveness. Care is also necessary in speaking to naïve listeners, for the initial impact will order the listeners' minds and determine a major part of their response to subsequent information. If the sequence of events is not clear to them, they may be unwilling or unable to understand some crucial concepts in the message. Narration tends to appeal to sequentially oriented minds that prefer to store information in chronological sequence.

Exposition seeks to explain the components of a situation, object, or event. It may proceed through simple description, or it may use narration to clarify the elements but deal primarily with components, such as the relationship of smoking to cancer, the various individuals who make up university personnel, patterns of communication in teen-age marriages, the nature of industrial capacity of Japan, etc. Exposition seeks to clarify, and consequently proceeds, normally, from simple understanding to complex and sophisticated mastery. It may move inductively, from specific to general, or deductively, but it must take care to preserve necessary relationships and emphasis.

Argument seeks acceptance for a proposition or a course of action. The speaker has developed a goal and wants his audience to accept it. He proceeds to give the reasons why the audience should do what he wants them to. If he gives only his reasons, he may alienate his listeners. Consequently, he seeks to phrase his reasons so that they will fit needs his listeners have.

ANALYSIS

Analysis through definition is normally called for in any speech, because old problems require redefinition and clarification. The search for the nature of a problem and its causal structures requires development of categories and classifications that make sense to speaker and listener. The speaker seeks verbal "maps" that will best express his presentation of the structure of a problem as he understands it.

For example, the analysis of juvenile crime evokes different categories depending on whether it is being discussed by social workers, educators, lawyers, economists, preachers, or parents. An economist might look at such categories as "standard of living," "taxation," and "employment." A social worker might tend to view the problem in terms of "housing," "family size," or "recreation." A teacher might see it in "education of the parents," "cultural opportunities," and "facilities for special education." A lawyer might be interested in "law enforcement," "juvenile courts," and "probation." And a parent might be concerned only about "what my kid does." Clearer definition of words becomes more necessary as concepts become more abstract. When clarity of outline begins to blur, definition is necessary to make verbal distinctions that will help regain clarity.

There is a tendency for definitions to become strings of synonyms proceeding to higher levels of abstraction. They may go around in circles, becoming more and more vague—that is, one undefined term may be explained by another undefined term indefinitely. Definitions should be accompanied by illustrations and by reference to specifics. A better isomorphism occurs if illustrations precede the definition. However, no words may be needed for definitions if the object is at hand. Without support from lower order abstractions, however, definitional concepts often lead to interminable arguments.

Whatever point of view he takes, the speaker plans his message according to his commitment and purpose. What analysis he makes of listeners must be done from this standpoint of purpose. However, speakers have a tendency to assume others have the same concern and understanding the speakers do. This may cause a speaker to employ a "special rhetoric" of his commitments, and thus confuse or alienate his listeners. For instance, a layman will not support teachers' pay raises or oppose Medicare until he finds a reason in his own mind, regardless of how important the speaker's reasons may be to the speaker. A sensible definition of the problem in a listener's understanding assists isomorphism.

The effective speaker or writer approaches his task as a scientist. He determines where his vision is tunneled, and what must be done to broaden his own view. He then utilizes all resources to convey his understandings to others. Definition brings order and rigor into his composition, while it removes ambiguity and vagueness. Likewise, sound definition helps feedback make more sense, for the speaker is more certain that his listeners are responding to what he is talking about rather than to irrelevancies.

Putting together a message requires selection of materials with proper emphasis upon narration, exposition, and argument, with the abstractions ordered through analysis and definition. The speaker must do all he can to focus attention upon his message in order to make feedback more relevant. During preparation phases of the speech, the speaker must select ideas carefully with an eye toward their relevance to others. This process was called *invention* in the classical systems. His next procedure is to order the information into a sensible structure and arrange his supporting materials. The ancient philosophers called this *disposition*. Next he selects words and orders them, a process referred to as *style*. He stores the information in *memory* through the use of an outline, manuscript, or notes, and finally he *delivers* his speech to his audience. The classical contributors empirically understood the importance of these steps in the communication process, and what they wrote is as relevant today as when they lived, for they tend to accord with the natural processes of the human mind. All preparation centers around the theme, main idea, purpose, or central ideas of the speaker. Without some clear conception of purpose, all the speaker's preparation and effort may be in vain.

TACTICS AND THEMES

As a speaker learns more about his listeners and the situation in which they listen, he becomes more aware of his limitation in time and opportunity. His energy is limited, and there are limits to the staying power of his audience. As he speaks, he will become aware of distractions that compete with him for attention. He will understand that whatever he does must be done in a limited time—that he must get a "message" to his listeners as efficiently as possible, for he cannot predict when their attention may wane.

A theme is the product of abstracting a concept into the expression that best represents the idea the speaker wishes to leave with his audience. It may pertain to pressing problems, crucial situations in society, or to a specific concern of the speaker. A theme may be as precise as the details of a zoning appeal in a neighborhood, or as broad as a demand for interracial harmony or a plan to improve the economic status of a nation. Specific themes, like birth control in a specific family, may be subordinated to broader themes, for example, population control in a region.

A speaker's whole life career may be devoted to the development of one theme, like the "New Deal" of Franklin D. Roosevelt, the "New Frontier" of John F. Kennedy, or the "Great Society" of Lyndon B. Johnson. Literary themes may deal with the "spirit of man," "subjugation of peoples," or the "ascendency of the human spirit." Whatever the theme, it must be clear in the mind of the speaker before he can hope for any clear transmission to a listener.

There is one basic ground rule that all speakers must follow, which is: We must take responsibility for what we say. The most important commitment a speaker can make is to "truth." For the mature speaker, this commitment soon becomes a way of life. There is in him a persistent striving to help others to a better isomorphism with their world. His commitment becomes built into his feedforward activities. He knows that resistance to learning and change demands a *strategy* to achieve the goals on which his efforts focus. As a communicator he becomes a scientist to the extent that he makes effective predictions; he becomes an artist as he moves the hearts and minds of his listeners toward involvement and understanding.

Strategy refers to the major decisions about the construction of a speech and its delivery. Strategy includes selection of themes and the isomorphisms that will be used to implant them in the listeners' minds. *Tactics* refers to the selection of the precise materials to be used, and the specific use at a given moment with a particular audience. Tactics is concerned with sequence and timing of ideas used to support the main themes, strategically organized to raise the probability of reaching as many minds as possible.

Successful implementation of strategy depends on reception of feedback and its proper interpretation. Considerable care may be taken in the preparation of a speech developed to fit the anticipated audience. The speaker must have several clear alternatives, however, for the audience may be quite different from what was expected. To retain the strategy originally developed may mean certain failure, while adaptation of the strategy to particular requirements raises the probability of success.

In preparing a communication, a speaker will make inferences about how much definition is needed, for example, and where it will fit. He must determine what concepts must be made concrete through example and illustration. He will infer which ideas can be best clarified through use of statistics, which through citations of relevant authorities, and he will infer which authorities will be relevant to the audience. Once he confronts the audience, however, all of the speaker's expectations can be dashed. The audience may not behave at all like the speaker expected. They may get considerably more involved with a part of the speech the speaker thought would be dull, and they may offer resistance to what the speaker thought would be the most exciting part.

The speaker will look for overt signs of response from the audience, and he will discover modalities of behavior and make inferences from them. An experienced speaker can sense friendliness and hostility in his audience. He will be able to eliminate what is trite for the audience and elaborate on whatever stimulates them. He will take care to emphasize old ideas with new insights. He will avoid being more technical than the knowledge possessed by the modality of the audience will permit, and he will augment his definitions with illustrations or visual representations where necessary and possible. Eventually, he will begin to function in harmony with the audience feedback, so that even those people in the audience who oppose him and his message will testify to his competence.

The novice speaker attempts to develop a plan and stick to it no matter what. Most textbooks on public speaking seem to imply that careful planning is the road to successful speaking. We do not wish to demean the concept of careful planning. It is indeed essential to plan the development of the theme carefully, and to order the parts so that they make sense. But all the planning in the world will be useless if the target population does not behave as anticipated. Every speaker must be equipped with alternatives, and every speaker must develop a collection of strategies that will enable him to function regardless of how closely the audience hews to his impression of them.

Much of the speaker's effectiveness will depend on what the audience thinks of the speaker as a man, his *ethos*. Every successful adaptation to feedback will increase ethos. Each time the speaker clings to his original plan despite the feedback, his ethos will be reduced. Even if an adaptation is not fully satisfying to the audience, virtually all listeners can recognize effort. Often, they will demand little more from a speaker than clear evidence that he is trying to reach them. If the speaker gives this evidence, the audience will "come along" and increase their efforts to reach the speaker and discover what he is saying.

This is particularly true in the teaching process. All of you have had professors that "turned you off." The quality of their behavior that alienated you was their apparent unwillingness to try to reach you on some level you could understand. Those who excited you were the ones who tried to present material on your terms.

The preparation and planning of the spoken message calls for considerable application of scientific principles and techniques. The actual presentation of the spoken message calls for considerable empathy, quickness of adaptation, personal commitment and involvement, and simply cannot be programmed. Once again we see the sense of referring to speech as a science-art. This is particularly important as we examine some of the problems people have when they try to communicate and discover the importance communication has in developing a successful personal life.

SUGGESTIONS FOR DISCUSSION

1. There was some discussion about how children learn to talk in this last chapter. You might get considerable insight into the problem if your class tries to invent a language. Work out a simple language with, perhaps, a 100-word vocabulary. Make it a language you can use in the class. Be sure there are references in it to the commonplaces in the classroom. After you have experimented with your language for a while, see if you can come up with some general propositions about the nature of language and the problems encountered in learning it.

2. Scientists often use the concept of *operational definition*. What is the difference between an operational definition and a dictionary definition? See if you can find a dictionary definition and an operational definition for the following words: communism, flunk-out, dog (referring to a type of coed), Greek (as in fraternity man), potato, banana (as in "my love for you has made me bananas"), professor, student. Try writing an operational definition of "Glork" from the following statements: "Every time I see you, I glork all over. Her sweater was sort of a soft glork. My mouth feels like it was full of glork. It is one glork of a day today."

3. Many of you have been told about a potential blind date, "she has a nice personality." Using that sentence, develop a *concept* of the phrase "nice personality," and see if you can explain it to another person. Then go out on campus and see if the two of you identify the same people for whom the term might stand.

4. Aristotle said that the use of analogy was a sign of genius. Divide yourselves up into teams of three and find out what kind of geniuses you are. See if you can make some analogies between Faye Dunaway and Mae West; your girl friend and Kate Smith; your boy friend and Boris Karloff; Russian potato soup and Siamese cats; an electric typewriter and a fan dancer; a red Alfa Romeo and Muriel cigars; Barry Goldwater and Jack E. Leonard; Rowan and Martin and Damon and Pythias; a file cabinet and a diaper; an Airedale puppy and your professor; Godzilla and your college president; an electric wire and a football; any other unlikely combination you can think of.

5. Working in groups, see what kinds of classifications you can develop for: students at your college; faculty at your college; courses at your college; recreational activities at your college; cultural enrichment activities at your college; various geographical regions at your college; historical milestones in the development of your college. Make up a name for each of the categories and write a definition for your category words that would be clear to someone on another campus. Be sure you identify the similarities on which your groupings are based. Now see if you can identify some characteristics at which we might look for differences.

6. Now go on with your "category job" and try to discover how category systems reflect the culture of our society. What does it reflect about our culture when we classify students into freshmen, sophomores, juniors, and seniors? How about classification of footgear into wedgies, flats, brogans, boats, hushpuppies, loafers, boots, etc.? If you were to tell an anthropologist from Nepal that he could learn to understand our culture by looking at the categories we use for things, what genera would you point out to him and what categories would you ask him to note?

7. An interesting exercise is to have someone make up a list of abstract words like "progress," "courtesy," etc. (5 or 7 words will be enough), and give a free association quiz, with each member writing his immediate associations with the words on a slip of paper. Then go through the answers and see what commonalities and differences you can find in the associations. Which list do you expect to be longer—the list of commonalities or the list of differences?

8. As an introspective exercise, it might be a good idea to examine some of your own multi-ordinalities. For example, is there some minority group you hate? How important is it to keep hating them? If someone wanted to change your mind about the minority group, would it be more useful to present facts to refute your biases or show you that it is socially unacceptable to have that kind of hate? Continue this kind of analysis with some of your other pet loves and hates. It's interesting to submit these as anonymous papers and read them around.

9. Is there any difference between the words "discriminate" and "prejudice"? If President Nixon appointed you administrator of race relations, would you find it more effective to work to prevent prejudice or discrimination? If you had to develop a program to combat both, how would the programs differ?

SUGGESTIONS FOR FURTHER READING

Rudolf Flesch, *The Art of Plain Talk* (New York: Harper and Brothers, 1951). Another of Dr. Flesch's useful books, this one has some excellent thoughts on abstraction and symbolism in Chapter 5.

Rudolf Flesch, *The Art of Readable Writing* (New York: Harper and Brothers, 1949). *Time* magazine called Dr. Flesch the "Mr. Fixit of Words," and this time he presents day-to-day examples of isomorphism in action. Read Chapter 2.

Aldous Huxley, "Word and Behavior," *Readings in Speech,* ed. Haig A. Bosmajian (New York: Harper and Row, 1965). Read this once for the information; then go through it again, at leisure, to enjoy the beauty of his presentation.

Harry Weinberg, *Levels of Knowing and Existence* (New York: Harper and Row, 1959). If you have already read Chapters 4 and 6, review them. If not, treat yourself to some good reading.

8

The Vast Range
of Communication
Disorders

The change of vapor in a cloud into rain that is turned into electrical power at a hydroelectric plant is a transformation. A change that goes on from generation to generation—a cow to a calf to a cow to a calf, etc.—is an isomorphic transformation. The basic structure is retained from stage to stage, but the form changes.

The principle of change can be applied to the communication process as man relates to his environment. The life facts he perceives are transformed into counterpart semantic structures, which, in turn, generate symbols, language structures, and behaviors. Personal outputs in the form of behavior produce further changes in the environment, and the cyclic communication process continues indefinitely. What we communicate is kept in correspondence with what we perceive through conscious abstracting, plus the ordering of these abstractions by means of negative and positive feedback; both are integrated through feedforward.

We infer this communication process in the human species, but it can be measured accurately in only a few respects. We can, for instance, measure acuity of hearing and vision, but not the valuative impact. We can measure *quantity* of verbal output, but we are especially deficient in the measurement of *quality*. About all we really know is that most tests, inventories, and case studies yield only tendencies, averages, and norms. Our efforts to measure quality are about as accurate as prognostications of the weekend football scores. While interesting and often rewarding, they lack reliability and validity because of the difficulty in defining where a part of the communication process joins another part operationally and where these two parts join with the whole process. Wholes have a way of being more than the sum of the parts, especially where man is concerned. Where does personality stop and vocalization begin? How do the ideas of one person accord with the ideas of another? Do ideas reverberate through our audiences? Where is the saturation point? These questions are made more knotty, because of the difficulty of phrasing them precisely enough to make a useful answer possible.

Messages are rarely received at the same level of abstraction at which they are sent. A speaker's summary may be only an example to one listener, or a simple description may be perceived as a generalization. For example, messages about birth control offend some, while enlisting the cooperation of others. People in India, though they and their children are starving, refuse to eat beef in spite of the most "logical" appeals. *Segregation* has a different connotation at the operational level of the landlord in Cicero, Illinois, than it does to a committee in the South African legislature or to the sociology seminar in a northern college.

Since we all must live and succeed in our world by predicting about our particular enterprises and cultures, we assume some norms against which performance may be judged, as we endeavor to make sense out of each person's unique communication. We shall examine some possible communication deviations and attempt to propose methods whereby the deficient and/or mediocre speaker may move on to excellence and from there to creativity.

History, a great laboratory for the study of interactions, offers many examples of problems that have arisen from difficulties in communication, and the longer a problem remains unresolved, the greater become the communication difficulties. Habits of thinking tend to solidify, so man constantly has to struggle through the vicious circles that he has such a propensity to create. We learn, for example, that war resolves nothing, that it is not possible to win, yet leaders continually offer war to their people as a potential solution. Words about war have entered our language, so that we use them habitually. Language habits can crystallize into pathologies, which complicate the possibility of finding solutions.

What we are saying is that simply possessing the requisite mental or biological equipment does not guarantee success as a communicator, just as the inheritance of sharp vision, acute hearing, and delicate neurons does not guarantee acquisition of learning or the power to generate more and better ideas. Sometimes superior equipment only multiplies the troubles that the "superior" person creates for himself and for others, as anyone who has known a prime "know-it-all" has discovered. We all know intellectual fools, those persons educated beyond their own intelligence who are the "geniuses" incredibly learned in a few areas and incredibly handicapped in most other areas of human interaction. At another terminal, we have the apparently handicapped person, like Charles Steinmetz, who becomes what we term a genius. What makes the difference? Why does one smart person cause trouble while another solves problems? Why do feedback activities of evaluating and symbolizing become over- or underdeveloped? How does an injured organism bring itself into new balance to heal itself?

Educators generally tend to label the 1 percent of our population who have intelligence quotients above 132 as potential geniuses. Persons with an IQ of 125, plus drive and ambition, fall in the same category. Out of every 100 students, educators expect the 8 they grade "A" to be in this genius group, but educators are frequently surprised by the achievements of the 32 graded "B" and baffled by the accomplishments of a few of the 24 who received "C" and the ? percent who flunked out. This should not be too surprising to you, if you recall what was said in an earlier chapter about human behavior not being totally predictable. In addition, we have many late bloomers whose abilities are slow in developing. Much data supports the notion that the communicative capacity often is increased in persons who undergo sufficiently deep, wide, and varied experiences as their years go by.

Most so-called retarded readers, writers, and speakers are the products of educational deprivation, poverty, or the mental ill health that such deprivations tend to produce. Our methods of evaluating intelligence, i.e., traditional IQ tests, depend on the capacity to manipulate symbols. We might well raise a question of the potential effect on "intelligence" that increasing communication skill might have.

SOME GROSS SPECIFICATIONS FOR THE "PERFECT SPEAKER"

Consider the requirements postulated by our Western culture for the "best" possible speaker. Such an individual would be adequate in *all* his associations with all people. Even such noted speakers as John F. Kennedy, John Gielgud, or Winston Churchill were not always adequate to the situation. In addition to superb vision, hearing, tactual and other outer senses, the perfect speaker would need to have supersenses through which he could abstract from every event all relevant data to maximize the influence he can exert over the environment. His inner senses would need to be similarly sensitive to the functioning of his body. He might even be clairvoyant or have extrasensory perception. His knowledge and memory would be such that he could tap experience as necessary, but he would be able to use great discretion in their use, depending upon changing situations.

Our perfect speaker would incessantly probe apparent chaos and disorder to find structures upon which predictability depends, and he would be completely open-minded to new knowledge from a changing world. From such a reservoir would come a free flow of ideas, inferences, and predictions—always subject to the checks of critical thinking and all relevant to his purposes. He would not be inhibited in speaking or acting as the situation made it appropriate. However, he would balance feedbacks for frequent clarification of immediate and long-range goals. The endless energy of his healthy body and mind would produce continual advances from goal to goal.

Our miracle man would be able to focus attention on what is important to him and to others. He would be able to perceive both outside and inside himself, ranging from complex and detailed specifics to the most esoteric and theoretical abstractions.

Such a "perfect" communicator would be able to examine unlimited possibilities in his use of words and language to suit each situation. He would continually evolve new and more exact statements out of his vocabulary. His release of ideas would swiftly alternate between thoughtfulness and self-criticism as he derived more appropriate statements. He would be powerfully persuasive, but not overwhelming, because of his awareness of his own fallibilities. He would be accurate in pinpointing his own responsibilities and in attempting to assume them in cooperation with others, or as a leader in bringing people and their resources together.

Eventually, our model speaker fades into the misty sunset, because, as you well know, the perfect person just does not exist—despite the claims of some pretenders to the title. However, it is a useful goal upon which to build models of excellence. Any striving toward the goal, however, must be entered realistically.

SPEECH PROBLEMS REQUIRING THE SPECIALIST

As we've said, none of us is a "perfect" speaker. We are all subject to countless disturbances. We can *see* physical injuries, retardations, and abnormalities in others, feel them in ourselves, and sometimes take action to correct them. However, hidden reticences, hostilities, self-deceits, and other communication cripplers are what impede the necessary balancing of freedoms and restraints essential to effective communication.

While some children are born with deficiencies in those organs that must work together for communication, the limitations of inheritance and environment are seldom as serious as the limitations and handicaps into which we talk ourselves as we become older. Many have demonstrated that they can overcome disorders for which they were not responsible. Blind persons tend to make up for their defect in visual perception with sharpened sound, tactual, olfactory, and kinesthetic perceptions. Those who are born blind almost never learn to speak intelligibly, but the late Helen Keller—born both blind and deaf—learned to speak and communicate many inspiring ideas. Ludwig von Beethoven, the great composer of symphonies, created his most beautiful patterns of sound as deafness closed in. His masterful and lovely "Moonlight Sonata" was, in fact, composed after he was deaf. Abraham Lincoln made up for his educational deprivations by studies he imposed on himself. With his glorious sense of humor, he made assets of his homely features and awkward motions. Franklin D. Roosevelt, once a powerfully strong, athletic man, had been crippled by polio before he became spokesman for the Western World. The late Dr. Martin Luther King, Jr., "handicapped" to many people because of the color of his skin, gained the respect of the world as a leader and man of peace.

People who rise above their handicaps have determination and persistence in propelling themselves, for letting themselves be propelled, toward their goals. They have active feedforwards and effectively utilize feedbacks. They employ the superior intelligence expressed in the old adage, "Know thyself." It is not feasible here to list some 3,000 diseases to which human beings in childhood, adolescence, maturity, or senescence are subject. Most of these eventually involve the voice, breathing, or other parts of the communication apparatus. The weak and slurred speech that is characteristic of leukemia, the wild incoherence of schizophrenia, and the husky, erratic, and very labored speech of emphysema victims are only three examples.

The dangers that beset us from our high-velocity, crowded environments, from our poisoned air, polluted water, and highway accidents, continually mount. Repair of the resulting injuries and disabilities comes within the province of the medical specialists. But because so many disabilities involve the speech and communication apparatus, cooperation is required between speech and communication pathologists and the medical profession.

Five percent of the United States' population, or more than 10,000,000 people, suffer from some sort of communication disorder. Twenty percent of these are labeled stutterers, because their speech fluency is interrupted by blocks or repetitions in pronunciation. Fifteen percent have vocal disorders, such as breathiness, harshness, exclusively high or low pitch, or monotony. Forty percent have articulation or pronunciation difficulties. In about 20 percent of the children who have disorders, intelligible speech is delayed beyond expectations, while 5 percent cannot comprehend as they attempt to listen or read, or they are unable to express themselves orally or in writing. Language disorders like these constitute some of the various forms termed *aphasic*. In addition, 5 percent of the disabled population have a significant hearing loss. Thus many potentially capable communicators with much to contribute are unable to assume roles for which they would otherwise be qualified. Also at present, there are about 6,000,000 mentally retarded. The number of emotionally disturbed people whose ability to communicate competently is severely impaired runs into the millions.

Vast cadres of professionals are needed to differentiate the causes and to propose remedies for the many kinds of communication disorders. Furthermore, the statistics presented here include only the more severe barriers to communication. The relatively few available specialists are overwhelmed with the task of repairing the disorders, and little or nothing is done for those who are inadequate but not distressed.

An even greater potential loss grows out of the unused potential of people with superior intellect who have been deprived of cultural and educational stimulation or who are the victims of the pressures of their environments. Furthermore, children from better economic backgrounds often grow up without guidance and run wild, until they encounter the realities of a world with which they cannot cope. Inability of the ghetto child to communicate with society has already led to social violence. Inability of upper-class children to do so has led to neuroses.

Frequently severe physical damage occurs as the embryo develops and is born. Disease in a parent or accidents during birth may damage delicate brain mechanisms and result in cerebral palsy or damage to the parts of the brain upon which symbolizing depends. The injuries may not be recognized at the time of birth, and only later may be identified as causes of retardation and speech ineptitudes. The high fevers caused by childhood diseases sometimes have similar effects. Such injuries may be reflected in marked inability to recognize spoken or written words, inability to formulate statements for speech or writing or to spell or to remember.

The damaged child may become hyperactive, impulsive, or high strung; he may have poor muscular coordination, a short attention span, difficulties in reading, writing, speech, and arithmetic. Problems of perception may appear, which may result in "spotty" behavior—high ability in one area and total ineptitude in another.

The communication pathologist may classify the problems with which he works into one or more of the following three categories:

1. Physical injuries (traumas and lesions), structural defects in the organs that must work together for communication, or abnormalities in the development of these organs;
2. Deficiencies in isomorphism and evaluation;
3. Interferences in coordination, feedback, and regulatory phenomena.[1]

Few, if any, communication disorders are simple enough to be treated with exercises and drills. The relationship between physical and psychological communication disorders has become clear in recent years. We now know that communication disorders rarely exist alone; most affect personality in some way. Most psychological problems manifest themselves, at least in part, through speech. And both physical and psychological disorders frequently affect the operations of the body. It is for this reason that specialists in speech pathology have become general students of the human condition.

Communication problems in society may be viewed in much the same way, with causes sought in physical and social conditions as well as in the behavior of the individual. The assassination of President Kennedy can be construed as physical injury, while the equal-rights conflict is a social problem. The general student of the human condition is needed for "normal" as well as "pathological" man.

To help solve some of these problems, speech and hearing pathologists are now founding coordinating teams from various health and educational services to work to remedy the *whole* person in the environments out of which his communication disorder has grown. They are drawing on people from medical science, speech and hearing science, anthropology, linguistics,

[1] Elwood Murray and Joseph L. Stewart, "Communication Disorders Viewed as Disorders of Relationships"; paper delivered before special education groups at University of South Dakota, February 1965, and Idaho State University, February 1965; available at University of Denver.

psychiatry, and general semantics. They weld their skills to do a more effective job to improve man's mental well-being.

ISOMORPHISM AND MENTAL HEALTH

Mental health is as important as physical health. While neither can be considered as an absolute, a fair share of both kinds of health is essential to a productive, satisfying life. Physical disabilities need not impair intellectual output, for the world has known great speakers and thinkers who have suffered from physical disabilities. However, since competency and adequacy results basically from the degree of isomorphism between man and his relationships, mental illness must be considered as a basic threat to speech and thought. The most dramatic breakdowns in purposive communication occur among the mentally ill. Communication is not necessarily cut off entirely; but the mentally ill are so classified, because their isomorphism is so low that their symbolism appears irrational, obscure, or dangerous to others.

At the lower end on the scale of isomorphism, representing about 1 percent of the population, we encounter the so-called insane who apparently have little contact with reality for most of their lives. Such people are incapable of finding and expressing meaning that makes sense to others. In fact, many are like silent "vegetables" and must be moved physically from place to place. There is no way to "get through to" them, even though their sense organs may be without discernible defect. Their apathy or violent resistance make them liabilities to themselves and society. Yet recent psychiatric data indicates that defective communication is at the root of their trouble.

Farther along on the scale are those who misinterpret who they are and have little or no conception of time and place. They live in a world of delusion and fantasy. Because of their desire to escape a reality with which they cannot cope, they symbolize, literally talk themselves into living entirely inside their own minds. They are out of phase with the *what, how, when, where,* and *why* of life. Their speech may deteriorate into babbling incoherence or express wild fantasies; they may plunge into deep depression and silence, then suddenly shift to exhilaration and euphoria. Such tragic people are dramatic examples of communication and semantic disorders. Unhappily, there is little that present therapy can do for them.

A more reasonable approach to the communication problems that characterize mental illness is to prevent the problems by doing the very best job possible in extending the ability of everyone to talk sensibly of reality and to use speech to solve their personal and social problems. A look at our "normal" population, however, will reveal the magnitude of this task.

A large proportion of our population is quite competent in the routines of everyday living, though they exhibit a narrow range of flexibility in coping with new problems. These people tend to ignore "distant" events, which should be of importance, while they become overly disturbed by minor problems in present time. Many feel they failed only because they were "discriminated" against; they seek simplified explanations for complex problems. Others preoccupy themselves with trivia, perhaps devoting their entire lives to the cleanliness of a home in the hope that other problems will pass away. They conform to the "norm" because it is easy to do so. However, they may deteriorate when their system breaks down. They are usually poor listeners, read only what is absolutely necessary, say too little or too much, and often have difficulty seeing deeper relationships. They avoid precision in their own thinking and respond to issues with repetitive cants. They are easily "taken in" by smooth persuaders and are sheeplike fodder for charismatic movements and speakers. Their condition illustrates incapability to interpret feedback, with extremely vague feedforward. Of course, care must be taken in generalizing so as to avoid the famous quandary of "All the world is daft but thee and me, and I sometimes wonder about thee!"

Isomorphism is the goal of competent, productive, and creative people who want to maintain the ability both to respond to life facts and to abstract deeply. Such people represent the optimum, for they are able to use languages well, and their questions are penetrating. They make the most of their experiences and are fast and thorough—but highly selective—readers and intent listeners. By insisting on precision in their quest for information, they insure maximum flexibility in their choice-making. They are not prisoners of creeds, nor must they respond to events in unitary fashion. They represent the goal to be sought by those of us who would use language well. The meaning and order of that goal remain to be studied.

DANGERS OF INTENSION WITHOUT EXTENSION

People apparently derive their meanings and order their lives in two main ways. The individual tends to think and act as a result of his training and inheritance, but his orientation is made up of both *intension* (note the "s") and *extension*. Whichever predominates will determine effectiveness.

Those individuals who are oriented by *intension* react mainly to what they generate in their own minds. They often tend to make *connotations* (which are the feelings, fancies, and associations triggered by a word) the focus of their attention, so that evaluation of an event becomes more important than the event to which the word actually refers. Relationship of one word to others, as determined by grammatical rules, guides them more than their understanding of the relationships to which the word might guide them. On the other hand, persons who are oriented by *extension* separate connotation from *denotation*, which is the specific meaning that the word should consistently evoke. To distinguish further, whatever exists must *extend* in space-time, even if it is not accessible to abstraction by the senses. There are countless things that influence us whether or not we are aware of them. We must assume that these likewise *extend* in the *extensional* world.

Extensionally oriented people try to remain aware of the realities that influence them. If a physical object or situation is accessible, they point to it by the words they use. These people try to go beyond the connotations of words to the reality that the words are about. Instead of acting *as if* the words and the things they stand for are the same, they recognize that words are pointers and organizers of life facts and events. They do not place excessive faith in definitions, because they understand that all words have a connotation potential that can cloak an event in emotion. They attempt to improve the isomorphism between the word-maps and fact-territories. They seek connections among things while they relate them to what is stored in their minds, so that reality can provide an antidote to fantasy.

The more severe semantic disorders of the mentally aberrant illustrate intension without extension. For example, those who do not talk at all seem to have blocked out feedback entirely. The ones who respond irrationally seem to be unable to distinguish between the real and the imaginary. Both, however, separate their internal from their external environments. Their inability to communicate with reality often makes them dangerous to others, because they respond to what is not real. Intensionality and blocking of feedback is also found in those who feel aggressions, hostilities, inhibitions, rigid prejudices, or unreasoning fear in new and strange situations.

In each case, the victim shows some unawareness of reality and an inability to receive and process data from outside. He may interpret suggestions from a teacher as hostile arguments; he may assume that any group of people who are talking are talking about him. His wife's smile at another man may be interpreted as adultery. The young victim may not be able to see the potential future; he may respond only to the stimuli of the present. In every case, the victim of a semantic disorder responds more to the world inside his head than to the world outside. While it is important to process and evaluate the information received from the outside, it is foolish and dangerous to block information or permit it to become so distorted that it makes reality unreal. The word *permit* is used advisedly. Such authorities as Ernest Becker and Thomas Szasz regard mental illness as volitional or voluntary. The victim has used the inside of his own mind as a refuge from reality, and he has made a withdrawal from reality in order to simplify his understanding of the world. The withdrawal is not an accident, and it can be prevented by learning to manipulate language intelligently.[2]

THE CREATIVE POWER RELEASED FROM EXTENSION WITH INTENSION

As extensionality increases and isomorphism improves, intensionality becomes an asset rather than a liability. That this is possible is demonstrated by the fact that most of the population is teachable to some extent. Unfortunately, however, people often have to be coerced into extensionality, usually by dire experience and the shock of disaster. Intensionality is com-

[2] Ernest Becker, *The Birth and Death of Meaning* (New York: The Free Press, 1962). See also, Thomas Szasz, *The Myth of Mental Illness.*

fortable; extensionality is threatening. But intensionality, well coordinated with extensionality, provides depth to data from the outside world and can add the spark of creativity to man's thought.

Even in the best of times man has limped forward under a load of ignorance, superstition, fear, selfishness, plain human orneriness, ubiquitous tendencies to quarrel, and guilt about his own behavior. Arnold Toynbee analyzed twenty-five great civilizations that had disappeared and concluded that their demise resulted from the inability of their leaders to overcome the inertia of the citizens faced with the need to change. It was, apparently, easier to dream intensionally of the past than to take an extensional look at the present so as to preserve the future. Thus societies display the semantic disorders that afflict their individual citizens.

History measures a leader by his foresight. He is great if his prophesies come true and his actions prevent disaster. In semantic terms, his extensional look at the present synthesized with his intensional understanding of the past enables him to exert appropriate feedforward. Such men are often rejected by their society, for often they must speak of threat. Men such as Edmund Burke, John Quincy Adams, Abraham Lincoln, and Woodrow Wilson were attacked by their fellows but were proven correct by history. The "blood, sweat, and tears" speech of Winston Churchill before the disaster of Dunkerque showed how a speaker can mobilize the actions of other men to avert destruction. The exposure of the personality of Senator Joseph McCarthy in the radio-TV hearings in the early 1950's made it possible for thousands of people to make an extensional contact. One of the most constructive uses of communication is to increase extensionality. However, all too often it is used to perpetuate one man's intensional myths. The recent campaign for the presidency by certain unscrupulous minority candidates showed clearly that Americans are not immune to myths.

It is not possible or desirable to block the operation of intensionality entirely, because data from outside must be evaluated. The problem is to extend the amount and quality of the data received, and to train the mind to react to it—and not to a distorted image of it in the mind. Each individual has the tendency to reshape what he perceives to make it fit what he already knows. This distortion can make intensional the most precise extensional information. Learning can be enhanced by establishing situations that require that ideas be tested against reality and in which each individual learns to doubt his evalutions so that he can achieve capability to revise them when necessary.

The truly great speaker, artist, or scientist is never satisfied with his product. The man who succeeds has learned to doubt. He does not blame his failures exclusively on a "hostile" society. Rather, he understands the possibility of his own failure to acquire sufficient data and to use it effectively. The successful man utilizes feedback to develop feedforward, which tests the reality he perceives. The speaker or, in particular, the writer desires to make his communication correspond to the situation about which he speaks or writes. Conversely, the paranoia of extremist movements is the result of data that corresponds only to the inside of the communicator's mind. Those who predict accurately and propose solutions that work do not need paranoia as a refuge from reality. They need not blame others for their failure; they need only the ability to correct their feedforward and try again.

Creative artistry is somewhat more intensionally based. Yet, the creative artist is futile if what he produces strikes no chord in others. Even the artist must concern himself with the way others will respond, for to generate art only out of the inside of a mind is to guarantee critical oblivion. Art like this is produced all the time by inmates of mental hospitals. Such production may be considered mental ventilation, but it is not communication. It may make the artist feel better, but it can exert no influence on others, unless there is correspondence to the extensional world and the development of a common ground against which all perceivers can check reality.

MAJOR SEMANTIC DISORDERS

Severe semantic disorders are often caused by physical impairment—a destroyed larynx, a cleft palate, diseased lungs, deafness, severe birth injuries. Such disorders, of course, cannot be remedied until some physical repair is accomplished. In this section, however, we are concerned with the severe communication disorders that can be remedied by learning to communicate more effectively.

We are concerned with the child who has no brain injury yet is unable to recognize words or to formulate thoughts into coherent statements. We are concerned with those who cannot speak their thoughts fluently, those who stutter, and those who choose to remain silent because of fear. And we are concerned with those who say words well, but whose ideas are disorganized or are out-of-phase with reality. We are very much concerned with helping people who have the ability to speak; we want to better their communication. These people are not physiologically impaired, and any psychological problems are of a minor nature. In other words, we are concerned here about the average student or person who wants to better his oral communication skills. In short, this book is primarily directed to "normal" people who need to improve their speaking so as to improve their influence on society.

For example, those who try to help others may be defeated by *their own* inept communication. This is apparent in the efforts of parents, speech pathologists, psychotherapists, doctors, teachers, and good friends. However, it is increasingly apparent that each of us needs to help and be helped by others. We do this mainly through our communicative contact. Each of us, professional or nonprofessional, may help or injure others by the way we talk to them. One instance of this is stuttering, which appears to be triggered partly, at least, by the evaluations of others.[3] This disorder originates in the semantic environment of the child—the thoughtless labeling by parents,

---

[3] See Wendell Johnson, ed., *Stuttering in Children and Adults* (Minneapolis: University of Minnesota Press, 1955), Part II, ch. III, pp. 37–74.

peers, teachers, and others of the normal nonfluency that many children display in learning to speak. As the advice and pressures to improve mount, normal development in reading, speaking, writing, arithmetic, and other symbolizing is distorted or inhibited.

All too frequently trained personnel in health and educational institutions are similarly inept. Too little attention is devoted to readjusting the verbal output of people with problems. Those who are physically ill must learn ways to speak and think of their ailment realistically. Similarly, those who are mentally ill have become classified that way because of distortions in their ability to symbolize. Much of their therapy must be devoted to relearning ways to receive information from their environment and express sense in their talk about it.

Most of us find it awkward to talk with a handicapped person. We do not know whether to respond directly to his impairment or to ignore it. We do not know how much of his speech is a result of his own response to his difficulty. He, in turn, may interpret our remarks as hostile or patronizing and respond with hostility. Semantic disorders displayed in those who are mentally ill evoke a similar reaction. It is as though they come from an alien culture whose language we do not understand, while they remain in a state of frustration because of their inability to motivate in us the response they desire. The only commonality between any two people communicating lies in the extensional world. It is only when both parties to a conversation learn to refer their talk to external life facts that a degree of understanding can be achieved.

There is a tendency among people to evaluate others. Our own behavior is often a standard against which we judge the people around us. We call those who are not interested in the things we are "apathetic." We call those who dress differently "hippies" or "clods." We call those who disagree with us politically "fools," and we have choice epithets for people of other races and religions. Most of us find it hard to avoid evaluation, and most of our evaluation is totally intensional. When an associate verbalizes a problem to us, we are quick to condemn him for getting into trouble in the first place, and we are almost as quick to prescribe a cure. Rarely can we accept deviation and difference. It is almost as though the word "different" implies some kind of vertical scale. A person cannot be "different" without also being "better" or "worse."

Because of this tendency to overuse evaluation, most people soon learn to keep some kind of a mask up, as a defense against evaluation. Most of us are afraid of social situations because we do not wish to expose ourselves. Most of us are unwilling to concede a "hang-up" because we know that the admission that we are troubled will evoke an evaluation from someone, and the evaluation will very likely ruin our chances to achieve our goals. As a result, most of us, at one time or another, find ourselves in a situation of "quiet desperation," quite unable to ask for help because we are fearful of what others will say to us in return. The social fear that comes from defective communication can be considered the major *semantic disorder*.

Semantic disorders thus permeate the entire population, preventing people from realizing their goals and objectives and reducing their effectiveness in society. Perhaps the most prevalent type of semantic disorder, one which affects all of us, is *identification*. It appears generally in one of three forms:

I_1 is the tendency of people to identify themselves with a teacher or parent and base their behavior on what that person would have done.

I_2 is the tendency to identify with the hero in a book or play and to develop the emotions and values of that person.

I_3, the most prevalent, is the tendency to confuse responses to words with the responses to the things the words stands for.

Each of these represents a refuge from life facts, a way to avoid or reconstruct reality.

Whenever a person responds to the stored memory associated with a word, rather than the life fact that the word ostensibly points to, there is a strong possibility that isomorphism will be blocked. Words are indicators, pointers, and devices used to make the manipulation of data more complete. Those people who will not talk of "cancer," because of their fear of the *word,* will be quite unable to cope with the phenomenon of cancer. Those who spin words into webs and respond to "conspiracy," "revolution," or "disaster" will be forced into an intensional bind that will deny them the ability to predict events with a high degree of probability, and, hence, they will not be able to cope with them very well.

I_3 insidiously intrudes on our evaluations to block our thinking. This is especially true in our reactions as we listen to, read, or speak words. Many persons have permitted this semantic disorder to determine their careers and to continue throughout their lives to restrict the fulfillment of their potential.

To recognize the power that I_3 exerts is not easy, because without careful introspection we may not be aware of what is happening. We tend to remember the reinforcements of reward and approval when we were learning to speak, spell, write, and read, but we tend to suppress the experiences of failure, punishment, derision, and disapproval. We continue to confuse what *was* or what *might be* with the *now* of today. In short, I_3 keeps us in a state of intensionality.

We must rely upon examples, if we are to be able to understand, and hence do, anything about the I_3 disorder. Soldiers frequently faint while waiting in line to be vaccinated. Their I_3 may be confusion of the piercing of a needle with the imagined piercing of a bullet, or they may simply fear a needle. However, our abstracted inference is from a possible future situation *as if* it were occurring at the present. The soldier does not respond extensionally to check for differences between the present and previous situations of which he has memory and from which he might be abstracting. He reacts as if what he imagines might happen in the future were the same as previous situations wherein he was in pain from some injury.

Psychologists tell us that no experience is completely forgotten and always has the potential to affect perception, evaluation, and action. It is because of stored memory that communication has such a high potential to motivate human behavior. Negatively, communication can cause confusion through an I_3 response. For example, confusion is present if your mouth begins to water as you read the following: "I just had a most delicious breakfast: buttermilk pancakes with plenty of butter and pure maple syrup, a perfectly fried egg, real country sausage, and coffee with thick cream. Was it good!"

You might expect your mouth to water if you could see and smell the food, even if you were only slightly hungry. But the salivation induced by the written or spoken word is the *as if* identification behavior—a response which has no isomorphism to the here and now.

I_3 can be compared to the conditioning of reflexes in the familiar experiment by Pavlov, the famous Russian psychologist. Pavlov harnessed a dog in such a manner that he could measure the secretion of saliva. When food was brought within sight of the dog, saliva was always secreted. Each time the food was presented, a bell was rung. When the dog associated bell and food, the bell ringing was sufficient to evoke secretion of saliva. This identification response in the dog did not cease until after he had been "fooled" eighteen times!

Advertising provides unlimited examples of this semantic conditioning. Consider such trade marks as *Carnation* milk, *Finish* detergent, *Pet'M* dog food, *Long-Last* mascara, *Candlelite* lighting. The seller's product is presented by *word association* with what has previously given, and hence will continue (through inference) to give, satisfaction to the prospective buyer. Advertising also uses subtle persuasions by presenting exciting color photographs of a desirable way of life to lead us *unconsciously* to seeing a situation the same as that presented. We are directly led into the hidden I_3 in which the advertised products *equals* (=s) the desired (fill in your choice), or (another beautiful consequence), etc.

Belief that whatever is, actually *is,* and belief that whatever is not, *is not,* acts to sell a product that is purported to prevent undesired occurrences or to remedy some unpleasant condition, such as headaches, "sour stomachs," or sniffling colds.

Many of us do not notice how prone we are to buy the definition rather than the real product. We find ourselves dedicated to—and living by—a logical, tight verbal system in which definitions fit together into ideologies and philosophies. Each incorporates a rhetoric and persuasion that, through I_3, dominates the lives of whole societies.

In this changing world, complexity is so great and chaos piled so high above the tall structures and organizations that there is no verbal system in which we may implicitly believe for all time. The communists are finding this out through their ponderous dialectical materialism from which they are having to deviate broadly. Belatedly, practically all the great religions are now recognizing this, and are slowly coming together in efforts to update and correct their massive verbal-philosophical structures. The reform we must have will be greatly expedited if we can achieve flexibility from the extensional orientation.

In industry, government, and education, flexibility is more apparent. We can solve our problems only to the extent that we evaluate from the basis that no process is *identical* with another process, and no process is *identical* with itself.

Another semantic disorder, severe in its consequences, occurs with the *is* of predication. In I_3 we equate a noun or pronoun (the subject) at the level of abstraction with another noun, e.g., "Man is an animal." The *is* of predication equates a noun (the subject) with a general characteristic (an adjective), evoking a private allness at a point on a scale far different from that which the sender intended, e.g., "John *is idiotic*," "Snow *is white*," "Love *is wonderful*," "Mothers *are good*." Such examples of the *is* of predication are ordinarily innocuous, but they are damaging to the extent that they stop thought, discourage discrimination, and induce misunderstanding. Other examples can stop many conversations or evoke heated arguments, which may develop into outright conflict: "Colored people *are inferior*," "Politicians *are corrupt*," "The president *is bigoted*."

History documents scores of situations in which the use of the *is* of identification has disturbed whole nations and brought terrible consequences. For example, "He *is* a sabbath-breaker" (Christ); "She *is* a witch" (Joan of Arc); "He *is* an atheist" (Spanish inquisition). Many necessary reforms have been thwarted by being labeled "That *is* communistic," or "That *is* un-American."

A third semantic disorder, called *allness,* is also influential in blocking the extensional orientation. Whether explicit in such statements as "He *is* a (all) criminal" or "That *is* (all) bad" or "Business *is* business (all businesses are the same)," the silent *thinking* implies finality.

A difference between I_3 and the *ises* of predication is illustrated by the statements "John is a fool" (I_3) and "John is foolish" (predication). The allness of the forms may not be intended in an absolute sense. In the latter sentence, the statement is open to many degrees of "foolishness," but receiver and/or sender may be thinking *all.* Both block out the *is not* which close inspection of the facts reveals in almost every *is.* In a proper evaluation, the *is not* must always be considered, because avoidance of allness leads to explicitness and greater extensionality by forcing a look at now rather than at words about now.

A sort of double *allness* is implied in the either-or fallacy. While allness ties our thinking to a complete identification and only one perspective, either-or binds us to two ways, one usually the opposite of the other. A situation must be "either (all) good or (all) bad." "There are two sorts of people, the haves and the have nots." "The proposed law either is or is not socialistic." Everything is either black or white—and no attempt is made to discriminate among the many shades of color in between.

Whenever the voice and attitude imply *all,* we must look below the superficiality for a not-so-hidden allness assumption interfering with evaluation. Up to a point, there may be credibility that should not be ignored. The static allness may not even be in the context of the words; instead it is often carried in the silent levels below consciousness, where it still can block the forward progression of discussion.

At this point, we must point out especially that the semantic disorders as defined here are disorders of the underlying silent abstracting, ordering the abstractings, and evaluating. They are the enemies of sanity and, in principle, dangerous. *Is* and *allness* words need not be detrimental, when they do not contribute to misevaluation. When the talk concerns unimportant and routine matters, overly precise statements would be obnoxious. The use of *is* should be reduced in direct proportion to the importance of the situation to the person who evaluates it, and according to the necessity for accurate and precise statement.

Qualifying statements such as "In my opinion," "From what was said," "As I see it," or "Perhaps" are frequently necessary, but their overuse becomes awkward if not ridiculous. Hence, it is necessary to retain the style of the language, while training the mind to a more satisfactory interpretation of it.

I_1 and I_2 represent an aggregation of many semantic disorders rolled into one. In a sense, these two forms of distress are the normal man's schizophrenia. There is nothing more pathetic than the middle-aged ex-football star who fancies himself still an athlete; the effete, acneed youth who regards himself as a great lover; the uneducated man who regards himself as an intellectual. Many studies have indicated that children try to pattern themselves after models which they find either in life or literature. While some modeling is, of course, quite desirable, taking refuge in the character of another person is most dangerous. We must examine people and take from their life style those characteristics which are *useful* and *doable*. Extensionality, however, requires that we make a judgment about the compatability of the characteristic we admire and our own life style. Awareness of I_1 and I_2 can act as a brake on the rampant tendency to borrow life styles and may, perhaps, prevent our eventual refuge-taking.

Those with semantic disorders emit signals.

1. They may talk too little or too much.
2. They may keep their conversation on the same topic or the same level.
3. They may become aggressive in their attacks on others, defensive when their own ideas are challenged.
4. They may resort to euphemism in order to avoid unpleasant topics.
5. They may become gross in their talk about horror, distress, or sex.
6. They may become excessively personal and bare too much of their lives to casual acquaintances.
7. They may discover panaceas and become true believers; selling a creed like vegetarianism, general semantics, or a particular brand of religious or political commitment, as a solution to everyone's problems.

Each of us will do some of these things, some of the time. But the person who does one or more of them consistently reveals his semantic disorder, and is communicating a request for help. For many of the people around us (and perhaps for ourselves), future adjustment and capability depend on how others respond to their request and on their eventual development of the capacity to talk about problems as they exist in life, extensionally, without the necessity to resort to intensional refuge, avoidance, evasion, fear, anxiety, or mental illness.

SUGGESTIONS FOR DISCUSSION

1. The word "isomorphic" has been used extensively throughout this book. Do you have an operational definition for it? How similar must an idea be to the fact in order for it to be isomorphic? What is your attitude on borrowing terms like "isomorphic" from the sciences and applying them to studies like speech?
2. Is an isomorphism a one-to-one relationship, a point-to-point relationship, a relationship of picture to thing, a relationship of abstract picture to thing? Or what?
3. Have a beauty contest (if yours is a coed school). Have each man in the class select the most "beautiful" girl. Have each one prepare an anonymous list of the criteria he used for his selection. Combine the lists of criteria, agree on a common list, and run the contest over again. Was it any easier to pick a queen after you had agreed on the criteria? Does this help explain why it is so difficult to handle questions of value? Try some other judgment questions, such as the criteria for choosing a course; the qualities of an outstanding professor; the characteristics of a good student (your instructor might want to participate in this one); selection of a student body president or a president of the United States, etc. Remember, your job is to agree on the criteria *first!*
4. What is the relationship between intelligence and communication skill? Do you think the best talkers are the brightest people? To what extent does our society base its evaluations of people on the way they talk? There is some reason to believe that people who come from ghettos or poverty areas have difficulty competing in school because the school system is rooted in middle-class speech styles. What is your attitude on this idea? If you agree with it, what are the implications for revision of public school curriculum, testing procedures, evaluation procedures?
5. Why does a clinician treat the "whole person," if only part of the person is damaged?
6. There are many good articles on the speech of the mentally ill. (See Brendan Maher, "The Shattered Language of Schizophrenia," *Psychology Today*, Vol. 2, No. 6, November 1968.) Read one or more articles and try to prepare a short brochure on the topic, "How Mental Illness Can Be Avoided Through Communication Training." This is a good group project.
7. One theory of mental illness declares that a person who is mentally ill doesn't suddenly start acting peculiarly. Rather, mental illness is an accentuation of a behavior already characteristic of the person. What do you think of this idea? If you were planning to become mentally ill, which of your behaviors do you think is likely to become accentuated? How does a psychiatrist use communication to diagnose mental illness?
8. Zorba, in *Zorba the Greek*, told his young boss that he was too reserved and needed "a little bit of madness." Is it possible to have a little bit of madness? Do

you? Your friends? From this notion can you derive any advice for success at communication?

9. Do you believe the folk-myth that geniuses are also "mad"? Does the "madness" of genius have anything to do with the "madness" Zorba was talking about?

10. Gather in groups and draw up a chart, putting mental health on one side and mental illness on the other. Now subdivide your chart so that you have headings "extensional behavior" and, "intensional behavior" on both sides under each main heading. Working together, list the characteristics of mental health and mental illness under the intensional-extensional classifications. What advice can you derive from this listing about "talking your way to mental health"?

11. Many psychiatrists believe that mental illness is a volitional act, that is, a person becomes mentally ill because he has been rewarded for being sick in childhood and chooses mental illness as a refuge from a reality he cannot face. What are the rewards for being mentally ill? What are the hazards? If one can will himself mentally ill, do you think he can, without assistance, will himself back to mental health? What conditions (social and otherwise) do you think caused people to choose the peculiar behavior? What are they avoiding? What is the price they pay for avoiding it?

12. Write a personal profile of yourself for yourself (don't pass it around) in which you identify your own personal I_1, I_2, and I_3's. If possible, pick a few and throw them, anonymously, into a hat. Is there any commonality among you?

13. How can an extensional orientation make you more isomorphic to your environment? If you were more isomorphic to your environment, would you be more sane? Is sanity merely a good relationship between a person and his environment? If so, can it be sane to be insane? Using your campus as an environment, what behaviors would you classify as most healthy? Which most unhealthy?

14. You go to the doctor and he says you have "chronic infectious rhinitis." You get worried about it and go to bed, and you suffer and prepare to meet your end, and generate all kinds of new symptoms. How is this like stuttering? What is a semantic disorder?

15. Prepare a brief handbook for the class that will explain how semantic training can make them more analytical, logical, and rational. What form would their training take? See if you can spin this handbook into a syllabus for a course called "Practicum in Semantic Training."

SUGGESTIONS FOR FURTHER READING

Paul Chauchard, "Speech and Consciousness," *Language and Thought* (New York: Walker and Company, 1964). This section contains some excellent material on verbalization of thought.

Israel Goldiamond, "Self-Control Procedures in Personal Behavior Problems," *Control of Human Behavior*, eds. Roger Ulrich, Thomas Stachnik, and John Mabry (Glenview, Ill.: Scott, Foresman Company, 1966). This psychology-oriented reading presents the problem of disturbed communication in the light of a different discipline.

John R. Kirk and George D. Talbot, "The Distortion of Information," *Communication and Culture,* ed. Alfred Smith (New York: Holt, Rinehart and Winston, 1966). This is an extension, with different examples, of our topic in this chapter.

Thomas S. Szasz, *The Myth of Mental Illness* (New York: Hoeber-Harper, 1961). Dr. Szasz presents some remarkable information about people choosing mental illness as a tension release. His book also gives a good insight into people's semantic mental health.

9

The Improvement of Isomorphism

In Chapter 7, we discussed the principle of isomorphism and how it relates to effective speech communication. In the preceding chapter, we discussed its relation to the common communication disorders. Our goal, as you'll recall, is to improve speech communication, so in this chapter we will examine some ways in which to improve isomorphism, which is one aspect of betterment.

Obviously, it is possible for someone to be trained to achieve an extensional orientation and to improve isomorphism. Several devices have been suggested to focus attention on *what, where,* and *when* and to divert attention from cosmic implication. Called *extensional devices,* these can be used as we listen, read, speak, or write. Thoughtlessness and impulsiveness become virtually impossible when extensional devices are incorporated into our daily language, because the devices serve as mental punctuation marks that delay our overt responses, while we contemplate the meaning of the vague and ambiguous.

FIVE EXTENSIONAL DEVICES

There are five basic extensional devices that we will consider in detail.

1. semantic indexing
2. semantic dating
3. The etcetera device
4. mental hyphens
5. quotation marks

Semantic indexing attempts to focus attention on the specific examples from which a generalization was formed, so as to clarify the similarities among them *and* to delineate the differences among them. Let's look at an example: John's home is a ranch-type, split-level in the suburbs; Fred's home is a cottage on the beach; home $_{106}$[1] is an apartment in a lake-shore high rise.

The three homes are similar only insofar as they donate a space in which people reside. They are different because of their shape, form, contents, location, quality, etc. Thus, the use of the concept-word *home* focuses attention only on the similarities among the three in our example, and it is foolish to assume that the similarity extends beyond the precise quality that enabled us to classify a living unit into the category of "home."

For example, teachers give "home" work to students. The assumption which underlies this practice is that a student has a place to go to inside the unit he calls home, where he can sit in a chair, at a table or desk, under a light, and may proceed with minimal interruption with his work. This assumption is quite safe for most middle-class children, but for the slum child, the lack of space, furniture, and privacy makes homework a mockery. Such children could be materially assisted in their academic progress if a way could be found to offset the differences in their homes. Meanwhile they are frustrated in their work if their teachers can perceive only the similarities between "home" for one child and "home" for another.

By the same token, if I were bitten by the dog $_{\text{Fido}}$ while the dog $_{\text{Rover}}$ greets me with effusive joy, I cannot absolutely assign either hostility or friendliness to the category "dog." The category may derive from appearance or from scientific analysis, but the qualities in it extend only to the precise definition. Or, in another example, Communism $_{\text{Moscow}}$ is behaving quite differently from Communism $_{\text{Peking}}$ or Communism $_{\text{Bucharest}}$. Thus, a general policy directed at "communism" may be only partially effective. In this case, the classification "communism" is less relevant than the classification "foreign nation," for each of these countries must be reacted to as a separate entity, since their separate behavior belies the label that we commonly attach to all three.

Generally, any proposition that extends beyond the precise requirements of a category or classification is the result of defective indexing. The use of indexing enables us to separate specific from abstract statements. For example, we may take the word *efficiency*, the meaning of which may be quite unclear, and trace it down to the specific statements involved in it.

efficiency$_1$	efficiency$_2$
Japanese whaling fleet	gas consumption
rendering process	sedans
Captain Ogo's ship	my Pontiac

[1] Semanticists usually raise the dates following the name of an object or situation; they lower the word or index number to specify place or other circumstance. On the following pages a few examples are given.

The word *efficiency* could be applied to each specific case. The communicator normally has only one case in mind, however, and to understand him it is necessary to discover *his* specifics. If this is not done, you have no choice but to respond to *your* specifics, which might be vastly different from what he has in mind. Naturally, the speaker also has a great responsibility in this area, and the effective speaker is highly cognizant of the principles of semantic indexing.

Semantic dating focuses attention on changes *in* a thing over a period of time.

Often our perception of another person (or event) is affected greatly by our initial contact, and by the words we use. But people (and processes) are in a state of constant change. Virtually every college student returning home for his first vacation break will recognize differences at once, and the old grad going to his reunion is often disappointed because his old friends are not acting as he expected them to.

Semantic dating provides the flexibility necessary to cope with our world of dynamic structures and processes, and it allows a basis for forming inferences and predictions. It enables us to adopt our statements and actions to a universe of changing processes in which no process is identical with itself in the next moment and in which no process is identical with another process at any time.

The home in September is different from the home in December. Measles on Monday is different from measles on Friday; The communism of 1967 is different from the communism of 1935. Student before the exam is different from student after exam.

Obviously, as the value differences are changed by the passage of time, the various reactions, responses, and behaviors have to be modified. Semantic dating requires flexible thinking and behavior patterning on the part of speaker and audience.

Perhaps the most frequent semantic disorder suffered by most of us is the inability to keep our assumption rooted in time. Many of our disappointments arise because our expectations are based on previous experience, and we are not set for the changes that have come about. Four examples will illustrate this point, as follows:

The man who refused to eat liver explained that, in his early years, his mother had forced him to eat tough and tasteless liver, because it contained iron which "was good for" him. The revulsion evoked expanded so that he continued to apply it to liver regardless of how or by whom it was prepared. Some 30 years later he was able to overcome much of his prejudice, when he applied semantic dating to a specific plate of chopped liver prepared for him by Mrs. Birnbaum.

A four-year-old child screamed frantically whenever anyone dressed in white came near. She refused to go into a room with white walls. During her first two years, she had undergone three painful operations in a room with white walls and had been attended by persons dressed in white. Not until many years later did she finally learn to discriminate among the different whites.

A 40-year-old man became panic-stricken when he crossed the U.S. border into a Mexican town in which he heard no English being spoken. As a boy he had lived in a German-speaking community. He was left out of playground activities, and he was physically beaten several times by older German boys. The fears engendered remained to distort any situation in which he couldn't understand what was being said.

An adolescent ghetto resident was unable to respond to on-the-job training, because it took place in the school that he hated because he had been expelled from it two years earlier.

Of course, one of our most frequent disappointments is political. A voter may be disappointed if his candidate is elected and then does not perform according to the creeds of an earlier day—which is somewhat like expecting the Democratic Party of 1972 to remain isolationist because of the policies of William Jennings Bryan.

Semantic dating can prevent gross misevaluation by ameliorating such attitudes as "I can't do anything like that"; "This is the way it is"; "No one likes me"; "The South will never integrate"; "He will never amount to anything." A vehement allness statement implies: "That's the way it *was* (or *is* or *will be*), PERIOD!" Allness, as we saw earlier, begets allness through reaffirmation of errors. The respect and awe evoked by a charismatic speaker may actually be only gullibility. "He knows all." AMEN! Such speakers, often handsome and possessed by resonant speaking voices and magnetic personalities, are reinforced by the nods of approval and applause from the multitude of uninformed who hold similar dogmatisms. The few who have doubts concerning the sincerity and credibility of what is being said often are too timid to disagree, or they do not feel sufficiently secure to ask the vital questions that would expose the "slanted" information, or they become apathetic toward the dogmatism.

Futile arguments and disturbances are triggered by dogmatic, allness statements, which violate the allness assumptions of others to the point where tension, name-calling, insults, and conflict congeal prejudices. In the intensity of emotional and senseless panic, individuals go berserk, and groups generate themselves into riots.

However, there is usually a modicum of truth in even the most dogmatic affirmations. If the receiver has sufficient extensionality to delay his reactions, he may see that the statement "has some truth in it." When he applies semantic indexing and dating, he can ask the kind of questions that would tend to reduce distortion. Such questions are asked in a spirit of inquiry seeking more evidence and accuracy. If the person who made the broad assertion is sincere, he will correct it to improve isomorphism; at least he will qualify his statement by "This is the way I saw it," or "As reported to me," or "The data and authority I have available indicates . . . ."He may then present his evidence. This kind of exchange may continue with mutual correcting of each other's assumptions. Even the ignorant listener need not be gullible, particularly if he has the ability to use the extensional devices. Constructive and creative inquiry can take place, to the extent that unreality actually may be blocked out of the discussion.

Argument can arise from interpretations of facts and the attended predictions. "The cost of living index went up 0.2 percent during February 1970" is a far less controversial statement than "The cost of living is skyrocketing." Creative reasoning proceeds best without debaters and public speakers who do not add to the extensionality of their audiences.

The young child particularly suffers from nonuse of extensional devices. This is clear if he begins to say "I can't spell"; "Geography is too much for me"; "I hate arithmetic"; "I don't like poetry." In failing to notice fears that language can build up in a child, we permit intellectual crippling that will consign the child to a life of mediocrity, or even to semiretardation. Parents and teachers often are unaware of the ways they can either injure or help a child through the use or nonuse of semantic indexing and dating. "Failure" must be rooted in "when" and "in what circumstances." Otherwise it pervades the child's whole being, and he begins to act like his label. Many inadequate speakers got that way because of nonindexed evaluations made by parents or teachers.

The child who finds himself in a vicious circle of antilearning attitudes at home, school, and in the neighborhood rarely can overcome the effects without special help. We think of the influences as being at their worst among deprived children of the slums and backwoods country, but they occur with startling frequency in the most affluent states where the devastation is often hidden or unacknowledged.

The semantic dating device is especially potent in broadening the range of choice for intelligent persons who find themselves in "ruts." This is particularly true of those whose education and experience are narrowly specialized. When they reach a peak of accomplishment in their speciality, excitement becomes impossible because they are not sufficiently broad to find new involvements. Their evaluation of their work as "important" made all other things "unimportant." Their "therapy" should include a reevaluation of other activities by applying indexing and dating.

Perhaps the point may be best exemplified by a rather lengthy story, in which the semantic dating device enabled a schoolteacher to break through into a full panoply of relational and creative thinking. As she thought of an object in time dimension, she thought of a tree as it was in 1942 and in its changing situation through to the present. A flood of memories and ideas were aroused by checking the same thing to two different times. In 1942, as a schoolgirl, she remembered the scrawny, misshapen Russian olive tree growing next to the sidewalk leading to her home. When she took a course in biochemistry, she became concerned about the health of the tree and speculated about its composition and history. As a high school senior, she was concerned about the several diseases and inroads of insects which the tree had undergone. Between 1942 and today, the tree has grown into a well-proportioned and beautiful structure. Thought of the tree recalled other trees along the sidewalk; the huge oak under which cars parked . . . the people who came and went in those cars . . . for various business or social occasions . . . her sister's beaus . . . the roses they stole when she was married . . . the activities of her brothers . . . the awful time when Jim was ill . . . other problems and crises that her family had met and won . . . or lost . . . their beloved dog killed by traffic . . . the zoning problems in the community as the population of the city expanded into their area . . . their speculations concerning the beautiful young woman who moved into their neighborhood and seemed to love their olive tree as she passed on her way to and from work . . . it was the oak which drew her attention as the leaves changed color . . . that was the fall of 1951 . . . and they wondered what had happened to her when she stopped coming by . . . but the war had started . . . and other things were affecting their lives . . . the issues raised by the war in Korea . . . the changing demands upon education after the Russians launched Sputnik . . . standing under the tree and hearing of the death of a president . . . another war . . . !

Ideas, fancies, theories crowded in by the score about the tree and other things as well. Her life was filled with drama, newly remembered excitement. By doing some research, with further processing of these materials into plot or other organization, with revision and editing, she had sufficient materials for significant speaking or writing! She could form these materials into a historical novel, a poem, a movie documentary, or express them in music. Her conversation was bound to be exciting!

This woman could mobilize practically all her memories and knowledge into a unity around any specific theme she wanted to develop. Each object was more than unity. It had its designation, but was isomorphic as it changed in time and space and creativity was expanded.

The et cetera device comes into use because, implicitly or explicitly, communicators must show recognition of the limitation of their words. Any statement that can be made about anything can only express a part of what there is to say. A famous contributor to general semantics theory used to use a simple apple in his demonstrations. He would ask what there was that could be said about the apple: about its composition, its origins, its appearance, its deterioration through time, its relationship to other fruits, to other things, to people. Invariably his students would agree that here was no object about which it was possible to say "everything."

The tendency of speakers and writers is to focus on stylization, on the use of words and their connections in order to express a message. So much effort is expended that, frequently, in their minds, a message becomes *the* message. They are, consequently, unprepared for argument, disagreement, variation in interpretation. A piece of literary criticism, for example, has validity for the person who writes it, while it is potentially meaningful to the reader as another perspective from which he can evaluate and make decisions about his own actions. It is not the whole story about the work, however, and the critic appears arrogant when he demands allegiance to his words. Use of an implicit *etc.* would permit him to accept both the inquiries and the objections of others. Let's explore some examples.

An expression of a political view is not a statement of fact. The assertion that "Rockefeller would make the best president" is a summation of the world of politics as one person sees it at the time he says it. It may not represent his view a month ago or a minute later. Furthermore, there is a strong likelihood that virtually every other person will view the political world somewhat differently, although "they" may also conclude, at the moment, that "they" too favor Rockefeller. There is really more that can be said about Rockefeller. Indexing and dating helps us to discover some of the facts that entered into the expression of the evaluation. The addition of *etc.* helps us to understand that the statement is limited in scope to one person at a given time, and can be amended by the person who made it or by anyone else—including Rockefeller himself.

Adding the *etc.* indicates to us that words are only representations of thought which cannot capture the infinite relationships of which the mind is capable. While it is somewhat awkward to punctuate oral discourse or written text with *etc.,* it is a good idea to adjust your speaking and writing to include a silent *etc.* at the end of each thought unit.

Mental hyphens is the fourth basic extensional device to help us improve isomorphism. The hyphen is a warning to us to check our words closely to see that they define events and relationships rather than static entities. For example, we speak sometimes as though mind and body were separate units, each operating independently. The *and* that separates them seems to make this distinction. To show the relationship of mind and body, the hyphenated word *mind-body* better expresses the connection. Movement in space and time is more accurately expressed as space-time. It is possible to avoid arguments about which is more influential, heredity or environment, merely by connecting heredity-environment to show that each influences the other. Even the title of this book, *Speech: Science-Art,* uses this device to show that the artistic use of language cannot be separated from the scientific aspects of human communication codes, nor can the science become so precise that communication can ever be lifted entirely from the artistic base in the human mind.

Many of our English expressions make use of hyphens. The word *clear-cut,* for example, does not mean "clear" and "cut." Its meaning is more accurately expressed as "cut clearly," but even then, the adverb *clearly* receives less emphasis than the verb *cut,* and whole expression is adjectival in value. The relationship between *clear* and *cut,* because of the hyphenation, makes a new thought concept that cannot be expressed by any other relationship of the two words. In speaking and writing it is imperative to maintain connections where they exist, and not to allow words to mislead you into the belief that inseparable elements can be isolated either for conversation or study. This problem plagues research in human behavior, because in order to study a phenomenon closely, the phenomenon must be separated from the whole unit in which it is found. Yet the study of the phenomenon separately does not permit total reconstruction of the whole. Continued use of hyphens, either explicitly or implicitly, will help you to remember that often our separation of elements is a matter of linguistic convenience, which has no necessary correspondence to the reality of the thing about which you are speaking.

The use of *quotation marks* also enables you to build more isomorphism into your language. Words have many meanings, and the dictionary provides only a historical record of what words have meant. As we've said, it is not a catalog of current word use but is, instead, more of a historical document. In any given context, a word can take on a specific meaning which may differ from that given it by a listener. To show this differentiation in speaking, skilled conversationalists employ inflection of the voice. By utilizing the wide range of vocal power, you can, in your speech, reveal delicate and subtle nuances in meaning. And you can manufacture your own metaphors at will merely by endowing your words with meaning particular to the given context.

For example, the word *tough*, for most people in the "over 30" generation, means "hard," "difficult," "knotty," etc. But for yesterday's "teeniebopper," the word took on the meaning of "splendid," "delightful," "superb." What does it mean to you, today? There is no problem in understanding which meaning is meant when we listen to people speak in context, but redacting the speech—putting it into writing—takes the flavor from the word. The only understanding we can get comes from our own experience with the word. Thus, unless the new meaning is indicated in some way, we are in danger of misinterpreting messages. "Hey, that's tough!" would at least call our attention to the word and indicate that, perhaps, there is something special about this usage. However, this idea brings up that nasty concept of assumption again, and this often leads us blindly into trouble.

We tend to make two dangerous assumptions in our speaking and writing. First, we assume that our listeners will understand our understanding of relationship, despite the fact that our language expresses a dichotomy. When we talk of body and mind, we can affect the body, and it can affect our mind. In other words, one may work on the other, and the entire thing may work in reverse. Second, we assume that whatever specialized meaning we give to a word will be expressed clearly to the listener by the word itself. Unfortunately, only a good perception of the context of the word will convey the appropriate impression of meaning. We can assist perception of context by putting written words that have special meanings in quotation marks, and by speaking special-meaning words in such a way that our senses can at least perceive speciality and our audiences will look for new meaning. Let's look at some examples that hit close to the classroom.

Courses listed in college catalogs are classic examples of both verbal hair splitting and failure to show special meaning. The obvious separation of psychology and sociology or of English and speech encourages a kind of academic xenophobia, where disciplines contend rather than cooperate in the search for answers. Such words as *behavioral* and *laboratory* may mean entirely different things depending on which department uses them. Even the word *college* can have special meaning—as a part of a university, a separate unit, a political function, or a high school extension. But, this is a narrow example.

Most of society's serious issues—that is, poverty, racial integration, war —do not permit functional separation of the political, economic, and socio-logical issues. To approach those problems from only one perspective will lead to warped or incomplete conclusions. Mental hyphens—political-eco-nomic-sociological problems—each indexed and dated into operational ex-istences, help to bridge the gaps by revealing the interdisciplinary imperative of most problems. Even this book, written for students of communication, has not been able to separate the problems of speaking and writing. Further-more, many of the words we use, like *feedback* and *isomorphism,* have special meanings within communication which must be indicated, simply because these terms are used in other disciplines to mean other concepts.

It is rarely necessary or feasible to use *all* the extensional devices— *semantic indexing, dating, et ceteras, hyphens,* and *quotation marks*—at the *same time,* except when a new idea requires immediate and clear definition so that a line-of-thought does not start off ambiguously. But, the need for their use increases as more high-order abstractions are used, in order to pre-vent the receiver from pursuing a completely different line of thought than was intended.

Some speakers, captivated by methodology, overuse the devices and apply them overtly to *all* their statements, revealing a kind of hairsplitting that makes the speakers appear ridiculous, and which antagonizes the listeners. After reasonable understanding has been established, sparing use should be made of the devices, depending on the potential ambiguity of what is being said. Qualifiers such as "According to my information," "It appears to me," "Can you give me evidence of that?" "As near as we know," "You mean that as an inference," lead to dullness in style and "turn off" the listener. Skillful composition, based on semantic understanding, allows you to blend your concepts and symbols together into meaningful isomorphism.

The extent to which you openly use the devices depends on the require-ments of the situation and (after their use becomes a fine art with you) upon experience and intuition. This applies particularly to extemporaneous speakers because writers must plan the use of qualifiers beforehand. This book, itself, is an example of the quandary faced by communicators. There may be little consistency apparent in the use of extensional devices. We "think"—but not "always"! Their use depends on how we, the writers, anticipate the responses of you, the readers.

In our present undeveloped state of the communication science-art, we doubt whether complete accuracy and consistency is feasible. Speakers and writers must assume that there is some sort of semantic agreement with their audiences. We *assume* that both you and we *know* we are not speaking the *absolute truth* about *everything!*

As we really do not often deal in absolute truths, it might be well to look at some other communication problems around us. And, while you're reading, keep in mind that our chapter topic is "The Improvement of Isomorphism."

THE INDEXING OF SILENCES

We are surrounded, figuratively, by the heavy artillery of mass communication, and every single day our minds are the targets of a deafening barrage of words. The small-arms fire of personal communications peppers us daily, adding to the massive semantic attack. We have only thin shelter against this verbal bombardment, and many of us fall victim to some degree of "battle fatigue." On the job, through the mass media, even in relaxations, our days are spent trying to sort out meanings from words. The impact of semantic reaction upon semantic reaction sets off self-reflexiveness and contributes to our tensions. Our own talking escalates the word war. Tensions build as we permit inference to build upon inference, for our positive feedback may run wild if it is not controlled. We can get carried away with our own words or become locked in by them, if our negative feedback becomes hypercritical or dogmatic. Temper and depression characterize our modern communication.

Busy executives, teachers, and others whose work depends upon constant face-to-face encounters with others are hard put to find time for relaxation and meditation. Honest silence is hard to come by, yet without some time for silent reflection, semantic saturation—which may be looked upon as a sort of communicator's combat fatigue—may set in, and alertness will be dulled and inefficiency increased. A point may be reached where silence is intimidating and solitary thought becomes threatening.

Without quiet and calm relaxation, however, we are unable to examine our data processing and correct the ordering of our symbols. We may remain insensitive to the manner in which we project the distorted silent assumptions we have generated from our internal environment.

The reduction of inner turmoil helps us become conscious of abstracting, and it permits us to analyze the symbols we use as we think. For this reason, most of the great religions set time aside for meditation, contemplation, and silent prayer. Contrived silence permits development of abstraction into new perspectives, which offer insights into error and help us to avoid acting as if our inner world were perfectly true and correct.

Silences also communicate, and no two silences are identical. The speaker must perceive silence with the differences among them. Here are examples:

Rusty, watching the situation comedy "George and Vera" on his television set at 8:30 P.M. is not the same behavioral unit who perceives that program at 8:42 P.M. He is not the same unit as the final commercials roll at 8:58 P.M. To the actors, of course, he is a silent perceiver.

Bill is speaking to an antique automobile club, and he is not the same Bill who was speaking to them five minutes before. Likewise, his audience of five minutes earlier (tired-bored) is not the same group now (entertained-enthused).

The meaning of silences differs for each individual, and in the same individual from moment to moment. Speakers often grossly misinterpret the meaning of their listener's silence. A speaker should concern himself with the meaning of silence and catch its nonverbal cues. He must cultivate the ability to understand what his listeners communicate to him by their silence. He can do this best, perhaps, by understanding the wide range of potential meaning in silence. A listener must appropriately interpret the silence of a speaker who is asked a question. His silence may mean confusion, desire to think out an answer, or it may merely reveal the normal speed at which his mind operates. A writer projects to a silent audience, and one that he never sees. Few people, apart from editors, "talk back" to books, so the writer must predict the state of mind of his silent reader. The reader is "spoken to" by a writer who can only speak through the silent symbols on the page. Any questions must be answered by the words that are there, not by direct contact with the writer.

There are more ways of communication than through the ear. The eye, the skin, the nose, and mouth present messages to us that are in many ways more important than those that come through the ear. Words can be stylized. Often they can be used to conceal, rather than clarify, messages. What is seen and touched, tasted and smelled, may convey more of honesty. Effectiveness in communication is, in many ways, dependent on extending the number of senses employed in the act of communication. Skill as a listener implies skill as a viewer, a toucher, a taster, and a smeller, for it is in the perception of silent data that messages about the integrity of the communicator are to be found. Silent understanding is one way to penetrate the "wall of words" and to help improve total communication. But, let's look further now that we have established *silent understanding* as an aid to bettering communication.

RELAXATION WITH AWARENESS: THE ECONOMY OF ENERGY

Self-reflexiveness generates tensions. What someone says, what we read or remember, a word, or even a look may start a chain of semantic reactions inside our head. We can silently talk ourselves into hostility, anger, rage, love, dependency, depression, etc.; we place ourselves in a variety of evaluative states that are often inappropriate. Intension that blocks extension incites us into committing stupidities and causes increased tensions. Control of silent reflection, however, can have the reverse effect, enabling us to receive and process data more clearly.

Controlling intensional symbol manipulation by constant input of extensional data helps keep general tension at a minimum and, conversely, enables a more effective mobilization of tension where necessary. When danger is imminent, all human resources must be mobilized to assist in overcoming the *particular problem*. Unspecified tension, however, can turn into terror and render a person incapable of coping with threat.

The impotence we sometimes feel at times of great crisis illustrates this point. The missile crisis of 1962 left most of us in a state of shock. Forces were loose in the world with which we were powerless to cope. Sending telegrams to the President, and close attention to the news media were not particularly satisfying activities, and, in fact, probably increased tension. Our fate was not in our own hands, or was it? It was possible during those critical days to work oneself into a state of panic. Internal manipulation of symbols could lead to thoughts of total holocaust and complete destruction. The feeling was, perhaps, something like the feeling of the man who is afraid to ride in an airplane, though he is not afraid to pilot one. The passenger in an airplane has no control. His destiny resides in the skill of the pilot and the mechanical quality of the plane. The pilot, on the other hand, has a number of specific alternatives for action. He is skilled in manipulating his machine and totally trained in what to do in times of crises. In fact, part of every pilot's training includes actual emergency situations, as well as simulated ones. When danger threatens, all the passenger can do is become tense and fearful, while the pilot can take action.

Understanding of these simple extensional facts sometimes helps alleviate tension. As another example, the act of electing a man president vests tremendous authority in the hands of one man. Once he is in office, it is necessary to observe him act with the knowledge that your choice has been made. When protest or complaint is in order, contemplation of the most effective and efficient channel is far more useful than thrashing wildly around with demonstrations and picket lines. The objectors to the Viet Nam war, for instance, reveal generalized tension in their protests. They do not focus on a kind of action that would bring about a change in policy or in the activity of their leaders. Vain and blind protest most often heightens tension in the protestors while it polarizes antagonism to them and subverts attainment of their goals.

Virtually any interpersonal act carries with it a degree of tension. There are some people who are completely threatened by confrontations with others. They are unable to exert an influence, because their fears make them feel that pleasure will make them appear foolish, and thus destroy their "image." Skill at interpersonal or public communication comes from satisfactory management of tension; through an understanding of how to control intensional tension with extensional data in order to achieve focused and intelligent behavior.

The amount of energy that can be mobilized against a given obstacle varies in each individual. Efficiency is limited by biological inheritance, metabolism, digestion, and other factors of physical health. Efficiency is further limited by the effects that intensional data processing can have on the physical body. For instance, internal stresses and strains can severely impair the body and prevent it from achieving its full potential to act. Generalized tension over a long period of time results in a state known as anxiety, in which the individual is prevented physically and psychologically from coping with the problems that he confronts in daily life. Any major threat, physical and social, can throw the person into a state of confusion. The end product is mental illness, which is an evasion of normal behavior.

Magda Arnold has described four levels of efficiency of *general* and *specific tension*. The greater the general tension the less brain and muscle energy will be available to focus on the work demanded by society. The less the general tension, the more specific tension available for the work of the musician, the actor, the diagnostician, the orator, or the problem-solver. As a rule, general tension concords with semantic disorders and leads to mental illness. Arnold's four levels are:[2]

1. *Low general tension, High specific tension:* affords greatest efficiency in skills and problem-solving. It is the level of greatest adequacy and productivity, characterized by minimal communication difficulties. Spontaneity, creativity, and high intelligence permits utilization of semantic devices as needed in associations with others.

2. *Moderate general tension, Moderate specific tension:* leads to effort greater than achievement. The person is usually adequate in situations of ordinary difficulty, but not so capable in confronting the unusual. Using semantic devices may be especially helpful in retraining him to keep from settling into ruts. This person is capable of learning, and represents the closest approximation to the norm.

3. *High general tension, Low specific tension:* leads to inefficiency; effort is disproportionate; disturbed communication is displayed in many situations. This person needs guidance, counseling, and close but permissive supervision. He is likely to regard semantic devices as a religious creed, if he does not reject them totally.

4. *High general tension, No specific tension:* characterizes a sick person. His behavior is characterized by accidental and awkward specific tension, emotional outbursts, or disorganization of behavior. Communication is often bizarre and nonisomorphic. He cannot comprehend that he is ill, and he needs clinical and psychiatric services.

Maximum alertness and ability to cope is found in the person who will take the time to correct his internal symbol manipulation by making it isomorphic with extensional data. He will be able to feedforward as a sort of rehearsal to behavior in ways that will give him a high probability of

---

[2] Magda Arnold, "Tension in Relation to Breakdown," in *Papers on Second Congress on General Semantics*, ed. M. Kendig (Lakeville, Conn.: Institute of General Semantics, 1943), pp. 209–230. Reprinted by permission.

predicting the outcome of his various acts. He continually corrects his thinking by applying extensional devices.

These tension concepts have important ramifications for speakers. Private speech and voice coaches employed by the famous for fabulous fees have long advocated relaxation as a part of the training process. They have devised methods for relaxing the muscle and mind so that greater contact with reality can be made. One of the main aspects of the relaxation process is the blocking out of irrelevancies. In front of an audience, a speaker is confronted with a wild melange of stimuli which may distract him from his goal. They may threaten him if he misinterprets them as hostility, or they may make him ineffective if he infers that they mean support. The speaker's attention must be focused on his message and on satisfactory interpretation of the feedback he receives from his audience. He cannot afford to be concerned generally about the impression he is making, for that would lead to a generalized tension and subvert the attention to his goals and objectives. Of course, this presupposes that the speaker has carefully thought out what he wants to accomplish. This, too, is involved in the relaxation phase.

A writer, however, has a number of opportunities to "warm up" before he communicates. As the ideas begin to flow onto paper, he may feel somewhat the same way that athletes do at practice. With each revision, his tension becomes more specific, until his final product represents the best job he can do of expressing the ideas he wants to express in ways that will make them understandable and acceptable to his reader.

The speaker, on the other hand, really has only one opportunity to approach his audience, although he has gained partial *warm-up* in composition and gains partial *warm-up* during practice phases. Nevertheless, his failure can be immediate, and he has few chances to correct. Consequently, he must be able to understand the possible range of positive and negative feedback, and be able to feedforward to control his own behavior. He must provide himself with options, i.e., enough ways to approach his task to cope with whatever the audience may do. He must be set to focus tension on both the best and the worst possible situation. In a sense, the speaker must be relaxed while he speaks—in the sense that he is no longer concerned or threatened by anything other than the elements of the communication situation. He must be able to bring his total mind-body to focus on the problem of communicating effectively.

Once he has achieved a relationship with his audience, his task becomes easier. As he experiences feedback he becomes more accustomed to the range of behaviors of a *specific* audience, and his tension becomes even more specific. He begins to use words, body, and eyes to make even closer contact. He can interpret the frown in the second row as a request for more information; the wriggling in the third row as involvement, not boredom. He will come to understand that the fixed gaze of the person sitting in the fifth row is not close attention but something akin to sleep. He is able to bring information to bear on his topic, and on his listener. He evolves a speaker-topic-listener relationship in which the major elements of the speech act are working in synchrony.

Such rapport is impossible when a speaker is so centered on his own fears and anxieties that he cannot separate them from his task. Whether or not the audience "likes" a speaker is really immaterial. The question is, Will they understand and believe? By the same token, in a social situation, liking may be a legitimate goal to which persuasive impact may have to be sacrificed.

The extensional devices are not panaceas for success in oral communication. They can act to improve it, however. To achieve the optimum of your own speaking skill, practice in the use of the extensional devices is necessary. This can be most effectively achieved through programmed contemplation, making use of your own silence to bring your intensional and extensional worlds into the closest possible harmony.

However, introspection is only part of improving communication. We've seen the need now for silence and for relaxation. Let us now go back to the noisy, action-world words and see how some betterment might be possible.

FROM INHIBITION TO SPONTANEITY

Movement and action in nature do not occur until the conditions of interaction reach a critical point. Once started, though, action continues to trigger further action until energy runs out or a restraint is imposed. Sometimes the sequence is as sudden, short, and violent as an explosion, while the action of an acorn becoming a full grown oak can take centuries.

Action may be interrupted or diverted by changes in the environment of the organism, change inside the organism, or interaction of change in both. Without the proper chemicals and moisture for example, the oak will slow down in its growth or die, while with the addition of fertilizer and water it will grow to greater height.

The process of progress is called *reflexiveness*. For most things on this earth, reflexiveness is relatively predictable. The chemist who makes the explosive can predict the influences one chemical will have on another. He understands what is necessary to trigger the explosion, and he can predict, relatively well, its outcome. The problem of insuring that the acorn will grow into an oak is somewhat more complex, for there more variables are involved. However, there is still a high probability that selection of the proper soil, treatment with the proper fertilizers, and consistent watering will lead to growth. Of course, if the explosive happens to land on the oak, the process is drastically changed. In any case, neither the chemicals in the explosive nor the acorn have any choice or decision-making capacity that will enable them to alter their fate. Only the human has the power to make changes from within. Only the human has the power to alter his own behavior in response to situations he perceives around him. In one sense, man's environment is at his mercy, while, as we've written earlier, man can also easily be at the mercy of his environment when he is stripped of his symbol and signal weapons.

Nowhere, though, is reflexiveness more characteristic than in the act of human communication. The human being is fantastically flexible. He has an almost infinite range of choices and decisions he can make. Because of this, many human encounters are relatively unpredictable. We really do not know what will trigger anger in another person or, for that matter, in ourselves. We cannot predict with accuracy the frame of mind even of the people we meet daily, nor can we assess with certainty what their needs are as they interact with us. Consequently, we must remain ready to change our own behavior to make it better adapted to changing conditions. Unfortunately, the information we get about changing conditions is also uncertain. We must learn about the extremes and the likely, and we must remain ready to adjust to both. An educated and trained policeman puts this important kind of information into operation every time he approaches a person suspected of a crime. The untrained, unskilled officer will react with violence. A trained professional at anything will consistently expand his skill. What separates a professional from an amateur, a dilettante, or a failure is capacity for constructive reflexiveness.

Behavioral looseness is essential to permit maximum constructive self-reflexiveness in communication. The speaker cannot be *locked in* to a policy from which he will not deviate. When he is, he is not too different from the growing oak tree. Perhaps this is why schizophrenics who have withdrawn into their own verbal world are often termed *vegetables*.

As words generate more words, the rules of grammar and habit become negative feedbacks. They restrict the output so others can understand and accept. When rules have not been well learned, the speaker's background is revealed, and it may alienate the listener. In some of the "intellectual elite," the rules may be so deeply internalized that the rules become ends in themselves—and the speaker may be unable to adapt his speech to practical, down-to-earth situations. In sophisticated speakers, awareness of vocabulary and grammar hovers on the fringes of consciousness, available for use as necessary.

Uncontrolled self-reflexiveness may be compared to the action of a moth flying close to a hot lamp. Each flap of the wings triggers another flap and another and another as the moth rushes toward self-destruction. Through the positive feedback in the wing movements, the moth stimulates itself. Self-reflexiveness "feeds" upon itself until its self-contained energy runs out; information coming in, is stopped; a negative feedback—heat—restrains it.

The human being, too, is often subject to destructive self-reflexiveness. We literally talk ourselves into gross stupidities. As words generate more words, as identification and the allness of prejudice and dogmatism become more vehement, as the unrestrained semantic reactions assume reflexive action, our behavior becomes no more intelligent than that of the moth—even though it may be more complicated and ingenious. Chain reactions multiply into fright, sadistic fury, fear-ridden panics, and flight.

Self-reflexiveness as a descriptive term carries no value connotations by itself. Activated by positive feedback, uncontrolled by negative inhibition, it has served and still serves to abet the development of pernicious ideas, such as those which, sustained and refined in past ages, result in human sacrifice, slavery, and incredible torture. For example, while the deliberate destruction of an entire population was not a new idea, genocide reached new efficiency in the Nazi cremation ovens at Auschwitz, Dachau, and Buchenwald during World War II. A murderer because of creed does not respond to negative feedback. Neither does an habitual fool.

Conversely, reflexiveness can be constructive. In spite of chronic resistance to change, self-reflexiveness has served and still serves the development of good ideas, those that lead to reform, furthering knowledge, and inspiration. Self-reflexiveness sustained the writing of our Constitution, the Christian love of fellowman, the integrity in holding to "the facts," the wise evaluation, the creation of the artistic, and many scientific discoveries. The list is endless, obviously.

Productivity results from spontaneity. Spontaneity is a state of looseness of the mind in which all available resources can come into play. If the results of productive thinking are nurtured, then fed by isomorphism with extensional data, they can be called *creative*. If they are fed and nurtured only by more symbols within the mind, they are bound to be destructive. Even the most artistic productions must eventually be tested against reality by using the extensional device, if they are to have meaning to anyone other than the artist.

In communication, spontaneity means the ability to pick up understanding about the responses of others, and to react to them quickly by adjusting the form of the message. In writing, it means anticipation of response, based on previous experience and careful analysis of the potential audience. A mental warm-up period, as we have previously said, is useful to both speaker and writer. The warm-up serves to trigger memories of previous experience into action, so that it can be reinforced by feedback and adjusted to meet immediate needs. It may be compared to the briefing sessions for pilots before they go into combat, or to the "skull session" before a football game, where the coach reviews the behaviors of the other team as well as those of his own.

Warm-up is not necessarily only rehearsal or practice. While rehearsal may sometimes assist the warm-up process, it can also fix responses in the mind in such a way that they cannot be adjusted in practice. A speaker's rehearsal should be similar to a writer's first draft, with the series of rehearsals comparable to a writer's successive copy drafts in which he cleans up and sharpens his messages. Take care, though, for excessive rehearsal can make the message "cold," and coldness may dissipate the specific tension necessary to succeed with the task.

In any event, regardless of the medium of communication, the creative process must be assisted by data. If knowledge is only verbal and not associated with a life situation it cannot be activated. You will not learn to speak well or write well merely by reading this book. If that were possible, the book would be a best-seller and not a text! The only way to become skilled at communication is to communicate, and permit the resulting feedback to adjust your style and behavior. This book should serve as a guide to things to look for while communicating, and it may offer you some values and ideas to test. In the final analysis, however, your skill will be a function of your theory *and* your experience, though experience *alone* may result in cluttered, disorganized, yet perhaps vital, behavior. Theory *alone* will result in dullness and conformity to rules, which may earn you a grade, but will not make you generally effective.

Your goal should be spontaneity, controlled by data. The data must include knowledge of your own capabilities, assessment of the possible range of attitudes and behaviors in the audience, solid knowledge of the subject, firmly structured organization of ideas, a storehouse of words plus the ability to put them together so they make sense, and integration of the vocal mechanism. Furthermore, in practice, the system must remain open so that it is possible for you to revise your understanding of yourself, change your impressions of the audience, call on relevant information where needed, change structure to meet needs, alter words to achieve understanding, reshape sentences for impact, and improve control over voice and diction to maximize comprehension. The elements of the process of the preparation are also relevant to the process of presentation. Feedback of extensional data, interpreted correctly into positive and negative feedbacks inside your head, provides the feedforward necessary for isomorphism.

On the other hand, concentration only on extensional data leads to dullness. Neither listeners nor readers normally are interested in prosaic recitations of dry facts, unornamented. No one will listen to a speaker who does not give him a reason for listening and who cannot sustain attention. In a like sense, no one will read the works of a writer whose sentences are dry and lifeless. The creative process permits the making of metaphors, the use of literary devices that make communication sparkle for the receiver.

Remember, though, that identification and allness can block spontaneity. Each tends to set off blockage and inhibition: "I just can't think of anything to say," or "They won't like me anyway."

In the extreme, such inhibitions may produce pronounced timidity and reticence in persons who might otherwise be very competent communicators. Such people do not stand up well where they must "hold their own" and are open to criticism—that is, they tend to be silenced by the assertiveness of others. They avoid situations in which they need to think "on their feet." They lack confidence to speak extemporaneously, and even discussion intimidates them. They need more data about themselves to break the block of allness. By exposure to a series of small successes, they may be assisted in revising the ideas about themselves that inhibit spontaneity. This is when the teacher who is sensitive to the needs of such people can make a wonderful contribution to the betterment of human communication. In addition, this fine teacher will also recognize other communication problems and know what to do to help the people who have them.

Uncontrolled spontaneity can also be a barrier to communicative effectiveness when self-reflexiveness is uncontrolled and runs wild as overexuberance or oververbalization. For example, the unusually "bright" person may dominate a conversation or discussion because he has become oblivious to reaction, unresponsive to feedback. Regardless of how effective he may be at abstracting in his topic, he has misinterpreted the situation concerning his listeners, and thus loses his effectiveness. Those of lesser abilities are likewise prone to talk too much when they get "wound up" and have assured themselves that they are being received with approval.

Finally, creative people need to be alerted to avoid self-centered *passion*, the arrogance the Greeks called *hubris*, lest they have inordinate difficulty in their relationships with others. The feeling that the personal act of creating is so important that it cannot be interfered with may trigger an allness of egocentrism. It may happen that a way-of-life defense of the act takes so much energy that none is left over for real work. Paradoxically, creativity may create its own sort of blindness and deafness to feedback. The creator who becomes the victim of his own hubris may be unable to reverse himself and will generate obsessions beyond which he will not see, and will not listen. His passion prevents his giving real attention to reason with which he disagrees or seeing merit in alternatives. He recklessly disregards moral laws and restraints and makes life miserable for his associates, who can do little but leave him alone.

Withdrawal from life is not a necessary accoutrement of artistic creativity, and withdrawal hardly meets our goal of bettering human communication. So toward that purpose, let's move along.

SUGGESTIONS FOR DISCUSSION

1. Your authors gave you a brief list of extensional devices, but in their research they came across over 50 of them. You might want to check some of the writings by Alfred Korzybski, S. I. Hayakawa, Irving Lee, Harry Weinberg, Bess Sondel, or Samuel Bois to see how many extensional devices you can list. If someone really followed all these extensional devices all the time, would his life improve or would he be mentally ill? What makes an extensional device "extensional"?

2. If you are relatively normal, you daydream every so often. For your own information, list some of the things you see yourself doing when you daydream. Is it possible for you to do any of these things in reality? See if you can develop a plan for actuating your daydreams that are possible of achievement, and see if you can build your impossible daydreams into short stories.

3. The novel *Tristram Shandy* by Lawrence Sterne is called a "digression on digressions." If you have read the novel, what does this have to do with self-reflexiveness? What does Uncle Toby have to say about "riding off on hobby horses"? What does this have to do with extensionality? If you haven't read the novel, would reading it be an extensional device?

4. See if you can create an extensional device that no one has thought of before. Show how it would improve communication between people.

5. Pair off and sit facing your partner in absolute silence for about five minutes. Now see if you can estimate what the other person was thinking. Write it down. Compare it with what he thought you were thinking. Test it against what he was really thinking. Does silence communicate?

6. Nonverbal communication has not been thoroughly studied by anyone. Conduct your own personal study of nonverbal communication. What expressions can you

detect that give you more information than words? Are you able to read moods by observing faces? If any of you are camera enthusiasts, you can prepare quite a photo-notebook of nonverbal communication.

7. Magda Arnold described four kinds of tension. Can you find examples of each of the tensions in your personal life? How would you describe the tensions in words? How do you go about describing any "feeling" in words? Using words like "embarrassment," "uncomfortable," "nervous," "jittery," "afraid," etc., see if you can talk specifically about what you feel. Avoid the use of words like "I feel funny." What do you feel in your stomach, your head, your legs? How do your "feelings" differ from those of others? If you express common symptoms, can you be sure you have the same feelings?

8. We have advised you to warm up and relax. If you knew someone who needed one or two shots of whiskey before he could face his audience, what would you tell him about how he might be able to train himself to do it without the booze?

9. Is an inhibition part of conscience? Where do your inhibitions come from? Separate your social inhibitions from your psychological inhibitions. How would you go about overcoming an inhibition? Suppose you were hired as a consultant to a school district just about to integrate their classes and one of the teachers remarked that she had strong inhibitions about talking with black people. How would you go about training her to overcome her inhibitions? (Or would you fire her?)

10. How much of your life do you control? In November 1968, half the country felt an earthquake. Suppose some great scientist predicted that earthquakes were about to become frequent and that your locality could expect in the near future earthquakes to register about 7 on the Richter scale. What steps would have to be taken to protect the community from the danger of earthquakes? What changes would this bring about in the normal life of man? It is said that the masters in a slave society were more enslaved than the slaves. What do you suppose this means? Given all of the mechanical gadgets around us as slaves—how free are you because of their assistance?

SUGGESTIONS FOR FURTHER READING

John C. Condon, *Semantics and Communication* (New York: Macmillan, 1966). Review appropriate sections of this book as they fit your needs.

Harry Weinberg, *Levels of Knowing and Existence* (New York: Harper and Row, 1959). Pay particular attention to Chapter 3 as it relates to our present topic.

Joshua Whatmough, "Words and Meanings," *Language: A Modern Synthesis* (New York: St. Martin's Press, 1956). In this brief section of a very learned book, Professor Whatmough compares semantic maps with human territories in several languages.

10

The Growth of a Speaker:
From Mediocrity
to Excellence

It is easy to become a mediocre speaker. Most of us achieve that by merely being alive, well, and talking. Obviously, the better speaker you are, the more influence you will exert in your environment. This seems like something worth working toward.

The past chapters have dealt with various concepts and perceptions of thought and of communications processes. So far, you have been dealing mainly with ideas and images. Now, you will become involved in a more personal sense, for our emphasis in this chapter shifts to people speaking.

While we will be dealing with reluctant speakers in much of our writing here, just keep in mind that no one is yet a perfect speaker. If he were, there would be no need for him to read this book or to take a speech course.

THE MESSAGE: SEMANTIC OVERLOADS AND UNDERLOADS

An easy way to lose contact with your audience is to present new or complicated information too quickly. You should realize from your own experiences as a listener that even one new word or new technical phrase can block attention to an important message. Each of us has his own level of input for new information, and anything that goes beyond that level is *semantic overload*. The result is a blown fuse in the brain, which sends out blocking signals saying "I don't get it" or "That's beyond me." At this point, communication quickly halts. And if the speaker is perceptive, he will note the negative feedback and attempt to correct the semantic overload by connecting the new idea with an existing memory or an experience stored in the receiver's memory bank.

The thing for you to remember is not to crowd ideas on top of each other so quickly that your listeners cannot assimilate each meaning fast enough for comprehension and still keep up with your delivery. As an intelligent speaker, you will pace your delivery by regulating your rate of speaking, pitch, and vocal modulations to keep the semantic patterns you are evoking in phase with your isomorphisms. Keeping pace with your listeners, allowing them to evaluate and comprehend the isomorphic concepts of your message, is an excellent measure of a speaker's deliberation, and deliberation is a meaningful measure of the speaker as an artist.

As you'll recall, we cautioned earlier about professional or occupational specialists who cloud listeners' minds with technical overload, e.g., the electrician speaking of "ohms," "nuvistor," and "diodes"; or the pilot speaking of "Omni," "VFR," and "IFR approach"; or the academician who speaks of "underachievers," "heterogeneous grouping," and "comprehensive evaluatory experience" to the local Rotary Club.

You, as a student fairly new to the world of communication, should be cautioned against using many of the new terms we have covered in this book merely to impress your less-fortunate friends who have not yet discovered us. Such frightening words as *allness, isomorphism,* and *entropy* are enough to frighten away most people and induce barriers to communication even among your own peers.

Semantic overload may be reduced by the use of diagrams, by role-playing, by familiar examples, or by various visuals. In one way or another, you must always attempt to build a communications bridge across the semantic barrier between you and your listeners.

In addition to overloading your listener and blocking your message, you can find your message ignored through *semantic underload.* This happens when your listener recognizes your message as "old stuff"; redundancy immediately sets up a chair for boredom to sit in. When this happens, you also lose the listener.

Granted, some repetition of any idea may be necessary to establish meaningful communication. When more than one person is in your audience, your risk of semantic overlap and redundancy is greater. However, you must minimize this overlap as much as possible so as not to lose your group. Naturally, the more highly educated and sophisticated your audience, the less tolerance they will have for overlap.

The artful speaker succeeds in keeping himself balanced upon a tightrope, with the obscurity of overload on one side and the boredom of underload on another. In baseball, the successful base stealer knows just how much or little lead to take on the pitcher, and in speaking, the same knowledge applies the same way—that is, if you stay too close to the "base," you won't advance; if you get too far off, you might be tagged out.

Perhaps our best advice here might be: watch your words as carefully as you watch your step.

AWAKENING THE SLOW LEARNER: HE FINALLY MAKES IT

There is a vast difference between the slow learner and the retarded person, yet both may be more intelligent than initial contact would indicate. In the case of the slow learner, his problem usually is one of assimilation and comprehension, which seem guarded by a barrier of unresponsive lack of ambition. The retarded person, on the other hand, is usually a victim of a birth injury, childhood disease, or other physical abnormality.

In the case of the slow learner—and there are thousands of people of all ages in this category—the major problems are cultural deprivation; lack of stimulation, social contacts, and motivations; a strong antilearning environment; and self-inflicted semantic disorders, e.g., the "I-can't-learn" feeling.

While the retarded have been aided greatly by both medical specialists and special-education people, the slow learners have been less fortunate in many cases. In instances where the special-education professionals have been able to work with slow learners, the progress in attainment has been marvelous. One of the most exciting ideas to come along in recent years is that the traditional IQ test measure of a person's intelligence is not a static quantity, and that a person who scores badly on an IQ test is not necessarily doomed to second-rate citizenship and mental inferiority for the rest of his life.

In the great gray "prisons" of our nation's slums and ghettos are children who have never been to a zoo or to a museum. They are hemmed in economically and socially, and they live in utter monotony, isolated from the rest of the world by neglect. No wonder they become hostile to the constructive, educational influences in society. Once in school, failure is heaped upon failure. For most, even a feeble showing of desire or curiosity is derided by peers or parents or squelched by an insensitive teacher. These rejections result in a loss of identity, and the youngster falls under the example of his peer group in his desperate search for "Who am I?" This is the classic life cycle of the dropout and delinquent and is an extreme case, both in polar terms and numbers, because there are so many of these young people in our society today. They are easy prey for extremists who mobilize youthful anxieties into pointless violence.

Other slow learners come from low- or middle-class homes and don't live in ghetto areas. They, too, may be culturally deprived, and they often have emotional problems for one reason or another. While their problem is different and ostensibly less extreme than that of the ghetto child, it is no less distressing and often harder to overcome. In both cases, it is the communicator's role and the teacher's job to knock down the barriers to communication and learning. Let's look at these problems a little more specifically.

Slow learners typically abstract less than their capacities warrant, yet they notice and retain only a meager amount of information. They are dull in the discrimination of differences, and their inferences stop at the lower orders of abstraction. Obviously, because of the deprivations they have, they possess less with which to abstract. When self-reflexiveness is a factor, their predictability and evaluating become twisted and inadequate, and their abstraction of similarities soon becomes I_3, activated by unpleasant past situations. Their "allness" attitudes are based on hopelessness, if not open hostility. They are often predominantly intensional in orientation.

As we've stated, release from these semantic disorders requires specialized help from schools and from community. Many slow learners could be pulled from the morass of mediocrity by cooperative teamwork among parents, teachers, and others within the community and its school system. The basic problem is twofold: placing the child in decent personal relationship with his situation and showing him how to think relationally about what he could write or speak. Obviously, as his experience deepens, his reading and speaking take on fuller meanings, and his deprivations will begin to wash out of his active mind. As he begins to understand comparison and analogy, he sees meaningful relationships, and he begins to learn how to abstract, and his awareness deepens. In a reward sense, he finds his personal influence over his environment growing as his abilities grow.

Perhaps you wonder about the relevance of so many sentences about the slow learner. Perhaps you can identify only partly with his problems. Please recall that the term "slow learner" is a relative term, and we have given you only the darker side to show that nothing is impossible when it comes to communication and education. What application does this have for you? As a future teacher? As a speech student right now? As a businessman in a few years? As a civic leader later? As a housewife? As a human being? Only you can answer the question about your relationship to the slow learner— and we bet that somewhere in your mind you are already doing so. With that, let's take another step up the educational ladder in our quest for communication betterment.

FROM RETICENCE INTO LEADERSHIP

The reticent speaker is not a slow learner in the sense of that term as we have just covered it. He is a person who, for one reason or another, would prefer to remain silent and uncommunicative. Part of this attitude may lie within the person, e.g., he just has nothing to say for one reason or another. The major reason, usually, is a lack of confidence in ability to speak to others. For fear of failure, the reticent speaker shrivels his communication with others, and lets the less inhibited monopolize conversations.

Study of case histories of the reticent speaker indicates that little failures tend to escalate into bigger and bigger failures. Sensitive to the failure to meet the goals, the person begins to narrow his attempts, and a self-negating pity begins to take over. How often have you heard a student express such attitudes as "I'm no good at . . ."; "I'm afraid of . . ."; "I couldn't do . . ."; "I just know I'd fail . . ."? Or how many times have you said something like that yourself?

This student passes up verbal opportunities, and often takes refuge in another type of activity, always seeking some means by which to win recognition. Oddly, some of the more reticent become excellent writers of theory and history, because they can "hide" in libraries, do research and writing, and let someone else promote their work.

To some degree, the reticent speaker recognizes his problems, and although he may not face up to them immediately, at least he knows he has a communications problem. Some authorities suggest that semantic indexing and semantic dating are possible solutions for the problem of reticence, in that both reduce the damaging assumptions of I_3 and "allness" attitudes. The goal is the gradual increase of extensionality, which will cause the past influences to fade, and the spontaneity of thought, speech, and action to blossom forth.

What we are saying, of course, is that the person who is reticent needs to have his confidence developed. He should recognize, and so should his teachers, that this comes about gradually, with a block of success here and a block of success there . . . finally, someday, forming a solid foundation from which the newly successful speaker may address his peers. As this process is going on, however, the circles of influence widen as the speaker gains more and more confidence.

A college speech class probably offers the finest opportunity for the reticent to make progress in communication growth. This shouldn't surprise you. After all, do you come to a speech class as perfect speakers, only there to amaze each other with your oral grandeur, or do you come to learn and practice? The more useful speech classes will offer an assortment of activities for students, including many channels for the reticent to interact with others similar to him, and with other students too. For example, role-playing has been demonstrated as an effective aid in developing confidence in reticents. Oral interpretation of drama and other writing has helped these communication-shy persons too. Hundreds of young men and women, for instance, have diminished their speech reluctances by taking the roles of Romeo and Juliet in the famous balcony scene, and have gone from there into more difficult areas that strike more directly, and actively, at their semantic disorders.

In addition to the above techniques, case studies and practical situations may be designed around the family, job, church, fraternity, sorority, or the community. Valuable preparation and involvement may be gained for the reticent when he takes part in these sociodrama situations. Of course, sociodrama is not truly real life, but it comes close, and it will at the very least provide a familiar referrent when the student does find himself in the "live" situation.

A similar activity that will aid the reticent in improving his ability is to take part in public speaking, discussion group, and debate activities. These are active and potent means for him to improve his speech personality, and they will enable him to build confidence in his own ability.

Unexpected bonuses await the student who is willing to admit he has a reticence problem, and is even more willing to try to do something about it. We've listed a few examples of those "somethings" above. His reward? Improvement in relations with others is a direct result of improved speech communication. And, with better relations in oral communication, the entire academic and social world suddenly becomes much brighter and more rewarding to the individual.

FROM CRUDITY AND AFFECTATION . . . TO ART

Speech, like other disciplines, has several areas of specialty. Public speaking, discussion, and debate often have been called "applied arts," while oral interpretation and drama are classed as "fine arts." The time has passed when this dichotomy served any useful purpose. All of us have been present at speeches, discussions, and debates—in person or on TV—that for ease, grace, wit, and finesse we called "art." Whether they were "applied" or "fine" art was unimportant.

Such men as John F. Kennedy, Winston Churchill, or Adlai Stevenson represent maturity of communication. Their "art" was far more than simple refinement and skill in language, logic, and persuasion. They achieved a pinnacle with their "art" because no one could seriously doubt their honesty, sincerity, and integrity. They seem to fulfill the classical concept of the speaker as a "good man who speaks well." They could stand up to judgment on both their purposes and their means.

This is very important to success at communication. Men who understand themselves extensionally have no trouble with their own identity. They understand what they can do and what they cannot do in a given situation. They are able to utilize many resources as they present their message. The expression of integrity or *ethos* from such men makes them appear credible, believable, to their listeners. True credibility cannot be achieved merely by sharpening skill.

The highest degree of wit, polish, and cultivation can become an instant and hostile interference with communication if there is the least suspicion that the speaker is not fully committed to what he says, particularly if the audience suspects some selfish motive or vested interest is concealed in the message. This was the problem faced by President Lyndon Johnson when he confronted the "credibility gap" issue, for many Americans suspected him of deceit, though little tangible evidence was offered by anyone to prove it. The late Senator Robert Kennedy encountered the same kind of suspicion in his tragically short campaign for the presidency in 1968. Many labeled him an "opportunist," a charge from which he never fully recovered. Thus, neither position nor sophistication seems to be sufficient to establish credibility. The most scientific selection of words and phrases, the most carefully selected, tailor-made ideas, beautifully enunciated, still do not raise the act of communication to the status of "art."

The man who is skilled, but is not fully credible is called a *sophist*. This uncomplimentary epithet implies that the audience regards the speaker as a "slicker" or "con artist." This inference is made often, and unjustly, about able and articulate speakers who appear crude and uncoordinated.

Whatever their validity, a speaker must live with the evaluations of his audience. The reputation lives and transfers to other times and other situations, for it cannot be assumed that the typical audience is capable or willing to use the semantic devices. Part of development of skill, therefore, demands the development of a strong *ethos* capable of carrying the speaker through the most threatening situations of negative evaluation.

Many of us react negatively to certain speech styles. We label a cultured tone as "phony," "put on," "ivory tower," or "theatrical." On the other hand, many listeners may be overawed by this same sophistication. There is a tendency to equate smooth and fluent delivery with superior intelligence. These people, according to Wendell Johnson, overvalue delivery without subjecting it to critical evaluation. It would appear that the intellectually snobbish, then, are no less gullible as listeners than those persons with educational or cultural deprivation!

At that lower end of the cultural spectrum, you find the crude, gross, and uncouth mores of language and speech. Vocabulary is meager, and repetitious slang hangs heavy in the speech patterns; grammar is ignored; mispronunciation abounds; and profanity and vulgarity run rampant through conversation. There is no model of personality that these persons can follow to better their communication patterns.

Of course, a great deal of communication at this level is rebellion by young people against the standards demanded by their family and school situations. This rebellious use of crude patterns differs greatly from the slum-area patterns, although the results are likely to be self-defeating. While it is clearly understood that profanity, for example, can be a natural part of a man's style, the normal listener will still evaluate it negatively.

The only way to bridge this semantic gap is through face-to-face communication and a "selling job" on the idea that there is a better way to communicate, and that it really is better! In this respect, the mass media can do much to aid communication betterment. Television is widely criticized because it does not meet the cultural standards imposed upon it by various self-proclaimed literati who feel the medium must conform to their set of rules. However, the success that television has had as a mass medium can be attributed to the fact that it does not conform to these elite ideals; instead, it is a natural idiom couched in the language and imagery of the mass population. Television "talks" the language of a far larger percentage of our population than do the literati who deem the medium a cultural desert or vast wasteland. While we could debate the honest and sincere motives behind contemporary programming practices, there is absolutely no doubt that television communicates effectively.

You, of course, share a great deal of responsibility in this area too, and this betterment of communication might just be one of the debts you owe your society. Think about it.

WHEN SCIENCE AND ART JOIN IN SPEECH

An *art* is generated by the semantic responses of the person who involves his relationships with that which he beholds. Art is a value judgment, and an appreciation based on past experiences related to present perceptions. This does not mean that a man seeing Edward Steichen's photographs or hearing a Beatles' composition for the first time cannot appreciate either as art—although he must have something in his memory bank with which to associate the new perception in order to identify and evaluate it. Remember, though, that in communicating about any art, you are as subject to reactions and to semantic disorders as you are to what the objects themselves symbolize.

We are saying that art is a series of abstractings of value judgments made on the symbolic worth—to the perceiver—of objects and ideas. Many speech students are blithely unaware of confusing orders of abstraction as they engage in futile arguments about what *is* or what *is not* art, what *is* or *is not* a speech disorder, or what *is* or *is not* good television programming. In discussions, and often in loose-format graduate seminars, speech students are prone to carry their rhetoric into even higher orders of abstractions after only the most meager analysis, and with little specific reference to the topic itself. This develops into unintelligent, generalized, intensional complaint about a concept into which the critic has little insight. Such emissions cannot be considered "art" regardless of the vehemence with which they are uttered.

If a message is not to the point, directly relevant to speaker and listener concerns, it cannot be art. Some speakers try to cloak their remarks in long words, attenuated and contrived phrases, hoping, perhaps, to overcome deficiencies in reason through the power of words. But words have little power if they do not point to extensional data. The typical audience responds to such a speech as "arty," and withdraws into a semantic stupor, hiding their real feelings with devastating remarks like, "isn't that interesting?" A more frequent reaction, however, is a noncommittal, negative silence.

Response to an artistic performance is displayed through a change in our personality. An exciting speech, a truly great play or musical performance excites us, and we cannot help but express our understanding and approval. A speaker can estimate his own approach to the quality that would make him artistic by taking an extensional view of the response given to him and his message. When he is specifically aware that the audience "understands" and accepts, then he can feel secure in continuing. Messages of confusion or rejection require that he alter his style. It is imperative, when speaking to others, to make them the prime focus of concern. The speaker's task is to relate audience and topic. His personal concerns must be minimal in order to bring this about.

Every idea has its own rhetoric, sources of persuasion. The speaker must discover in an idea elements that give it appeal *for the audience*. Part of this can be done by organizing or structuring it into a form that makes it easy for the audience to understand. The language with which the idea is expressed must be carefully selected so that words do not confuse or distract, and the delivery of the message should be coherent and appealing. Each of these isomorphisms represents a harmonious expression of the idea, a reinforcement that helps drive the idea through the various resistances that an audience can raise against it. The speaker is the medium, and he and the message combine to reach the minds of the listener. The speech becomes an "extension of man" in the best McLuhan sense.[1]

Now that we have found the art, the next logical step would be to draw some boundary lines around it. But there are no precise measures to separate the crude, the vulgar, and the tasteless from the beautiful and the cultured. It is functionally impossible because so much depends on the tastes of the listeners and the demands of the situation. Just as there are disagreements about what object is worthy of being in an art museum, there is discord about the qualities that make a communication "sublime." Of course, we will probably always have self-styled censors who would impose their own, often neurotic, whims and tastes upon us all. And, there will always be blind prejudice against new and startling ideas, forms, and styles. Critics will continue to be critics, usually unaware of what they are doing, as they blindly abstract and segment the communication process in their critique of various art and social forms and concepts. Surely, though, there must be a better way!

Perhaps, in the future, we can utilize scientific methods to help define the art of communication at operational levels. We have been discussing these operational levels in each chapter of this book so far, and we have been trying—almost desperately—to point routes along which the two forces could proceed toward unification at the great common denominator—human interaction in the search for truth and authenticity.

It has been said that the greatness of a message lies in the *truth* it manifests. This word *truth* needs much indexing and dating, because there are as many truths as there are communicators and receivers to symbolize; everyone has his own truth. For example, truth may lie only in fidelity to the drives of the artist as he creates, without reference to others who might experience it. Art may lie in the capacity of the communicator to achieve goals, though this perhaps might be called "expediency." Art may refer to elevating the emotions, though this might be termed "demagoguery." Each definition that we make of art can be called by another name, a pejorative designation.

[1] Marshall McLuhan, *Understanding Media: The Extensions of Man* (New York: McGraw-Hill, 1964).

When scientific propositions are applied to an understanding of art, the production often loses its vigor. It does not help much to attempt to explain DaVinci by detailing the chemical composition of the colors he used on his canvas. By the same token, even the most careful examination of the nature of the words and phrases used by "artistic" speakers will offer little insight into what made their speaking great.

If we try to operationalize our investigation, we find some useful precepts. For example, we can be quite certain that effectiveness in speaking is related to the amount of understanding of, and concern for, the audience that the speaker shows. We know that effectiveness has something to do with the speaker's unwillingness to compromise his personal belief, even while he adapts it to his audience's capacity to understand and believe. We know that propriety has something to do with effectiveness; that communications which appear awkward, disjointed, or out-of-phase with the occasion or audience do not succeed well. We know that the artist-speaker must show more concern for a specific audience than the artist-writer, for the reader can put down what he finds unpleasant or obscure, while a listening audience often has no choice but to hear it out.

What we do not yet understand is the relationship between effectiveness and art. It appears, at this moment in time, that scientific investigation of the communication process can help us to become more effective. We do not yet have a way to pinpoint the elusive quality that carries us beyond effectiveness to art, and thus, we find ourselves still rooted in the term science-art when we talk about learning to speak well.

There are many texts which offer specific instruction for achieving success. This particular text will make no such suggestions. In the first place, the authors would have little more to offer than can be found in many good books. The Bobbs-Merrill Series in Speech Communication, for example, examines many types and styles of speaking in detail, and covers the same ground we would have to cover, if we were attempting to give such advice. There is nothing to prevent a student from picking up these books and examining them, provided he understands that even though it appears that "rules of success" are being offered, the individual human is so crucial in the communication act, that the eventual result is a unique methodology, necessarily your own!

And so we repeat our one bit of advice. Learning to communicate well proceeds best through communicating, not in the form of isolated exercises, but with real people, about real issues, in real situations. Each experience can display improvement if the speaker carefully admits the maximum information (feedback) from his audience and processes it in his mind in reference to the reality. Consciousness of the goal, improvement of communication, helps the student speaker develop his own methodology for improvement. It seems to us that this is the only rational way.

Whatever happens, we must know that whatever change we make in our communication style will also change our personality. Or, do we have to change our personality to alter our communication style? Perhaps the next chapter will help us to answer this.

SUGGESTIONS FOR DISCUSSION

1. Have you ever experienced a Dale Carnegie Course? The late Mr. Carnegie wrote a book called *How To Win Friends and Influence People.* Get that book or one like it (sophisticates might try *Gestalt Therapy* by Perls, Hefferline, and Goodman). Try some of the exercises. What has to go on inside you before the exercises start working? What can you get out of reading this book that will help you improve your communication? Why do we offer exercises? Why did we suggest that you devise your own exercises? Do you have any comment to make about a book one of the authors recently saw in a bookstore, the title of which was *How To Be A Successful Lover?*

2. Collect some samples of assignments given orally by various professors. Make a long list of them and evaluate them carefully. How many of them are clear enough for you to go out and do what was requested? (You might make a similar analysis of the exercises in this book.) What advice would you give a beginning teacher pertinent to making assignments to a class? What would you want to tell him about information overload and underload? Would you have any suggestion about how he could use extensional devices to improve his assignment-giving? If you are working out your own assignments in this course, take care you heed your own advice.

3. Speech is often divided into three parts; speaker, message, and listener. Which do you think has been the focus of this book? How is it different in focus from some of the more standard speech texts available? Think back on your writing course that you took last term or in high school. Did the advice given you about organization, grammar, punctuation, and spelling help you express your thoughts more clearly? More vividly? Do you think anyone really wants to read what you write? Can you apply some of these ideas to the act of speaking? Do people really want to listen to you? How do you suppose you could best learn so that people would want to read your writing and listen to your speaking? Would concentration on communicator, receiver, or message be more important to you?

4. Are there areas in which you are a slow learner? What is the difference (in your mind) between slow learner and retarded? Consider the area in which you consider yourself a slow learner; what would you have to do in order to speed up your learning? Does the term slow learner imply anything about the quality of the learning? That is, does learning become more important because it is done in a shorter period of time?

5. Do you think you have become more intelligent as you have progressed through school? How intelligent do you expect to be when you are 35? Would you agree that intelligence is a function of age? If so, you'd better not disagree with your professor. He is older than you.

6. Write a brief case history of one or two of your failures. What precisely happened to you that led you to classify the experience as a "failure"? How much of a recovery did you make after the "failure"? If your failure concerned a person of the opposite sex, has it stopped you from trying? What did you learn from it?

7. In this chapter we told you that a slow learner abstracts at a lower level of abstraction, and the person who is mentally ill is usually functioning on a high level of abstraction. Doesn't that mean that the slow learner is the sanest of all?

8. Are all learning problems really problems in communication? What responsibility does a classroom teacher have to communicate with his class? What responsibility does the class have to communicate back? What form should the class's communication take?

9. How much can you trust a professional actor?

10. If you haven't tried role-playing yet, this is the time to try it. Work out some simple cases and play them out. In the evaluation that follows, note the difference between the grossness of role-playing and the subtlety with which we act in real life.

SUGGESTIONS FOR FURTHER READING

William Brigance, "What Is a Successful Speech?" *Quarterly Journal of Speech,* November 1925, pp. 372–377. Classical success comes from classical methodology, and this meaningful jaunt into speech history will show the way.

Orrin Klapp, *Symbolic Leaders* (Chicago: Aldine Publishing Company, 1964). This fast-paced book discusses the personality-leader society we live in today. It discusses the subject of the latter portion of this chapter in some detail. The fact that you will enjoy reading it helps prove the author's thesis.

Irving Lee, "They Talk Past Each Other," *How To Talk with People* (New York: Harper and Brothers, 1952). Here's truth about the old axiom differentiating monologue from dialogue. Lee's forte is cutting down on semantic overkill, which is why he was a good teacher and author.

11

Communication and the Development of Personality

Mr. A talking to Mr. B is a deceptively simple affair, and we take it for granted to a fantastic and tragic degree. It would surely be true that our lives would be longer and richer if only we were to spend a greater share of them in the tranquil hush of thoughtful listening. We are a noisy lot; and of what gets said among us, far more goes unheard and unheeded than seems possible. We have yet to learn on a grand scale how to use the wonders of speaking and listening in our own best interests and for the good of our fellows. It is the finest art to be mastered by men.[1]

This fine philosophy of Wendell Johnson's presents a delightful preamble to our attempt to show you how oral communication makes you what you are. This chapter will deal with your development, and some of the "what, how, when, and why" concepts that lie behind your communication patterns. We feel, of course, that you are your own best spokesman; however, you are not always solely responsible for the quality or quantity of your spokesman's position, as you will discover later in this chapter. Yet how you handle this role, as Johnson suggests, can be one of the finest arts of accomplishment.

If communication and interaction were a science, we would have unambiguous units that could be accurately measured in the precise language

[1] Wendell Johnson, "The Fateful Process of Mr. A Talking to Mr. B," *Harvard Business Review* (January-February 1953), p. 56.

of mathematics. The natural sciences have unequivocal units of weight, size, shape, velocity, temperature, frequency, etc. The numerical outcomes of such measurements can be processed according to the statistical method, and predictions can be made with considerable accuracy about the effect of one force or object on another. In communication, however, it has been impossible to define exactly what is to be measured, and we cannot even guess at the validity and reliability of such measurements.

Despite the handicaps, considerable research effort has been devoted to measurement of what is measurable. Scientists are now able to synthesize the human voice by duplicating its phonetic components. Voices can be analyzed spectrographically and on the oscilloscope, and accuracy is said to be so precise that authorities claim that no two voices are exactly alike. Their methods let them isolate and identify individual voices in much the same manner and with the same degree of accuracy that fingerprints can be identified. In addition, attempts are currently being made to achieve similar precise analysis of the components of language under the rubric of linguistics. In general, much of the information derived from these kinds of studies is useful in deepening our understanding of the scientific and grammatical aspects of communication, but what has been done so far has little relevance to the understanding of communication meaning. There have also been a number of studies made of persuasion hoping to discover what succeeds and what fails.

What seems to be the logical base unit for the study of meaning in communication is the influence of an expressed idea, a semantic pattern, as it takes place in interaction between persons. For example, we use the scientific references in our metaphors, as in a "heated" argument, a "heavy" gloom, or a "negative" attitude. But this use of scientific jargon provides no valid insight into the science of meaning.

Unfortunately, our tools for really discovering the influence of ideas on people are exceedingly few. In most instances, our most efficient and productive "tool" for investigation has been the case history or individual investigation and analysis. Behavioral psychologists have attempted to produce instruments of many kinds, but they have succeeded only in measuring group attitude changes and, even then, in a limited way. The most productive information about the effect of meanings on human beings comes from psychiatric studies, but here the studies are of people classified as abnormal. It is doubtful that generalizations can be made to the general population. Furthermore, so few individual studies have been made and the modes of investigation are so inconsistent that it is virtually impossible to isolate common propositions. Even the computer has not helped much in the scientific study of communication, for human interaction is so holistic it is hard to find viable units to analyze.

For these reasons we must retain the notion of science-art in any present examination of the communication process. Communication may be considered an art about which more scientific information is needed, and it may also be considered an evolving science, which will remain partially artistic. Conclusions about communication based on availability of present knowledge cannot be drawn from scientific evidence alone, nor is it reasonable to rely on the judgment of the artistic critic. Even with our limited information, a synthesis must be made between what we know because we have measured it and what we know because it represents the consensus of the best judgments of qualified critics.

Now that we have expressed our credo of melding the science-art concept into speech communication, let us explore you and your personality by taking a look at how you got that way.

FROM SUPERFICIALITY TO DEPTH OF INTERCHANGE

Most of our associations with other people are casual, routine, and quite superficial. If our first appearance is favorable, if our habits of speech and manners are not irritating, if we listen even a little, and if we avoid argument, nothing much happens with the person we encounter.

We may work side by side in the classroom, on the job, in the community, and in the church and still have only a superficial relationship, a façade of neutrality or surface friendliness, which provokes no complaints about our work or about us as individuals. We may even be spoken of as "wearing well," if we expend a little extra discipline.

Friendly, good-humored, even if inane, chatting at which most of us are quite adept may lead to deeper, richer, exciting, and significant levels of interaction, or it may very well go in the opposite direction. As our contacts extend, then likes, dislikes, irritations, frictions, and other emotions begin to affect the manner in which we view each other. With some care, making the effort to listen, and using our knowledge of our own communication process, we can often make these contacts reach deep levels of mutual satisfaction and benefit.

The magic process by which deep friendships or severe hostilities emerge between people is not clear. Part of communication between people is, of course, nonverbal. As we pointed out earlier, the first appearance of a person before you evokes images from memory of other people that appeared the same way. Thus, the labels you can apply to the new people whom you meet evoke a host of internal evaluations. Each of your new contacts is, in a sense, the prisoner of your previous contacts with others. The reason is that we tend to identify the unfamiliar with the familiar. Developing positive contacts calls for considerable personal effort. While a few individuals seem always to be able to evoke positive responses, most of us find the process of improving interpersonal relations arduous and tension-evoking. Being nice all the time just isn't easy!

Once a continuing friendship has been established, it is still characterized by friction. There are some who believe that all relationships between people are essentially competitive—that is, each person seeks ascendancy and dominance over the other. As we've seen, like most other theories about communication, this proposition cannot be proved scientifically. However, your own observation should tell you that those around you seek behaviors from you that will satisfy their own aims and goals. If you ignore expressions of these wants and needs, then strain and hostility enter the friendship. On the other hand, if you pay them too much heed, then the friendship becomes sycophantic; it may even approach a kind of interpersonal slavery and martyrdom, which is akin to blind hero worship. You also must have your needs satisfied. The process of communicating with another person for purposes of interaction must be characterized by mutual concern for satisfaction of needs.

Many people seek to resolve their tension about interpersonal friendships by immersing themselves in a clique or social group. There are a number of theories about this behavior. Probably the most prevalent is that offered by David Riesman, who characterizes people as inner-directed and other-directed.[2] *Inner-directed* man, according to Riesman, is a person who acts out his own inner programming without reference to the demands of social context, while *other-directed* man has a built-in radar that enables him to perceive cues from others and respond to them with considerable skill and Machiavellian adeptness. By acting in other-directed ways it is possible for a person to be socially accepted, yet be entirely alienated, because an other-directed society gives the individual no opportunity really to satisfy his personal needs and wants. Thus, the person who communicates the most friendliness and appears to have the most friends may internally be anxious, for what he really seeks cannot be satisfied through his communication behavior. He is living a sham of success.

In twentieth-century America, it is necessary for an individual to build a kind of communication pattern that enables him to live in close contact with others, while retaining a sense of personal integrity that will prevent his total loss of identity in the crowd. Communications in our century have been characterized of late by greater and greater reliance on social creed, which depends on the norm of behavior set by the mores of society. It is interesting to note that the same theory of social creed holds forth both in the establishment society and in the anti-establishment society. Despite the extremes of their polarity, both groups adhere staunchly to their own social creed, often to the point of being totally dogmatic and unreasonable. The attendant sacrifice of personal autonomy is reflected by the rising incidence of mental illness, because living by a social creed is not necessarily personally satisfying. What a society believes is a norm (which is a watered-down synthesis of the beliefs of many) is the least common denominator of value that permits the people in the society to live close to each other, but does not necessarily permit any individual to be satisfied in his personal drives. Government is also characterized by this sort of alienation in the midst of the crowd. As population increases and the size of population centers multiplies, direct access to the governing power becomes harder, and people must seek influence through representatives—if, indeed, they can find them. Communication is characterized by a downward flow, with many messages emanating from governmental units and agencies to the people;

[2] David Riesman, *The Lonely Crowd* (New Haven: Yale University Press, 1950).

but few messages come back, so there is little feedback contact between those who receive the messages and those who transmit them. It is for this reason that governments are often out of phase and unaware of the needs and wants of the people they govern. This, of course, is the source of the harried cry of the young dissenters as they picket and protest against the various governments across our earth. But many of the people who are governed, just sit and sulk in sullen resentment about the way they are ignored by those whom they helped to elect to office.

The weedlike growth of business, industry, and government as mass employers has created communication problems. For example, employment advancement is also characterized by what might be considered competitive remoteness. The individual who wishes to advance in salary must achieve an appropriate position in the company hierarchy. In order to do this, he must prove himself to be the person who can make decisions superior to other possible contenders for the position. Sometimes it is more expedient to build one's own reputation by sacrificing or denigrating the reputation of others. This represents a signal for interpersonal combat that is particularly discomfiting, because it takes place among people who have to work cooperatively with each other on a day-to-day basis.

Many attempts have been made to map these kinds of interactions, and it is possible to draw some fairly exact pictures of the ways in which communications flow in neighborhoods, communities, businesses, and governmental organization units. The most important proposition for personal behavior that we may draw from an analysis of these communication flows is that the individual who is immersed in competitive communication needs a personal release in some form of expressive communication. There must be some place or some set of circumstances where the individual can act out his needs and wants as an individual rather than as a representative or agent of some larger unit of society. To be more explicit, every individual needs a relationship that goes beyond the casual and the competitive. Each of us needs deep-level, involved associations that permit us to act as ourselves to another person, who has the privilege of assessing the extent to which our needs and wants may be satisfied. Everyone needs someone willing to become involved in his personal problems, and everyone is needed by someone else for the same reason. What is needed is a friend in the personal and communicative sense. Each of us needs someone to talk to and someone in whom he can confide. A psychiatrist or clergyman can be a paid friend in the sense we have been discussing. A glance at the institution of marriage reveals a relationship in which these criteria can be satisfied. But the high incidence of divorce indicates clearly that the marriage contract often is used to structure another situation in which the superficial or competitive aspects of communication are stressed to the sacrifice of communicating about personal needs and wants. Thus the mutual effort to achieve satisfaction of needs and wants by both parties to a marriage is lost by both.

Obviously, when one becomes involved in a need-communication relationship of this sort there are many hazards. The deeper the relationship, the more each person has at stake, because a shattering or disruption of the relationship is hard to take. Hostility emerging in a superficial contact is well within the realm of possibility, while hostility emerging from a competitive relationship is to be expected. But, when hostility emerges from the deep relationship between husband and wife or friend and friend, the disruption may be so severe as to be disabling, e.g., divorce or a bitter parting. Yet, to avoid these deep associations makes personal communication ineffectual in virtually every important situation. This is especially important to anyone who would lead others, in particular to parents, teachers, and counselors whose job can best be done through deep rather than superficial relationships. The art of public speaking, which is practiced by parents, teachers, counselors, and others, is characterized by the quest for involvement, for only when a listener becomes deeply involved with both the personality and the ideas of the speaker does he make progress toward achievement of his ends Only then does the listener achieve any satisfaction of his needs and wants.

If you would establish this precious relationship, you must exert effort and maintain awareness. To meet the vicissitudes of deep-level communication requires equal effort and also discipline; and sometimes a certain "toughness" is required if respect and dignity are to be maintained. Both parties must have an ability to resolve misevaluations and quarrels and to handle difficult episodes without breaking off or harming the relationship.

We must bring the full panoply of communication factors to our day-to-day associations if we are to achieve maturity. In this sense, *maturity* is characterized by self-control of abstracting and extensionalization, correction of assumptions, and holding to ethical and proper evaluations based on our reason and judgment.

THE SEMANTIC HYPHEN IN "INHERITANCE-ENVIRONMENT"

Each of us is the product of the interaction between inheritance and environment—the influences we exert in interplay and the influences exerted upon us. For an understanding of *why* we communicate as we do, we need an undistorted view of the situation from which we have emerged.

Almost from the moment of conception, the individual begins nonverbally to influence his surroundings. For empirical verification of this, ask no further than the nearest mother! At the time of birth, the inherited body, the first-order environment, begins interacting with ever-widening relationships into the inherited but changing environments. Living is a continuing cycle of interchange, nonverbal and verbal, with inheritance-environment. This relating process goes on as ONE. It continues operationally unsplittable, regardless of our physical-mental health and regardless of the labels we use in attempts to dichotomize the two.

If we do not find a way to connect inheritance and environment in our minds so that we do not split them erroneously, we are likely to begin to believe that the one can be affected without influencing the other. The best of scientific evidence indicates that, regardless of biological inheritance, the environment can drastically shape the life of the individual; yet, regardless of how nourishing the environment, the individual will make no progress without some reasonable biological inheritance. Consequently we must connect inheritance and environment by using the semantic hyphen, so that inheritance-environment emerges as one word and one concept.

Man is born with capacities and limitations. He strives toward his goal of health and happiness, functioning to the limit of his physical and mental capacities as they are tested by the world he encounters. A high capacity that goes untested will never have a chance to emerge, just as a low capacity that is excessively tested can destroy the individual. Although we know a great deal about generating stronger strains of wheat, we know little about how to generate stronger people, and the implications of controlling the biological functionings of people in their interaction are too threatening to be taken lightly. We must deal, then, with the person as he *is* and the world as it *is* when he lives in it.

Mind can be viewed as the development of a storage vault for images and symbols about the world, so that these can be processed and used in each subsequent encounter with environment. You will recall the mind/computer analogy we used earlier to describe the functions of the mind. In addition, we have already examined in previous chapters the effects of physical health upon mental health and vice versa, and you understand how physical energy can be used to generate semantic disorder or semantic adjustment. What you now need is a way to control input and output, so that your symbolizing capacity can be used constructively to help you to achieve your aims and goals. Since the process of using mind to control outputs involves sensible input and output, extensionalization and awareness of reality in the world are essential to your growth as an individual. Charles Woolbert, a great speech teacher, once pointed out that the mind depends upon what the body is doing. Further, we know that what the body does is largely controlled by the mind. Modern concepts of communication, including feedback and isomorphism, can thus help you to understand what goes on when a man communicates with his environment, and the environment communicates with the man.

We create another connected concept, that of mind-body. In speaking to others, we understand now that we seek to influence environment to make it more comfortable and acceptable to our lives. If we do not receive intelligent and intelligible messages from the environment, our attempts at communicative control will be futile. Hence, you should now understand why realistic assessment of your audience is so essential to the success of your communication efforts. If you do not have sufficient funded experience to guide your decisions and choices about what you communicate and how you communicate it to your audience, your attempts will be equally futile. Using these concepts as a model however, we can assert that communication is a process of synchrony between self and environment, in which the concerns of internal self are as important as the needs for survival within the environment. Communication must be a process that succeeds in exerting influence as well as a process that is personally satisfying. Unfortunately for many of us, communication is forced and ineffectual, and no satisfaction results from it. Such communication arises from inadequate extensionalizing about personal needs and the strictures of the environment. Ideals set too low or too high, distortion of data to fit internalized creeds, egocentric concern for self exclusive of environment, all contribute to disrupted attempts at communication and lead to the frustration that comes from failing to achieve what one seeks to achieve. Care must be taken to distinguish between the desirable and the do-able in setting goals.

The crucial variable, then, is feedback. This is the message we receive from the people with whom we interact. Feedback provides us with the data for the assessments that we make, which lead to our behavior, which is effective or ineffective, depending on the accuracy of the evaluation.

THE EFFECTS OF OVER- AND UNDERSTIMULATION OF FEEDBACKS

Self-regulation and self-control affect the operation of the communication process:

1. *self-regulation,* which is primarily subconscious, aids the growth of the human body-brain—the great symbolizing apparatus—toward a satisfactory maturity;
2. *conscious self-control,* which is vitally necessary for the formulation and correction of ideas as individuals relate to each other; and
3. *deliberately conscious self-control,* which occurs when the individual is capably directing his further evolution by his own regulation of self.

The interactions of these levels are interesting, although not surprising. The subconscious operation of the body regulates, among other things, the brain, which receives data and controls response to the environment. If the regulation remains subconscious, then response is signalic, unmediated, uncontrolled, and inexpedient. Conscious self-control guides the behavior of the body in response to what is seen, heard, or experienced through one of the other senses. This kind of control, not possible in lower animals, enables us to discriminate, for example, among various kinds of threats and prevents us from freezing or running when it is not expedient to do so. Deliberate self-control adds feedforward, helps us to formulate a goal and enables us to select from many alternatives the alternative which appears to us to be most potentially satisfying. The mind then sets the body in motion, an action is carried out, a response is received, which in turn is evaluated and another action results.

In a communication interaction, a remark may be threatening, which stimulates the body to produce adrenalin which causes tension. Rather than respond with violence or flight, self-control mediates by reminding us of the social exigencies. The mind can then be applied to the phrasing and uttering of an appropriate response designed to carry on a counterattack, soothe the troubled waters, or break off the engagement. Whatever alternative is selected will evoke a reaction from the response which again must be answered on all three levels.

DEVELOPMENT OF SELF-CONTROL

At this point, we are primarily concerned with the second and third levels, the development of self-control; that is, with the rule of inner feedbacks and how a child attempts to cope with his environment, the effects upon the language he learns, how communication becomes incorporated in his personality-character, and what it does to his behavior.

Most serious communication problems stem from failure of communication in the family, school, and community. Cases of deprivation of affection, lack of opportunity to form attachment to a mother-figure, or changes from one "mother" to another during infancy, are at the root of mental illness and personality distortion.

Children have an uncanny way of knowing whether they are accepted, and immediately they sense pretense. A child must feel secure in the affection of both parents, who are comfortable with themselves and with each other. Parental agreement on what is important for the child's welfare, even though the child may not always agree, is at least one firm basis upon which a child gradually can expand his relationships with others outside his family.

Children reared in an *overload* of conflicting demands and expectations become pressured into disturbed communication because they find it too threatening to cope with others. Children reared in the midst of an *underload* of expectations—neglect, deprived environment, lack of stimulation to exercise their communication capacities—rarely learn to compete well with those around them. Parents who are preoccupied with outside concerns and are oblivious to the strains developing in the child as his searching proceeds and his misunderstanding piles up, often neglect the obvious necessity for maintaining a warm two-way communication among the members of the family, a communication, that could preclude or ameliorate such strains.

"Brat" behavior, for example, designed to receive attention, can defeat attempts to communicate affection even in parents who are most sincere in assuming their responsibilities. Some children carry refined versions of brattiness into adulthood, and we're sure you could name examples among your friends.

There are parents who, in an *allness* of admiration of everything their child does, ostensibly approve of a kind of reverse punishment that their child metes out to them, and which may develop into subtle, fantastic "games" between child and one or both of the parents, with the child usually emerging as winner. For a concrete example, think back to the last time you were "put down" by a child using your rules in his game. You lost the game!

When parents openly quarrel before their children, they present the worst possible models of communication. In such displays of his parents' own semantic disorders, the child falls under conflicting pressures to please both parents. These frequently become unbearable for children in situations where divorce, a patent failure of communication, is impending, because of the competition by both parents for support or custody of the children.

In families where there is insensitivity and thoughtlessness on the part of one or both parents, the child may find himself in the midst of diabolical pressures that he cannot resolve. A resultant mental "illness" will have corresponding effects upon many areas of communication in the child. A child may become trapped in what Gregory Bateson referred to as *"double binds,"* which may be looked upon as a perversity in which argumentative and ignorant parents place the child in the role of judge of their dissonance. Then his only way out is to *deny* the reality of what he experiences, from which he learns to take refuge in an intensional world. These intolerable pressures occur when the child is faced with the possibility of having to infringe upon a family prohibition. For example, in a mixed religious marriage, the child may use atheism as a response to both. In other sorts of conflict, the child may seek new contacts, hopefully more nurturing; or, he may resort to lying and deceitful activities designed to defend himself against the pressures.

Another influence that may lessen the child's ability to carry on speech coherently and logically results from the parent's responding to the child's messages by going off in irrelevant tangents to the expected answer or in side remarks. For example, little Georgie comes running in the house to his mother. He has a big nightcrawler clutched in his grubby little hand.

"Mom, look, I caught a big worm!" is his joyous greeting.

"Go wash your hands, they're filthy, and get that ugly worm out of my house," is mother's tangential reply in a dry, pleasure-smashing voice.

Georgie is smashed too. His ego is deflated, and he is disappointed and confused. His mother could have reacted very differently, pleased Georgie, and still have achieved her goal of getting his hands cleaned, if she had replied:

"By golly, Georgie, that's really a big worm. But I'll bet he'd be happier outside in the soil. Why don't you put him back in the ground? Then please come in and wash your hands. OK?"

Teachers also "turn off" communicative exuberance in children by forcing them to adhere to spurious classroom regulations.

Excessive freedom or restraint beyond the necessary "do's" and "don'ts" cannot resolve the child's need for the security of affection. He must feel secure if he is to develop respect for discipline he may require. Harsh discipline tends to build abject dependency and conformity, to kill initiative and creativity and perhaps stimulate sadism, while softness and pampering tends to make for irresponsibility, obnoxious aggression, and ototoververbalization. Lack of parental, or even teacher, firmness at times critical to the welfare of the child may leave him confused, without a basis for anything certain, before he gradually learns how to be secure and to cope with uncertainties on his own. Without some exercise in exploring uncertainty and developing constructive feedforward, he may be unfit to face the uncertainty of the world.

The responses of the people in a child's environment do a great deal to shape his communication style and, through it, his personality. The child who learns deference because he is repressed will continue to show excessive deference to others. The child who learns to struggle to be heard because he is ignored will struggle equally hard against the rest of the people in his world. The child who is excessively rewarded for trivial contributions will expect similar rewards from the people around him. It is sad that we have so little control over the development of our communication style and consequently our personality, but it is possible to extend new kinds of controls, deliberate conscious controls, to alter our communicative outputs, and thus alter the responses that people make to us, which, in turn, can alter our personality.

CRISES IN THE EMERGING SELF-IMAGE AND IDENTITY

What we do in relation to others is controlled by mind. If sensible feedback has been obtained, which enables positive feedforward to take place, we may interact effectively. But, if feedback is negative, and feedforward is positive, the individual may blunder through his transactions, exerting no influence at all. An obvious example is the unfunny comedian whose jokes keep "laying eggs," yet he continues his behavior toward the hostile audience. He ignores their negative feedback as he continues to feedforward. Now if feedback is positive, but feedforward is negative, the individual may retreat from a successful presentation and thus lose his chance to exert influence. This is exemplified by a talented young pianist who blushingly refuses to perform before an audience, despite their verbal pleas for her to do so.

The key to effective feedback and feedforward in our attempts to control our environment through communication lies in *self-image*. *Self-image* is what one thinks himself to be. Sometimes this is closely related to what he is becoming, and it represents accurately to the person his own standing and potential with others. It includes assumptions that he makes about his ability to relate to others, the success of the relationships that he carries on, and how others see his worth and importance. At the center of his self-image is his view of self as a communicator. Each individual has some idea of what he can say and how effective it will be, and this serves as a basis for feedforward in the form of social confidence, courage, and stability. If someone thinks little of himself and his ability, then he will proceed without confidence and without ability to enhance his image through success.

One of the goals in communication instruction is your development of a strong self-image as a communicator. There must be no misunderstanding here. This strong self-image does not imply that you must believe that you are able to exert control all the time and with everyone. A strong self-image is characterized by a solid understanding of the problems you are likely to encounter when you communicate, together with a willingness to make the effort with some hope of success. You must be aware of both strengths and weaknesses.

There are many threats to self-image. Children, for instance, are particularly influenced by gaps in their relationship with the people around them. An overburdened teacher may appear indifferent to some of her pupils, particularly toward those who don't appear to have problems yet do not distinguish themselves as being especially bright or talented. Such a teacher regards the communications of these children as sufficiently normal so that special attention on her part is not warranted. However, such a child interprets her response to mean that he is not important in her eyes, and wonders what it is about him that might be disturbing. A parent involved in the problems of making a living, paying the bills, etc., may often ignore the attempts at communication made by his children. Specifically, a child, who as an infant received considerable attention, may be distressed by the withdrawal of that attention once he is able to come and go on his own. He may interpret this to mean that he doesn't have sufficient power to influence his parents to feel that he is important. In another dimension, peers tend to bully those who appear weaker or not quite so aggressive, so that in youthful peer associations rigid hierarchies often emerge, putting some children off to the fringes and making them appear impotent in their own eyes. In addition to all this, the typical attitude of adults toward children is that children are not to be taken seriously. It is almost as though adults assume children do not notice and cannot understand when they are being ignored.

The state of affairs, however, is actually quite contrary to this false belief! A child's sensitivities are as deep as those of adults, though children have considerably less experience to use in managing their feelings. This means that children have their self-image reduced much more easily than do we adults. And this reduction is so much more hurtful and damaging to children. For example, the dressing down given by a neighbor on whose lawn a child steps, the brushing aside of the child waiting his turn in the grocery store, the bumping into children without an "Excuse me"—all are so characteristic of day-to-day living. Each of these activities renders the child less able to communicate in ways designed to cope with the environment.

When we fail to *listen* to the child, or when we ignore his messages, discipline problems in the home and school multiply. In the dissonant semantic environment of increasing alienation, estrangement, and widening distrust, there is the potential to drop out, go delinquent, or become mentally ill. These choices are made by children whose easily bruised self-images have been hit hard in one way or another, as we've just described. The child will carry the ramifications of his choice into his adult life, and maybe for the rest of his life, usually with very unfavorable results. We ought to keep this in mind when we communicate with children, and attempt to place our influence in their environment.

As the attitudes and orientations that will guide his life into the future are being formed, the child interprets and attaches them to *language*—by far the most important instrument he has to influence his way of life. Alienation from the teacher carries over into rejection of what is being taught, coloring what he can and will read, what he will listen to, his speech and writing behavior patterns, and, finally, may carry over into the semantic disorders described earlier.

As success and/or failures are incorporated in his self-image, his communication future is built. At stake is the right answer to the big question: Will his attitudes toward the use of language keep him open to continued development? Or will *identification*$_3$ and *allness* force him to avoid speaking, reading, writing, and listening?

We can see the same kinds of patterns emerging in the modern university. A student comes to a university, presumably, to grow and develop, yet, for the most part, he is forced into a lock-step environment, where the whole society of administrators and professors continually communicates to the student a strong sense of noninterest. It is this feeling, perhaps, that lies at the root of student revolt. The academic environment must, in some way, give the student an opportunity to test himself as a person, and then offer opportunities for improving in areas of weakness. Without the chance to talk, the effectiveness of talk cannot be measured. Without the chance to present ideas freely to interested listeners, feedback is inadequate, and sensible feedforward cannot be developed.

Training in communication should pervade all academic areas. Students should be given the opportunity to present their ideas about history, political trends, social movements, no matter how foolish or immature these may seem to the professors. There is no point to demanding adherence to "revealed wisdom." Any student who would buy the professor's opinions uncritically is too weak to be trusted if those opinions are ever challenged. The typical student performs a ritual. He memorizes the professor's biases long enough to parrot them back on an examination, taking care not to let them get rooted too deeply. Several studies have indicated that faculties really have very little influence in changing attitudes and behaviors of students.

If this sad picture can be believed, then it is absolutely imperative that ways and means be devised to provide opportunities for students to learn to take communicative control over their activities and beliefs. Training in communication must be extended beyond the classroom, and the professors pressured into honest dialog with the students whose right it is to have it. Here is a real communication problem for students to sink their teeth into.

DIFFICULTIES IN MAKING AND ADHERING TO COMMITMENTS

Student bodies today are brighter, better informed, and far more critical about what is going on in their communities than at any earlier time in history. However, demonstrations and riots directed at communication gaps among students, instructors, and administration create public backlashes that threaten both the freedom which students must have to test their ideas and the financial support which is necessary to sustain the university.

The openly bizarre speech behaviors in which some college students indulge are not new phenomena. What is occurring now on the campuses is only a continuation in new and strange forms of existing communication disorders. In generations past they were manifested in outrageous pranks, flagrant violations of regulations, ridiculous initiations in fraternities and sororities, panty raids, and other relatively nonviolent disturbances in the academic community. The coonskin coats, zoot suits, bermuda shorts, and t-shirts of the more affluent, collegiate playboy types evoked an image of students interested only in trivialities, rather than men concerned with the important questions they faced as they entered their careers.

Today's demonstrations and riots aim at different and more significant behaviors, because they are directed at many of the great issues of the times. As the colleges permit more and more freedom for discovery and learning, student responsibility is often ignored or forgotten. The students, lacking perspective and unable to test the extensionality of clashing verbal systems and philosophies, are unable to sort out the orders of abstraction as they are applied to issues in a complex world. In this situation, many students remain in confusion. They are not able to perceive what they can achieve and thus confuse what is *desirable* and what is *do-able*. They demand more than can be given and are disruptive when they do not attain their objectives.

Each individual must make commitments to many other persons and to himself. Without commitments, it is difficult to develop sufficient feed-forward to achieve purposes. Often verbal systems force people into commitments that are unrealistic, ephemeral, and disruptive. With the decline in influence of traditional religion, many students have found it necessary to seek other kinds of systems to which they can adhere. It is clear, however, that the world is so complex that no single system encompasses all the answers, and consequently the most desirable of citizens are those who can sit with others and reason out the most appropriate solution for whatever problem is at hand. Knowledge cannot be acquired critically in operational ways if it must be forced to conform to some system that presently serves as the great gyroscope governing the behavior of man.

Much of our talk is directed toward development of systems of belief and behavior. Our parents attempt to instill in us their rules of virtuous behavior, which frequently conflict with the rules of social success that prevail among a particular peer group. To reject parental rules means violation of whatever trust and confidence exists between child and parent. To reject the values of the group, however, means isolation and loneliness. Much of our behavior, however, is unthinking. Sufficient time is not taken to talk things over and to reason out. The bull session in the dormitory, student union, or local pub provides an excellent arena in which to test moral values and potential behaviors. But our system tends to discourage this kind of interaction, particularly while it tends to demean the verbal contribution the student makes. Actually, it would be most useful to self-development if students were permitted to discuss their commitments honestly and freely, with professionally qualified listeners present to raise questions and to offer critical analysis. Sensible commitment must grow out of feedforward to a goal that can be achieved. Only if goals are selected and achieved can an individual find the feeling of success that is so necessary to the development of his self-image.

SUGGESTIONS FOR DISCUSSION

1. You now have enough information to make up a list of the scientific and artistic aspects of speech. Organize into groups of three. Take a sheet of paper and write "Artistic" on one side and "Scientific" on the other. Now list the distinctly scientific features of speech and the distinctly artistic features of speech in the appropriate columns. For each of the "scientific" aspects of speech, see if you can discover a device by which they can be measured. For each of the "artistic" aspects, come up with some criteria against which they can be evaluated. If you find this exercise unsatisfying or frustrating, see if you can come up with a list of criteria to evaluate "speech effectiveness." Try using the criteria as you evaluate a few speeches. How do you account for the inconsistencies in judgment between you and your classmates?

2. Is "science" a method, a body of knowledge, a way of life, a religious commitment, a method of copping out? What are we talking about when we talk of science? Why do we all seem to express the notion that "scientific information" is of better quality than any other information? Is it possible for a scientist to have "insight"?

3. Is art generally useless, i.e., in order for something to qualify as artistic it cannot be applied to the solution of any of man's problems? Can you think of any artistic productions that were useful? If they were useful, why weren't they called technological innovations?

4. Another good group exercise at this point is to use what you know about communication to make some communication models of what goes on in your local college, community, and, perhaps, the nation. Show who communicates with whom, the direction in which communication flows, and what kind of communication is characteristic of each relationship. When you do the model of your college, locate yourself, the student, and list the ways at your disposal to communicate with the top administration, the faculty, service personnel, etc. If you wanted to organize a protest about some fermenting issue on the campus, where would the most vulnerable spot be in the communication diagram?

5. Write a case history of a friendship of yours. Detail the way you got acquainted, the testing period, the development of trust, the breakdowns of the relationship, the accommodations you made to preserve it, the points of contact at which there was friction. Write this with fictitious names. Gather the case histories from the whole class and read through them. What are the commonalities and differences between them? Using these few case histories as a research sample, what general premises can you establish about "how to preserve a friendship"? What channels of communication were most frequently used? What topics of conversation were most common? What differences can you detect in meaning of the word "friend" as defined by the various case history writers? What relationship does the word friend have with the word communication?

6. To what extent do you listen to yourself? Can you talk yourself into things? Do

you ever carry on conversations out loud with yourself (in private, of course)? To what extent do you think the words you say to others compel you to develop attitudes? A recent piece of research demonstrated that in Nazi Germany the act of saying hateful things out loud (even by people who did not believe them) would heighten real hate and eventually would enable people to do unspeakable things to the object of their hate. Do you think there is any analogy here with the common talk about the establishment, about Afro-Americans, about communists?

7. Why is it that our self-image is rarely the image that others have of us? What is your true image? To what extent does your true image depend on the way other people see you and respond to you? How do the responses of others affect your behavior?

8. If you haven't had much action on your campus lately, you might want to try to stage a demonstration. Pick a topic that is not too threatening. Something like the food in the dorms, or the price of activity tickets. Put up a soap-box on a busy corner and run through a series of protest speeches. Be sure to have some signs. What kinds of people are attracted and how seriously do they immerse themselves in the action? Who objects to what you are doing, and why? (For this exercise you had better have the approval of your college administration!)

SUGGESTIONS FOR FURTHER READING

Robert Ardrey, "Cain's Children," *African Genesis* (New York: Atheneum Publishers, 1961). This is an interesting, and somewhat deflating, view of who we are and what we are doing on Earth. After you read this chapter you will have a better understanding of why we stress human communication and relations.

Hans Toch, "The Psychology of Seeing the Light," *The Social Psychology of Social Movements* (Indianapolis: Bobbs-Merrill, 1965). This section is an excellent summation and overview of perceptions as they relate to the development of personality.

Goodwin Watson, "Culture and Personality," *Social Psychology* (Philadelphia: J. B. Lippincott, 1966). Chapter 9 is an interesting approach to various models and theories that act as catalysts to the human communication process.

12

Deepening Perceptions—
Defeating
Self-defeat

In this chapter we will be concerned with how the long-run effectiveness of the speaker develops new and complex problems for him, and how development of success raises the risk of failure through defective interpretation of new challenges.

The labels "effective," "successful," or "failure," applied to a speaker and his career do not represent definite indexes. George Wallace, for example, was a successful speaker to his followers, no matter what he did, and equally, he was a failure to his opponents regardless of the "quality" of his speaking. It is hard to conceive of an evaluation of a speech made without reference to the speaker and the occasion. Furthermore, to avoid "allness" we must take care not to apply such labels generally. Even the most famous speakers have had their ineffective moments, and many of those who do not fancy themselves speakers at all have had their moment of glory.

Improving speaking means accepting new challenges. Those speakers who never fail probably have a good record because they have avoided particularly sticky communication situations. Virtually anyone can be assured consistent success if their remarks are sufficiently bland and trivial and the occasions on which they speak sufficiently neutral. All they must do is take care not to be trivial and neutral too often, and they will win a reputation for being pleasant humans. A speaker who attempts to persuade a hostile audience about a critical issue, however, raises the risk of failure.

Failure, on one occasion, does not mean defeat. Many of our most famous speakers, men like Edmund Burke, Abraham Lincoln, and Winston
Churchill, had their moments of distress, but because of their early failures,
their chances of success when the issue was truly crucial were raised. Many
speakers are not really aware that mistakes can be profitable learning experiences. Those who are defeated by a few failures, and those who refuse
to recognize the existence of failures destroy their chances for success.
Thomas Dodd and Adam Clayton Powell were both oblivious to failure and
received the censure of their colleagues. And we do not even know the
names of the millions upon millions who were so defeated by a few initial
failures that they never tried again.

The inference that a speaker draws from total and continual success tends
to root him in habits that might spell failure in other circumstances. $Time_1$
is not $time_2$ and $audience_1$ is not $audience_2$. Any child knows that appeals
that work on the parents may not work on the teacher, but the child who
is continually successful in getting his parents to do his will tries to persev-
erate his behavior in school and loses. Yet, he will not recognize the loss.
Furthermore, to continue to utilize speaking techniques that were once
successful but are not effective any longer means that the capacity to receive and respond to feedback has atrophied.

Poor impressions are hard to reverse. Whether it is rational or not, many
decisions are made on first impressions. People tend to shape their later
evaluations to make them conform with the first impressions. A negative
impact fades slowly. A positive impact helps the next interaction. The man
who has built a reputation of trustworthiness has an easier time of defending
his cause. A man with a taint on his record faces insurmountable odds.
Eldridge Cleaver is a good example. In an early book Mr. Cleaver made
some statements frightening to white people. Now, in a more mature career,
his pronouncements taken out of the context of the man make eminent
good sense, yet the white majority will not accept his new ideas largely
because of the fear instilled in them by his first highly unstrategic remarks.

The main question, of course, is how deep is the desire for success? If
the goal is clearly developed out of sensible feedforward, if it is worthy and
if it can be accomplished, then speaking to achieve it demands mobilization
of strategy. It is pointless, for example, to win a verbal encounter with a
heckler, if it means losing the entire audience. Often, the defense of ego is
placed ahead of defense of cause; words and tension escalate. The speaker
may be momentarily satisfied, but he may have defeated himself by jeopardizing the achievement of his goal.

We are thus confronted with two main problems for speakers. Some
cannot develop a feedforward that will give them a successful self-image;
consequently, they do not risk. Whatever worth and merit their ideas have
becomes irrelevant, for those ideas will never be displayed before other
men's minds. The other problem speaker is the man whose success image
is so strong that his objective becomes the defense of the image rather than
the cause. Worthy ideas may become putrescent as the man speaks to maintain his position and power.

Many of our present-day problems show signs of this kind of self-defeat. Rivers and air are polluted, and men are dismayed by it, but those who are disturbed have not yet taken the platform with sufficient vigor to mobilize their fellow citizens to take action. Ecumenism in the church has suffered because men of good heart and good will have not spoken strongly enough on its behalf. And on the other side, weird and wild causes burgeon and flourish throughout the land, because demagogues and extremists have mastered persuasive oratory and have learned the art of moving the hearts of men.

WILL ENTROPY WIN OUT?

Some historians and scientists, observing the self-defeating actions of man, are pessimistic as to our destiny. Others point out that many problem situations have germinated their own solutions as men have devoted their minds to the discovery of new ways to alleviate them. There is capacity for both solution and destruction, but what is clear is that the entropy that seems to spell our doom can be reversed by the negative entropy of human communication.

Pronouncements on the accumulating pressures of neglected problems blare from almost every TV newscast, newspaper, and magazine. We have become so supersaturated with crises that, like the citizens of ancient Pompeii who were fruitlessly warned of disaster so many times, we remain unmoved. We have become saturated with talk of danger. There is no meaning. We don't discriminate among the problems, and we don't assign them realistic priorities. We cling to old assumptions or make no new inferences whatever; we take refuge in saying, "everything will work out somehow."

Refusal to listen is characterized by the apathy and inertia of psychotic vegetable man. The shutting off of stimuli by individuals is typified by the isolation of slums or backward nations where "outside" ideas or "foreigners" are viewed with hostility. Failure to exercise the abstracting abilities, living only on the level of sensual perception, leads to continuing deterioration— to the ultimate death of meaning.

In virtually every situation, some failure of communication is inevitable, especially when speakers fail to meet the challenges that provide the greatest opportunities for effective communication. The most crucial impediment to communication that confronts speakers who would bring about change is created by the apathy, indifference, and insensitivity present in the networks of vested interests, personal commitments, and habitual interests characteristic of those who hear but do not listen.

Perhaps the ominous way in which communications' people use the word *entropy* will make the point more specific. It refers to loss of organization, clarity, and sharpness of a message. The speaker can control for entropy by careful preparation of a message so that it will reverse disorder. Entropy of communication is the death of meaning and of prime concern for anyone who speaks. Loosely, when you say "Everything is going to Hell," "My life is falling apart," or "It was another one of those days," you are suggesting a form of communication entropy. When you change your mind only in order to win the applause of the mob, you have surrendered to entropy.

Apathy, indifference, insensitivity, and devious refusals to present or to accept information are all examples of entropy; they create mounting misevaluations and eventual deterioration of interaction. The validity of this statement has been documented in the massive *Study of History* by Arnold Toynbee.[1] Inability to rise to the challenges of their times and failure in communication characterized the 23 great civilizations that no longer exist. From Toynbee's analysis, we may infer that no civilization had been entirely bereft of competent and informed persons, but each failed to face and comprehend the challenges and to activate the necessary problem-solving forces.

Some of the civilizations had leaders who were recognized as great orators, despite the fact that they were unable to break the barriers of semantic stupor that existed among their people, and we can infer that the civilizations also had men who were capable of solving the problems who did not rise and make any attempt at all.

There appears to be a paradox here. The man who tries often fails, and the man who does not try cannot fail, yet out of risk of failure comes eventual success. The "courage of failure," discussed so aptly by Paul Goodman in *Growing Up Absurd,* is a prime requisite for anyone who wants to succeed in any kind of interpersonal transaction. To meet new people calls for courage, for first contacts do not always succeed. To face a group, a crowd, or a mob is both psychologically and physically threatening, for disapproval or unconcern are more likely responses than acceptance and belief. Yet, it is clear that without extending the effort to meet people, you will meet no one, and without attempting to change the minds of men, minds will not change. The question is, will the men of good will continue to leave the platform to the machinations of those who seek to control minds in order to gain personal power?

LEVERAGE POINTS FOR EXERTING INFLUENCE

Most of us, if we were perceptive and persistent, could exert far more influence than we do.

In the too-often feeble half-life of the majority of our organizations, there is need for and many opportunities open to informed, tactful, and communicative leadership. The impotence of many organizations extends into the grass roots of our democracy, e.g., to local institutions of government, education, religion, and social life. In community after community, the work is carried on by a handful of "work horses" who are not necessarily the most informed or the most competent, but often merely the most hyperthyroid or power hungry. The rest of us just sit back.

[1] Arnold Toynbee, *Study of History* (New York: Dell Publishing Co., 1946), TM674623, Vol. 1.

Democracy is defeated when local leadership fails; real power shifts upward, and citizens look to state and national leaders for amelioration of their problems. What willing reliance is being placed upon the federal government to solve our problems of poverty, education, health, and law enforcement! All these are problems that ordinarily could be prevented by adequate person-to-person and organization-to-organization local communication about the situations that create them. The solution to these problems must eventually occur in operations at the local level; but the more we evade responsibility at that level, the more we must contend with delay, waste, and inefficiency as the lumbering action of the larger organization takes over.

So often we can effectively engage our efforts to improve the evaluations being made and the removal of obstacles to evaluation. There are many leverage points at which a minimum of effort may overcome a maximum of inertia. A pound of "push" multiplies in power and can move a ton of indifference, confusion, and indecisiveness. Factual information and skillful persuasion must be applied at the right time at the right points, but in such a way that the persons concerned move themselves out of their indecisions. Just the right question or just the needed statistic may be all that is necessary to break an impasse. Ideas introduced too soon, too late, or with improper emphasis trigger those old semantic disorders that keep minds closed and arouse hostilities. The problem is that you can't know whether *your* remark would have solved the problem unless you made it, no matter how much you daydream it when it is too late.

Because the skilled speaker observes the deficiencies of communication, he can help a group to become alert to the issues concerned. He can deftly improve its perception of a problem and its abstracting of the essential meaning in both the small and the large picture, and he will contribute to the wisdom of group action. On such a speaker will fall more and more leadership and responsibility.

More and more, individual success is accomplished by the back-and-forth cyclic interplay between *speaker*-listener and *listener*-speaker. Advance emerges with the continuing improvement of semantic isomorphism to environment. When this basic requirement is met, success for the prepared speaker is effected with little or no effort on his part, because he is at the junction of forces that carry him forward, or because he has had the foresight to place himself in a strategic position whereby, with a maximum of skill, he can exert leverage with a minimum of effort.

Mrs. Rose West, a Denver housewife, was at a "junction of forces" when she found herself propelled into national fame because she initiated a boycott of the supermarkets a few years ago. Her active anger at excessive prices, contributed to by such sales gimmicks as trading stamps and promotional games, swiftly struck a responsive chord in thousands of other housewives. Reports in the mass media generated spontaneous reaction throughout the nation. Within several days, hundreds of customerless supermarkets were forced to cut prices on many commodities, and for a brief period the whole nation supported a binge of economy. The price "squeeze" extended into the entire distribution system from retailer to producer. Mrs. West and her little group of associates were overwhelmed by attention from many consumer and governmental organizations. Unhappily, they learned that because of their lack of preparation and their lack of knowledge necessary to force fundamental changes in the economic system, they could not buck the powerful pressures of organizations interested only in profits. Their efforts were defeated; high prices and the gimmicks were mostly restored within six months.

Two recently active speakers did, however, have the foresight to place themselves in strategic positions through which they could make success out of their failures.

1. *Lyndon B. Johnson, recognizing a current of hostility to him among his constituency, elevated his position in the eyes of many citizens by renouncing his claim on candidacy for the presidency in 1968, and used the apparent defeat in order to generate the victory engendered by cessation of the bombing in Viet Nam. He could have defended his ego and run for re-election, but his accurate assessment of feedback led him to the development of intelligent feedforward. He emerged both with strategic success in winning his cause and with his reputation materially enhanced.*

2. *Richard M. Nixon, losing the campaign for the governorship of California, resolved never to run again for office. Through the years, however, his loyal support of the Republican cause and of candidates who represented it built for him a legacy of goodwill and trust that led to his nomination against formidable contenders and mobilized for him the support of the men who were indebted to him so that he won his election.*

Both men employed strategies in order to win their cause. The word *strategy* is heavily laden with unpleasant connotations. Here, we intend it to mean technique, planned and applied to accomplishing a goal. There is nothing unethical about it! It is a function of sufficient openness to receive feedback, intelligent interpretation or intensional processing of feedback, and development of concrete and carefully planned feedforward. Strategies are our personal techniques to help us win our goal. A strategy is neutral. It can be employed by a bad man for a worthy goal; a good man for an unworthy goal; by an evil man for an evil goal; by a noble man for a noble goal. It is the man (spokesman) and the goal (cause) that we evaluate. Perhaps this is why Cicero defined the great orator as a "good man who *also* speaks well."

Application of strategy to the interaction of people and organizations can be compared to the *critical points* which determine outcomes in the physical universe. James Clerk Maxwell, an English physicist of the last century, pointed out that even in the simplest physical system, there are moments when exertion of an infinitely small force can bring about a change of unbelievable magnitude; as when a pebble starts a landslide. The words spoken at the right time, to the right audience, can be an "infinitely small force." The response of the English people to Winston Churchill's, "I have nothing to offer but blood, toil, tears and sweat," is an example of a change of unbelievable magnitude. Lewis Mumford states that Maxwell's doctrine allows for the direct impact of individual humans on the course of history.[2] One man may start the group that leads to the organization that changes the course of the nation. The time must be right; the situation must be correctly assessed; the intervention must be properly strategic.

The speaker who seeks to keep himself in sufficient control of a situation to exert that force when the time is ripe is sensitive to the nature of relationships and the responsibilities he must assume when he essays to change them. What could be less predictable than an audience? A speaker may apply the finest of logic to his planning, but his ability to capture the immediacy of a critical point represents the difference between success and ineffectuality.

Individuals who have achieved success at *human relations* seem to be able to say just the right thing at the right time. Because his remarks are usually appropriate and encouraging, people like him, believe him, want to have him around, and are influenced by him. Many who have this kind of interpersonal control are equally successful on the public platform. They are able to sense the crosscurrents of feeling and opinion and apply strategy like a lever, to move the majority. When speakers display this kind of sensitivity, speech moves to its most artistic level.

Once again the authors seem to evade their responsibility. What should follow now is a list of steps to success. But, lamentably, there is no such list. There are an infinity of recommendations listed in many good texts that you can examine at leisure. What you must know is that it is your responsibility to discover and to experiment with your own strategies, for in the final analysis, it is your personality that will exert the control. Sensitivity that can only be derived through continuous interaction is the essential for interpersonal achievement. Sensitivity can only be gained through practice at interaction, like the advice given to young writers: your only road to success is to write, revise, write, revise, write, revise. So, with speakers, the application of appropriate grammar, good word choice, fanciful metaphor, colloquial leavening, excellent organization, intelligent selection of examples, is not sufficient without the depth that comes from experimentation in many situations, even those in which failure is assured, followed by evaluation of the situation, analysis of the failure, and discovery of the strategy that works. Our recommendation is to read some of the texts available. (Your instructor can recommend many.) And then, interact, talk, experiment! Try your hand at meeting new people, learning to know strangers, opening yourself to other personalities. Appear on the platform. Speak out at meetings. Ask questions in class. While at the beginning you may not get the responses you want, the only way you can achieve isomorphism is through your own test-

[2] Lewis Mumford, *The Transformation of Man* (New York: The Macmillan Company, 1956), Ch. 8.

ing process. Remember that it was the failures that led to the eventual success of virtually every great man in history.

Perhaps there is no place for such sermonizing in a textbook, which, by rights, should be both dry and austere. But we are writing of a science-art! We have discussed the scientific aspects of communication. Art cannot be achieved the same way. Science-art can only be achieved through immersion in the theory, in the act, and in the critical analysis of both together!

Those who have achieved success at directing the activities of others have learned their skill by discovering through experience the limits of their control. Most administrative controls are exerted through communication. The act of directing involves at least as much persuasive impact as the act of motivating. Such clichés as "use channels" appear to be highly important. Successful military leaders discovered that discontent among their underlings was the effect of failing to use channels, and when discontent began to grow among enlisted men, it became necessary to change the channels.

The concept of democratic leadership implies extension of communication channels. The autocrat maintains a downward flow. He receives little feedback; he assumes that his directives are carried out and acts accordingly. Thus his feedback is restricted and his feedforward is based on intensional data. The democratic leader, however, is receptive to upward flow. He utilizes existing channels or creates new ones so that he can get more information from those he supervises. Thus, he has constant feedback, and considerable extensional information to work on. People tend to commit themselves more vigorously to goals they have had a hand in shaping. They respond to leaders who respond to them. Thus, an autocrat must maintain his control largely through force and bribery. When the payoffs are not high enough, support withers away. The democratic leader sustains himself in power by encouraging communicative contact. For the person interested in developing communication strategy, an effective idea to work on is that of maintaining feedback.

THE PRINCIPLE OF NONADDITIVITY

Communication transactions do not expand in complexity arithmetically. Addition of one person to an interacting group does not increase complexity by +1, but rather by a geometric figure. For example, in any relationship involving 3 people, there are three basic relationships, each involving three possible conditions of contact. A is related to B and to C, and C is related to B. A can talk positively or negatively to B and to C, and the same is true of C to B, and the conversation can flow the other way as well. Furthermore, there may be no conversation at all. To calculate the complexity of an interaction transaction use the formula $\frac{(N[N-1])}{2}$ where N is the number of people involved. More subtle analyses can generate a virtual infinity of different types of two-way relationships. Furthermore, if we expand the model to include the possibility of one man speaking to more than one man, we can expand the formula by *N!*, or in a case of a 5-man interaction, $5 \times 4 \times 3 \times 2 \times 1 =$ possible interactions. A little mathematical "fiddling" will show you how inserting a new face in a group can complicate the transaction. Furthermore, in the case of an audience, it is rarely clear who is interacting with whom. Presumably the speaker has an effect on each listener, but the speaker's effect is altered by the effect that the listeners have on each other. The speaker can never know whether the look of disapproval on the face of the man in the sixth row had any impact on the man in the fourth row who was looking around to find an exit, or whether the rigid attention of the people up front has any influence on the restless ones in the back.

Additive thinking about any living organism becomes uncertain because of possible interactions and the different influence that changes in environment might have. In any observed relationship there can be degrees of affiliation or hostility. These cannot be estimated according to any finite scale, yet they are pertinent. The mild assent one man gives to another may have little influence on his behavior, but the imperceptible nod he gives to another man, more influential in his life, may spell defeat for the speaker. A relationship involving 2 women and 3 men cannot be described in $2 + 3 = 5$, particularly if female *A* is fond of male *C*, and dislikes male *D* intensely and dislikes male *E* mildly; but male *C* adores female *A*, and is neutral to female *B* who in turn likes him very much, despite the fact that male *D* likes her and dislikes male *C*, etc . . .

A student who fails a test in English, and then fails another test in English has failed two tests in English, and may conclude that he has failed English. Add to this failure on a chemistry test, and the student may not conclude that he has failed $2 + 1 = 3$ tests, but that he is a *failure*.

Teachers who maintain good communication with their students know that addition or subtraction of one student in the classroom affects the learning process of the whole class. When Susie the spark plug is out sick, the class seems leaden and dull, but when Bernie the disrupter is ill, the class displays real excitement about learning. Furthermore, there are days when Susie is more effective than usual and when Bernie is more disruptive than usual, so that their normal influence on the class is magnified, thus altering every other relationship in the room.

Once again, strategic considerations would seem to suggest that an effective speaker is perceptive of crucial relationships. He attempts to discover who exerts influence in the group; he stylizes his appeals to influence those who can influence others. He attempts to take advantage of nonadditivity, instead of trying futilely to influence each individual one at a time.

The speaker who perceives all the parts or units of his listening audience as equal is in trouble. The speaker who expects the same response from each listener raises his probability of failure. Awareness of difference of kind in relationship, as well as difference in intensity, will inform the speaker that members of the audience might, at any given time, respond to influences other than himself. Furthermore, they will respond in different ways. Their responses will reveal their style of responses, and only after time and careful observation will a speaker be able to distinguish between a nod which means real approval and a nod which is habitually given but which holds no evaluation. He will learn that some people wriggle when they listen, while others sit rigid, but when a wriggle-listener sits next to a still-listener, the wriggling might distract the still-sitter so that his attention is taken off the speech. The look of disapproval the speaker thinks he sees on the face of the still-sitter may well be a response to the wriggler next to him, and have nothing whatsoever to do with the speaker and his message.

Disregard of the impact of relationships often is the cause of difficulty suffered by many speakers and administrators. Politicians and poll-takers (at least the successful ones) are aware of this. If Richard Nixon had assumed that his 16-point lead in the polls was permanent, he would not have invested the final three million dollars in television advertising in the last week of the 1968 campaign. He could not assess the differential influence of a hard-campaigning Hubert Humphrey, and a vigorous George Wallace (and it was even possible that Dick Gregory or Eldridge Cleaver might have had some effect), and of course, it was not clear whether individuals who became disaffected with Wallace would join the Nixon or the Humphrey cause, and if they did join one or the other, what might be the pyramiding, differential effect on the other followers. Consequently, there was continual poll-taking right up to the day of the election to sense the changes in mood and relationship, which in turn changed the nature and intensity of the message beamed to the voters. The triumph of Richard Nixon and the fine showing by Hubert Humphrey were tributes to extensionality and awareness of the deep complexity of relationships in an audience.

SHARPENING PERCEPTION OF ORDER

Discovery of the vast complexities of an interacting world requires imposition of some kind of order on rampant phenomena. A speaker needs some kind of system with which he can arrange information and respond to it. To attempt to take each perception and evaluate it as a single impact would require more data-processing capacity than any of us really has. Sometimes speakers develop such rules of thumb as, "the mind can only absorb what the seat of the pants can endure." This folk wisdom is confirmed empirically by the discovery that the average mind can absorb information in approximately 20-minute units. The application of this adage means that the speaker must select strategies to alter the listening condition (and thus the relationships of his listeners) periodically to keep their attention on his message. If they expect a 50-minute speech, for example, he ought to give them 47 minutes, but not 30 minutes and not 52 minutes. The 30-minute speech would alienate a good share of his audience, for they may not have made plans for the additional 20 minutes. The additional 2 minutes might also alienate those people who made plans to go elsewhere. You know your own response when a teacher lectures overtime.

Furthermore, built into the speech must be diverters, devices to break the tension, coming sufficiently frequently to prevent restlessness at least in the majority of the listeners. Jokes, narratives, even digressions are important to sustain the listening attention of the audience. However, the speaker cannot expect that each device he uses will strike every listener the same way. What he must do is master a general (scientific) principle that describes the modal or most probable behavior of a listener, and then plug it into the specific situation in response to his perception and evaluation of the feedback he receives (art).

Most important in developing these strategies is maintenance of a sense of order in the presentation. Human minds differ in their cognitive ability. Some minds can perceive things connected together in time; others do best when they can see a visual or spatial diagram. The speaker needs to develop his remarks in orderly sequence, the order being dictated as much by the demands of the audience as by the demands of the material. In speaking about a complicated and influential medical center, the historical growth may seem most important in the light of the material, yet a good share of the audience may simply be more receptive to an understanding of how the wards and examination rooms are laid out, or perhaps they want to know the present impact on the community. An effective speaker is prepared enough so that he can shift from a historical exposition to a spatial description in order to meet the needs of his audience as he assesses them from observation of feedback.

We are all subject to acting on precept. We evaluate knowledgeably and properly take care to have priorities laid out well in advance as to what we say and what we say first, second, etc., and to whom. We can't add the eggs after the cake mixture is in the oven, nor can we save the horse if we lock the barn door after the horse is stolen! Inability to perceive order, to bring about order, and to distinguish priorities results in chaos. Rigid and blind adherence to plan in defiance of feedback, however, is self-defeating.

Space relationship is as important as time relationship. Shifting one digit or decimal point in space changes an entire concept. 1965821 and 9165821, or .918 and 9.18 are vastly different. Shift the letters in t-e-a to e-a-t, and you transform a noun into a verb of totally different meaning. "My mother-in-law had a nasty fall" changed to "My nasty mother-in-law had a fall" could raise havoc!

The order and placement of digits and letters in respect to each other can be made in random order. The result is abstract, final, static, and absolute. Take s-c-r-o-j and call it a "dirty word," and you have a dirty word. Rigidity in relationship can be ameliorated by thinking in terms of *dynamic* connections. Space-time allows for more change than space and time.

We speak of integration as a situation. Immediately, we have to know where-when (space-time). The information about a move of a Negro family into a white suburb in Denver is not enough, for example: this had a far different connotation in 1950 than it does now. The explosion of a hydrogen bomb *in China in 1967* changed policies and programs in a measure not calculated when only China's neighbors were concerned about the explosion of an atom bomb in 1960. And when China tests a rocket, everyone shudders.

Individuals may easily assume that they are in complete agreement with each other as they talk about the "same" thing at the "same" level of abstraction. If their conversation continues without regard for each other's abstractings in the lower levels of description, their unconscious deception often ends in utter disagreement. Or dialogue may proceed amicably, but innocuously, until applied to something specific at levels in which meanings are generated, and then it becomes intense. The argument becomes interminable as each speaker silently, and often unconsciously, refers to his private abstractings of the same event. The possibilities are so vast that special effort must be made to discover special meanings.

Disturbance of the communication process in these circumstances is quite frequent. Speakers *start* with generalizations and work toward the specific: a process defined by logicians as *deduction*. Much of the agitation would be avoided if the speaker started with *induction*, which works from specific to general. With sufficient knowledge of the specifics and by using examples as they ascend into the higher abstractions in the natural order of evaluation, they could avoid communication disturbance. Proper evaluation and workable agreements require that unsplittable and circular induction-deduction be constantly corrected to the descriptive levels. On the other hand, deductive speaking seems more clear to the audience. Thus, an inductive-deductive approach must be taken.

The most serious interference to evaluating is failure to predict and anticipate the resulting order at any level, but especially at the first order of abstracting. Ability to predict patterns of sequence depends upon the perception of order, and any control we exert is based thereon.

Unless we are inert and indifferent to the problem, we will be imputing and inferring *causes*. Man has advanced from the primitive stages as he has been able to test the validity of his assumptions as to order.

We, along with the grammarians and linguists, are concerned with the sequences and order in which words are put together in sequences. "The rain fell on the pedestrian" makes sense, but any violation of the order or the sequence of those specific words will evoke disorder among the semantic reactions. If we are to "make sense," nothing is more important than the order in which we arrange our words.

PENETRATING INTO FUNCTION

Skilled communicators regard the perception of function as imperative— one fact so related to another that it is dependent upon and varies with that other. This means that they must be prepared to alter strategies directed to the whole audience when a part of the audience shows movement. Not all evaluation will be made in perceivable feedback. The impact of influential behaviors on other listeners can indicate a function that provides valuable data about how the whole audience can be reached.

Skilled speakers often find audience data hard to come by. Often they call upon research teams and computers to determine functions, and they withhold opinion until they can obtain up-to-date information concerning the causes of the problems they confront. They realize that there may be many causes for serious problems. Unfortunately, all of us are prone to look for a single cause of trouble which will permit a simple solution, and we tend to assign what is only a precipitating event as the sole cause. The immediate function is usually the converging of many causes back through long chains of influences that cannot be specifically allocated. The act of pulling the trigger to kill oneself had its origin long before the act itself. Riots in a slum are the result of long-standing and complicated conditions for which there is no one solution.

Thus, nothing of importance is really isolated. A vacuum is filled almost as fast as it is created. Physical gaps serve as media to carry countless influences of magnetism, polarities, radiations, and inductions. In the fields of invisible activity, everything seems to influence everything else given enough time-space. For example, in the summer of 1967, French President Charles de Gaulle was on a state visit to Canada, where he made the remark, "Long live free Quebec." He was urging French-speaking Canadians to take their destiny into their own hands. Apparently he permitted the delight and adulation of a small minority to becloud his perception of the immense social forces inherent in the Canadian population. He disregarded function. He grossly neglected the variables, changes of quantity, magnitude, and quality aspects that have transpired since the French first settled in Quebec, and he ignored the interaction of those variables upon each other in the inevitable manner in which one variable depends upon another. He didn't see that he would anger French manufacturers who depend upon Canadian buyers, as well as French hotel keepers who depend upon the continuing influx of American tourists who, incensed by de Gaulle, might omit France from their itineraries. Economists could have provided for him relatively accurate measures of these correlations and of their reliability.

De Gaulle blindly abused the hospitality of a great nation of which he was an invited guest. He earned himself a shattered image as a statesman, and he created a disturbance that was multiplied in nonadditive ratios by the mass media. History will probably never exonerate him from the stupidity of his misevaluation. His stubborn refusal to apologize disturbed even the broadminded who might otherwise have excused his transgression.

MOBILIZING OUR KNOWLEDGES IN OUR SEARCH FOR STRUCTURE

Farmers order their planting and harvesting of crops according to the seasonal cycle, and they know the general pattern of climatic changes in their particular localities. No farmer would try to grow oranges in North Dakota, nor plant rice in Arizona.

Doctors have become more and more precise in their diagnoses as they have learned to recognize the hidden causes of the fevers of infection. There was a time when most fevers were treated with the same few remedies. Later when doctors could differentiate among diphtheria, polio, smallpox, etc., for all of which a high temperature was a symptom, they ascertained differences and could prescribe widely differing remedies to cope with the unique structure of the disease. Even then, no prescription was routine until the effects had been established and it was determined there was auspicious similarity in the results obtained.

Prediction becomes more reliable as the knowledges of a specific situation in a specific location fall into patterns. For example, the seeming disorder of the new media is really segmental, in that we obtain no more than *partial* views that the editors think will hold our attention. We often remain ignorant and misinformed of the complete event, of the sometimes world-wide ramifications engendered, and of underlying invisible and inaudible structures that are emerging. We are aware only of symptoms and superficial manifestations of a random event. This editorial phenomenon was termed the "gatekeeper effect" by the late Dr. Kurt Lewin, who made extensive studies of the editor's role as a selector of which news is reported in the media. Others, such as Wilbur Schramm and David Manning White, have refined the "gatekeeper concept." We do not observe and study long enough and deeply enough to discover the *pattern*.

The critical point may be specific location in space-time, or it may be specific data in time-space. For example, socialist and communist demonstrations regularly occur in many parts of the world on May 1. Likewise, we can predict with certainty that many celebrations will take place in the United States on July 4. There is prescribed regularity in the meetings of state legislatures at a certain time in certain place. Old Faithful spouts faithfully in Yellowstone National Park.

In studying any structure of activity we must determine precisely that aspect wherein the pattern is discernible. Only when we observe maintained patterns do we discover enough of the actual structure to help us plan. As we ascertain regularity in structures, we have a basis for estimating probabilities—thereby improving predictability.

There is patterning in the way your automobile motor functions, even though you turn on the ignition at irregular intervals, i.e., if the unity of activity is maintained, there is structure. Therefore, we can predict the motor will start. And if it doesn't?

We must realize that we recognize and understand patterns and structure only if we have the ability to recognize similarities in the differences, in the repetitions which occur in apparent disorder. To discern similarities is not always easy, for the abstracting of similarities is the abstracting of wholes in comparison with other wholes in our memory patterns. Of course, the converse immediately becomes true. If we do not see the differences in the similarities, our perceptions will be unreliable, because our observations have been superficial or our memories inaccurate.

Analogy powers the whole symbolizing process, but any analogy becomes false at some point, because two things are never totally alike. Similar yes, alike no. Failure to notice when similarity veers to dissimilarity can ruin the evaluation. At some point during our perception and the pondering that corrects it, we need to have a spontaneous insight into structure, which is reliable for prediction. Subsequent hypotheses and assumptions may or may not correct for isomorphism and form the basis of our message.

Most patterns and structures are not "sensed," because the segments accessible to our senses extend far beyond the relatively narrow spectra to which our senses respond. Some range into the submicroscopic; some range into and beyond the galaxies.

Relatively few of even our more intelligent and better informed speakers are able to realize the potential of their knowledges. Many readers bypass an author, because they "freeze" at one level of abstraction, while what they read was said or written at another order. Semantic rigidity permits no translation of jargon or terminology, because there is no meeting of minds at the nonverbal levels. The unity of the first-order operations and relationships perceived, together with the transformations, order, and functioning, are segmented, or are left in limbo.

We all so often remain semantically "blocked" when we most need to assimilate our knowledges for an all-at-once application. Our badly needed symbolism, in memories or in the libraries, is halted, and we remain inflexible, and unable to bring about that ordering of abstractions which releases our thought processes. Major areas of our sources are left unused and our knowledges are demobilized. We fail to grasp the message; we can't or won't see the pattern; we talk without awareness of structure; we evaluate on the basis of parts; we ignore the wide perspectives of wholes; and we fail to delve into the relevant.

Specific operations and relationships are, at least theoretically, connected, and are in interaction with everything else via transformations. Therefore, everything is relevant to everything else. An incoherent speaker, however, can try to make everything—past and present, remote and near— have an impossible equal relevancy. The creative speaker permits his thoughts to range far into the most remote relevancies, but he rigorously restricts his expressed thoughts to what is directly and immediately relevant to his situation and purpose.

We are confused as we listen to the speaker who sees only the similarities and erupts in a flood of verbal incoherencies. We are disappointed in the speaker who has a narrow absorption with differences only, because he does not see much that is relevant either. When the two inadequacies are combined, our frustration is almost complete!

The innovator will not succeed in getting his ideas accepted unless he is quick to correct his analogies—bringing clearly into relief the differences in the similarities with the use of precisely supported facts and logic. He can correct his aberrations and impracticality, *unless* his I_3 and allness reactions are too formidable. The academician is often accused of being unable to express what he feels are significant theories in pragmatic terms.

The astute critic, aware of similarities in the differences, performs his most important function by bringing the innovator down to the earth of extensionality. But a critic whose perceptions never rise above the minute differences—the nitpicker dedicated to the status quo—may remain unmoved until a changing world detours him from the mainstream of human affairs.

Persons whose knowledges are specialized, whose vistas are circumscribed by the routine terminologies of a single vocation or profession, tend to remain unadjusted to the complex world of today. Often they are unable to discern patterns and to appreciate and evaluate the great structures of the universe in which they exist. They belong to the myriads who are preoccupied with distorted self-images. They oscillate between indifference to change and rebellion against it. But life may become an exciting challenge for those specialists who break through their verbal cocoons to operational levels outside of their immediate professions. For example, professional football star Frank Ryan earned a Ph.D. in mathematics; CBS-TV's news chief Richard Salant is a lawyer; playwright Robert Ardrey is a recognized ethological authority; Dr. Ernest Becker is a professor adept at many disciplines; and Dr. John Kenneth Galbraith is an economist who is also at home in politics, history, political science, sociology, and as a writer and satirist.

Thus, the illumination of a structure increases as we deliberately explore it from as many modes of perception as possible, such as looking for transformations, looking for order, and looking for function, which requires looking into the often invisible and inaudible levels of operations. To do this, we need to employ as many of the different forms and media as are available, the messages of which are relevant to the situation concerned. Poetry, painting, music, drama, and the other arts bring an indispensable balance into the illumination derived through rigorous and exact scientific description. Action based upon the purely factual and the tightly logical may proceed crudely to hurt people, if the speaker does not have the sensitivity to human values that the arts are supposed to induce and that immersion in them often brings about.

The words *transformation, order, function, structure* are being used to help us extend our perceivings, so we may overcome narrowed and blocked abstractings. As with any other avenue of exploration, we must not permit these words to divide the indivisible and so cause us to think of the *one* as being of separate parts. There is no such thing as a transformation without order or one that is separate from its functioning. Things may appear separated but only to the nonperceptive man.

SUGGESTIONS FOR DISCUSSION

1. How are the influences on a speaker "nonadditive?" What does nonadditive mean? How does it apply to the communication act? Why does nothing succeed like success? Have the Green Bay Packers ever won ball games simply because they are the Green Bay Packers? (Ask the Dallas Cowboys!) Do you know any people that seem to succeed all the time in social interaction even when they seem to you to be acting foolishly? Can you think of any nonadditive influence in your life? Can we call Joe Namath "nonadditive man"?

2. Try some exercises in role-playing the effect a personality has on history. Suppose Adlai Stevenson had been Emperor of France instead of Napoleon. Suppose Richard Burton had been a presidential candidate on the Democratic ticket in 1968. Suppose Al Capone had been general of the British Armies in India at the time Mahatma Gandhi was striving for independence. Suppose Nikita Khrushchev

had been ruler of North Viet Nam at the time of the Gulf of Tonkin incident. Make up your own supposes, and act them out. How is the course of history affected by the presence of the right person at the right time? What kind of personality do we need as a national leader now? Where is he?

3. How is it possible for one person to enter a group and take over? Do some observation of groups on your campus and see if you can map the influence that individuals have over the way the group operates and how well they succeed at their task. How does the principle of nonadditivity help explain the reason for their influence? How would you go about developing a nonadditive influence for yourself in a group of which you are a member?

4. The case of the men who succeed in more than one field is very interesting (cf. Rowan and Martin). Is it possible that they succeed in more than one field because there is some common analog of success, i.e., a structure that will inevitably lead to success no matter where it is applied? The idea of common structure or analog ought to be explored deeply. Can you find any commonality in structure between physics, botany, sociology, and drama? Try some other combinations. What commonality does a lawyer have with a plumber? A physician with a bootblack? A poet with a streetcleaner? A "hippie" with an "activist"? A "Greek" with an "Independent"? (Try all the combinations you can find.)

SUGGESTIONS FOR FURTHER READING

J. Samuel Bois, *Explorations in Awareness* (New York: Harper and Row, 1958), and *The Art of Awareness* (Dubuque, Iowa: William C. Brown Company, 1967). These books give many interesting insights into our problems of getting and managing knowledges.

Rudolph Flesch, "One Language After Another," *The Art of Plain Talk* (New York: Harper and Brothers, 1951). While this chapter reads like comedy, it makes a very cogent point about language and communication.

Harold D. Lasswell, "Strategies of Inquiry: The Rational Use of Observation," *The Human Meaning of the Social Sciences,* ed. Daniel Lerner (New York: Meridian Books, 1959). Dr. Lasswell, a pioneer in communications research and effects, takes a long look at the rise of specialized knowledge and its relation to human communication.

Harry Weinberg, *Levels of Knowing and Existence* (New York: Harper and Row, 1959). Review Chapter 5, which is about additivity, logic, and rational thinking processes.

13

*Bringing Unity Among
the Dissonances—
Inner Listening*

In the preceding chapter, we concluded that communciation becomes more adequate through discipline of the self to achieve deepening perceptions of the world. Our freedom to explore unknown ideas depends upon breaking through our inhibitions to curiosity. The flexibility we develop in freedom depends upon our ability to overpower restraints that impede our thought and action. Thus, as increased ideational power is made relevant to our purpose, we become more productive as speakers in more complex situations.

This art of expression, which overlays the science we can bring to self-control, is needed most in our everyday person-to-person associations as we live through changing situations, which so easily can disrupt our routines and which may lead to stress and emergency. "Keeping in tune" with another person all the time in every way has probably never been achieved in the relationship of any two people. Complete semantic compatibility would require that the behavior of both parties emerge from identical inheritance-environments. So, our responses to others and their responses to us occur on the shaky basis of our individual perceptions of each other. Many times our impressions are unreliable, because of incompleteness in our abstracting, distortions of our inferences, and façades behind which we conceal our real selves.

The order we bring into our relationships with others depends upon harmony of the uniqueness within ourselves—upon our self-control. No achievement will be bestowed upon us, so our survival depends on personal concordance. Persons in concordance with themselves tend to induce concordance among their fellows, with corresponding good return to themselves. Persons discordant within themselves make for discordance among their fellows, regardless of whether or not they intend it, with corresponding trouble for themselves. In simple terms, all we are saying is that people with pleasant personalities seem to be able to have more friends than people with angry or somber personalities.

Discordance-concordance is built into our personalities. No one is able to completely escape his past. We emerge from it, and it builds us in somewhat of an additive sense, but voices out of the past may make enough noise to block out new signals. Our problem is how to make our past give greater meaning to the present.

CONCORDANCE-DISCORDANCE INTERFACES

As the interchanges between two healthy communicators proceed, there is involvement, understanding, and tolerance. As each responds to the other, they clarify expectations, increase trusts, and make mutual commitments. In every relationship, however, there are bound to be vaguenesses and ambiguities. Persons concordant with themselves are confident that most misunderstandings can be worked out, so they are careful to let each other know where they may not be able to meet expectations. This is meaningful communication.

On the other hand, persons discordant within themselves misevaluate grossly. They harbor conflicting allness attitudes; they tend to expect too much of others, and demand that these expectations be fulfilled. When the fulfillment does not occur, they swing to reluctance to trust others about anything.

A satisfactory communication relationship can continue on an even keel indefinitely, provided there is constant effort, mutual thoughtfulness, and concern for changes through which each must live. If one party becomes hypersensitive about some point, careful evaluation of the change in relationship is needed. We know that disagreements tend to fade if we allocate them within their specific dates, and recognize their potential for changing relationships. Before attitudes become hardened, ambiguity should be clarified to preserve trust. The mature communicator is careful not to let his relationships with others fall into disarray. By keeping the reservoirs of good will full, he puts himself in position to receive unexpected collaboration and "good luck" in the future.

Persons who are concordant within themselves are able to explore their semantic disorders with each other, and to accept commitments and responsibilities which come as communication relationship deepens. In short, they are able to communicate about their communicating! In no realm is this more important than in a courtship or another relationship that requires long-time association and will be subjected to frequent "testing." To evade genuine communication or to fail to take time to achieve it is to guarantee multiplication of frictions and fractures in relationships.

We have noted before that two-way communication is the most difficult level of communication, and it is the level that requires the greatest discipline, including discipline of delayed reactions by at least one of the parties, as well as permission of freedom of expression without recrimination. The build-up of self-reflexiveness and positive feedback, which demands that expectations be fulfilled, is dangerous to a relationship, because it leads to quarrels. The immediate comfort of verbal explosions carries a high price, usually the rupture of contact. Once a party to a relationship explodes, the process is irreversible; scars remain even after apparently successful attempts at forgiveness and reconciliation. As Benjamin Franklin wrote, "Anger is never without a reason, but it is seldom a good one."

Our personal interchange can be summarized in the following four categories of overlapping behaviors:

1. The most difficult relationship exists between two persons each of whom is discordant within himself and discordant externally. Such persons, severely ill mentally, are usually under institutional care, which prevents them from damaging themselves and others. Because of their alienations from everything and everybody, only the intervention of specialized health counselors or psychiatrists can possibly effect even momentary communication of acceptable relationship. Devoid of self-control, two discordant persons will have only bizarre relationships and conflict may be expected, so that any accommodation to personal needs is accidental.

2. When *discordance*-concordance person meets *discordance*-concordance person, viable relationships cannot be expected. The relationship is characterized by frequent flare-ups, threats, coercion, and displays of temper, with the result that cooperative enterprise is impossible. As their involvement in communication deepens, matters become worse, even dangerous. Self-reflexiveness is triggered in each, which, in turn, intensifies suspicion, envy, hate, anxiety, and fear. To remain safe, communication is usually frozen at superficial and formal levels that, of course, can do little to resolve the problems of either. For example, when personal problems are mentioned, a crisis is precipitated. Finally, in their ambivalence, both parties may vacillate from casuistry to irrational emotion, doing whatever is necessary to preserve the shreds of their fragile self-esteem.

3. When *concordance* meets *discordance*-concordance, the superior self-control of concordance can conserve relationships indefinitely, but frequently without satisfaction to either party. Concordance must work too hard to protect *discordance*-concordance to be concerned with satisfying his own needs. The semantic disorders of *discordance*-concordance, the anxieties, hostilities, and guilts, tend to overwhelm the trusts, loves, and faiths needed for adequate communication. *Concordance* must retain a high degree of tolerance and discipline to permit the relationship to survive the emergencies that arise.

4. When high level of *concordance* meets high level of *concordance*, there is sufficient understanding and sensitivity present for each to satisfy some of the needs of the other. Their interaction is characterized by a freedom for careful analysis of their interactions. However, because of their sensitivity to each other, this is necessary only when they discuss the vital questions in their lives. Their argument will be characterized by logical reasoning and a search for more facts. Their decision-making is a give-and-take relationship based on mutual freedom to correct and improve their evaluations.

Only highly *concordant* people are able to help those who are less concordant to help themselves. Such people are in great demand in the professions, particularly health, education, social work, management, and communication. They are especially important to aid in resolving the great problems of management-labor relations, mental health, racial integration, poverty, and war and peace. The *concordant* person is most likely to be innovative and creative, and his interpersonal communications and interactions may be interesting.

The four categories just discussed may enlighten your judgment and provide you with some practical insight into the "why" of communication failures between people. Contact between people is maintained through communication that reflects concordance-discordance. If you keep in mind that discordant personalities tend to heighten communicative disturbances, and that concordant people do the opposite, you will recognize how imperative it is that guidelines be employed to permit people to become more consonant as they work together, to bring unity among the dissonances.

An analogy may perhaps clarify this concept. As we attempt this musical analogy remember that we have said before that all analogies fail at some point. If a person is to "make music," he must have the skill to keep in key with his own melodies and those played around him. A few players are able to transpose from one key to another, while others play only in one key and never are able to harmonize. To achieve the fullness of communicative "music," we must be able to make our sounds consonant with others. Whatever our role, accompanist or soloist, we must take the other into account. Instruments must supplement and complement each other in a communicative duet. However, exact duplication would be wearying. Coordination of overtones enriches the performance of each player, so that harmony can be brought out of their diversity. *Together* they produce beautiful music, where alone they might be discordant. In a musical duet, the participants usually "speak" in synchronization; in speech they alternate in various interchanges. The rhythm must be consonant, however, and each player must explore the extent to which he harmonizes with the other. Do I *listen* to you before I speak? Do you really *listen* to me? Are we "in phase" with each other? Our semantic symphony over, we now turn to the animal world for additional comparisons in communicative behavior.

Association and communication in the animal realm are based on efforts to meet the needs for survival. Associations that are not in the best interest of the group are met with rebuffs and hostility. For example, the animal that seeks gratification at the expense of the group is expelled from the group.

Specifically, in colonies of wolves, no single wolf can eat until provision has been made for the pack. Monkeys who seek sexual gratification out of season are cast out from the colony. Serving the ends of the group guarantees satisfaction of individual needs.

Human society is organized for essentially the same purposes, and antisocial people are either isolated or destroyed. The adhesive of the units of human society is, of course, communication, and each person seeks gratification by communicating with others. However, unless the gratification is mutual, neither party can be satisfied. Expression of high-pressure demands may achieve compliance or acquiescence, neither of which is as gratifying as agreement. Thus, in any human relationship, communication must be in "phase," i.e., synchronized so that both parties meet their needs. This calls for careful attention and control by both parties.

Keeping in phase is impossible, for example, if listening is superficial. This lack of listening is quite evident at cocktail parties and other social gatherings, during which superficial discourse is the order of the day. It has been suggested that everyone either talks or thinks about what he will say next while the other person is speaking. Thus, no one really listens. And the scores of recall tests, if given to cocktail-party guests, would no doubt be quite low. However, in deeper relationships, where communication becomes meaningful, more is required than mere hearing of the spoken words. There must be deep inner listening that abstracts what the speaker intends to say and what he is unconsciously saying about himself at the same time. Listening to voice modulations, rate of speech, and hesitancies must be combined with seeing and sensing nonverbal bodily postures and demeanor. Careful observation and abstraction can provide cues to the needs the speaker is expressing, so that responses can be directed to inner needs— not merely words.

But no two persons can be perfectly compatible about everything all the time. Even the most devoted lovers have their irritations. We may easily be rubbed the wrong way, and we may tend to be oblivious of the silent frictions we cause in the other person. We would often be shocked if we became aware of the damage our words do. Recall, for example, our discussion of the effects of our words on children (see page 184). Thus, when these effects are escalated in adults, disruptive conflict may occur, if we do not take care to investigate the effects of our communication. The difference between communication and rhetoric is in degree, not in quality, and intelligent analysis can improve both. For example, your recognition that each person is a unique individual may assist, rather than impede, your relationships. When the differences are not noticed and you expect one person to behave like another, your relationship with that person may be disrupted by semantic noise. Successful communication is characterized by careful analysis and response to the unique personality of your listener, as reflected in his responses to you.

Although there have been many hundreds of volumes written about *human relations,* it becomes more and more evident that there is no clear prescription for improving them. Virtually everyone agrees that virtually everyone else ought to improve, however. Consequently, we will not regale you with a long list of attributes or a spurious list of techniques. We will assert, however, that attention to the following points can substantially assist you in developing sensitivity to others:

1. Be aware of uniqueness. Do not expect similar responses even from people who appear to be similar.
2. Be aware of complexity of relationship. Remember that insertion of one more person into the relationship can pyramid the difficulty, and removal of the "right" person from the relationship can materially alleviate it.
3. Remember that *there will be trouble*. It cannot be avoided. Much of interaction is devoted to remedying difficulty.
4. Avoid attempting to analyze variables out of context. Personality must be considered in a social milieu as influenced by physiology. A hard chair and an allergy to smoke can disturb a relationship even when both people are men of good will and the social conditions are comfortable.
5. Remember that success comes through proper application of strategy. This can only result from substantial feedback (extensional) intelligently processed (intensional). Keep the feedback coming in by listening carefully and observing closely.
6. In processing feedback, be careful to discriminate between the desirable and the do-able. You may not get a Catholic to denounce the ban on birth control, but you can get him to understand why you approve of birth control. Set your goals so that you have some chance to achieve them.
7. Try to avoid making a combat out of conversation. Seek ways in which both parties can win by achieving their goals. It is easier to achieve mutual goals than to destroy another person while achieving your own.

LEVELS OF AWARENESS CONFRONT LEVELS OF AWARENESS

When individual personalities meet, much of the interrelationship is concealed beneath the audible and visual levels, because it is impossible, at first glance, to perceive individual inheritance, background, unique experiences, and talents. But what we say can provide this information if it is attended to, because we are not able to conceal our personality from a careful listener. Both our strengths and weaknesses are communicated. Furthermore, our attitudes toward the "other" are also revealed, and we attempt to infer how our listener is responding. However, we are often concerned more with the response to us as a person than to our ideas. Often we try to classify our inferences by labels, thus permitting I_3 to impede the relationship. If our labels apply only to the superficial, we are prevented from becoming aware of deeper personality traits. The following illustration is offered to help you become aware of a communication relationship. Mr. *A* and Mr. *B* interact in respect to the problem of air pollution and lung cancer (APLC).

1. The first level of awareness is in *what each "knows,"* or what each individually has abstracted about APLC. What *A* and *B* know *is not* APLC; what they know *is not all* about APLC; and what each knows has a different bias. In their inferences and self-reflexiveness, their judgments are not free of distortion. The majority of people rarely rise above this awareness level of meager and secondhand information generalizations, and of unchecked and untested assumptions. Such awareness may result in direct collision, quarrels, and tensions. As Mr. *A* talks to Mr. *B* complications arise if one or the other remains at this primitive level of awareness. Their attention to each other is clouded by inferences about the other. For instance, Mr. *A* feels there is no connection between AP and LC. Mr. *B* accuses him of owning stock in an air-polluting company. Thus, inference has taken over, and the real issues about APLC begin to recede as personality conflict increases.

2. A more sensitive level of awareness is *what each "knows" about his "knowing,"* which is the extent to which each is conscious of his own abstracting about APLC. Mr. *A* begins to see that he might not have all the facts about APLC, but Mr. *B* continues to criticize Mr. *A's* personality. While Mr. *A* seeks better isomorphism with APLC in his talk, Mr. *B* remains frozen in his bigotries. Mr. *A* can now control what he says *and* remain open to feedback. He can resist becoming hostile to Mr. *B*, because he can understand why he behaves as he does. But Mr. *B* continues to attack Mr. *A*. He has lost the issue of APLC, and his talk reflects his problems in abstracting. Meanwhile, Mr. *A* is able to define his own communication deficiencies. He wants to ask questions about what he realizes he doesn't know about APLC. Mr. *A* has a base from which he can control his communication. He can respond both to ideas and audience.

3. The third level of awareness is *becoming conscious of abstracting in the other person.* It requires intense listening, sharp observation of others, and of himself. Previous acquaintance with people who were unable to move beyond the first two levels, people such as Mr. *B*, helps him to interpret what is happening under the façades. For instance, Mr. *A* may infer that his questions may have threatened Mr. *B*. Mr. *B* ignored his question. Why? Was he afraid his cough might indicate the beginning of lung cancer? Was he inferring that Mr. *A* thought this, even if he hadn't expressed it? Was he attempting to justify smoking by making AP the prime cause of LC? Mr. *A* will now take care that Mr. *B* obtains reassurance and support for his self-image. Mr. *A* can ask questions or make statements designed to help Mr. *B* into an evaluative state. He may show Mr. *B* his personal stake in the issue of APLC, and he may also indicate the reasons for his own questions and show Mr. *B* why it was impossible, initially, to accept a casual relationship with the limited evidence. Mr. *A* may reinforce Mr. *B's* self-esteem by motivating him to find the missing facts. Thus Mr. *A* moves the conversation back to the issue and away from personal conflict.

At this third level we can go beyond the discussion of issues. For example we can perceive more of what a wife, friend, or boss may be trying to get through to us. Potentially embarrassing situations can be avoided by understanding the potential for threat and spotting it early, so that our conversation partners can be protected and assisted in moving up one level in their awareness. Achievement of the third level means increase of mutual influence.

4. A fourth level of awareness, which is rarely achieved and then only briefly, depends upon expansion of the third. The fourth level is the level of speculation by a speaker about what a group thinks about his ideas and about his personality. The few who are adept at this level—for example, "highly charged" executives, educators, clinicians, preachers, and politicians —succeed in getting their ideas adopted and carried through. People with this skill are mature observers of the effect of social pressures. Sometimes, however, attempts to win acceptance are not accompanied by concern for the ethicality of ideas. The ability to win the minds of others does not necessarily go along with wisdom. Skill at selling a solution does not endow the solution with truth. Thus a speaker's *charisma*, his "Pied Piper" image with his audience, may be powerful, while his ethical image may be somewhat suspect.

It is exceedingly difficult to make judgments about the ethicality of a man or a cause. Because it is so difficult, we must assume a certain decency and rationality in humans, and infer that if they are given the opportunity to hear the various sides of an issue and observe many different people representing the views with equivalent skill, they will be able to distinguish between the genuine and the sham, the personal self-seeker and the man committed to human progress. This, perhaps, is the most legitimate goal for speech training; to prepare as many humans as possible to assume the task of speaking out to the best of their ability, so that all of us can be better informed and have a better perception of the issues and problems involved in the various decisions with which we are confronted.

These, then, are the four awareness levels. They do not divide neatly, for they lie on a continuum. It is possible for a speaker to step back and forth across the borders of the various levels. Although speakers are quite capable of performing up and down the levels, we hope that the hypothetical progress report will show you how to complete the steady climb to the fourth level. This is the abstraction level you want to attain when you speak to an audience or interact on a person-to-person basis. However, there are other forces that enter this system, and one of them is *silence*.

Through the various levels, silence speaks. We reveal much by what we choose not to talk about! Silences communicate; they are potent in stimulating inferences. They may be used deliberately to persuade.

"I wonder why he didn't say something about that?" you ask as frequently as you ask "I wonder why he said that?" Such inference questions show a lack of understanding at a given moment. Increasing communication maturity helps us to withhold inferences, to listen longer, and to observe silent behavior to obtain more information.

ROLE INTERACTING WITH ROLE

In terms of communications, *role* may be described as the semantic costume in which a speaker dresses himself to meet the expectations of his audience. A good example of this is the manner in which entertainers change characters for roles. Tommy Smothers is actually a rather sensitive, yet sardonic, young man, but his expected TV *role* is that of a bumbling, inarticulate sibling to his brother Dick's smooth performance. Politics can supply another example of *role*. When Lyndon B. Johnson was president, he perceived his expected role as that of a "humble servant, quietly dedicated to helping America along the path to greatness." Once out of the public eye, though, his manner was much more forceful, his tactics effectively shrewd, and his communication often direct and crude, according to those working around him.

On our various levels of awareness, we assign roles to ourselves as well as expect them from others. The other person may not see himself as you do, nor does he see you as you see yourself. One person may attempt to play the role of wise man, only to appear a sad fool to another person who sees himself as wise. Obviously, discrepancies between role perceptions can distort or complicate a communicative relationship.

Roles are often fixed by using labels. "Doctor," "preacher," "teacher," "laborer," "citizen," "mother," "student"—all define sets of behavior we have learned to expect from persons who carry those labels. We tend to develop prototypes of label behavior in our mind and are disappointed if the "other" does not conform to our expectations. Unfortunately, the other may have a different prototype in his mind. We may expect a "doctor" to act like Jim Kildare, while "doctor" sees himself as a Gillespie. The variation in expectation can subvert understanding and act as a serious barrier to communication.

On the other hand, understanding may be enhanced if we seek to respond to the other person as he sees himself, rather than attempt to force him to perform as we expect. Finding the role the "other" seeks to play calls for careful observation, control of inferences, and performance, by us, on the fourth level of awareness.

We may also have problems if the behaviors we want other people to perceive are inconsistent with the roles we have defined internally for ourselves. Inconsistency between actions and goals makes it difficult for us to wear a convincing mask. There must be consonance between external action and internal goals. Dissonance between them is often classified as insincerity, because the behavior does not ring true. Thus, the child becomes suspicious when the father tells him the spanking is for his own good, because he can perceive the need of tension-release by the father.

The adequacy of a speaker may be measured by the number and variety of honest roles he can assume and sustain in the generalized perceptions made of him by others. This flexibility is necessary to the artist-speaker, reader, actor, or discussion leader, and also by teachers and clinicians. A few actors become famous for one outstanding role, but most professionals can make many kinds of roles ring true. The actor learns techniques of external control, but for most of us, internal commitment is essential to the appearance of honesty.

Discordant persons have difficulty in sustaining any role believably. They may tend to accept I_3 derogatory labels, such as "failure," "bookworm," "dolt," "unstable personality," "atheist," "socialist," "conformist," "radical." Sometimes they rationalize by saying, "If you have the name, why not the game?" Unfortunately, it is virtually impossible to internalize an external role conferred on you without becoming mentally ill. Honest communication requires the reverse, which is externalization of internal roles.

The effective speaker manages to avoid accepting labels. He seeks approval of his behavior only as he behaves it. He is careful to fulfill the roles he undertakes as precisely and thoroughly as necessary, to satisfy his internal goals. He tends to be indifferent to labels, because he seeks to establish his identity as a unique, autonomous, meaningful person. For such a speaker, no label will hold for long, because he will be evaluated as the unusual, dynamic, many-sided person he is.

Fiction and dramatic literature provide a vast heritage of materials for role study and for the development of oral interpreters and actors. At the same time, these materials provide examples that throw light on communication in its whole range from disorder to creativity. Experience in these activities provides opportunities to develop and to obtain new speech skills, as we explored earlier. But let us expand on that theme here.

ROLE-TAKING AND ROLE-PLAYING

There is probably no better experience in the development of two-way communication and listening than practice in taking and sustaining different roles, i.e., *role-playing*. Role-taking requires that the speaker put himself in another person's shoes, personality, and life. To accomplish this successfully, the speaker must forget himself, and then give full attention to what the character whose life he fills will say, and do, and feel, although he will continue to suffuse his role with his unique personality.

The best role-players go beyond the specifics and details supporting the plot. Through inference and imagination, they fill in the gamut of emotions justified by the context of the play—extensionalizing the character into their own world beyond the bare details prescribed by the playwright or director. The best of actors plays his role as no other person can, for his role is a synthesis of playwrighter's lines and actor's perception, yet the acting-out internalizes empathy for the role.

Offstage, the most basic experience in role-taking and interpersonal communication lies in putting oneself into the lives of everyday associates in real life. It is the special responsibility of older persons and of those in positions of authority, e.g., the parent or teacher who is not aware of the inner feelings of the child, the bully who "lords it" over his younger siblings or peers, or the boss who bulldozes those he "controls." All should expect trouble, for without stepping into the role of others, these self-centered people have no basis for feedback or interpretation of the messages dispatched to them.

The ancient *commedia dell'arte* gave public presentations of situations, themes, and questions presented to the cast by the audience. The highly imaginative actors took the suggestion, assigned themselves roles, and developed a play from that point. This required a tremendous spontaneity and versatility. Such ability *can* be developed through practice, and it is critical to development of empathy leading to intelligent interpretation of feedback.

Taking the role of the other person demands the widest latitude for spontaneity. Formal attempts to achieve this in the classroom, such as sociodrama, often fail, because the instructor does not permit unique stylization of roles. Achieving success at this kind of semistructured role-playing calls for considerable practice, and often teachers do not take the time to provide this practice.

Learning to play roles in order to build empathy is important to every speaker. Even more important is cultivation of ability to understand natural roles. The word *sincerity* is an abstraction, which is hard to pin down, but for the speaker it means consonance of roles within, as well as outside, the speaker.

THE SELECTIVE ACTIVATION OF MOTIVATIONS

A satisfactory communication relationship is characterized by perceptive coordination of needs and gratifications. Normally, people do not receive advice concerning their needs unless they ask for it, and sometimes not even then. More often, advice given to others is relevant to requests for behavior that would satisfy the needs of the advice-giver. The verbalization of a need *is not the same* as the need. Our language often leads us to misevaluate our needs, for verbalization of a need distorts our perception of it. There are similar gaps in our perception of the gratifications we might supply for another's need. This is consistently evident in such activities as the campus dating game, in collegiate politics, or in the student press.

What we say someone needs may not be *his need*. The gratification we think we provide not only may fail to meet his need but may, in his terms, be wholly wrong. Perhaps the greatest challenge to our interchange of messages is in the mutual correction of our assumptions, speech, and action to a better isomorphism with what specific individuals basically need.

It is essentially futile to try to pin down general or specific motives upon which we can rely for persuasion. Hundreds of motives are stated at various levels of abstraction in psychology books as well as in works on rhetoric and persuasion. Motives are sometimes referred to as *drive, instinct, urges, wishes, desires*. Our various terms mean essentially the same thing, and which label we use is unimportant in the relative sense of labels as images of meaning. What is important, however, is that the specific act of persuasion is unique, and it depends on concordance between appeals and needs. For instance, what motivates one person often repels another, and a speaker may incite action in part of his audience and obtain just the reverse response from the rest of it. Deep and extended communicative relationships, however, tend to reduce error and permit greater precision in motivation of behavior. Compatible husbands and wives know how to motivate each other to do what is desired. It is the specific appeal to the specific person that is effective.

Specific appeals, however, are developed out of general categories. These categories, not necessarily in rank order, are as follows:

1. Need for physical safety, physical comfort and well-being, and gratifications of urges, including sex.
2. Need for fuel to maintain body action, i.e., food, water, and air necessary to human survival.
3. Need for resources such as abilities and money, to function adequately in our society.
4. Need for self-esteem, sense of worth, protection of self-image and identity, status, power to influence others, love, respect, dignity, recognition—all important to personal homeostasis.
5. Need to satisfy curiosity about the unknown or mysterious.
6. Need to communicate and to understand basic to human development.
7. Need for status, position, or a secure niche in a social hierarchy.
8. Need for conceptual explanation of a complex world.
9. Need for the aesthetic and beautiful for creative expression, to fulfill altruistic impulses and to inspire others.

Animal behavior specialists suggest that all kinds of animals, including man, have a need for survival, conservation of species, excitement and stimulation, and possession of territory. Some psychologists add that humans develop a need to "grow" to make better use of their potential. They offer this as a basic motive as well.

There appears, however, no single list of universal motives, and the list the authors have given is only as good as the reasoning offered by those who propose it. Speakers who seek to appeal to basic motives will have to compile their own lists experientially by analyzing what seems to work with other individuals and why.

ROLE, STATUS, POWER, AND COMMUNICATION

The concept of *territoriality*, recently developed by ethologists, has appeared in many forms. The concept of *pecking orders* in the barnyard has been used as an analogy to explain development of status-order role in human society. Conflict for position and acceptance of assigned roles are characteristic of animal societies, and much of human behavior can best be understood by examining it in relation to this concept.

Power is an underlying force to achieve status in our society, and power rests on your ability to manipulate your environment and circumstances around the following criteria: change and sustained action; personal technology; tools and resources possessed; personal attraction or repulsion to ideas; symbols used; rewards won; plus many other reinforcements of the personal image of power.

Thus, as our civilization has advanced, roles and behaviors have begun to meld into the occupational specialization we now have in this country. However, communications have become more distant and more complex, creating problems in status-power-relations roles for people in business, industry, and government. In our own economic structure, we have seen individualism submerged in those vast aggregations we call "Big Capital," "Big Labor," "Big Military," "Big Media" "Big Transportation," "Big Government," "Big Education," "Big Religion." In fact, you could place almost any word after "Big" and have the term make sense. This largeness has placed tremendous responsibility on the leadership role, particularly on the ability to communicate with people in the face of this mighty onslaught on nonindividuality. This massive problem creates tensions, at both ends of the structure.

Tension and frustration at the lower-workers' echelon is reflected in tardiness, illness, accidents, slow-downs, disloyalties, sabotage, pilferage, strikes, and vast lack of pride in work. In the executive suite, and on the way up to it, tensions are a measure of communication failures, office (or suite) politics, and the barriers between status levels that act as barriers to effective communication. The payoff is ulcers or breakdown.

As tension and frustration begin to take over at all levels, rumor and gossip start to clog the communication channels, and what starts flowing along the lines is an effluvium of misinformation, untruth, and other damaging semantic noise.

The ultimate result is that status positions are bypassed, leadership becomes confused, disorder follows, leading to chaos, with the final disintegration of the organization the dying gasp of communication suffocation.

PHYSICAL-SEMANTIC DISTANCES

Physical distance exists between two people as they exchange messages within a field of space limited by one or all of the senses at any specific time. On the other hand, *semantic distance* extends beyond the immediate area of influence to include the acceptability people evoke in each other's communication when they are not within physical sight and sound of each other. Thus, physical distance deals in space and senses, while semantic distance deals in time, memory, and image-sense. Obviously, then, semantic distance may be widened while people are less than two feet apart. Semantic distance may be shortened although the communicators are thousands of miles apart, as any ex-GI who ever got a "Dear John" letter could tell you.

The concept of physical-semantic distance begins at birth, when the two distances are almost one. However, as the child grows, his experiences with the various physical and semantic distances of other people and things affect his perceptions of his interrelationships. As he matures, he begins to judge his physical-semantic distances, and begins to make use of this concept, usually without being aware of it.

Therefore, when there has been a deep, meaningful, and communicative relationship between people, the influences they will have on each other do not weaken or cease, regardless of time or physical distance. However, there are times when physical and semantic distances must overlap, e.g., during personal interviews for jobs, making political agreements, courtship, settling labor disputes, etc.

The public speaker can achieve both physical and semantic intimacy with his audience, despite actual physical distance, when he is personally extended by the mass media, particularly television. Franklin D. Roosevelt, John F. Kennedy, and Edward R. Murrow, for example, had semantic union with their audiences, who felt the intimacy of what was being said, although the physical distance separating them was usually very great.

There are times when you might wish to control distance. Controlling physical distance suggests a plethora of methods, most of which are unfriendly, even hostile, but usually effective. Semantic distance may also be controlled, usually nonverbally, by mobility of the face, expression in the eyes, bodily posture and movement, or by gesture. A great deal depends on the perception of your audience as to your success with controlling semantic distance. For example, a discordant person may not notice nonverbal cues, or he may misinterpret them and react in a hostile fashion. A concordant person, however, is not likely to lose his control, although he will probably recognize the cues and possibly react to them.

Just as there is a relation between physical and semantic distances with regard to control, there are also taboos. Various nations and cultures have physical-distance taboos as well as semantic areas that are not considered polite subjects for conversation. In the United States, narratives of sexual prowess are fair game for young males. In Spain, however, to discuss such topics is an ungentlemanly breach of confidence. Concern about discussing income varies from person to person and community to community. To the upwardly mobile, news about increases in income signals rise in status. The secure member of the middle class, however, feels that it is demeaning to discuss income and keeps his a carefully guarded secret. Questions about topics that are not proper for discussion can be regarded as intimidation, breaches of privacy, and a sign of grossness on the part of the questioner. Obviously, then, questions about the wrong topic are often a prime source of hostility and disagreement between people.

THE IMPORTANCE OF EQUILIBRIUM

To resolve his inner needs, man strives directly and indirectly for *equilibrium* in himself and his affairs. He is trying to achieve what the computer people call a *steady state,* which is what the ethologists call homeostasis, which is what we might call "peace of mind in that which is pleasing."

For example, being praised for an outstanding speech, selling a feature article to a magazine, getting your name in the paper for gaining a business promotion, are all instances where a healthy and ambitious person will have a full and satisfying feeling of well-being, or equilibrium. This temporary feeling is, fortunately, habit-forming in most of us, and we strive for more successes. Each additional success reinforces the image of future success potentials, and creates a positive feedforward. On the other hand, failures tend to pull down this image of satisfaction, and too many failures create confusion and personal turmoil. The answer to this, of course, is to make your successes gradually, but steadily, and not try for the "home run" on every swing.

In summation, we can say that you cannot accomplish a task unless you truly perceive yourself doing it. This perception may be within the self, and not at all verbalized. For example, we all know students who claim, "I just know I flunked that exam," and who manage to compile one of the highest grades in the class. This student admitted his ability to himself, although he verbalized something entirely different to his peers. Even with this contradictory situation, you find that the building of the image is totally intrapersonal and highly symbolic. To a very large extent, the interpretation of success or failure is controlled by the use of symbols and particularly within the process of abstraction. In a more personal sense, this means you literally create and control your own systems of punishments and rewards. Your own developed sense of extensionality and your developing ability to abstract intelligently will assist you in developing your own capability. Your interaction with others, then, becomes the critical arena where you put your abilities to the test of reality.

Perhaps now the underlying means by which better human communication is possible are beginning to classify themselves more clearly in your brain. If so, don't just file them away to gather dust in the attic of your mind. Put them to use to better yourself and your environment. Get out and talk!

With the permission of Dr. Alton Barbour, University of Denver, Denver, Colorado, we present the following breakdown of role-playing techniques, as well as some instructions for procedures.

Standard Socio-Psychodramatic Techniques

1. *Role-playing:* The portrayal or enactment of a character or a pattern of behavior deemed appropriate to a character. This is the most common and most important technique for both sociodrama and psychodrama.
2. *Mute technique:* A dramatic pantomime or portrayal without words, but with actions. Used to study nonverbal or paralanguage, to create imagery, to suggest visibly the personality of a character, to show inner thoughts and feelings, to foster spontaneity and involvement.

3. *Collective role:* Participants do not act out the roles of individuals, but of types, classes, or groups of people. This technique might be looked upon as an intentional stereotype on the (supposed) commonalities of mothers, fathers, policemen, Negroes, Communists, foreigners, etc.
4. *Soliloquy:* Used to reveal hidden or unspoken thoughts; it allows for the role-player to raise his hand to stop the action and enables him to "speak his mind" directly to the audience, tellings his intentions, explaining his behavior, etc.
5. *Harvey technique:* The role-player projects animation into an imagined or inanimate object; thus the imagined object is endowed with the ability to respond to the role-player. The reply is not voiced, but the role-player responds as if it were, allowing the imagined voice to say things to him, and replying to it.
6. **6.** *Role-reversal technique:* In any dyadic relationship, this technique allows both role-players to trade roles within the scene and to attempt, by representing the other role, to understand the other person's values, attitudes, beliefs, and motivations.
7. *Mirror technique:* The sociodrama or psychodrama represents the individual or group to itself; this is behavior demonstrated and played back.
8. **8.** *Auxiliary ego* or "double" technique: While one person represents the behavior of the person, another may represent the "auxiliary ego" by speaking as the conscience or inner self, delineating desires, conflicts, and inner feelings.
9. *Extension technique:* An individual role-player is in a scene with two or more auxiliary egos who interpret his role from different aspects of his personality, different points in time, etc. It can show the "many faces of man" by representing the individual as a father, husband, worker, group member, etc.

Director-Centered Socio-Psychodrama

I. WARM-UP (Up to twenty minutes if desired. The audience can participate and offer suggestions if the warm-up is done in front of an audience.)
  A. Decide on the topic or situation and analyze both content and characterization.
  B. Participants should be picked by virtue of their manifest interest and attitude. (Ideally, the participants will eventually assume responsibility and the director will do less and less.)
  C. Complete description, including physical location, time, props, physical and mental characteristics of characters in the situation, and background of immediately preceding action.
  D. Atmosphere of acceptance and permissiveness is helpful in the transition from preparation to enactment.
II. ENACTMENT (5-10 minutes except as therapy)
  A. Should be aimed at involvement and spontaneity.
  B. Direction should not be supervision, but facility, assistance.
  C. "Good acting" and imperfections are not important. The enactment is intended to be exploratory rather than definitive.
  D. When the enactment ceases to render meaningful insights, the director should "cut" the action and move to discussion of the enactment.
III. FOLLOW-UP (10-20 minutes)
  A. Should be discussed in view of the reality of the roles of the individuals involved and also in terms of the totality of social significance. Should allow for both catharsis and analysis.

B. Discussion should be construed to assist participants and audience to realize motivations, purposes, behavior, implications, values, relevances, etc.

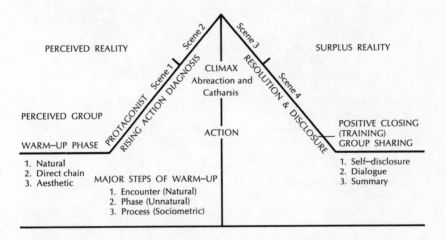

Figure 13–1. *Hollander Socio-Psychodrama Model*

Reprinted by permission of Mr. Carl Hollander, Director, Evergreen Institute, Evergreen, Colorado.

SUGGESTIONS FOR DISCUSSION

1. Are increased spontaneity and self-discipline contradictory goals? What do you think? Are self-control and "flexibility" contradictory goals? Is it possible to have both? Give examples.
2. How could "lack of control" cause us to lose contact with reality or lose contact with our friends? Could lack of flexibility or lack of spontaneity do the same thing? How? Would your lack of self-control assist or inhibit your control of others? Explain.
3. Does discordance-concordance have anything to do with intensionality-extensionality? Explain the relationships, if any. Could concordance be explained in terms of interpersonal sensitivity? How?
4. The authors say that communicative relationships between people are "irreversible." What does that mean and how is it used? A mountain climber sometimes takes a route that is irreversible—meaning he cannot get back the way he came up. Is that a good analogy?
5. How can we go beyond listening to what people say, to listening to what people mean? What sort of distance is there between what is said and what is meant? When Mr. *A* fights with Mr. *B*, how much of what goes on between them is a "content problem" and how much of it is a "people problem"? That is, if they agreed on content, would they agree?
6. How can our speech conceal or reveal "what we are"? When we talk, do we "expose" ourselves to others or do we "erect barriers"?

7. Are there people who "have charisma"? Can you name some? Do these people influence others because of who they are or what they do? Are you really what you do?

8. If we interpret human behavior in terms of role theory, how can we explain the wide variety of behaviors a single individual is capable of in a variety of settings? How many roles are you capable of? How do you communicate your role to others? How do they communicate to you what your role ought to be? What, if anything, does role have to do with status or the "pecking order"?

9. Is there some sort of distinction between role-taking and role-playing? Is one more "real" than the other?

10. Explain "semantic distance" using one of the models or theories presented thus far.

11. What do taboos and secrets have to do with roles? What violation of role is it to break the taboo or tell the secret?

12. What do balance, equilibrium, or consonance theories have to do with concordance-discordance or with extensionality-intensionality?

SUGGESTIONS FOR FURTHER READING

Daniel J. Boorstin, "From Ideal to Image," *The Image* (New York: Atheneum, 1962). Put into terms of modern persuasion and mass-image life, the author's words highlight a path to interpersonal disbelief. He offers no great solutions to the communication-image problem, just gives common-sense suggestions.

Hans Gerth and C. Wright Mills, "Symbol Spheres in Society," *Character and Social Control* (New York: Harcourt, Brace, and World, 1953). This is an early work explaining ideas and examples behind symbolism, allness, and images as they relate to communication within society.

Elwood Murray, *The Speech Personality* (Philadelphia: J. B. Lippincott, 1937 and 1944). This is the first textbook to associate personality development with speech behavior. It emphasizes integration of the speaker.

Elwood Murray, Ray L. Barnard, Jasper Garland, *Integrative Speech* (New York: Dryden Press, 1952). The thesis of this book is that the chief function of speaking is to bring about social integration.

Walter Lippmann, *Public Opinion* (New York: Macmillan, 1922). This is another classic, presenting pioneering information about communications. Read the section on stereotypes, pages 59–70, and note the applications in current society.

14

The Strategies of
Games, Ethics,
and Morality

So far, we have noted relationships among people, and written largely in theoretical terms about how these relationships could be bettered through betterment of human communication. We turn now to examination of some specifics in interaction, especially the results of people talking and listening to other people. You should be able to profit from the successes and failures presented in this chapter, and come away with an appetite to "try it" for yourself. If so, "Good Show!" We've done our job, and you'll soon be doing yours.

GAMES, COMPETITION, AND CONFLICT

Using communication terminology, we can begin by saying that most human communication can be regarded as a *game*. The concept of game is widely used, widely quoted, and widely misunderstood, which results in an oversimplification of the activity to which it is applied. According to mathematical games theory, action in a conflict situation proceeds as a *game* in which each player seeks to maximize his opponent's losses while mini- mizing his own. Each player is assumed to be a totally rational being, capable of assessing risk. To the psychiatric games theorist, a *game* is a regularized transaction established by two or more people that is maintained be- cause there is a potential "payoff" for the participating parties. While neither approach seems to be directly applicable to the communication process, interaction between people does have many aspects of a *game*. One possible view of human interaction, for example, is that people participate with others in order to "win"—that is, there is some stake involved and communication is used as the move calculated to win that stake. In such a view, each participant seeks superordinacy over the others. Obvious examples would be the businessman who makes it to the top office in the executive suite and the adman who wins the big client away from his old college roommate who now works at another agency. Once a hierarchy has been established, moves regularize, and communication can become a *game* in psychiatric sense. The leader uses his ploys to sustain his leadership, while the followers use their ploys (competition) to maintain their security, as followers holding firm positions in the hierarchy. Or the follower may choose to contend with the leader, attempting to seize some of his power, e.g., the race for the deanship among college professors. In some cases, the communication ploys may be calculated to lose the ostensible objective; i.e., winning power, in order to achieve a more viable stake, i.e., winning the name of gallant but defeated warrior or the profitable underdog. Remember the "we're only number two" theme of the Avis ads of a few years ago. In other cases, the drive for leadership may be sincere. The leader's responses, however, may be calculated to provide stimulation and challenge so that he sustains vigor among his followers.

Societies tend to regularize transactions through tradition or law. In such cases, the approach to the *game* could take on mathematical overtones, where interactions formally subsumed under law court or senate chamber must conform to strictures about behavior. Rules are provided stipulating who may talk when and in what context, and "referees" are provided to see to it that the rules are upheld. Combatants in such circumstances direct their words to their goals and control them through application of the rules of combat. In the United States Senate, for example, name-calling is interdicted by the tradition of the body, whereas in the British House of Parliament controlled insult adds status and effectiveness to the argument.

The specific communication activities we carry on, both inside and outside ourselves, can be regarded as attempts to "win," regardless of whether or not we use the concept of game to analyze them. A rhetorical view of communication behavior asserts that even the simplest phatic communion is calculated to bring about some gain. This might be the good will of the other party to the transaction, or it might be prevention of a negative evaluation on the part of the other person.

Such communication activities as teaching, clinical treatment, political participation, selling, and seducing are distinctly persuasive. One human seeks to bring about behavior in another in order to satisfy some goal. The persuader moves most efficiently when he can perceive the goals of his subject for persuasion, and effectively harmonizes them with his own. Persuasion is more complicated when goals differ. Then it may be necessary for the persuader to cloud his own goals or confuse the goals of his subject. In any case, a behavior change is what is sought, and communication is the tool by which the change is brought about.

In the example of a simple seduction, the desire for sexual pleasure on the part of the male leads him to seek to change the behavior of the female who resists the goal and who, therefore, receives the persuasion. Her resistance is developed through social conditioning, which she seeks to defend by uttering symbolic words about morality, or she seeks to take the attack by motivating a proposal of marriage as the price for successful seduction. The male may seek to cover his own goals by appealing to the sense of altruism in the other party, perhaps portraying himself as a pathetic figure needing nurturance and love. The female may then defend by rewarding these verbal ploys with nurturance and love in the form of soft phrases and, perhaps, limited physical contact, pointing out that ultimate contact would only stimulate feelings of guilt and would therefore hurt the persuading party, regardless of his present view of its potential. And so the semantic dueling goes on. One party or the other will achieve the goal of the transaction, or the game will end in a stalemate, with frustration on both sides. Such games can take place over periods of a moment or two, or they can take place over the years, as in a marriage, where it is never clear who is the "authority" in the household.

Often the nature of the game is clouded because participants are not clear about the goals they seek. A husband who successfully seeks total submission by the wife may discover that a completely humble woman is a bore, and that he has lost rather than gained in the transaction. Small children often contend vigorously for such goals as toys or candy rewards, only to find them ultimately unpleasant. Likewise, adults may struggle to achieve a promotion (or a social position), only to find it exceedingly unpleasant once it has been attained. This "taste of ashes" provides the substance of subsequent mental illness, withdrawal from competition, frustration, and, at minimum, ineffective personality.

The human who can clearly perceive his goal, and who is *sure* of its worth, can proceed most effectively through the rhetoric of games. The salesman who values his product is sure of its worth, understands its defects, and is aware of the ethics of the selling situation tends to have the highest sales volume and the healthiest conscience. The clinician who understands the strengths and limitations of the clinical system he uses is normally most effective in bestowing treatment. To believe in the product or the idea is the way to "win." If your "product" is the self, then communication must be accompanied by belief in the possibility of success in order for it to be successful. Unfortunately, the most carefully planned campaign of seduction or salesmanship can fail, because it is not clear what constitutes the best interest or course of action. Obviously, there are many ambiguities built into the rhetorical game, i.e., there is no analysis that can be made of individual or group that is infallible. The concordant persuader, however, is aware that his campaign might fail. Furthermore, he understands that his game often cannot be played directly, because other parties may be playing by different rules—even playing different games. Conclusion: The act of winning may take time and considerable verbal effort.

One reason is that the addition of another person to the communication complicates behavior inordinately. Now there are two persons, each very likely in conflict within himself, who must reach some kind of synthesis of ideas. One must win, the other lose, unless both are able to perceive their goals clearly enough for compromise or accommodation to be worked out. And, as more and more people enter the communication game, it becomes necessary to formalize some rules of behavior, sometimes as laws. Each player is then restricted in his behavior, because deviation from the social or legal rules means "loss" without regard for the merits of the case.

When groups begin to communicate with groups, societies with societies, and nations with nations, both general and specific codes of communication conduct must be synthesized. For example, two diplomats at the conference table must first reach each other as human beings, then as representatives of their respective cultures. It is no wonder that it is so difficult to reach international agreements, to make binding contracts, to find solutions to the many problems of conflicting human interests throughout the world.

The negotiations in Paris over the end of the Viet Nam war are a good case in point. The relationship between the United States and South Viet Nam is not clear. South Viet Nam has to preserve the image of being in control of her own destiny. The leaders need to sustain the fiction that the war is entirely theirs in order to hold power over their citizens. The Viet Cong (NLF) claim to be the legitimate government of South Viet Nam, yet they hold no ostensible accoutrements of power. To be accepted as a government at the conference would confer legitimacy on their claim. The United States cannot afford to confer legitimacy on the NLF, for to do so would put her in the position of negotiating with an inferior authority and would jeopardize relations with South Viet Nam. North Viet Nam has steadily maintained the fiction that her forces are not present in the South, yet it is clear that they are and that some direct contact with the United States is imperative to the solution. The myriad of claims and conflicting counterclaims must be resolved by human negotiators, who have to be concerned with protocols of manners, good form, and order. Such problems as who enters the door first and who sits next to whom at dinner cloud the more cosmic issues. To add further to the confusion, virtually everyone has to maintain the fiction of working through an interpreter because to engage in the language of the other party is considered demeaning. It is no wonder that resolving international conflicts takes so long, and is sometimes so unsatisfying.

The same sorts of problems also affect interpersonal communication between humans. The interviewee for a job must maintain a demeanor of security and confidence. He cannot admit that he needs the job. He seeks, rather, to explore personal gain. The interviewer cannot afford to admit that the interviewee is needed, and so he makes inquiry about what the interviewee can "contribute" to the company. Each verbalizes around personal goal because the search for a mutual goal would jeopardize the "face" of the two parties. The sparring continues, often with an unsatisfactory outcome.

Most of you have encountered such situations in your interactions with professors. The student who talks to a professor about a grade that was "too low" must maintain unconcern with the need for the grade and keep the talk on a level of fairness. The professor cannot afford to admit, however, that he made either an error or a misevaluation. He must maintain the fiction of altruism; he changes the grade only for the benefit of the student, but it must not be construed as a real evaluation. Once again, the problems of status and protocol prevent both parties from saying what is really on their minds, and once again, the interaction is manifestly unrewarding.

THE GAME OF ARGUMENT

The process of conflict through game is often referred to as *argument*. This word carries unpleasant connotations, for it implies clash, although clash need not be unpleasant. Indeed, verbal argument is necessary for survival of the human whose only weapon, normally, should be words. Much has been written about argument, formalizing rules and offering suggestions for manipulation of logic in it. But it must be remembered that argument is not a purely logical process. Any time two persons conflict in words, the entire personality is involved. Argument thus becomes more than a formalized interaction, and it has no clear outcome. The most convincing items of logical persuasion are futile if they do not reach a sympathetic personality capable of accepting them. The person who twists the facts may not feel he is twisting them at all, because it may be the way he perceives them, or it may be necessary for him to distort in order to protect his self-esteem or homeostasis. The speaker who relies solely on the logic of the case presumes that he is working in a formal milieu that does not really exist, and his logic may be lost in the ambiguity of perception with which his opponent is operating.

The very nature of the games we employ creates many ambiguities. For example, there are the misinterpretations which A expects in B, and B also expects in A as to *who* is playing or not playing, about *what* and *when* they are playing, and how *serious* the game is. In the final resolution of the ambiguity, and in the revelation of the nature of the plot, you'll find the fun, humor, and excitement of the situation. The ability to enter spontaneously into this sort of game is the sign of the mature speaker. For most people, it is very necessary and welcome in the wear and tear of our daily association. It's safe to assume that persons generally concordant within themselves have the necessary discipline to contribute an optimum of humor and excitement in these associations. Discordant persons, however, have difficulties in entering into such games. When they do, they lack the flexibility that is required and that grows out of the higher levels of awareness and the separating of orders of abstraction. Their participation is not fun, not exciting, not stimulating. Often, their personalities become so involved that the stakes are raised intolerably.

To cope with these game situations, we must know what is going on, and how the situations develop. Do you remember the order of the words in the heading of the first section? *Games,* a chief characteristic of which is "play," emerges into *competition,* characterized by "rivalry to surpass," which merges into *conflict,* characterized by "struggle to defeat." It is impossible to define in this merging just where games end, competition begins and ends, or conflict begins and ends. We can say, though, that rules begin somewhere within free play and increase in number and complexity through competition and on into conflict. When rules are violated, disturbance increases. Simple roles appear along with play, and increase in number and specializations along with the different levels of status in competition and conflict. For example, apparently purposeless dialog can escalate and become grim or even deadly in conflict. All these phenomena may be interpreted as manifestations of the tendency toward *equilibrium,* a state of mind we fight to defend.

ARGUMENT IN THE ENHANCEMENT OF THE EVALUATIONS

As good advice, we say that you should heed the warning never to argue *if* circumstances provoke argument only at a superficial level, where one or both parties have hardened assumptions on the subject. If there is violation of personal commitment, if there is threat to pride and self-image, if mutual respect is lacking, or if your role or status in a situation makes it inappropriate, do not argue.

Further, it is inadvisable for a lower-status person to argue with a higher-status person unless he is expected and invited to do so, or he knows what he can lose. And it is inadvisable to argue with someone about his professional role. However, in light of the uniqueness, different backgrounds, and the vast differences between and among us in our perceived needs, it is ridiculous to assume that we are able to or should avoid all argument. Sometimes it is necessary to psychic survival. But when argument is necessary and warranted, the parties to the argument must take care to avoid escalation into battle.

The constructive question of how we can best evaluate differences now arises. How are we to attain the consensus necessary to advance together? Perhaps most of the answer lies in our knowledge that intelligent and thoughtful argument is imperative as people come into closer contact and become more dependent on each other. The more mature and knowledgeable we are, the more we feel the need for critical interplay to confront and correct our assumptions, to fill an abyss of ignorance, and to sharpen the issues we face. For example, we know that friends who cannot discuss differences amicably are not of much value to each other; a family in which argument is squelched or forbidden impairs the development of its members; an enterprise in which there is no discussion concerning differences of opinion and policy is probably destined for deep trouble; a school that denies the freedom to debate controversial issues does not rate as an educational institution; and governments which prevent or widely censor argument become tyrannies—and tyrannies spawn violent revolution or divert inward pressures into foreign aggressions.

Persons who lack the discipline to restrain their words to those relevant to the issues and themes of discourse, or whose semantic disorders interfere with rapid thinking, are rarely in the debate finals, rarely involved in discussion symposiums, and rarely seen on television, and certainly they would be barred from the councils of the policy-makers. Yet no one should be deprived of formal experience in such activities because of the potential they hold for gaining new insights into our communication process and for acquiring new rational, critical, and creative powers. Actually, argument can bring us into better unity and consonance with each other and with our world *only* in direct proportion to the reliability and mature use of our knowledges. This is just as true when the occasion is intimate association with another or when the formal situation requires that we speak within complex rules.

Our whole way of life is predicated upon the assumption that our problems can best be resolved through the conduct of argument and controversy at a high level. Faltering increases disorder in our affairs.

MAKING, IMPROVING, AND FULFILLING AGREEMENTS

When we enter into competition, we take risks, sometimes more than we can afford. Of course, the more mature look to all the possibilities and probabilities of winning or losing, preparing themselves to take the consequences. However, in any competition, be it games, business, or society, we risk the impairment of relationships with other persons involved. The very ambiguities on which games are based give rise to some of our most bitter quarrels. The defeated party all too often isn't aware that he *is* in a *game.* The winner risks being labeled "crook" or "thief"; the deal becomes a "fraud"; the loser has been "taken in." Yet we can scarcely bear much association with the dolt who will never risk anything or enter into some kind of game, and we compete.

If we tacitly agree that each will do his best to surpass the other, *within the rules,* the relationship need not be affected regardless of the outcome. The harder, then, we compete, the greater mutual respect we earn. But, as we've said, there must be initial agreement as to the extent rules may be changed. Between a learner and a teacher of the game, it is particularly necessary that the teacher scrupulously live up to his role. Some teachers proceed from the allness that they must not in any circumstance permit themselves to be beaten at anything by anybody. The better evaluator, of course, will accept defeat after defeat if it is warranted without jeopardizing his will to participate. In the decision-making before and during games-competition-conflict, we should carefully assess the *will power* of the other person and of ourselves. What is the extent of endurance in resources and power? How far are the contending parties likely to go to win? We know that will power connects and holds the positive and negative feedbacks to the feedforward goals. Thus, will power propels the concordant speaker, who is aware of the extent of his preparation, to clinch the persuasion. Will power is not expended on trivialities and misperceptions. Its energy is not exhausted for the sake of winning, irrespective of more important facets.

Conversely, discordant speakers vacillate between taking on any opponent about anything, irrespective of the inherent power, or avoiding the game and running away at the crucial moment. They tend to "go to pieces" at the point when a little more give or take could determine the outcome, or they blunder into disagreement without regard for consequences.

The making, improving, and fulfillment of agreements proceed at the same three levels of games-competition-conflict we described in the preceding section. At each level, character and autonomy as a personality are at stake. In the relationships with other people, achievements, fortunes, and happiness are at stake, while in the interaction of power group with power group, the fate of the world is at stake.

Speakers concordant within themselves have the sensitivity and foresight to avoid unnecessary complications. Their sense of responsibility engages them in trying to solve problems not of their own making. They are aware that lives, enterprises, and the welfare of whole societies depend upon the networks of *agreements* people make and fulfill.

The very word *agreement* is in itself a multi-ordinal term, embodying all the dangers of vagueness unless, and/or until, it is tied down to the descriptive level. That this is highly important is demonstrated in the threat of often-unread fine print that delineates the exact responsibilities to which a person who signs a contract has committed himself. In short, a contract or agreement may have implications not understood at the time of signing and commitment!

Of course, circumstances can change the basis of, or the factors within, an agreement. But we must fulfill our promises, unless we can persuade the other person *to his satisfaction* that a change should be made in the responsibilities assumed. We can often improve previously made agreements, if we use due care in our interchanges. However, we must keep our premises, tacit or otherwise, if we cannot revise them and improve them in light of new facts. Otherwise we cannot be at ease with ourselves or with the other person. And, if this happens, we find ourselves more and more left out of the larger responsibilities we would like to have.

The formal rules of public speaking, debate, and discussion constitute a technology of agreement about what is required in a situation, but they do not extract from the participants all they should from the deeper levels of commitment. Classroom exercises of any sort lack the air of reality, and consequently the sense of involvement, that real issues contain. What is learned in the performance classroom can carry over into real stress situations only if the participants understand that more emotion, more involvement, and more perception are involved. Life plays for keeps, while in the classroom, we are often permitted to pick up our marbles and go home. Once again, learning benefits to the extent that the students can make the classroom into a real situation.

Agreement-making begins at the unspoken or tacit level, from non-verbal cues, and with silent, unconscious and conscious assumptions. And an agreement made by no more than a nod, a frown, a raised eyebrow, a shrug, or a smile should be as binding as the formal agreement made in a signed contract. We base our agreements upon what we read into or infer from actions or words, the commitments we have seen made and fulfilled, the degree to which we see the agreement consistent with each other's needs, and its appropriateness for each party to fulfill.

We must have wide flexibility in the agreements of involvements into which we do or do not permit ourselves to enter, as well as a strict control over the range from impersonality to intimacy therein. For instance, when we meet rashness and impetuosity in another person, we help him delay his reactions by being impersonal in our reactions toward him. A detached, but friendly, attitude in emotionally charged situations is often the most persuasive.

There is a definite art in applying the restraints of impersonality and formality in our roles, status, and power relationships, and as tools of this art, the ideas of etiquette, protocol, and tact are highly important. The more controversial the subject, the more necessary it is to match sensitivity with the sophistication of speech, manners, and erudition encountered. Mature speakers are usually able to avoid difficult situations, but when they permit themselves to be involved, they use the utmost discretion in *what* they say, *when* they say it, to *whom* they say it, *who* overhears it, and *whom* their message will reach in unintended or third-party channels. In the social life of our establishments and power structures, etiquette and manners are often critical. If the spirit underlying good manners is violated, warm two-way communication becomes unlikely. But if trivia are made excessively important, matters of serious import cannot properly be discussed, and agreements will never be made and kept.

HOW MUCH SELF-DISCLOSURE?

Some birds, fishes, and insects camouflage themselves as protection against predators. The biological duplicity that enables them to blend into their environments and keeps them from being noticed by their enemies is necessary for their survival. But man is capable of and does exercise far greater duplicity—and not usually for survival of life. Of all living creatures man excels in deviating from what he seems to be. He is far different from what he indicates by his talk and by his actions.

The mature speaker has under control what he conceals as much as, or more than, what he discloses in his messages, in the roles he assumes, or in the games and the competitions he enters. He is the great actor, the great role-taker, and through discretion, humor, and the freedom in what he displays and what he covers up, he brings an art of a high order into his own life and into the influence he has upon others.

Only a person concordant within himself is able to accomplish this art. *What* he will disclose and *when, where,* and to *whom* are fine questions successfully resolved by the adequate speaker, whether in private or public occasions. This is a point well worth remembering in your own lives.

Discordant people cannot control *negative spontaneity*—the freedom to conceal in their speech—even in the areas of their lives where it is desirable and necessary to conceal. As with the other facets of their communication behaviors and their personalities, the extent to which they reveal themselves to others is subject to gross misevaluation. They usually take, and may even seek, every opportunity to expound or "gush forth." Their main purpose seems to be to expose their deepest inner perturbations. However, they chronically defeat themselves because their hearers inevitably become bored.

For any kind of discourse, we need to know something about the other person, and he needs to know something about us. We need to share the viewpoints each has of the other, the biases that may be present, the semantic disorders, and any lack of extensionality. What must be revealed are the barriers in the communication process of each. In a real sense, when we are communicating about communicating, we try to amplify our abstractings and correct our inferences. We learn the aspects in which we are similar and where we will differ. Plato suggested that to persuade others, we must first know ourselves. In short, if you are to convince another person of what you are like, you must search yourself for the truth about yourself and use feedback from the other to show it to you.

The pressures under which we live today make it imperative that we have friends who are not directly involved in our problems but whose suggestions we can trust and respect, and in whose confidences we feel secure. Everyone needs associates upon whom he can rely and with whom he can feel comfortable in revealing matters that he would be reluctant to unburden even to someone who is very close. For example, many successful executives find an older person of wide experience with whom they can discuss problems of impending decisions. The more competent young people sometimes resolve their problems by asking for candid but constructive criticism from a peer. New perspectives, new solutions, and new confidence in self-abilities may accrue, as may the courage necessary to "carry through."

Countless people go through life in close proximity to many people yet never permit themselves to be known truly by another. They never know the great satisfactions of deep-level communication or the joys of deep friendships. A courtship does not succeed between an attractive and otherwise eligible man and woman because they cannot communicate. Likewise, neighbors in apartments or associates in the same office, church, farm, or classroom environments may keep a wide semantic distance. There are married couples and whole families who do not reveal their feelings about themselves to each other, who frown upon revelation, or who do not listen if and when such approaches are made. The result, inevitably, is hostility, conflict, and the building of additional personality discordance.

Conversely, some husbands and wives know each other so well, some mothers and teachers know their children so well, that words are almost unnecessary. Unfortunately, this is seldom the case in the vast majority of our associations. Cues from facial expressions, bodily movements, and vocal emphases are revelatory indicators of inner emotion, but they do not always enable us to read with accuracy the mind of another.

WHEN WE WOULD PERSUADE—HINTS FROM BIOLOGY AND PSYCHOLOGY

What we call *persuasion* is embedded in many species of life. Plant-animal, plant-plant, and animal-animal relationships are as vital in this realm as are those which occur within and among human beings. Look and listen to a meadow in bloom, and you'll see that plants strive for a position in the sun, to be seen and heard, to attract the pollen carriers. Consider the persuasions of a peacock as it spreads its fabulous tail. Animals also respond to similarities and differences in vision and noise. Built-in persuasion sends the butterfly or the bee to the right flower. Uniformity of size, shape, and color carries individual and unique characteristics, so that robins live with robins not with gray sparrows. The light of the firefly signals love or dinner.

Animals and plants respond to each other to satisfy mutual needs. Sometimes symbiosis results, a host providing nurturance to another animal in return for services rendered, like the small bird that rides the back of the hippopotamus: it earns its residence by picking the fleas off the hide. Man is also persuaded by signals and symbols that seem to offer satisfaction for his needs and drives, though the symbolic process immensely complicates human transaction even while it raises it to a high level of potential.

Man seems to differ from animals in these respects only in the number of rituals and superstitions he has multiplied beyond measure. In primitive societies, rituals are used to persuade the gods to make seeds grow, to bring the rain, and to protect the warriors. Witch doctors and priests have used rituals and incantations to maintain their power. Even in our so-called scientific enlightenment today, such methods of persuasion persist.

The salesman closing his deal, the public speaker obtaining approval of his resolution, the son who gets permission to use the family car, the teacher who induces an interest in a complex formula—all are examples of people using persuasion. But we must persuade or influence the other person to persuade himself! The audience's state of readiness to respond will determine the ease with which a speaker can trigger self-reflexive action in them. Persuasion has a crude similarity to the growth of a plant. Growth occurs according to the purposes programmed into the seedling that "decides" to grow because the outside influences (persuasion) of water, temperature, and soil chemistry are appropriate.

Persuasion is nearly synonymous to communication in that it involves relating, influencing, and interacting, although persuasion formally refers to change *purposely* induced. In this broad sense, persuasion includes our messages which influence others and/or messages by which we are influenced, whether they be verbal or nonverbal. Down through the ages, influencing of people has been treated as rhetoric, the discovery of the available means of persuasion. Modern students of rhetoric often regard communication and persuasion as identical, for all communication seeks change and is consequently persuasive.

Success at persuasion is measured by what people can be and are *induced to do,* e.g., what they put into the cash registers, what new relationships they form, what old relationships they delete, what thought-to-be-set goals they modify or change, what they learn.

Advertising and public-relations professions exist because their members persuade sufficient acceptance of products. They are perhaps the most potent specialists in knowing people's whims, and how to persuade people to action. However, the uncertainty of "persuasibility" is as great as the differences within personalities. Predictability of the outcomes of persuasive efforts is most unreliable when persuasion is applied to discordant personalities. On the other hand, concordant people are more amenable to what is reasonable. Their knowledges are relational, more logically assembled, and fit together in correspondence to an operational level. Their strategies of persuasion are in the selections of important themes appropriate at the time, and they talk and listen to the more significant matters. Their tactics of persuasion lie in asking questions, gathering information, weighing evidence, testing assumptions and premises, and application of conscious abstracting in predictions. They readily communicate about their communication processes. They ask each other about what each is abstracting; they reveal viewpoints and outlooks they want to be understood; and they help each other become aware of factual gaps and distortions. In addition, they are amenable to change, and they respond to extensional facts. Argument tends to improve their evaluations. They are able to compromise and to act on consensus. Since concordant people are autonomous, they are less persuasible by what the crowd is doing or saying. Concordant people participate widely in the larger issues of their communities and societies.

TYPES OF PERSUADERS

Professional entertainers are masters of persuasion. Don Rickles, for example, manages to persuade his audience to accept his insults and find amusement in them. Jack Benny persuades us that he cannot play the violin, and we listen to his abominable playing and are amused by it. Many movie stars persuade us that they are young and vigorous long after they have passed middle age. Many entertainers have developed sufficient charisma so that they can enter other arenas of persuasion. Ronald Reagan and George Murphy are perhaps the best examples of this; though many others like Paul Newman, Robert Vaughn, Dan Blocker, Bob Hope, Harry Belafonte, and Dick Gregory have utilized the image they developed as entertainer to make an impact on the world of politics or social welfare. So enticing is the union between entertaining and political action, that some politicians, Everett Dirksen for example, have tried their hand at becoming entertainers.

Persuasion that proceeds through charisma is often dangerous, however. There is nothing in the life of Yogi Berra to make someone assume that he has knowledge of shaving sufficient to qualify him to endorse razor blades, yet people are persuaded by his testimonial, and he receives money for his endorsement. Great numbers of people in our society are easily persuaded by transfer of authority. Demagogues have found it easy to mobilize emotion in some segments of society to build large and threatening movements ranging from the John Birch Society to the Black Panthers, and including the many fringe political movements that subvert our two-party process. The demagogue capitalizes on the discord characteristic of large numbers of our citizens. The tendency of discordant people is to act impulsively, to accept an idea because of their liking for a man, or even worse, to accept a man merely because he agrees with their idea. As George Wallace found out in the 1968 campaign, however, such believers are capricious. Their support cannot be counted on.

But not all persuasion takes place on the stage, in the political arena, in the courtroom, or through the advertising message. Some of the real persuasion in our society is carried on by the teacher and the clinician. The teacher's mission is to revise the behavior of students by motivating them to accept changes in knowledge possessed, and to inculcate attitudes about that knowledge that will lead to healthy and productive behavior. When a teacher loses sight of the persuasive task, he fails. Many teachers assume that dissemination is teaching, but it is clear that listening to teacher lecture is the most ineffective method of learning. The live teacher talking to a class seeks to motivate, to involve, to fan the spark of interest that exists in all students.

The clinician also seeks a behavior change. His efforts are directed toward guiding a patient to a recognition of his problem, and then developing with him methods to overcome or suppress the difficulty. Once again, blunt descriptions like "you're nuts" are worthless. The clinical process proceeds through the most subtle utilization of the available means of persuasion in the best Aristotelian sense.

Many times the most intractable attitudes are toward the words that are used, rather than toward a rejection of the actual situation. Advertising is especially aware of this, and the profession must use words or labels that will sell the product. It constantly searches for the right attention-catching and persuasive image label and is quick to change a label as its potency fades. In a commerical sense, convictions are not too difficult to change, unless total acceptance of a brand, product, or label has become part of the personality of the individual. On the other hand, advertisers constantly try to get us to change from a competitor's brand to their brand—or attempt to keep us loyal to their brand in the face of competitive advertising. Recognize the game theory?

To change long-held convictions is possible, but the persuader must expect the change to be gradual at best. Psychiatrists help their listeners review the history of their beliefs, obtain new perspectives, and bring their assumptions up to date with their changing world. They seek a better isomorphism—helping listeners to become aware of ways of observing, abstracting, and improving their evaluating. This is perhaps the most important contribution a speaker can make whenever there is resistance to the search for, and acceptance of, unpleasant facts. Speakers who can reach into the minds of others to bring misevaluations into the open for conscious revision are truly orators and educators in the highest sense.

THE SEMANTICS OF MORALITY

If the word *immorality,* or its equivalent, could be removed from the communication process, it would be eliminated from society. This becomes a possibility as we achieve extensionality in, and sensitivity to, the influence we exert in the interchange and complexities of interpersonal relations.

Most sins of commission and omission are in communication behaviors. Morality remains crude to the extent that we remain indifferent to changes which can hurt our fellowmen, and morality becomes immorality to the extent short-sightedness exists in the relationships we influence. If we look beneath the surface into the transactions and interactions going into our evaluations and communication, we find moral implications at almost all levels.

Credibility, the extent to which the speaker and what he says is to be trusted, is an integral part of morality and ethics. Morality is ingrained in what we say and in how we speak, and we ought not to separate morality and ethics from our communication processes. Morality is not going to be improved, unless we try to look upon it as it exists in the process of one human mind interacting with another human mind in every order of abstracting and evaluating.

In determining the moral act, we must recognize the semantic operations of the mind from which the act emanates. Here is the essence of the communication process and the integrity of the personality itself.

None except the credulous is going to change his belief, *unless* what is said is compatible with what he perceives as generally true. But *even what is most honestly perceived is not necessarily in isomorphism with the existences that a speaker assumes are being conveyed in his messages.* There are bound to be gaps between the event and the perception of it. Complications arise in our most earnest endeavors to be believed, inculcated in the very nature of what we call information. There is no real informing unless there is inclusion of something new to the person being informed, because anything else is a redundancy that rapidly evokes boredom in the listener. However, without some repetition or redundancy, the speaker risks inadequate comprehension by the receiver because of his limitations for immediate intake of the new. While "snowing" an audience with a plethora of words may impress listeners momentarily, it results in unacceptance or disbelief eventually.

The conscientious individual assumes responsibility for what he says and for what he hears, and he offers little or no room for ambiguity. His responsibility is in direct proportion to the import of the information he gives or receives, so that he has as much responsibility for what he does *not* say as for what he *does* say. He must be accurate, lucid, and sufficient, and he has the right to expect these same characteristics in the messages others send to him.

What further is meant by *responsibility?* Part of its meaning lies in the many decisions a speaker must make—for example, to whom and about what he will speak, when he will talk about himself and his affairs, the degree of necessary self-disclosure to others, the extent to which he will seek out and keep on increasing his information, and the extent to which he will disclose, censor, or withhold knowledge pertinent to and about others. How far he will open the gates to positive feedback, and how far he lets himself be carried away by his emotions are of vital importance also. If his trust is misplaced, if his cathartic outburst is overheard by persons who do not understand, or if his self-exposure becomes public, then possible damage may follow. Appropriateness and evaluation require fine distinction.

The dire consequences that may follow when information is withheld or the speaker lacks candor concerning himself was illustrated in the case of then U.S. Senator Richard Nixon, when later provision of demanded information almost retrieved a critical situation in which the Republican party suddenly found itself, but the damage could not be eradicated. Specifically, Mr. Nixon's vice-presidential campaign in 1952 was seriously jeopardized by accusations that he personally benefited through unethical practices of financing. Allegations cited by his opponents in the mass media resulted in his being labeled "Tricky Dick," an image so tarnished with the public that Dwight D. Eisenhower, titular head of the party, was required to decide whether Mr. Nixon should even remain upon the ticket. After Mr. Eisenhower's affirmative decision, Mr. Nixon spoke to the public with utmost candor and finesse when he delivered his famous "Checkers" radio talk, one of the most self-revealing disclosures ever given to the American public. Mr. Nixon talked about his own credibility and showed he was *not* a liar. He spoke of his dog Checkers as being a good fellow, like his hearers, and he forthrightly stated facts which had been hinted at obscurely, and had damaged his credibility and public image. He tried to meet an almost incredible curiosity for information by *communicating.* That he was not entirely convincing doubtlessly contributed to his successive defeats, particularly his campaign ten years later for governor of California, when the question of his credibility was revived. That he finally overcame the charge was testified to by his victory in 1968. Richard Nixon learned the isomorphism of communication.

Just as the insufficient release, or too-late release, of information accrues adverse consequences, so too does the release of too much information or of information with which recipients are unable to cope or of information which is untimely. A remarkable example of this was in the furor resulting when Jacqueline Kennedy decided that she had told too much to William Manchester, author of *Death of a President.* She requested that the book not be published when she belatedly decided that too much of a personal nature concerning her family and its associates in government had been exposed. The semantic disturbance her request provoked mounted in non-additive fashion, through the mass media, into world-wide proportions. In a poignant failure of extensionality, she acted, without having read the manuscript, upon the suggestions of friends to whom she had assigned the responsibility of reading it. After the curiosity for information had been partially satiated, the frenzy abated and the underground gossip network subsided. This is a clear example of

1. The effects of the release of too much information;
2. The effects of threatened withholding of demanded information;
3. Publicity regarding efforts to withhold or censor information to insure that it will be demanded. (The issue as to whether Mrs. Kennedy made deliberate use of this factor for personal reasons is irrelevant.)

In both the Nixon and Kennedy episodes, the pinpointing of specific responsibilities goes far beyond the principal actors. The reporters, editors, and broadcasters willfully enhanced the vast curiosity focusing on these people. Who can determine how ethical they were in overplaying and underplaying the actual facts in their efforts to sell their own "product"?

Lack of candor is often a measure of self-deceit, which is the mask, subterfuge, or duplicity used to conceal our thoughts and actions and to confuse our roles. However, departure from the isomorphism of what we say about our true selves is not the primary concern. We commonly defeat ourselves by continuing *to believe and to act upon* what we say about ourselves, regardless of its accuracy. In other words, we behave as if our masks were not masks, and therein lies our greatest danger.

Decent relationships are not possible among persons governed by and restricted to limited ways of looking at themselves, at others, and at situations. In labeling an utterance or act as "good" or "bad," "right" or "wrong," "guilty" or "innocent," "true" or "false," or any *is* or *is not*, we commit a degree of immorality, *if* we have no tacit agreement with the people to whom we are speaking that we are not taking our words seriously. The lack of morality and ethics is in proportion to the importance of that which we attack, or to which we attach labels.

No one is guiltless of damaging another person, sometimes by no more than thoughtless speech. We speak and act from the midst of frustration, inadvertently, and without realizing we are inflicting a hurt. Those prone not to treat others decently are discordant personalities, deficient in perception and with numerous I_3's. But ignorance does not condone impulsive and inappropriate utterances, so that each of us is responsible for what we do and what we say. Poverty of love for our fellowman will inevitably result in alienation because of unsatisfactory interpersonal communication.

People have abused and continue to abuse the freedom they have—and thereby thwart their desire for freedom. The inevitable result is more restraints, more prohibitions, more codes of ethics, more laws to protect the group. Most tyrannies, as history attests, have grown out of accumulated abuses to fellow citizens, which has resulted in breaking established order.

Verbal construction of laws and codes is often so oversimplified that justice becomes a crude affair or is even defeated. That which is "right" or "wrong" or "good" or "evil" by specific definition *is not* the behavior or the relationship under question, nor does it cover the ramifications of the occurrence. Extensional and concordant personalities have the sensitivity, the self-discipline, and the flexibility to make the necessary distinctions.

Quite frequently we hear that the ethics we apply should be "relative to the situation." Unfortunately, the loudest proclaimers of this theory seem to use it to condone the free play of impulse and desire, as well as gross lack of perception of the deeper relationship in a situation and a violation of our precious freedom. These are the people who beat up an antiwar speaker and call him a "commie"; they are the students who hold a professor hostage because they feel their civil rights are being violated. In their low-order abstractions and in their hostile behavior they forgot that others have freedom and civil liberties also.

We talk of "cultural relativism." We argue that morals differ from culture to culture, and that what is believed to be wrong in one group is approved in another. That this is true has been established many times, especially in studies of primitive cultures. There is an implication that what everybody else is doing is right and that it is impossible to live happily in a group if we don't do what everyone else is doing. This assumption simply overlooks the fact that what many a culture, large and small, has done resulted in suicide. Specifically, at one time or another human sacrifice, slavery, gladiatorial circuses, and child labor have all been generally approved.

"Everybody is doing it" is a refuge for paralyzed evaluation. Evaluation must be kept active and positive! This is essential, because, no matter how hideous his history and despite the vast indifferences of the older generations, man is saved when he not only knows but also experiences in his emotional nature that union of contrasts which is his destiny.

The union of contrasts requires that the dissonances in our situations be defined to bring the clashing overtones into concordance. Then, the communication process itself becomes the highest of human values.

A new generation that can rejoice in the union of contrasts must take over and make itself heard—as it communicates.

SUGGESTIONS FOR DISCUSSION

1. What aspects of human communication can be interpreted in terms of game theory? How does game theory differ from all the other theories of communicative behavior thus far presented?
2. How can one "be understood" and yet "lose" in his relationships with other people?
3. What "rules and regulations" associated with "fully informed" games (such as chess) could be applied to any conflict situation?

4. Students at American military academies are often schooled in game theory. In what way is a military battle similar to a game? Can you explain the World War II Battle of the Philippine Sea in terms of game theory?
5. Can you apply the previously discussed topics of goal-setting and decision-making in the context of game theory?
6. Distinguish between a "game," "a fight," and a "debate." In what sense is a game "play" and in what sense is it not? In sports played in England, players are often said to regard "the game" as being the most important, while in America, players regard "the competition" as being most important. Explain this distinction.
7. Could all communication be said to be an attempt at persuasion? In what way? What could game theory have to do with persuasion? When we persuade, do we win? What does balance, congruity, or consonance have to do with our "credibility" or the extent to which we are persuaded?
8. Based on previously explained models and theories, how would you explain such values as "right-wrong," "just-unjust," "moral-immoral"? Where would they belong in the model? Are they extensional?
9. Use your role-playing skill and act out some typical communication games.

SUGGESTIONS FOR FURTHER READING

Eric Berne, *Games People Play* (New York: Grove Press, 1964). This very readable book presents some cogent and useful material.

Orrin Klapp, *Heroes, Villains, and Fools* (Englewood Cliffs, N.J.: Prentice-Hall, 1962). This well-written book concerns the changing American character and how we found ourselves living in the cult of the personality.

Orrin Klapp, *Symbolic Leaders* (Chicago: Aldine Publishing Company, 1964). Glance through several of the examples of symbols and leaders, then review our chapter again.

Hans Toch, "Gain Through Community," *The Social Psychology of Social Movements* (Indianapolis: Bobbs-Merrill, 1965). In this section, Mr. Toch presents some interesting theories and examples about social games and sociocultural living.

15

The Voices Around Us: Mass Communication

You would probably agree that face-to-face discussion is the ultimate in interpersonal human communication. Unfortunately, contemporary society is far too complex to function only through this direct communication between individuals. To be actively effective, many daily messages must reach many different people, often simultaneously. In this sense, mass communication has become an extension of interpersonal communication.

From a definitional standpoint, *communication* is derived from the Latin word *communis,* which means "common," while *mass communication,* the plural form, refers to the process of achieving communication among the masses of people, regardless of the medium used to disseminate the message.

One epic of American rhetoric was compiled in 1919, when President Woodrow Wilson spent 22 days touring 17 states and made 40 formal, yet extemporaneous, speeches on behalf of United States' membership in the League of Nations. In the face of heavy Congressional opposition to the League, Wilson took his hopes and his persuasion directly to the American people, and lost both. Years later, Hugh Baillie, a United Press reporter who had covered the tour, wrote:

If he'd had radio and television to carry his message and personality to millions rather than to thousands, the history of the world might have been different. With television, I am convinced, Wilson would have carried the country for the League.[1]

What Baillie was saying about the effects of radio and television on people is so taken for granted today that we accept it almost without question. How often do you stop to think specifically of a motion picture, a televised speech, a newspaper column, a textbook, a magazine editorial, or a radio commercial as a form of mass communication? Most of us look on movies, radio, newspapers, and magazines as "things" that are there, ready for use when we are ready to use them. Is this the unspoken relationship you have with the mass communication industry and its media?

Much of what we have presented in the preceding chapters concerned interpersonal communication, although we have at times written about speakers talking to large audiences via television. In this chapter, we shall present *mass communication* as a specific topic. By *mass communication* we mean one person talking to many or many people talking to many other people, as well as the media through which the audiences are reached. The basic difference between interpersonal communication and mass communication, at this point, is that the latter involves dissemination of a message to a vast, faceless, unknown audience with small capacity to note immediate feedback of impact.

Unfortunately, much of the world's problems come from misunderstanding, suspicion, prejudice, hatred, and violence. All of these problems are at least a partial result of the lack of adequate mass communication among people. There are four major obstacles to effective mass communication between the people of our world: illiteracy; language barriers; censorship and suppression of ideas and information; and a variety of prejudices. When these basically semantic obstacles are removed, people will communicate more effectively and we will have a more meaningful world.

Our purpose in this chapter is to present a survey of basic information about the models, theories, media, and roles of mass communication in our contemporary world. When you apply the knowledge and techniques learned in previous chapters to the problems of mass communication you will be contributing to the removal of those obstacles that impede effective human relations.

Successful mass communication may be looked upon as person-to-person contact repeated thousands of times simultaneously. The speaker who engages the mass media to disseminate his message should be aware that his effectiveness as a communicator will depend on his application of the principles of interpersonal communication. These same principles we have been sharing for fourteen chapters will also be applicable to the material in this chapter.

Only 30 years ago, the term *mass communication* was new to our vocabulary, although a few social scientists were beginning to study the

---

[1] Hugh Baillie, *High Tension* (New York: Harper and Brothers, 1959), p. 49. Reprinted by permission.

phenomena to which the new term referred. Today, borrowing data, theories, scholars, and practitioners from sociology, speech, anthropology, psychology, journalism, political science, advertising, computer science and statistics, general semantics, English, art, and almost any academic area we might mention, mass communication is emerging as a separate field of study. Its definitions and theories, however, remain as many and as varied as the number and orientation of the men who study mass communication. But, while the search goes on for parameters of this polyglot field, the importance of mass communication in the modern world cannot be denied by anyone who lives within its influence.

MASS COMMUNICATION MODELS

Mass communication researchers are great model builders, and they delight in making complex flow charts to show how people communicate to and with each other, using mass channels of dissemination. We have already presented illustrations of several basic models. Now, we will present a brief outline of five of the current mass communication models to give you a representative sampling of what is being used. There are other models, and as we suggested earlier, you may wish to examine these before making evaluative judgments about mass communication, or you may wish to design your own model.

1. *The Individual Differences Model.* Based on environmental behavior theories, this model describes mass communication effects that vary from person to person. It differs radically from the models which are designed to show that mass communication has a uniform effect on the population. In any case, more emphasis is placed on environmental factors causing behavior in the individual differences model than in other models. This model is a modified successor of the classic stimulus-response (S-R) model, differing only in that it includes the individual's own self as an intermediate step. Thus, it now becomes the stimulus-(intervening-self process)-response model.

2. *The Sociocultural Model.* This is primarily a persuasion process model, based upon the idea that mass communication effects are influenced by the social interactions a person has with others in his environment. This model is used to explain advertising appeals as well as other forms of mass persuasion. It allows a great deal of personal interpretation of, and involvement in, the message by the members of the audience. It is a strongly environmental model, and the idea behind it is oriented toward a consensus society, and is designed to leave you with the idea of "keeping up with the Joneses."

3. *The Psychodynamic Model.* This is the alternative to the idea of a consensus society that is predominant in the sociocultural model. Here, the individual differences among people are subject to persuasion by the mass communicators. The psychodynamic model is a refinement of the individual differences model in that it is an attempt to interject individual psychological need into the flow of the model. For example, a television network may

attempt to reduce discrimination, which is overt behavior, by showing a powerful documentary program designed to reduce racial prejudice, a covert attitude that leads to discrimination. Messages that conform to this model are usually emotional in nature, like the advertising writer noted when he said: "The way to the mind is through the heart."

4. *The Social Categories Model.* This model often overlaps the individual differences model. The basic idea is that groups, blocks, or categories of people exist who will react uniformly to the same stimulus. Its various categories may be detailed by some sort of demographic distribution of the potential audience, e.g., sex, religion, socioeconomic status, fraternal membership, etc. This model is used heavily in mass media research, where it is assumed that, despite the heterogeneity of the general population, groups of people with similar tastes and behavior patterns are to be found. The model is well adapted for statistical studies of media use habits, opinions, etc.

5. *The Social Relationships Model.* In this model, the interrelation of various groups with predictable behavior is an underlying assumption. However, another variable, the *opinion-leader,* is inserted into this model as a message interpreter between the communicator and the audience. This opinion leader is a communication middleman, whose thoughts and interpretations of the media messages influence the opinions and attitudes of others in the audience. The opinion leader may be a legitimate source, or he may merely be a celebrity with great charisma. This model may be used to chart many of the appeals used in advertising, public relations, and other persuasive efforts.

You should now begin to match models and assumptions to some of the mass communication messages to which you've been exposed recently. Hopefully, we've shown that both interpersonal communication and mass communication are closely related, have common assumptions, and will work interchangeably in various models of communication.

However, mass communication does have certain characteristics which help distinguish it from interpersonal communication, as follows:

1. Mass communication is usually one-way. Other than the reaction of the newsmen present, there is no way for the President to judge the effect of his messages delivered during a news conference.
2. There is a great deal of selection in mass communication, as the communicator works carefully to select his audience, media, and message. A local beer distributor would hardly sponsor a church service broadcast, just as a candidate for office would not discuss the advantages of private firearms confiscation with a sportsmen's club.
3. Mass communication is capable of reaching vast audiences with great impact, despite the heterogeneity of the population. President Lyndon B. Johnson's decision not to run for office in 1968 was announced almost as an ad-lib "tacked on" to the end of a major policy speech, televised nationally. The impact upon the world was startling.

4. Mass communication is addressed to a common denominator of humanity. Right or wrong, this adage has been traditional. It was expressed by a newspaper editor who advised a young writer to "write for the guy who moves his lips when he reads."

5. Mass communication is a social-business institution, somewhat responsive to its cultural environment.

You have now read about some mass communication models, seen how closely interpersonal and mass communication are related, and also seen that there are differences. The next step is to consider the channels of mass communication, that is, the mass media.

THEORIES OF THE MASS MEDIA

Two basic, historical theories underlie the operation and function of all mass media in the world. While in current practice the two basic theories have been modified, the concepts are at the root of day-to-day dissemination of communication. The two historical theories are as follows:

1. *Authoritarian Theory.* This theory grew from the philosophy of the late Renaissance; it was based on the notion that truth for the people came from a small group of wise men who knew truth and could interpret it for the masses. This meant that the communicators were near the power structure of government, and that communication was from the top down. Obviously, the media were used to advance the cause of those at the head of government. In one form or another, the authoritarian theory governs media activities in Spain, Japan, and in many of the small nations of Asia and South America.

2. *Libertarian Theory.* Arising from the philosophies of such men as Mill, Locke, and Milton, this theory was adopted by England in 1688, and later by the United States, under the philosophical leadership of Thomas Jefferson and others. It is based on the concepts of man's basic rationalism and his natural rights to express ideas freely as he seeks truth. The purposes of the media operating under this theory are to inform, entertain, persuade, and sell goods and ideas through advertising. Control of the media is through the self-correction concept of ultimate truth and to some extent by courts of law. This theory was basic to the media in this country for many years, and to some extent was operable in modern times in Great Britain, Israel, Australia, and in several South American countries.

These two theories have been widely modified and now a great deal of overlap is present. It is also possible for a nation to switch from one extreme to the other extreme during a political upheaval. However, the twentieth century has seen the emergence of two current theories appropriate to current times and events. Although the basic authoritarian and libertarian theories may be clearly seen in the new concepts, the operational meanings have become more closely drawn. The two modified theories are as follows:

1. *Totalitarian Theory.* This theory was born when the Nazi Party decided the authoritarian theory was not controllable enough. From Germany, the iron hand of the totalitarian theory of media control spread to Italy and Japan, and in postwar years, to Russia, China, and other lands ruled by totalitarianism. The philosophy behind this theory has been expressed in the writings of Hegel, Marx, Lenin, and Hitler. According to these philosophies, the media are dedicated solely to the furtherance and success of the party-state. The media are state-owned and tightly, if not completely, controlled as to the contents of messages.

2. *Social Responsibility Theory.* Evolving from the libertarian theory in this country, this concept of media operation better fits the needs, roles, and goals of the media and society in the twentieth century. The constructive thinking of Hocking, Irwin, Sinclair, and The Commission on Freedom of the Press are largely responsible for the emergence of this theory. The basic purposes of the media are the same for this theory as for the libertarian, except that the idea that media have a responsibility to help build a better culture has been included.

Ownership is private, and with certain legal or emergency restrictions, the media people are free to disseminate what they please. This is now the major theory behind media operations in most democratic nations today. How well the goal of social responsibility is being met is another question.

MEDIA IN SOCIETY—MASS OR CLASS?

Mass communication media are common in terms of purpose and performance, although there are differences between them at the operational level. Basically mass media have three major roles in society today.

1. The media serve as the channels through which people are informed. Their role is both to influence and reflect public opinion. For example, the media can help unify support of a bond drive in a local community.

2. The media serve as a means for expanding the national economy in a productive growth cycle through dissemination of effective advertising. The amazing growth of Polaroid cameras from a hobby product for a wealthy, older-aged market to the inexpensive, youth-oriented "Swinger" of today is an example of advertising at its economic best.

3. The media influence, perhaps even shape, the patterns of our society. However, this influence often results in meaningless fads, such as the startling popularity of 1930's fashions following release of the motion picture "Bonnie and Clyde."

Thus, the media are a powerful and fundamental institution in our society. As our populations continue to increase and our planet becomes even more crowded, mass communication will assume even more importance in more serious matters. Ideas and information flow through the mass media and are spread among the various cultures of our world. For this reason, the media must be free of stifling censorship and political control. But they must also avoid becoming a mistress to economic interests. Free and responsible media are essential to the socially beneficial use of mass communication.

MASS COMMUNICATION AS A SOCIAL PHENOMENON

One of the early contemporary observers who noted the close ties between society and mass communication was Charles Cooley. Cooley concluded that modern society could not exist without mass communication, and that this communication could not exist outside a social system. His concept was reflected later by George Herbert Mead:

The process of communication cannot be set up as something that exists by itself or as a presupposition of the social process. On the contrary, the social process is presupposed in order to render communication possible.[1]

Mass communication, of course, is only one of the many phenomena that affect contemporary society. There are certainly others, for example, poverty, war, crime, weather, overpopulation, morality, political ideology, religion, greed, prejudice, in fact, our list could go on indefinitely. Mass communication, however, is the *only* phenomenon that cuts across every cultural line and every human problem. Almost every person in the world is exposed to at least one of the mass media, and the results show. This explains why dictatorships suppress the media as an initial military step. There are military historians who wonder what might have happened if Adolf Hitler had used radio as frequently and effectively as did Winston Churchill and Franklin D. Roosevelt.

On a more personal level, you've probably heard a four-year-old singing the latest cereal commercials from television. Perhaps you've walked into a neighborhood tavern and heard the "regulars" discussing the ball game that was just on television, the latest crisis just heard as news on the radio, or an editorial in the daily newspaper. Although there is likely to be more heat than light shed on the discussion, the impact of the mass communication media is definitely felt.

It seems intelligent to conclude that mass communication is important and effective, and then move to the question of how well the mass communication media do their job today.

RESPONSIBILITY VERSUS PERFORMANCE

The greatest strength of the mass media system in this nation is its relative freedom from control and censorship. In some respects, this very

[1] George Herbert Mead, *Mind, Self and Society* (Chicago: University of Chicago Press, 1934), p. 260.

freedom is also a basic weakness in that it makes the media dependent on the market place for support and defines no role for them. Indeed, it is a paradox, or maybe a blessing, that our Constitution guarantees freedom of speech and press, but sets down no guidelines for role and responsibility. Definition, interpretation, and implementation of that role and responsibility are left to the integrity of the men who control the media. For example, many media critics point out with alarm that the top management people in the mass communication industry are all businessmen first and communicators second. The inference is that management worries about their profit-and-loss statements first and their social responsibility second.

Another traditional criticism of role-performance in mass communication is the concept that mass media build a society of mass, popular tastes which are led and fed by the mass media use habits of the people. The idea was expressed by Harold Wilensky who classed people as belonging either in *high culture* or in *mass culture*. Most critics hold this same idea in more or less varying degrees of semantic acceptance. Most theories of mass communication and mass culture suggest that society tends to level out into the middle groupings of people, and that our society is not so much pyramid-shaped, but diamond-shaped. In most cases, however, the critics seem content to let the residents of the mass culture guzzle beer in front of the television set, while the members of the high culture sip wine and read *Saturday Review*. The consensus of criticism is that the media have largely ignored responsibility in favor of entertainment.

The question now arises: Who should judge the performance and content of mass communications? There are as many criteria for judgment as there are judges. Our history is filled with rapid changes in customs, mores, and laws. We are undergoing one of these evolutionary shifts right now, and it is difficult to set guidelines of performance when so many middle tones and parameters are shifting so rapidly. For example, nudity was never seen on American motion picture screens until only a few years ago. Now it is almost as universally accepted as popcorn. Just as the libertarian theory of media operation gave way to the social responsibility theory, standards of performance must also remain flexible.

In a democratic society, responsibility for improving society through mass communication is at least a corollary of freedom. Of course, how well the mass communication industry fulfills its social and cultural obligation is still a matter of unresolved debate, as we have just recounted. In any event, applying a lesson learned earlier in this text, it is no more fair to label the mass communication industry, *per se,* as "good" or "bad" than it is to label people with those same polar value-judgments. Perhaps it would be well for you to apply more of the science-art ideas about communication to your own experiences as a consumer of mass communication.

We are now in an era when communication satellites and interplanetary space exploration have opened new vistas and hold new promise for man. Yet, much of this space-age news is still pushed off the front pages by stories of social unrest, open violence, human ignorance, and other daily accounts of inhuman interaction. Once more, the obstacles to effective human communication make themselves known. We must defeat these obstacles so that the scattered millions who live on our planet may talk together as harmonious citizens of one world.

UNIFYING THE MASS MEDIA AS EXTENSIONS OF INTERPERSONAL COMMUNICATION

As you read a book you operationally and physically come into *relationship* with the author. Semantic reactions which went into George Washington's *Farewell Address* evoke counterparts in you as you read the Congressional Record which you have taken from a dusty shelf in a library. The responses in you are an extension of the speech personality of Washington. The analysis and synthesis you make from this reading is an example of the time-binding described in previous chapters of this book. Time-binding may also occur in the exchange of messages with our contemporaries. When this communication process is unimpaired, there need be no loss of knowledges and ideas. In this two-way communication, each party in a group may benefit from the experience of each other. This does not occur in ant hills or wolf packs. Did you ever hear of a society of cattle improving its organization?

The physical process of interpersonal communication, the interaction of person to person, of experience with experience, has many adaptations and special arrangements. The speaker who uses the various mass media to assist his purposes is aware that his effectiveness depends upon his application of the principles of interpersonal communication as far as possible. Whether or not the communicator is aware of the exact process, there is an extension of himself whenever he is responded to, whether it be to a business letter, a poem, a symphony broadcast, or a theatrical production.

In this communication process, which is common to all the specialities of communication and the disorders incidental thereto, lies the unity of the whole vast area of *communication*. As you become a leader in a corporation, school, or community, you will be able to administer the various fragmented media in a more economical and effective manner if you are aware of these relationships—a matter greatly neglected today.

Mass media provide potent extensions of interpersonal communication. With these media the leader of today may multiply his influence immediately and fantastically. As he does this, he finds himself contributing to those all-at-once happenings described by Marshall McLuhan in his *Understanding Media: Extensions of Man*.

Our goal in this book is to help you improve your communication with other people. If you work at this, you will contribute to improved social relations among humans. For the first fourteen chapters, we discussed this goal in terms of interpersonal communication. Now, we want you to try it in terms of mass communication for the betterment of all of us.

SUGGESTIONS FOR DISCUSSION

1. How might history have been different if Woodrow Wilson had been able to use television to reach the American public? How might the civil rights movement have been different if Negroes had *not* had the availability of television?
2. How did Marshall McLuhan's book, *The Gutenburg Galaxy,* explain the impact of movable type on the Protestant reformation? Do you agree?
3. The authors speak of interdisciplinary studies. Is there any single idea that you know of which is accepted in all (or even most) of the academic disciplines?
4. How did Marshall McLuhan's book, *Understanding Media,* explain the effect of electronic circuitry on today's society? Do you agree? Do respected sociologists?
5. The basis for S-R theory is the assumption that man is totally a product of his environment. Would you accept that as a basic premise?
6. What constitutes mass media? Is that the same as mass communication? Explain. Why would mass communication firms have on their staffs sociologists or social psychologists? What sorts of information could people from these disciplines provide for mass communication?
7. What do mass communication theories have to do with mass government?
8. Do mass media "cause" such things as antisocial behavior or are the mass media merely a "mirror" reflecting antisocial behavior back to society?
9. What sorts of content material do you think mass media (particularly television) should show, and why would you prescribe such content?
10. Explain the First Amendment in the Bill of Rights and censorship in terms of positive and negative feedback in our society. What kind of feedback did Joseph Goebbels provide for the German people during World War II? How good a communicator was Goebbels? How good was Adolf Hitler?

SUGGESTIONS FOR FURTHER READING

Bernard Berelson and Morris Janowitz, eds., *Reader in Public Opinion and Propaganda* (2nd ed.; New York: Free Press, 1966). This survey covers the area well, so pick an area of interest and enjoy your reading. This is a good source book, too.

Alan Casty, ed., *Mass Media and Mass Man* (New York: Holt, Rinehart and Winston, 1968). A definitive new collection of essays on the theories and criticisms of our current society and its mass culture.

Lewis Dexter and David Manning White, eds., *People, Society, and Mass Communications* (New York: The Free Press, 1964). Another collection of timely and interesting readings on how we communicate with each other, this book is a complete treatment of a large, interdisciplinary field of study.

Edwin Emery, Philip Ault, and Warren Agee, *Introduction to Mass Communications* (New York: Dodd, Mead, 1965). This is an excellent and scholarly introduction to the entire field of study that used to be called journalism. It is also a thorough reference book in the field.

Some Wild Card Exercises for Your Browsing Pleasure

The following is a compendium of exercises, cases, and questions from which you may want to select. They are not necessarily germane to a particular chapter in the book, but they could be made to fit any of the chapters with the exercise of a little imagination.

1. In those classes that feature formal speeches, instructors have been heard to complain bitterly about having to listen to the same speeches over and over again. Virtually every speech teacher has heard about "skiing" and "How to Take Good Pictures" until he is surfeited. We have all been regaled with arguments to legalize abortion, "pot," prostitution, and all manner of bawdy and licentious things. In every fraternity file, there is a resource book in boredom, a file of the B+ speeches that have been given in various speech classes. A group of us sat down the other day and came up with a list of speeches we would like to hear.

How Popular Music Reveals the Types of Mental Illness in Our Society
The Excessive Power Buildings and Grounds Have on Our Campus
Opposed to Involuntary Incarceration of the Mentally Ill
Does Man's Soul Reside in His Computer Card?
Are Modern Food-Processing Plants Like Upton Sinclair's Jungle?
Educational Needs of Our Local Police Force
A Comparison of the Relative Merits of "Pot" and "Booze"
Why Beauty Contests Are Like Livestock Shows
The 4–H Club—Corrupter of Youth
Why the Poles (Italians, Jews, etc.) Should Retain Their Ethnic Behavior
How Dirty Jokes Reveal Emotional Hangups
Should the Church Be Permitted to Own Tax-Free Property
Underdeveloped Nations Are That Way Because It Is Their Own Fault
Cancel Foreign Student Programs on Our Campus!
The Corporate Structure Is Essentially Socialist
Please Let Me Join the Establishment
The Mini-skirt, Destroyer of Personality
Solid-State Technology Made Simple
What to Do in Scenic Center-City Baltimore (Punxsatawney, Greeley, Sheboygan, etc.)
How to Operate a Strip Mine
How to Rig a TV Rating Service

The Technical Operation of the Political Polls
How the IBM Selectric Typewriter Works
Fur Trappers in the Twentieth Century
Professional Athletes with Ph. D.'s
What Is the Nature of Soul Music
How a Combination Lock Works
The Personality of Perry Mason (Nero Wolfe, Philo Vance, Ellery Queen, etc.)
The Rules of LaCrosse
How Paris Fashion Houses Make a Buck
How Bookies Set the Odds
Why Paper Pulp Mills Smell So Badly
Etc. . . .

In short, it helps to find a topic that interests your instructor, particularly if he is still giving you a grade. Finding an interesting topic is half the battle; an interesting topic is probably one he has not heard before.

2. It is a good idea, regardless of what the class is doing, to have some kind of critic-observer watching the proceedings and evaluating the operation. One co-author's class, for example, set up a Criticism Committee to feed back information to him about the quality of his lectures. This was most useful and assisted the instructor in revising his yellowed and crinkly notes, bringing them up to date and making them relevant. Certainly when the class carries on group activities, the observations of a dispassionate critic other than the instructor can be quite helpful to the participants. Content of discussion, structure of discussion, nature and quality of leadership, nature and quality of interaction, and recommendations for improvement are the obvious kinds of critical categories. More obscure areas can be examined, also, such as the roles taken by the various participants, the overt and covert conflict between participants, and how outside influences affect behavior of individuals in the group. If you rely too heavily on the instructor for this kind of information, you will find yourself playing to please him instead of working to learn the process.

3. Even though this book will very likely be used mostly in speech classes, this does not mean that speech is the only legitimate output or form of participation. Students should be encouraged to use various channels of communication. In fact, those who can't speak well might be more successful if they used some other way to get their opinions to others. At various times, the authors of this book have had students do excellent jobs of communicating through writing, song, art and sculpture, dance, film, photography, role-playing, etc. The option ought to be open. There are some ideas, perhaps, that cannot be talked about intelligently since they have such a heavy emotional base. A program in song, or an artistic representation, might convey the message more effectively. This option should be permitted the students.

4. Following are some general questions about the book as a whole. They might be suitable for a traditional final examination:

   a. How is successful communication "relevant" in your world as a student?
   b. Have the authors given you a different picture of what a speech course can

be than you previously had pictured? How would you describe "speech" now?

c. Since we all have been fairly proficient speakers since about age three, why are there courses in speech?

d. Will changes in attitude and in thinking result in changes in speaking proficiency?

e. What is a "non-Aristotelian" as opposed to an "Aristotelian" approach? What kind of thinking and knowing do we associate with Aristotle? Was he that kind of thinker himself?

f. Why have the authors offered a range of choices and options in explaining communication instead of a definitive answer?

g. What would you say is the philosophy of education of this book?

h. With regard to the process of communication, do the authors seem to be saying, "It is better to know than not to know—knowledge has value just being knowledge," or are they interested in practicality?

i. Do many of the suggestions made by the authors now seem to be common sense? Why was it necessary to organize and conceptualize them for you?

j. Can the suggestions the authors have made about speaking be applied just as easily to writing? What are the similarities between speaking and writing and what are the differences?

k. What is the teacher's role as suggested by this book? What is the learner's?

l. How true is the old cliché that when you cheat, you cheat yourself? How could you cheat yourself in your learning about communication?

m. The authors have suggested a number of approaches to learning which might accompany this book. Could you create another one which might be more suitable for you?

n. How do the authors regard criticism and grading? Do you agree? Explain your position.

o. If criticism is not an effective aid to learning, what would be effective "feedback" in a teaching-learning setting?

p. What did Aristotle contribute to "knowing," logic, science, drama, and rhetoric?

q. What would you say is the ethical commitment of a speaker to an audience?

r. How does conversational speaking differ from speaking to an audience?

s. Is the "authenticity" of existential writers at all like the relevancy that students desire now, or the extensionality that the authors described? How appropriate is the phrase, "Tell it like it is, baby"?

t. How can the "fiction" sociodrama lead people to a better understanding of reality?

u. What cautions do the authors make with regard to sociodrama?

v. What sort of "Heisenberg Principle" applies to classroom speaking? How can it be avoided or lessened?

5. Dr. Mario Pei of Columbia University says that there are approximately one million words in the English language and that the average man knows about 100,000 or a tenth of the total. Would these numbers vary to any great degree from

one culture to another? How many words would it take to be adequate? Find out about the Whorf-Sapir hypothesis.

6. Schools are often concerned about the vocabularies of students. How does the size of one's vocabulary influence one's thinking for better or worse? Write an explanation of how you think vocabulary would influence one's thinking or "knowing."

7. Possibly you've read the novel *1984* by George Orwell. Discuss "newspeak" as distorted communication.

8. In August of 1962, the Pentagon announced that it was spending $42,780 for research on a new sound to warn of enemy attack. It appeared that the Office of Civil Defense had a low opinion of bells and sirens, regarding them as "just a cheap way of making a lot of noise." They said that people were used to hearing bells and sirens, and that this new sound should be of a more "disturbing nature." If you were given this same job, what sound do you think you could develop that would so disturb people that they would wake from a sound sleep. This is a job of communication that requires some creativity.

9. *Although words exist for the most part for the transmission of ideas, there are some which produce such violent disturbance in our feeling that the role they play in the transmission of ideas is lost in the background.*

ALBERT EINSTEIN

Can you give some examples of the kinds of words that Albert Einstein is talking about, and explain your feelings about the words.

10. Henry Putsch, Director of the Film/Media Center for Communication in Philadelphia says that "Words have fallen on evil days." Why are these "evil days" for words? Why would a man interested in films say that?

11. List as many superstitions as you can think of. How many of them do you see some sense to? Why? Why have other people taken these superstitions seriously? Explain your position.

12. What is your opinion regarding ESP (extrasensory perception)? Is this science or superstition? Is your position the same as for the previous question or has it changed? What, then, *is* a superstition?

13. When we label something, do we at the same time categorize and evaluate? How are there evaluations in the following labels:

teen-ager	Republican	cowboy
addict	gangster	farmer
butler	movie star	alcoholic
Nazi	Democrat	criminal
nigger	churchgoer	Communist
Catholic	Christian	atheist

Write a brief essay discussing the dangers inherent in such labeling.

14. If the same book were sold under two different titles, *Sin for Pleasure* and *Amateur Prostitute*, which title do you think would sell more copies of the book? Explain why you think so.

15. Discuss the meanings *to you* of the following words. How do they differ from meanings assigned by others?

Democracy	fairness	beauty
pleasure	equality	intelligence
sin	patriotism	
prostitute	evil	

16. What are the qualities or traits that you associate with "Jewishness" or "Negroid"? How do you expect a "Texan" or an "Oriental" to behave? Discuss with your class your personal meanings for these words. To what extent do they constitute stereotypes for you?

17. Find examples in advertising in which you think words are particularly important in getting people to buy a particular product. Why are people influenced by such advertising? Concentrate on products such as gasolines, cigarettes, and soaps which are extremely similar physically.

18. General semanticist Alfred Korzybski said that "false knowledge breeds insanity." How could "knowing" something that is untrue or false to fact lead to being insane or unsane? Give some examples of "false knowledge."

19. Because it was believed that England was going to be on the side of the Confederacy during the Civil War, the Navy designed a speedy ship to be used against the British if the need should arise. The need never developed, and the construction of the ship was not finished until 1868. When it was finished, it was discovered that the Wampanoag was capable of a speed of seventeen knots at a time when the best ships on the sea were only capable of a speed of fourteen knots. It was the fastest ship on the ocean.

This was at a time, however, when the Admirals were more sure of sails than they were of steam; thus, they began to "modify" the design to allow for a mast. They removed two of the boilers, two of the smokestacks, and two of the propellers. The result was a ship that was no better than any other ship, so they junked it. The Navy was not able to design and produce a ship capable of seventeen knots for another twenty years. What does this tell us about not trusting the "unconventional," about resistance to change, and about compromising the old and new?

20. Write a paper dealing with any area of science which explains how a new discovery has come from questioning something that was previously "self-evident" and "needed no proof."

21. Can you list some "laws of science" which are no longer looked on as true? What entire sciences exist now that didn't exist ten years ago? What does this say about our "knowledge" of the world we live in?

22. *Though the comparison is not apt, we are human beings not by virtue of blood in our veins, but by virtue of the words in our mouths. Blood kinships related us to the animals. Word kinship relates us to each other.*

JESSAMYN WEST

Explain language as a uniquely human characteristic. What do anthropologists have to say about the connections of language and culture? Read Ernest Becker, *The Birth and Death of Meaning* (New York: The Free Press, 1962).

23. *Looking back to the religious hatred of the sixteenth and seventeenth centuries, its irrationalities are clear. Both sides spoke in the name of God, of Christ, of love, and they differed only in points which, if compared with the general principles, were of secondary importance. Yet they hated each other, and each was passionately convinced that humanity ended at the frontiers of his own position religious faith. The essence of this overestimation of one's own and the hate for all who differ from it is narcissism. "We" are admirable: "they" are despicable. "We" are good; "they" are evil. Any criticism of one's own position or doctrine is a vicious and unbearable attack; criticism of the other's position is a well-meant attempt to help them to return to the truth.* ERICH FROMM, *The Heart of Man* (NEW YORK: HARPER AND ROW, 1964), p. 82.

Expand on this idea of Fromm's and relate it to your own experiences (perhaps rival athletic teams and their fans).

24. Alfred Korzybski told us that words could be compared to maps, and the way that maps more-or-less accurately represented territories, words more-or-less accurately represented facts. In the 1953 ascent of Mt. Everest, Eric Shipton discovered that when they approached Everest from a different direction, the Sherpa guides believed it was a different mountain. The Sherpas had lived in these mountains all of their lives, but they believed that a different view of a mountain could be a different mountain, and thus gave it a different name. How good is Korzybski's map-territory analogy? How many words do we have for the same thing, and yet, how many different things are there for which we have the same word?

25. Edmund Taylor said, "The real enemy of mankind is delusion inside the heads of so-called normal people . . . delusion means the nonsense we talk to ourselves and believe. . . . These are dangerous because they are not known by those who hold them to be delusions." Respond to this statement of Taylor's.

26. *If language is not correct, then what is said is not what is meant; if what is said is not what is meant, then what ought to be done remains undone; if this remains undone, morals and art will deteriorate; if morals and art deteriorate, justice will go astray; if justice goes astray, the people will stand about in helpless confusion.*

CONFUCIUS

Are Confucius' warnings about the importance of language to convey meaning at all relevant in this day and age? Is it possible for you to give some contemporary examples to support his ancient claim about language?

27. A few short years ago a Denver father noticed a book that his daughter had brought home from high school. It was a collected volume of the poems of E. E. Cummings. In leafing through the book, he came upon some "pornographic poems." He complained to the Denver schools and their response was to withdraw this book from circulation in school libraries. A great reaction came from the Denver chapter of the American Civil Liberties Union, which claimed that this constituted "censorship." The Denver Public Schools head librarian issued a statement that in the best interests of the students, and in keeping with the requests of parents, they were practicing "book selection." A letter in *The Denver Post* from members of the English Department of the University of Denver noted that no matter whether you called something "mass murder" or "the final solution to the Jewish problem," the result was the same. Discuss the sanity of how the words that were used described the circumstances of the situation. What would you recommend should have happened? How would you have described it?

28. How much is the "generation gap" that we hear so much about a matter of semantics? Try the same question with black power and white backlash.

29. The figure pictured below is simply three interlocking rings. Could you describe the figure in such a way that someone hearing your description could accurately *draw* the rings if they had only your description to go by? Try it. What does this exercise demonstrate about the difficulty of reducing objective reality to words?

30. When faced with something unfamiliar, some people will ask, "What is this?" Others will ask "What is this called?" Are they both asking the same question or are they asking something quite different? Which are you likely to ask? How does the way you acquaint yourself with the unfamiliar reflect something of your "world view"?

31. To what extent is a college education extensional or intensional? That is, to what extent does it have some relationship to the "real" world and to what extent is it purely a world of ideas? Are the present demands of college students for "relevancy" at all justified, or are they just as intensional as what they are objecting to?

32. Modern city-planner Constantinos Doxiadis from Greece says, "All big cities of mankind are sliding into chaos." How do the authors corroborate that this is happening? What would you recommend to slow or reverse this entropy?

33. Much of the protest movement of today's society involves violent demonstration, boycott, and physical rebellion. To what extent does this "cut off" communication and intensify the problem? Or to what extent is this an entirely new kind of communication that is much laden with meaning if it is only understood for what it says? Explain your answer. Define your terms.

34. Many of us habitually appraise objects, people, actions, indeed everything that arouses our senses or thought process, in the following terms: good-evil, dark-light, sweet-sour, up-down, black-white, success-failure, cold-hot, permanent-impermanent. Make your own list of opposites. What is wrong with using opposites as measuring devices of what we taste, hear, feel, see, touch? Why might these opposites be inaccurate in evaluating ideas and morals? Have you ever heard of the "semantic differential"? What assumptions does it make about polar opposites and the measurement of attitude? Would you rely on conclusions drawn from its use?

Selected Bibliography

Barnlund, Dean C. *Interpersonal Communication Survey and Studies.* Boston: Houghton, Mifflin Co., 1968. Thirty-seven studies pertaining to channels of communication, verbal interaction, nonverbal interaction, therapeutic communication.

Becker, Ernest. *The Birth and Death of Meaning.* Glencoe, Ill.: The Free Press, 1962. Presents the self in relation to symbolic activity and historical change. Uses man's sentiment of self-value as a new direction in search of a science of man.

Bradley, Walter. *Modern Systems Research for the Behavioral Scientist.* Chicago: Aldine Publishing Co., 1968. A source book by fifty-nine authors on general systems and cybernetics on self-regulation and self-direction in psychological systems.

Bronowski, J. *Common Sense of Science.* New York: Random House, 1959. Implies an ethics of communication and indicates how science may be applied to improve human values to bring unity to our society.

Burrow, Trigant. *Pre-Conscious Foundations of Human Experience.* William Galt, ed. New York: Basic Books, Inc., 1964. The development of language as an integrative and cohesive factor in evolution of man and his societies.

Cooper, Lane. *The Rhetoric of Aristotle.* New York: D. Appleton-Century Co., Inc., 1931. The great classical exposition which is widely acclaimed as providing the foundation book for persuasion and rhetoric.

Deutsch, Karl W. *The Nerves of Government.* New York: The Free Press, 1966. An application of cybernetic principles to the self-control of human organizations.

Duncan, Hugh Dalziel. *Communication and the Social Order.* New York: Oxford University Press, 1962. Presents a theory of symbolic interaction applicable to relationships between superiors, inferiors, and equals. Art-works offer the best clues for the analysis of these dynamics.

Hovland, Carl I., Janis, Irving L., and Kelley, Harold H. *Communication and Persuasion.* New Haven: Yale University Press, 1953. Summary of research on effects of attempts at persuasion on credibility of the communicator, fear-arousing appeals personality and persuasibility, and other rhetorical factors.

Johnson, Wendell. *Your Most Enchanted Listener.* New York: Harper and Brothers, 1956. Explains how our mental troubles, phobias, frustrations, and general insecurity are the product of man's failure to talk fully and frankly to himself—in other words, to think clearly.

Koestler, Arthur. *The Act of Creation.* New York: The Macmillan Co., 1964. One of the greatest books of modern times on verbal creation—the art of discovery, wisdom, originality, the artist.

Korzybski, Alfred. *Manhood of Humanity.* Lakeville, Conn.: Institute of General

Semantics, 1950. Second edition. Describes the time-binding functions of language in the transmission of human experience from person-to-person and generation-to-generation.

Science and Sanity. An Introduction to Non-Aristotelian Systems and General Semantics. Lakeville, Conn.: Institute of General Semantics, 1950. Second edition. Original formulations of the general semantics discipline for human adjustment and evaluation. Provides background for the isomorphism variable of the communication process.

Langer, Susanne K. Mind: An Essay on Human Feeling. Baltimore: The John Hopkins Press, 1967. Volume I. One of the most important explanations of feeling and form, abstracting, and art in nature.

Lippett, Ronald, Watson, Jeanne, and Westley, Bruce. The Dynamics of Planned Change. New York: Harcourt, Brace and Co., 1958. The successes and failures of leaders trained in group dynamics in bringing about planned change in enterprises in which they were employed.

Moreno, J. L. Who Shall Survive? Beacon, N. Y.: Beacon House, 1953. The basic book for the measurement of effects of communication, for the use of psycho- and sociodrama in the release of creative power and productivity in individuals and groups.

Reusch, Jurgen. Therapeutic Communication. New York: W. W. Norton and Co., Inc., 1961. Communication is the central ingredient in all forms of mental healing. The student of social science will find useful discussion of personal leverage, therapeutic dialectics, or frozen communication—topics applicable to most social situations.

Sondel, Bess. The Humanity of Words. A Primer of Semantics. Cleveland: The World Publishing Co., 1958. Presents in capsule form the theories of communication of Ogden and Richards, Alfred Korzybski, Charles Morris, and her own field theory.

Weiner, Norbert. The Human Use of Human Beings. Cybernetics and Society. New York: Doubleday and Co., Anchor Book A-34, 1954. The regulation and control of human relationships as depending upon communication with the reduction of entropy.

Index